I0793464

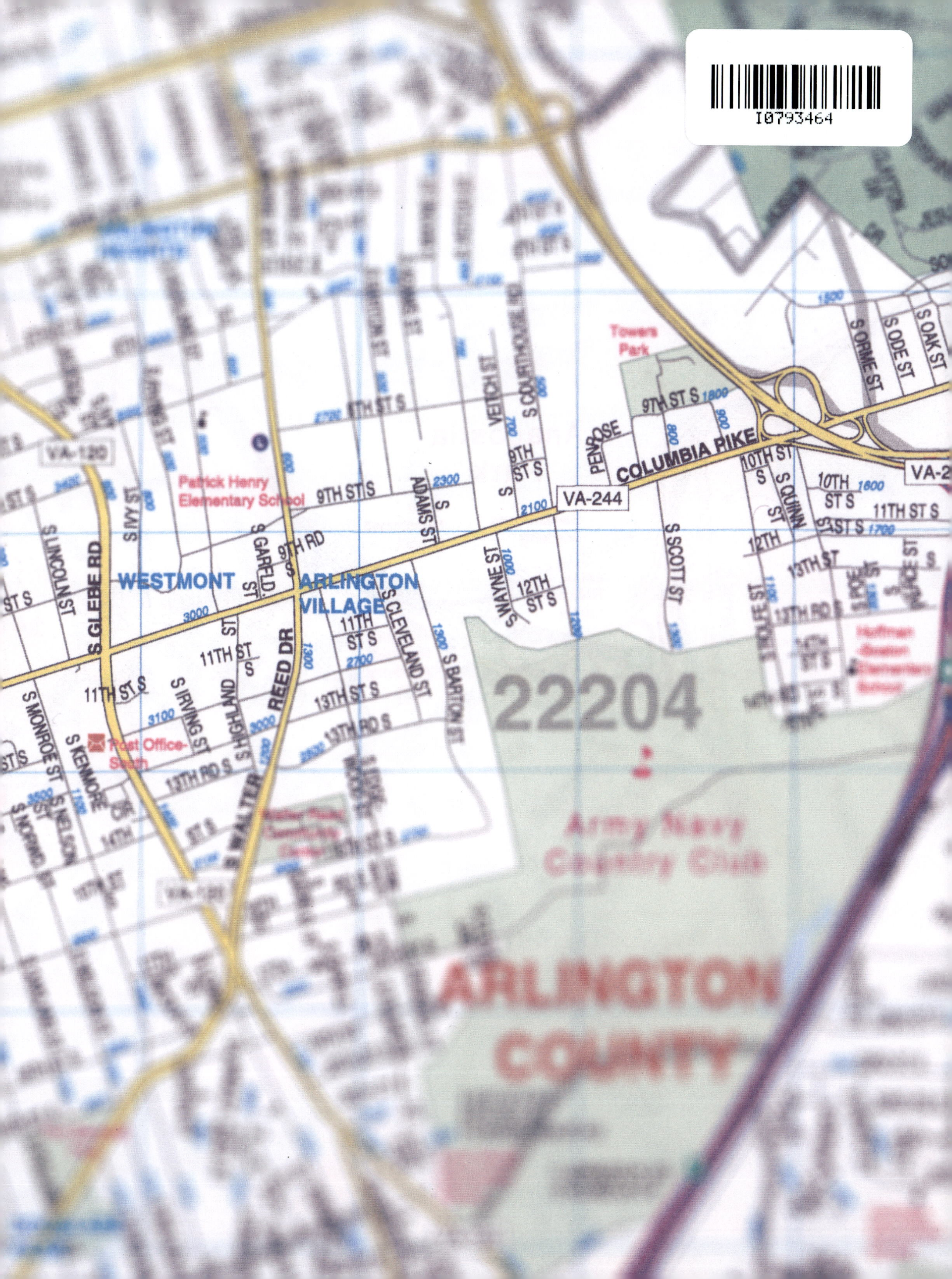
Towers Park
9TH ST S
1800
900
800
COLUMBIA PIKE
VA-244
PENROSE
S COURTHOUSE RD
VEITCH ST
6TH ST S
2700
Patrick Henry Elementary School
9TH ST S
ADAMS ST
2300
2100
9TH ST S
S GARFIELD ST
9TH RD S
WESTMONT
ARLINGTON VILLAGE
S GLEBE RD
S LINCOLN ST
VA-120
3000
11TH ST S
S CLEVELAND ST
1300
S BARTON ST
2700
13TH ST S
13TH RD S
REED DR
S WALTER
S IRVING ST
S HIGHLAND ST
3100
S MONROE ST
S KENMORE
Post Office-South
13TH RD S
S WAYNE ST
1000
12TH ST S
S SCOTT ST
22204
1500
S ORME ST
S ODE ST
S OAK ST
10TH ST S
S QUINN ST
10TH ST S
1600
11TH ST S
1700
12TH
13TH ST
13TH RD S
ARLINGTON COUNTY

Living Diversity

THE COLUMBIA PIKE DOCUMENTARY PROJECT

Lloyd Wolf   Duy Tran   Paula Endo   Xang Mimi Ho   Aleksandra Lagkueva

Living Diversity: The Columbia Pike Documentary Project

Photographs by Lloyd Wolf, Duy Tran, Aleksandra Lagkueva, Xang Mimi Ho, and Paula Endo

Forewords by David Bearinger, Lloyd Wolf, Audrey Singer, Marie Price, and Takis Karantonis

Book design by Matthew Langley / Basis Branding
Photo editing by Lloyd Wolf and Xang Mimi Ho
Text edited by David Bearinger and Lloyd Wolf

Published by the Columbia Pike Revitalization Organization
2611 Columbia Pike, Arlington VA 22204
www.columbia-pike.org
in conjunction with the Columbia Pike Documentary Project
www.pikedoc.org

Distributed by the University of Virginia Press

Printed and bound in India
FIRST EDITION 2015
ISBN number 978-0-9907988-0-4

Thank You

This book would not have been possible without the cooperation and help of many individuals and groups who have supported our work.

The Columbia Pike Documentary Project would like to particularly thank Takis Karontinis, the executive director of the Columbia Pike Revitalization Organization, for his guidance, cheerleading, good humor, wisdom, and financial, spiritual, and other substantive practical support. This book's advisory committee, Chris Zimmerman, Emma Violand-Sanchez, David Bearinger, Takis Karantonis, Lilly Mancilla, Dulce Carrillo, Christian Dorsey, Katherine Glennon, Dahlia Constantine, and Linh Ong also have made a real impact on this book becoming a reality.

As this work documents a large community, many others were of help to us. In no set order, and all vital in their support and cooperation for the work have been:

Jim Whittaker, Sarah Collins, Dr. Tsehaye Tefferra, Konjit Moges, and Chona Bravante of ECDC, Adriana Torres and Claudia Salazar of Café Sazon, Luz Stroh, Kerry Lutz, Nina Janopaul, Linda Kelleher and Liz McElwee of the Arlington Partnership for Affordable Housing (APAH), Dennis Jaffe of BRAVO, Dr. Elizabeth Fussell, Don and Juanita Zientara, Wuiping Yap, Achmed Osman, Bismarck Likambi and Veronica Minor of Ethio Café, Clint Hanover, Cathleen, Adam, Sarah, and Jordan Drew, Wayne Botts, Clinton Scott, Tsige Paulo, Abraham Yohannes Haile, Scott McKnight and the Jelly Rolls Mortals band, Rick Franklin, Grupo Awal dance troupe, Steve Sakole of Lost Dog Café, Jing Wei Maria, and Gary Shieh of Mrs. Chen's Kitchen, the Tran family, Daisy Lung, Angela Adams and Deirdre Ehlen of Arlington County Public Arts, Henrik Sundkvist of Art Outlet, William Alfaro of Domenick's Shoe Repair, the Honorable Walter Tejada, Mary Hynes, and Libby Garvey of the Arlington County Board, Cheick Hamala's Griot Street Band, El Pike restaurant, Mekbib Gebertsadik, Wodajo Gebretsadik Worke, Tadesech Tafferi Wube, Hossein and Meryam Mohammed, John Richardson of the Arlington Historical Society, Mike Morgan, Kima B. Norflet, Pan American Bakery, Mr. Zulkuf of Atilla's Restaurant, Sandra Claros of Abi's Restaurant, Roger and Yolanda of Vinny's Restaurant, Bob and Edith's Diner, Fernando Jordon of the Arlington Credit Union, Qui Bhui, Enrique Viscarra and Ranulfo Jimenez of Swank Custom Tailoring, Juan Chicas, Arlington United Methodist Church, Arlingtonians for a Clean Environment (ACE), Sybil Robinson of Twisted Vines Bistro, Rappahanock Coffee, Adam Lubar of William Jeffrey's Tavern, Kirsten Buhls of the Virginia Agricultural Cooperative Extension service, Diane Kresh, Jason Rogers, Judy Knudson, Ingrid Kauffman, and Peter Golkin of Arlington Public Libraries, Cameron Davidson, Scott McCaffrey of the Arlington Sun Gazette, Dr. Richard Kamenitzer, Toni Andrews, Leslie Cohen Scher, and Mathilde Speier of George Mason University, Cynthia Connolly and Ryan Holladay of Artisphere, Cecilia Cassidy of the Rosslyn BID, Susan Soroko, Mary Briggs, and Joan Lynch of Arlington County Cultural Affairs, Isabel and Karen Kaldenbach, Gary Chassman of Verve Editions, J. Akhtar, Dr. Deborah Lattanzi Shutika and her students, Jan

Kennemer, Roger Munter and Robb Farr of Arlington Video Network, Jackie Stevens of Arlington Public Media, John and Ginger Andelin, Amy McWilliams, Pam Holcombe, Samantha Wentling, Kay Plitt, JC Gibbs, Rita Wiggins, Stacey White, Randolph Elementary School, Randy and Anna Kelly, Jamie Daly, FotoWeek DC, Sedge Moss, Botanica Boricua, Susan Kalish and Nathan Spillman of Arlington County Department of Parks, Recreation and Cultural Resources, Judy Klevins, Aldwin Jones, Irene Wittig, Emilio Vasquez, John Moran, Kevin Irvin (JaziRock), Pryalal Karmakar of the Prio Bangla Festival, Northern Virginia Magazine, Dr. Linh Huang, Box Cartel band, Maria "Pete" Durgan and the Flores-Gambino family, Jim McCaskill, Pastor John Nicholas, Fetene, Wude, Yesak, Nico, and Sina Dubessa, Angel Morales and family, Chris Polk, the staff at Harvey Hall, Mary Nablusi, Francisco Mejia, Kim Hanh Nguyen, Beauty Fair Hairstylists, Mr. Buu, Emerson Doyle of Creative Martial Arts, Jeff Severson and Susan Swann, Patrick Bahn, the Yoga Mom's group, Kathy Anderson of Siena Park, Robert McPhail, Boris Borisov, Ivelene Ivenova, Jitka Jichova, Krasimir Pehlivanov, Martin Strba, Radek Kaczor, Polette Rodriguez, Milan Lukic, Radek Kaczor, Tania Stancheva, Viktor Nekoranec, Zuzana Jakobova, Zuzana Jakobova, and Stephen Lavery of High Sierra Pools, Vicky Sanchez and the staff of Le Touche Day Spa, Binyam Geb of Ledeta Gebeya, Michael Servello, Robin Armstrong, Eva Torres of Cassiel's, the Hussein family, Wanda Pierce of the Arlington Community Foundation, David Bearinger, Jon Lohman, Karenne Wood, and Jeanne Siler of the Virginia Foundation for the Humanities, Maria Cutipa, Justin Constantine, and Roger Boersma.

We hope we have not overlooked anyone, and thank you all for your kind cooperation and support in furthering the work.

For believing in our project, and their encouragement in bringing our vision to the public we wish to acknowledge director Mark Saunders and publicist Emily Grandstaff at the University of Virginia Press.

The Benefactors for this book from our GoFundMe campaign are:

David Blumenstein and Jane Pollner, Kevin Breen, Darlene Burns, Carol Post and Dr. Steven Dentel, Christian Dorsey, David Hafner and Theresa Moorleghan, Mark Herzberg and Rabbi Ma'ayan Turner, Dr. Scott Hunter, Betsy Nordland Wright, Elaine Reuben, Alex Trocker, Guillame Turpin, and the Urban Alternatives Foundation.

This book's Patron: Michelle Duell

The book's Angel donors: John Andelin, Ginger Geoffrey, and Rob Reiner of the George L. Shields Foundation

Thank you all. Without your generosity and belief in the spirit of this book, and of the value of history, culture, diversity, memory, and community, this book would not be possible. Our deepest gratitude to you all.

We wish to especially acknowledge the fine work of our historian, Todd Endo of Urban Alternatives, and of the terrific CDPD interns, Elayna Tursky, Maria Vasquez, Marina Ralph, Chloe Hollingsworth, and Ian Hardman.

And we finally wish to thank our financial sponsors, the Columbia Pike Revitalization Organization, The Virginia Foundation for the Humanities, PNC Foundation, the Arlington Commission for the Arts, the Arlington Community Foundation, The Rosslyn BID, Rosslyn Renaissance, JBG Companies, Performance Video Systems, the Circulator Bus System, Artisphere, and the Arlington Community Federal Credit Union, without whom this work could not have been realized. Your belief in our project is deeply appreciated, and we trust it has lived up to your hopes and expectations.

FOREWORD

Spirit on the Water
The Soul of Columbia Pike

DAVID BEARINGER

So we're sitting in a café up near the western end of Columbia Pike in Arlington, Virginia, *Café Sazon*, and I'm watching Lloyd Wolf slowly come to terms with the future.

It's early August, middle of the afternoon, hot enough to boil tea-water on the sidewalk.

The cafe is empty, and we're both staring out the front window, chairs kicked back. I glance over at Lloyd and he's got the look. As if sweet Destiny is hauling down the tracks right at him.

"You know," he says, it just might work...."

"Of course it'll work," I tell him. "This is a book whose time has come. All you have to do now is start climbing the Decision Tree and figure out exactly what you want this thing to look like."

"Thanks but, you know, seriously... do you think anyone is really interested in books like this anymore? Friends, sure; people who know the Pike, longtime Arlington folks; but who else?"

"Except that this is not *just* a book about Columbia Pike. The Pike is the lens, but the picture is so much bigger than that. You've said it yourself. The Pike looks like the future; it looks like the world. Besides, nobody knows the Soul of the Pike better than you do. If you don't do this now, you could end up regretting it later....It's where this project has been leading all along."

* * *

Lloyd Wolf is a hunter in the world of color, form, and space. He's also a truth-seeker and truth-teller, an inspired talker, citizen of the Planet—and of Arlington where he's lived for most of his life. And if you're holding this book for the first time, you'll soon see that he's also a brilliant photographer, a storyteller by the urban campfire; a traveler in the realms of the Spirit, shadow and light.

The same can be said of Paula Endo, Duy Tran, Mimi Xang Ho, and Aleksandra Lagkueva, all superb photographers in their own right and Lloyd's companions on this journey into the Soul of Columbia Pike.

Mimi, Duy, and Aleksandra have been Lloyd's and Paula's students in the past, and you can glimpse the relationship between them, lines of influence in this body of work. But you can also sense their independence, which is a teacher's greatest gift. The strengths of all five are impressive, individually and together, and the book is an unusual collaboration in that respect: between a team of artists, peers, teachers, students, and friends.

Of course it helps that they all share the same visual language: different dialects, different tones-of-voice, so to speak, different ranges, but the same vocabulary; and the same passion for the Pike and its complicated, still unfinished story.

* * *

Living Diversity is a book that matters, a book whose time has come, thankfully. And looking back, you can see it coming from a long way off. You can follow its roots back ten years, or even farther.

The Virginia Foundation for the Humanities has had a long connection with Lloyd, and with Paula and Todd Endo and the Columbia Pike Documentary Project. We supported the Project with a series of grants beginning in 2002, including publication of an earlier book called *Portraits from the Pike*.

I also had the good luck to be present at the conception of this new book, on that hot afternoon at *Café Sazon*. And the result, which you now hold, is a great gift—to Arlington, to Virginia, and to the World; a tangible and permanent record of what became, for a few years, in the span of our lifetimes, one of the most ethnically and culturally diverse nodes on the Planet.

I'd seen the early photographs, knew the broad outlines of the story; but it was Lloyd who first introduced me, in-person, to the Pike and its complicated, luminous Soul—a gift for which I will always be grateful.

* * *

Lloyd Wolf has lived in proximity to the Pike for more than three decades, and I think it's also fair to say that he and his cameras have lived *within it* for a good part of the past ten years. The Pike is in his Soul, and his Soul and heart are in the Pike, as these photographs make clear.

And once again, the same goes for the other photographers whose work graces and sometimes burns right through these pages. None of them has said the Pike is Heaven, because it isn't; but for a brief moment—the moment-in-Time this book chronicles—it might have been the New Jerusalem. Or something close to it.

Speaking of Jerusalem, Lloyd has traveled there many times, and he's also at work currently on another long-term book project designed to reveal that city's own complicated Soul. So I believe him when he says the difference between the Pike and Jerusalem is that "here, the diversity kinda works...."

* * *

I don't know what faiths the makers of these pictures profess; but I do know this is a deeply spiritual book. Because you just can't make images like these if you don't see God, or Yahweh, Allah, The Creator, or whatever else you might choose to call It in the faces and forms, the colors and movements of this material, human world.

Every place has a Spirit, often made of many spirits. And whether that Spirit is verdant and free-flowing or hard and desiccated, it's there to be apprehended and called forth.

But for an artist, especially a visual artist, this is a capture-and-release proposition. It has to be, because if you hold it too tight, or try to force it into street clothes or to fit some preconceived idea, the Spirit disappears. It's gone, moved on, and all you're left with is a dry, split-open husk, like the shell of a cicada hanging from the bark of a Decision Tree.

Which is part of what makes these photographs so rich, so life-giving; and why they have so much to teach, even to those of us who've never set foot on Columbia Pike, or been to Virginia for that matter. Their message, overflowing with the Spirit of this unique and wondrous place, is universal.

Which is to say, the Spirit of this book has no boundaries.

* * *

For the better part of fifty years, The Pike has been a *mecca* for new immigrants to the United States. They've come from everywhere: from Mali, Ethiopia, and The Sudan; Mongolia and throughout Southeast Asia; El Salvador, Guatemala, Ukraine, Egypt, Azerbaijan, Bolivia...the list goes on and on.

This is changing now, in spite of the best efforts of many in Arlington who place diversity among their highest *public* values and their treasured *private* hopes.

The end has not yet been written; but the forces of development—gentrification, some would call it—have already poured the footings and raised the scaffolds of profound change for Columbia Pike, and for its off-beat shops and quiet, still relatively affordable neighborhoods.

Today, along the four-mile stretch between the Air Force Memorial and Carlin Springs Road, much of the built landscape still looks a lot like it did in 1959 or '72. But you can also sense the fragility of these visual connections to the past and the power of what's coming, some of which is pictured here too.

Meanwhile, those who love the place continue to do what they can.

* * *

A few weeks before Lloyd and I found ourselves sitting at the café window, watching the sidewalk blister and dreaming about this book, a dear friend of mine (and Lloyd's), a longtime Arlingtonian and herself an immigrant to Virginia in the early 1960s, took me to a place called Pike Pizza.

You can't get a pizza there; but you can get great Bolivian food made the traditional way; and the owner, whose name many local readers of this book will know, spent an hour with us talking about her life back home in Bolivia and how she managed to buy this tiny restaurant space along the Pike. It was a miracle born of hard work and perseverance, the way most miracles are, and it's her piece of the American Dream.

So what happens to Pike Pizza and to other places like it when the wheels of development turn their way? What happens to the hole-in-the wall shops and low-rise apartment buildings and the faces that are pictured in this book? What happens to the street festivals and their outbursts of noise and color, and to the little girl in her handmade Bolivian dress? What happens to the old-style family diners, the *mercados*, to the storefront astrologers and the street-lamp assignations that are also captured here?

Most of all, what happens to the *living diversity* of this place when it looks like any other planned upscale shopping strip and condo village in America?

* * *

Nostalgia is a poison leaf; and anyway,"*change is gonna come*." Blake wrote: "He who binds himself to a joy/doth the winged life destroy/but he who kisses the joy as it flies/lives in Eternity's sunrise." So what can we do?

We can do what these artists have done here so gracefully and with so much evident love. We can record what we see in the moment, so that others who come after us will know what this time was really like, what it meant to those of us who lived within it, who witnessed it; and how the Spirit moved across the faces of the water, so to speak, in this place we call the Pike.

* * *

There's a passage in the Book of Ecclesiastes. It says, "...in this, my son, be admonished; of making many books there is no end, and much study is a weariness of the flesh...."

All you have to do to understand the wisdom of this is to walk into a chain bookstore pretty much anywhere in America. Any of the ones in Arlington will do.

Just about every time I go into these places, I ask myself; "does the world really need another book?" And on gloomier days, the answer always comes back, "no."

But then I see a book like this. And the dismal no dispels and recreates itself into a joyous yes. As if I'd just turned the corner and there's a beautiful woman singing under a street-lamp in the falling snow.

And so, remembering that passage from Ecclesiastes, I ask myself "instead of feeling weary and depleted, why do I feel so alive when I look at this book?"

I think it's because the people who made Living Diversity have lived and are living it themselves; because they've seen Life in the present and understood where it's pointing; because the Spirit of the Pike freely inhabits these pictures; and because the love that Lloyd and Paula, Mimi, Duy, and Aleksandra feel for this place is so evident, so unmistakable in their work.

Which is to say it's because they've looked deeply into—and really seen—the Soul of Columbia Pike, a place that is still, for at least a little while longer, one of the most diverse nodes on the Planet.

And because now, thanks to the Spirit moving on the faces of the waters of this beautiful book, you and I have seen it too.

David Bearinger
Virginia Foundation for the Humanities
Charlottesville, Virginia

So, Why Columbia Pike?

LLOYD WOLF

Awareness sometimes comes quietly and quickly.
I came of age in Northern Virginia in the 1960's. I attended a high school named for a Confederate general, JEB Stuart, just three miles from where I now live.

When I was growing up, there were just three ethnic groups in the area: Southern whites, Southern blacks, and government workers. My family belonged to the latter. I add the caveat that there were a handful of Cubano, Jewish (like myself), and embassy kids in the school, but we were tiny minorities, and strove to fit in without making ourselves distinct. Out of our 2400-plus student population, there were two Arabs (one the Egyptian ambassador's son), no Asians, no Central Americans, no Africans, no Russians, no Turks, no real diversity. We had a great - segregated - varsity football team, beautiful all-white cheerleaders, and an underground newspaper (it was the late 60's). This is what made up the community here, and what I thought made up most of America.

A couple of decades later, I was volunteering in my colleague Paula Endo's after-school photography program for immigrant teens along Columbia Pike, in Arlington, Virginia. Both Paula and I were veteran teachers in Arlington's public school system, and had experienced many changes in our classes' ethnic composition. The Columbia Pike Teen Photo Workshop was populated with teens from many countries. Under Paula's sensitive leadership, we worked with them as individual artists. They came from Cambodia, El Salvador, Eritrea, Mexico, Nicaragua, Pakistan, Thailand, Vietnam, and other places around the globe.

One day I was working with Weyni Ghebremedhin, a soft-spoken participant in the group. We got to talking about something other than her photographs. I assumed from her name and African origin, from the foods she ate, that she was Ethiopian, part of the large Ethiopian diaspora that was settling along Columbia Pike, and casually identified her that way in our conversation.

Weyni softly looked me in the eye and gently spoke, "No, I am not Ethiopian. I am Eritrean."

The two countries were at war at the time.

If I had been told three decades earlier that I would need to know the difference between Ethiopians and Eritreans (assuming I even knew of Eritrea's existence in my teens), and that I would be neighbors and friends of numerous people from both of these places, let's just say I would have been rather skeptical.

Awareness sometimes comes quietly and quickly.
The new awareness that arose in a flash from Weyni's gentle assertion brought me in that moment to a profound realization of the changes that had occurred in our community.

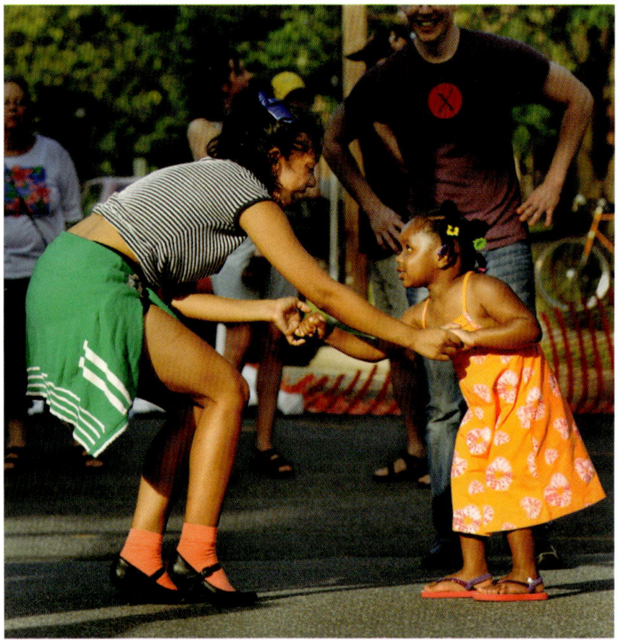

We talked for a while about Eritrea, about her mother's role in the Eritrean diaspora and the internal politics involved. After that I don't recall the conversation, but knew viscerally, and in that moment embraced, the full diversity of the many peoples that were now making their home along Columbia Pike.

My father came to America from Germany as a refugee fleeing Hitler's murderous regime, and my mother's parents had come to America from Eastern Europe to escape poverty and ethnic bigotry. As the child and grandchild of immigrants fleeing oppression and violence, it both made sense and was, in a way, reassuring, to know other people who came to our community for similar reasons. Shared origins...

And Lord knows, the food available in Northern Virginia was far better than it had been in my youth. Pupusas, injera, kebabs, pho, curries, salteñas, pad thai, falafel, roti, tamal de elote; a new vocabulary of tastes.

Columbia Pike was chartered by an act of Congress in 1810, to connect the new nation's capitol of Washington DC with a network of roads into Virginia and points west. The original tolls for travel along the Pike were 12.5 cents for a horse or mule with rider, 30 cents for a carriage with four horses, six cents for a led or driven horse or mule, and 20 cents for up to twenty head of sheep, hogs, or cattle. At the time, Arlington was part of the District of Columbia. The area was remanded to Virginia before the Civil War, and split off from Alexandria City in 1920, as Arlington was considered too rural for city status. During the Civil War, tens of thousands of Union troops were stationed along the Pike, and Freedman's Village was established nearby, on Robert E. Lee's family estate, to provide homes for newly freed and escaped slaves. A variety of communities - Johnson Hill, Barcroft, Nauck, Penrose, Columbia Heights, and others - grew up in the following years, but the area remained primarily pastoral until the 1930's, when FDR's New Deal brought tens of thousands of new workers to the area. This swift growth accelerated during World War II, with the Pentagon's completion and the massive influx of federal employees involved in the war effort. Housing for the new citizens was rapidly constructed, mostly garden-style apartments and small single-family homes which arose along the Pike corridor. The whole length of the road was paved. Several small strip shopping centers, primarily filled with local individual businesses, were established during this period.

This was largely the situation through the mid-1970's. At that time, Columbia Pike was a largely white, middle class series of neighborhoods encompassing a string of affordable rental apartment complexes and modest single-family houses, with some long-standing and historic African-American enclaves.

With the fall of Saigon, large numbers of Vietnamese refugees flooded into the area, many settling along Columbia Pike. The housing was decent, inexpensive, and the community was generally welcoming, both in attitude and in providing needed social services and educational resources. Arlington has a modern history of tolerance, imperfect to be certain, but the County had broken Virginia's era of massive resistance to school integration in 1959, when four African-American students and a teacher entered Stratford Junior High School, protected by eighty-five Arlington County Police officers. The ideas and values of the long-established Arlington Way - of welcoming and consensus-building - made it easier for the newcomers to fit in.

At roughly the same time as the Vietnamese, Cambodians, and other Southeast Asians were arriving, large numbers of Korean immigrants began to settle, followed in quick succession by early groups of Bolivians, Peruvians, Indians, Pakistanis, and East Africans, primarily from Ethiopia.

In the late 1970's large numbers of immigrants fleeing the troubles in Central America began arriving, mainly from El Salvador, Nicaragua, and Guatemala. The Pike's modest and safe housing and its proximity to jobs and transportation, combined with Arlington County's open attitude and access to social workers, ESL programs, and the like, made the area a magnet for mass immigration. El Salvadoreans in particular made Columbia Pike their home, and their cultural expressions and businesses became very visible. Ethiopians, Eritreans, Somalis, Palestinians, Mexicans, Eastern Europeans, Afghans, Bolivians, Iranians, Sudanese, Azeris, Turks, Moroccans, West Africans, Peruvians, Thais, Mongolians, and others have since come and settled. There are well over 100 languages spoken in Arlington Public Schools, and the Pike corridor is the center of this diversity.

By 2000, Columbia Pike had become one of the most ethnically diverse neighborhoods on the planet.

A 2001 research paper by Brookings Institution scholars Dr. Audrey Singer, Dr. Marie Price, and others described the area as a "World in a Zip Code." It stated that the 22204 zip code, which encompasses Columbia Pike and its neighborhoods, had about 128 nationalities living within it. Wakefield High School, which draws most of its student body from the Pike corridor, is currently 82% minority - with an exemplary 95% reading proficiency, a 92.9% graduation rate, and 86% to

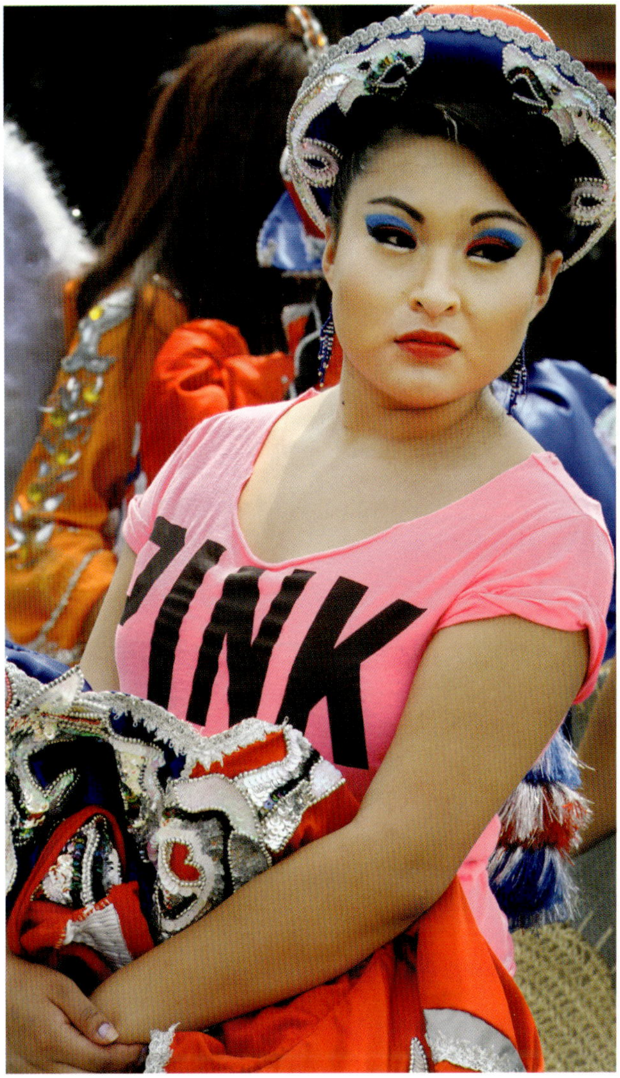

91% of its graduates going on to post-secondary education - despite the fact that 42% of Wakefield's students coming from economically disadvantaged homes. The Columbia Pike neighborhoods are a microcosm of the change from suburban to urban and from white to multi-ethnic and immigrant, which typifies many American neighborhoods in the last fifty years.

Unlike many other diverse communities in the United States, Columbia Pike has no specific ethnic neighborhoods; no Little Italy, Chinatown, or similar single-culture enclave has emerged. With the exception of a couple of older, stable, traditionally middle-class African-American neighborhoods, the new immigrants have settled evenly all over the Pike, in a mixed international mélange. Inter-ethnic strife, otherwise so prevalent in the history of the United States and of the world, is for all practical purposes non-existent on the Pike. What distinguishes the area is that in this extraordinarily diverse mix, vastly different peoples get along with one another quite well for the most part. This is true on both an individual and an inter-group level. So much so, that it is matter of strong local identity and pride. We are the whole world, and we like it. A lot.

I have a saying that I use, one of recognition and gratitude when I become aware enough to realize what's occurring in front of me.

"This is what peace looks like."

I have often said it along the Pike. I have been brought to tears of joy on numerous occasions while documenting the community. I particularly recall a Bangladeshi street festival, with its fireworks of astonishing colors and voluptuous scents, with the locally-based opening acts on stage being a Mexican dance troupe, a Chinese women's dance troupe, a Cambodian dance ensemble, and a group of Peruvian youth in traditional garb - all before the Bangladeshi pop singers went on to headline. Another peak moment was following 3,000-plus Bolivian dancers from thirty local groups marching down the street, a riot of color and sound; bells jingling, drums pounding, boots stomping, devil and angel costumes in a dazzlingly-impossible range of hues. Another awakening was when I first discovered that there was a quiet but vital enclave of Eastern-European Slavs running a highly-successful lifeguard business, with people from Poland, Bulgaria, Ukraine, Moldava, the Czech Republic, Belarus, Russia, and beyond, all making a living - and a life - here, pretty much under the radar of public notice. Other moments that have revealed the true nature and richness of diversity include a discussion with a Syrian-Sudanese Christian volunteer art teacher at an immigrant community center as she was teaching mainly Latina women how to paint plaster sculptures. Or Cheik Hamala, a local Malian griot and musician,

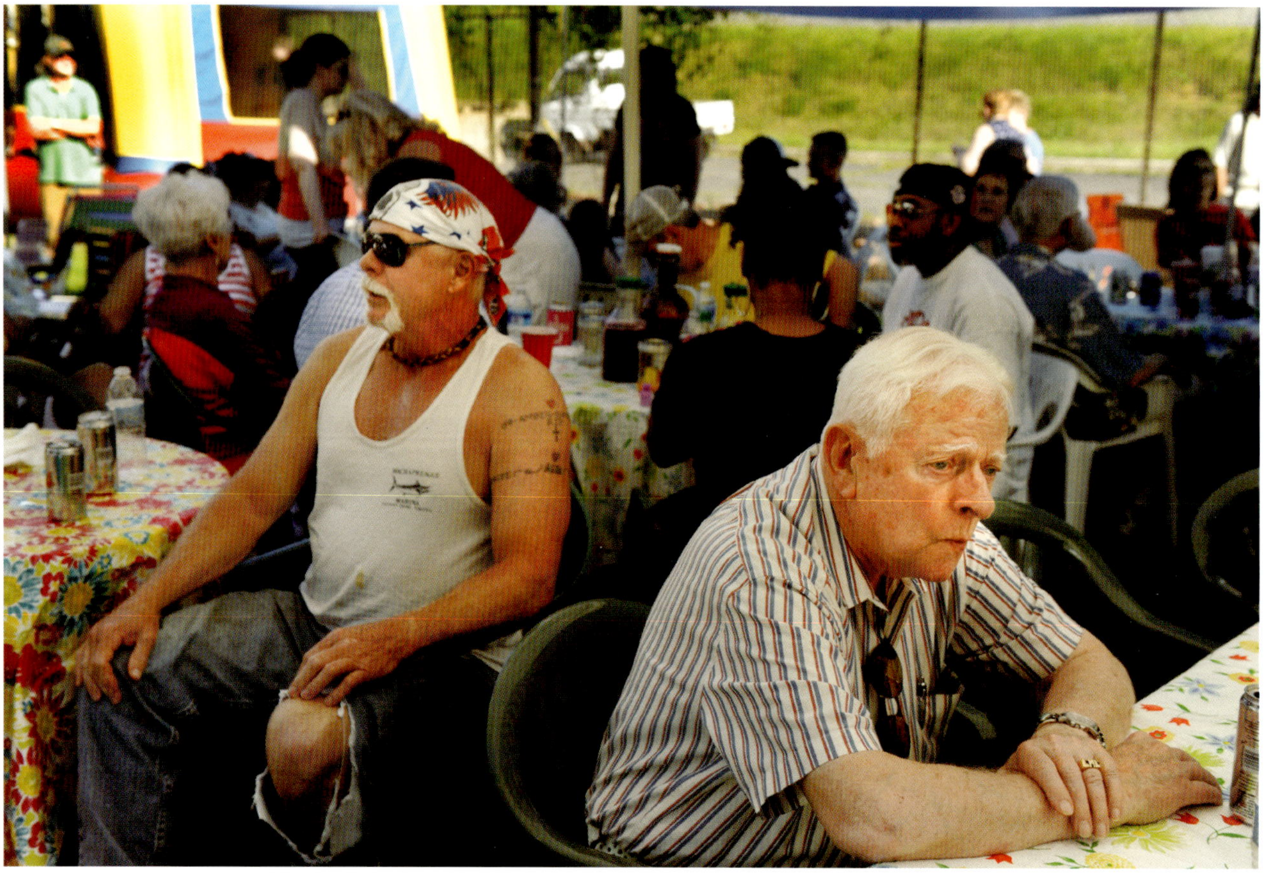

rocking the house with his Saharan blues at the Ethiopian Community Development Center's annual Christmas party. Beyond measure. Peace.

Peace between peoples is not something to be taken lightly or for granted. The whole time I have been documenting my home community of Columbia Pike, I have also been deeply engaged in a collaboration with writer Carol Grosman in documenting the ordinary citizens of Jerusalem, the ancient city holy to so many. There, the inter-ethnic conflicts can often be deadly, and even at the best of times, relations between the two main groups in the city is often fraught with tension, mistrust, and trouble.

An example of the difference peace and tolerance between peoples can make: One morning in Jerusalem the news announced a pigua, a terror attack, nearby. I sped to the site, and observed a smoking bus destroyed by a suicide bomber, and viewed the horror of eleven black bodybags lined up on a sidewalk. Glass from the explosion littered the streets. Rescue workers went about clearing the carnage. The working-class neighborhood was observing the scene, largely in silence, save for a few zealots shouting "maavet l'aravim," Death to the Arabs. These protesters were surrounded by city police to insure they didn't get out of hand, or potentially attack any innocent Arab passersby. The street was thoroughly hosed down, a few memorial candles were lit at the bus stop, and within a couple of hours after the explosion, people were in line waiting for the next bus.

Later that day, I was with a Sufi sheik, Ibrahim Abu-El Hawa, a vibrant Palestinian peaceworker from the Mount of Olives. Through his sobs, he said that not only had a local Arab family lost their child to the madness, but that eleven Jewish families were in pain as a result of the terrible attack. His tears were absolutely real. He understood that all suffered alike, and that no good came from this violence between peoples.
A few days later I was visiting Ibrahim for lunch. He asked me "Lloyd, you are from Virginia, yes?" I said, "Yes, I am." He inquired "do you know where is Bailey's Crossroads?" My jaw dropped wide open. "Why do you ask? I grew up there!" "My cousin has a restaurant there," was his reply. When Ibrahim visited me in Arlington the next year, we went to the restaurant, appropriately named 'Jerusalem.' It turned out that he has relatives all over the Columbia Pike area. We shared mint tea and creamy platters of hummus together.

As it has for so many others, the Pike provided peace, a welcome, and a home.

Why has diversity worked so well along Columbia Pike in Arlington, and why has it come about? It was not a planned outcome. The tolerant nature of Arlington has been a key element. Rather than shun new immigrants, here they get elected to office, start businesses, and are given a chance to succeed in school and to participate in community life on many levels. This tolerance and welcoming ethic is crucial, but so has been the availability of safe and decent affordable housing, and the lack of clustering into specific ethnic enclaves that might otherwise shut out recent immigrants or prevent them from interacting with their neighbors. The result has been a genuine pride in our internationally-based new American character, and a go-along, get along way of life. There is no single reason why this low-strife, respectful atmosphere developed. Perhaps, in this place and time, for now, "the better angels of our nature" have indeed come to create a peaceful and rainbow-hued home. It's a blessing, however it has occurred.

The photographs in this book were made by a team of photographers, all talented, and all with their own lens on the world. Co-founder Paula Endo is a life-long educator, originally from the West Coast, but long an Arlingtonian. Both she and her husband Todd were held in the infamous internment camps for Japanese-Americans during World War Two. This obviously affected their life-long commitment to the ideal of fairness for all, and to building a safe, just community. Paula has had numerous exhibitions in addition to her pioneering work in community building, teaching, and activism.

Duy Tran, who was born and has spent his whole life on the Pike, is the child of refugees from Vietnam. He is a multi-talented artist, with expertise in video and music, as well as an obvious gift for still photography. Xang Mimi Ho was born in a refugee camp in Thailand, and spent the first years of her life mostly in Vientiane, Laos. Her mother, hoping for a better life, settled her family on the Pike, and a new world opened. Mimi, now a professor of photography at area universities, is an up-and-coming fashion photographer in addition to her work with the Columbia Pike Documentary Project. Aleksandra Lagkueva grew up in the former Soviet Union, largely in Central Asia. An ethnic Russian, her family moved back to Russia in the 1990's. She came to the US on her own in 2010 and has made unique contributions to this project both as a person and as an insightful artist in her own right.

I have been privileged to serve as the project director and chief photographer for the Columbia Pike Documentary Project. I lived in many places as a child, but have been in Arlington for more than forty years, and in Northern Virginia since 1965. I am deeply concerned with issues of place, identity, meaning, and peace in my work, both personally and professionally. And with the secrets of making one's eyes dance.

There are many issues that must be addressed in documenting a community, whether through photography or any other medium. There is no way to create a fully objective and fully inclusive document, even with unlimited time, resources, and personnel. Time and the infinity of existence combine to impose fundamental limits on what one can see, portray, and share. What forms a community is its people, in addition to place and time. We as artists, as culture-workers, bring our individual lives, our idiosyncrasies, our biases, and our limitations to any such endeavor. The Heisenberg Principle, a basic axiom of quantum mechanics, also called the observer effect, holds that the measurement or observation of a system cannot be made without affecting the system itself. This principle applies in documentary work as well.

Photographs and interviews are limited, and a book limits their scope even more. Given that, we have done our best to be as thorough and fair in our coverage of the Pike as we could. Every single building was photographed. Many representative small businesses were photographed as well. Neighborhood events, public and private gatherings, schools, local government officials and programs, ethnic festivals and practices, representative street views, people's homes and celebrations, private and public moments, were all included in our documentary process. We strived to make contact with active non-profit groups on the Pike, and to cover the diverse population fairly – not an easy task, given the range of people who live in the corridor.

For several years we walked the Pike, made contacts, ate every conceivable cuisine, poked into nooks and crannies, and kept our

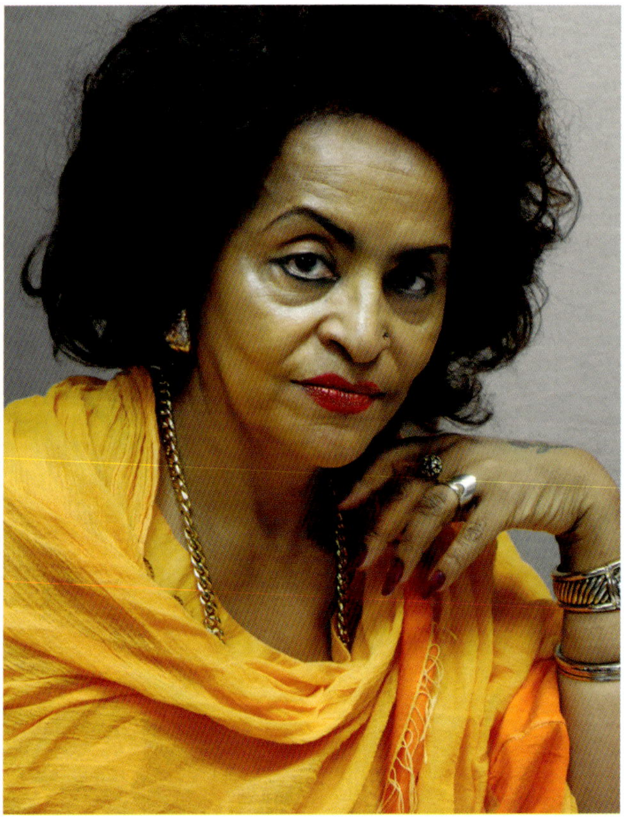

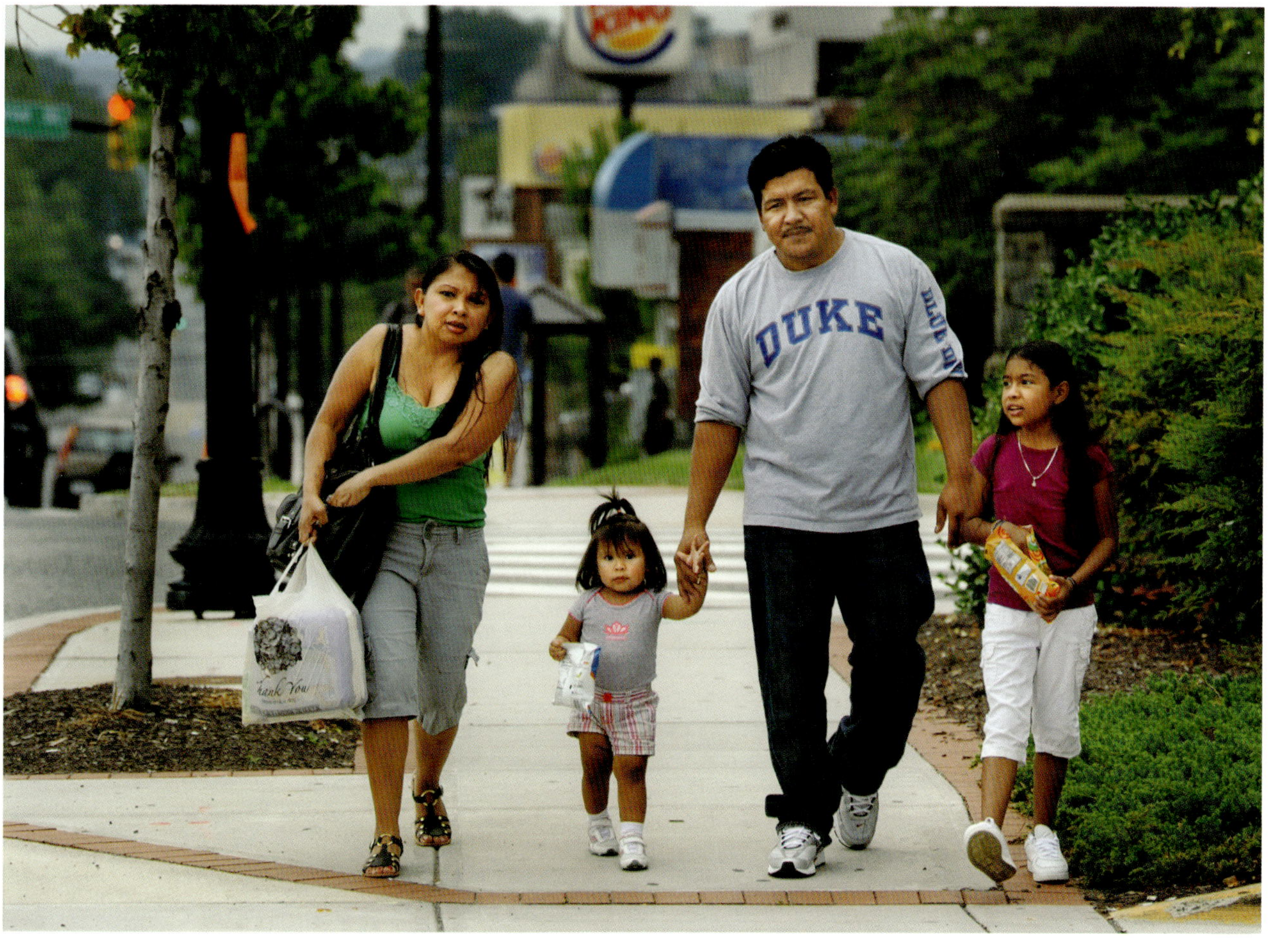

eyes and ears open to what needed to be covered, to the scenes and faces that best represent life here. We did our best to balance aesthetic choices with the demographic realities. These photos are in a sense our carefully-mined data, the distillation of what we have seen, felt, and learned through our life experiences in this diverse place, our home. To quote a museum curator friend, we have endeavored simply - and in complex ways - to make "good pictures."

The ethnic mix has begun to change again, rapidly, as the Pike develops. Luxury and high-end housing and retail establishments have grown up at the eastern and central sections of the Pike, and an affluent, younger, whiter population is moving into the area. This has increased pressures on housing prices in general, and there is widespread concern about the effects this new gentrification will have on Columbia Pike's rich cultural and economic diversity.

In the coming years, development along much of the Pike will continue, and the composition and character of its buildings, businesses, and population will dramatically change. With every day that goes by, the physical and the cultural landscapes of the Pike are shifting. Affordable housing is now something that needs to be planned for, if working-class and new immigrant families are to be able to afford to live in the community. And there is controversy about how transportation will develop, and about the shape of what the neighborhood wants and will look like.

Nothing is static... Our documentary project team has done our best to capture these ongoing changes along the Pike. We view the economic revitalization of the Pike as an opportunity to enrich the lives of all of its residents, if it can be done in a way that maintains the Pike's cultural diversity. In its official publications and websites, Arlington County expresses a

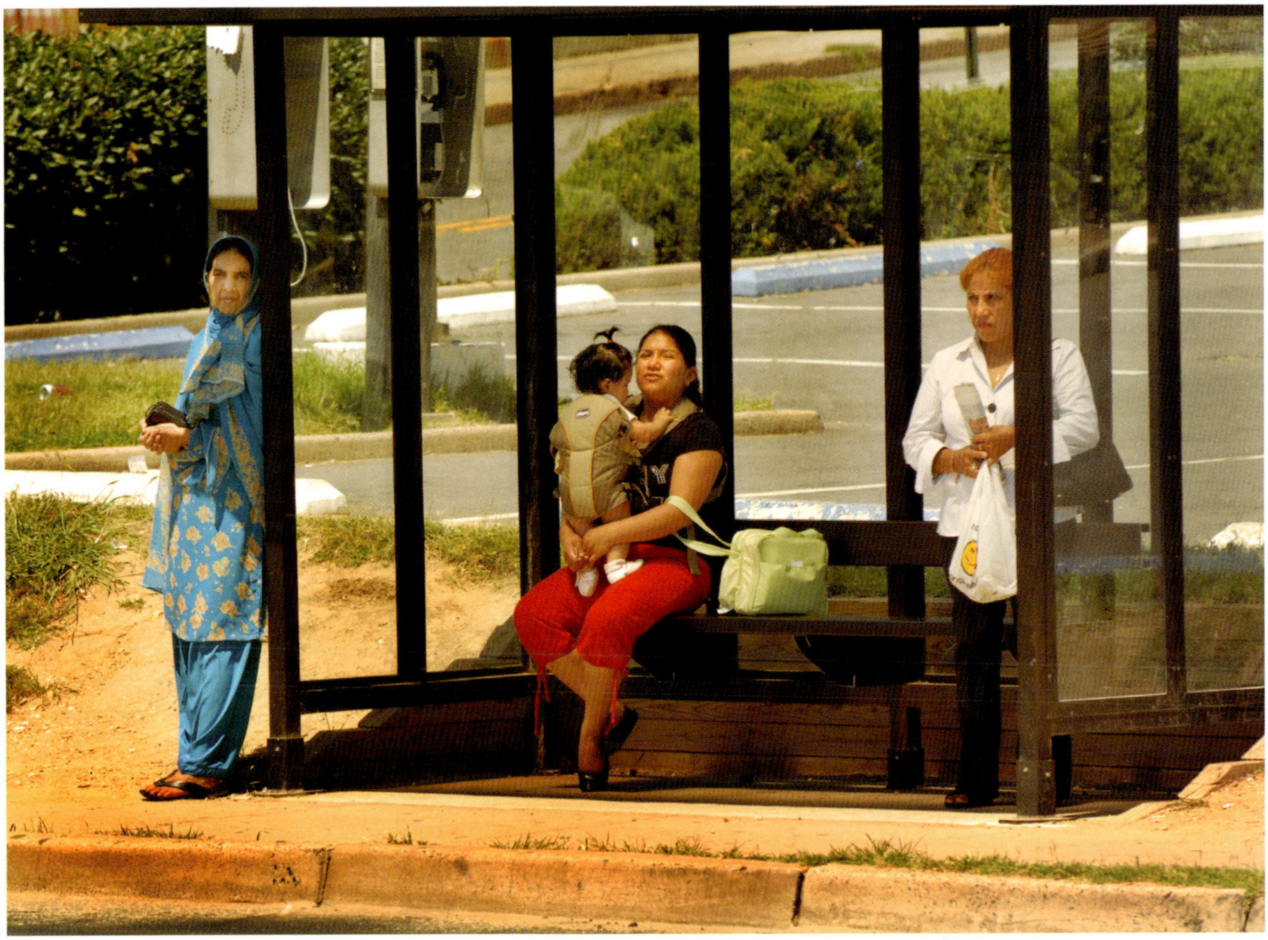

similar vision of community in these words: "Arlington will be a diverse and inclusive world-class urban community with secure, attractive residential and commercial neighborhoods where people unite to form a caring, learning, participating, sustainable community, in which each person is important."

Please look into the faces of the community. Get a feel for the neighborhood. Stay a while, learn, and be enriched by these people and this vital place.

These photographs, and this place called Columbia Pike, represent a microcosm of what America has become and is becoming. And perhaps the new face of the world, too. Living diversity.

We hope they will also inspire you to explore your own neighborhood, your own world. With eyes, mind, and heart opened.

Lloyd Wolf

Chief Photographer, Columbia Pike Documentary Project

Columbia Pike: Arlington's Artery for Newcomers

AUDREY SINGER AND MARIE PRICE

Sometime in the middle of the 20th century Columbia Pike in Arlington County ceased to be a major transportation corridor into and out of Washington D.C. and began its evolution into a distinct and diverse urban neighborhood. One of the oldest thoroughfares in the region, the Pike was built over two centuries ago. For much of its history it was Arlington's main artery moving goods and people westward from the capital city into the Virginia countryside.

The building of the Pentagon in 1941 effectively blocked direct access to Washington from Columbia Pike. Two years later the Shirley Memorial Highway opened (Interstate 395) and the Pike was no longer the major thoroughfare it once was, but rather a close-in urban neighborhood offering affordable housing for mostly white newcomers pouring into the region for plentiful government jobs. Just south of Columbia Pike lies one of the oldest African American neighborhoods in Arlington, Nauck, which had its origins prior to the Civil War. Much of Nauck's growth occurred in the mid-20th century as African Americans were also drawn to the jobs and opportunities in the nation's capital but limited as to where they could settle due to segregation.

To serve the demand for housing as more people moved to the area, hundreds of modest rental units, many in the garden apartment style, were built in the 1940s along Columbia Pike. Complexes such as Walter Reed Gardens, Fillmore Gardens, Arlington Village, Quebec Apartments, and the Dorchester provided homes for thousands. People who lived on the Pike could drive, take the bus, or walk to offices in Arlington or Washington, and they shopped locally at retail establishments such as those found in the Westmont Shopping Center, which opened in 1940 on the corner of Glebe Road and the Pike.

The economic and infrastructure investments that came to North Arlington and Crystal City with the construction of the Metro in the 1970s bypassed Columbia Pike. Yet the Pike's relative isolation from new investment, and its aging housing and shopping venues, proved attractive to a new international wave of residents accelerating the Pike's diversity beginning in the late 1970s.

Like earlier residents, these newcomers settled along the Pike because of its proximity to the urban core, employment opportunities, and relatively inexpensive rental housing. They came from El Salvador, Vietnam, Bolivia, Ethiopia, Peru, and the Philippines. Today, most of these countries-of-origin are still well-represented along the Pike, but immigrants from South Asia (India, Bangladesh and Pakistan) as well as Mexicans and Guatemalans have joined them, creating an ever-changing ethnic landscape along Columbia Pike. Together these origin groups comprise two-thirds of the immigrants in the corridor, which is also home to immigrants from scores of other countries. Currently, the Pike community is 37 percent foreign born. By comparison, Arlington County is 23 percent foreign born.[1]

Immigrants residing along the Pike numbered close to 12,000 in 1990, or approximately 29 percent of the total population. More immigrants followed throughout the 1990s. During that decade, new immigrants from 128 countries settled along Columbia Pike. [2] By the 2000 census, Columbia Pike was recognized as one of the most diverse areas in metropolitan Washington, and the metro area as a whole was considered an emerging immigrant gateway. By 2010, the extraordinary growth of foreign-born residents pushed the Washington region into the ranks of the "post-World War II gateways" along with Dallas-Fort Worth, Houston, Los Angeles, Miami, Riverside, and San Diego. [3]

All the while, Columbia Pike has maintained a fairly stable and affordable housing and commercial base serving local residents. Much of the physical infrastructure, including the automobile-oriented shopping strips, the post-War houses and garden apartment complexes, the vintage signage, and the general scale has the look and feel of a former time. This mid-century era retail space attracted immigrant entrepreneurs who opened ethnic groceries, restaurants, courier services, hair salons, and travel agencies, reworking and updating the Pike to fit their own needs. The inhabitants, shoppers and proprietors of the Pike have shifted over time as more newcomers arrive and some older residents leave, but the eclectic diversity of the Pike has endured. Where else can you walk into an eatery called Pike Pizza, where no pizza is served, and leave instead with a pizza box filled with Bolivian salteñas (meat pies)?

The Pike is a polyglot place, a multi-ethnic blend of the old and the new, something that *Living Diversity* so clearly documents. While blacks and whites have lived there for generations, immigrants and their children tracing their roots to Latin America, Africa, Europe, the Middle East, and Asia make up the rest of the population. Some arrived as economic migrants seeking employment opportunities, while others arrived as refugees from countries ravaged by conflict. Many located themselves on Columbia Pike because friends and family from their home countries directed them there. Community service organizations such as the Ethiopian Community Development Council, Bravo Tenant's Rights Organization, the Arlington Free Clinic, Urban Alternatives Foundation, and the Arlington Partnership for Affordable Housing, also developed to serve the changing population.

What Makes Columbia Pike Distinct

Columbia Pike cuts a wide swath east to west in the southern part of Arlington County, directly west of Arlington Cemetery, Fort Myer and the Pentagon. At the time of publication, the Pike is home to more than 47,000 residents or 23 percent of Arlington's total population.

Arlington County as a whole is a diverse, well-educated, and increasingly affluent jurisdiction bordering the District of Columbia. Since the mid-1960s it has been a welcoming destination for immigrant newcomers, especially in the areas around Rosslyn, Clarendon, and Columbia Pike. Yet today the Pike is the area where immigrant concentrations are the highest and where many newcomers to the region first settle.

The residents of Columbia Pike differ from Arlington's overall population in several important ways. First, the Pike has a much

1 To statistically define the Columbia Pike area we use a set of census tracts that straddle the Pike from three sources of data, the 1990 census, the 2000 Census and the American Community Survey 5-year estimates, 2008-2012 throughout the essay.

2 Audrey Singer, Samantha Friedman, Ivan Cheung, and Marie Price, "The World in a Zip Code: Greater Washington DC as a New Region of Immigration," Washington, DC: Brookings, 2001. In this study we use the 22204 zip code as a proxy for the Columbia Pike Neighborhood.

3 Audrey Singer, "Metropolitan Washington: A New Immigrant Gateway," Pp. 3-24 in Enrique S. Pumar (ed.) *Hispanic Migration and Urban Development: Studies from Washington DC*," United Kingdom: Emerald Publishing, 2012.

larger percentage of people of color, compared to Arlington County as a whole, and it has no clear racial or ethnic majority. Along Columbia Pike 30 percent of residents are Latino, 19 percent are black, 11 percent are Asian, while 36 percent are white. In Arlington as a whole, 64 percent of the county's population is white, while only 15 percent are Latino, 8 percent are black, and 10 percent are Asian.

Second, Columbia Pike residents are diversifying at a much faster pace than Arlington County. This diversification has not been a continuous trend, however. During the 1990s, both the Pike and the County saw fast growth in the Latino population while both experienced declines in the number of white residents. However, during the 2000s, both the Pike and the County experienced a decline in the Latino population (by 13 and 11 percent respectively) and the Pike's African American population also declined. During this period, the numbers of whites and Asians grew in both places.

Overall, between 1990 and 2012, the decline in the white population (by 18 percent) and the rise in Latino and Asian populations (by 87 and 38 percent, respectively) made the Pike a much more diverse place. In contrast, Arlington County's white population grew by 12 percent during the same period while the growth of Latinos and Asians ran in the opposite direction (by 36 and 80 percent, respectively). As the Pike receives more capital investment and new real estate development, the ethnic mix of the area may continue to shift.

Among its nearly 18,000 foreign-born residents, immigrants in the Columbia Pike area are more likely to be from Latin American and Caribbean countries (51 percent) or from Africa (16 percent) compared with Arlington County (39 percent Latin American and 12 percent African). However, only 26 percent of the Pike's immigrants are Asian, compared with 34 percent in the County as a whole. European immigrants are 13 percent of Arlington's total population, but in the neighborhoods along the Pike it's about half of that share or 6 percent.

The Pike differs from Arlington on a number of other measures as well. Half of the Columbia Pike community speaks a language other than English at home and one-in-six report speaking English less than very well. By contrast, 29 percent of Arlington County's residents speak another language at home and 9 percent are limited in their English proficiency. Income levels are lower in the Columbia Pike community relative to the County, but still high by national standards. The rate of self-employment is similar in both, but self-employment is higher for immigrants than for the U.S.-born population who live along the Pike. Both Columbia Pike and Arlington County have high educational attainment compared to national averages, but Columbia Pike has twice the share of people without a high school diploma, compared to Arlington County as a whole. Finally, the majority of the population in both areas rent rather than own their housing.[4]

Hyper-diverse Neighborhoods and a Changing Urban Scene

The images in *Living Diversity* capture the physical landscape and people who call the Columbia Pike neighborhood home. The portrait it creates is unique to Arlington but not entirely unusual for metropolitan Washington, or indeed for other major cities across America. In the United States today, immigrants account for 13 percent of the population, yet in many urban areas the percentage is more than double that figure. Immigrants today are more likely than earlier arrivals to settle in the suburbs of major gateways, rather than the urban core.[5] Thus Columbia Pike is representative of these trends.

4 U.S. Census Bureau, American Community Survey, "Selected Social Characteristics in the United States, 2008-2012," American Community Survey 5-year estimates, Tables DP02, DP05, and S0501 for Arlington County and ZCTA5 22204.

5 Audrey Singer, Susan G. Hardwick, and Caroline Brettell (eds). 2008. Twenty-First Century Gateways: Immigrant Incorporation in Suburban America, Washington D.C.: Brookings Institution Press.

Yet what makes Columbia Pike especially distinctive is its hyper-diversity. At 37 percent of the total population, its immigrant proportion far exceeds the national average. No one country of origin accounts for even a quarter of the Pike's immigrant stock, and Pike residents have come from all regions of the world.[6] Localities so diverse might seem common in places such as New York and Chicago, but are usually not associated with Virginia.

Hyper-diverse settings such as Columbia Pike are often characterized in polarizing terms. On the one hand they are portrayed as dynamic centers of cultural exchange and diversity that enhance an area's global competitiveness and attract new investment and talent. Yet, these same areas are also portrayed as localities of displacement with heightened tensions along racial and class lines. Columbia Pike tends to fit the first profile but not the second. And the area's diversity, relative affordability and proximity to the urban core suggest that it is poised for another period of rapid change.

The Future of Columbia Pike

In 2001, after nearly 60 years of business, Brenner's Bakery—a Pike institution in the Westmont Shopping Center—was forced to leave due to increasing rents. A trip into Brenner's was like walking into the 1950s with uniformed staff serving fresh donuts and various bakery treats. Today a mix of locally owned and chain store restaurants occupy the shopping center along with a new urgent care center. Across the street is an English language academy. On Sundays, a popular farmer's market is held two blocks from the Westmont Shopping Center, and a second farmers market has recently sprung up at the newly-rebuilt Arlington Mill Community Center. The current bakeries on the Pike are primarily Bolivian-owned and offer up sweets and breads distinctive to that culture. The Pike continues to cater to a diversity of newcomers.

The forces of economic development and growth are likely to put further pressure on Columbia Pike to change yet again. Already signs point toward greater affluence along the Pike as newly constructed housing tends to be more vertical and much more expensive. As the County advances new transportation possibilities along the Pike, some residents are concerned that such development will further increase housing and retail costs, while others welcome a convenient mode of transit.

At this moment, so eloquently captured in *Living Diversity*, the Pike's eclectic and hyper-diverse mix seems to embody Arlington County's aspirational vision to be a "diverse and inclusive world-class urban community." Living with diversity is not always easy, as witnessed by scores of xenophobic and anti-immigrant measures occurring in major immigrant destinations around the world. Residents in such hyper-diverse localities as Columbia Pike co-exist and thrive because of the purposeful inclusionary policies and institutions that exist in the region. As political scientist Robert Putnam reminds us, "The central challenge for modern, diversifying societies is to create a new, broader sense of we." The collaborative documentary process represented in *Living Diversity* is an affirmation of that new '*we*', we have become.[7]

Audrey Singer is a Senior Fellow at the Brookings Metropolitan Policy Program. Marie Price is Professor of Geography and International Affairs at the George Washington University.

6 Marie Price and Lisa Benton-Short. 2007. "Immigrants and World Cities: From the hyper-diverse to the bypassed" GeoJournal 68:103-117.

7 Robert Putnam. 2007. "E Pluribus Unum: Diversity and Community in the Twenty-first Century. The 2006 Johan Skytte Prize Lecture" Scandinavian Political Studies 30(2): 137-174, p 139.

The View From Within.

TAKIS KARANTONIS

Promenade

I wish there was a way to give instructions to the reader of this book, right on the cover: *"Do not to attempt to read it the first time you hold it in your hands!"*

Instead, browse through it like you would an illustrated magazine. Take in the visual impressions first. Then, return and read it.

It is comforting to know that the great advantage of photography books is that they seduce readers in exactly this way; and so the instructions might not be needed, but just in case...

I have had the privilege of spending of more than two years in the presence of many of the photographs from the Columbia Pike Documentary Project. Right now, several of them are hanging on the walls of my office on the Pike. Seeing them has become a daily ritual, and I sometimes find myself deliberately promenading past the pictures again and again.

There is a holistic quality that is unmistakable in the collection hanging on my office's walls, and in the larger body of work included in this book. Art critic John Berger attributed the kind of attraction I am describing to the way photography penetrates conscience, through memory or/and expectation.

Mapping the territory

There are the moments when I return to a particular photograph with the intention to "read it"; to go more deeply into the world it depicts.

Much of the work I do consists of reading and trying to more fully understand Columbia Pike. After all, I am also tasked with explaining and promoting the Pike to a large and constantly changing audience.

I use observation and analysis, economic and demographic data, housing and transportation policy documents, place making, urban development and zoning; all these tools and ways of looking at the Pike overlap like layers of a sophisticated map.

Mapping is an attempt to capture and reproduce dynamic processes with static means. Overcoming the limits imposed by static analysis is what drives my desire to return and immerse myself again and again in each individual photograph.

The project photographers are documentarians. They are also visionaries. Their work transcends the layers of an inventory of the Pike's communities because it also tells the story of the future.

Our own mosaic

The vast majority of the photographs in this collection are portraits. Landscape photographs are carefully added to provide context. They capture the physical environment of the Pike that surrounds the people who live and work here.

In some cases, both elements - the human and the built environment - merge into a single, harmonious whole, which is exactly what distinguishes the Pike from many other urban neighborhoods. When this happens, the pictures rise to a completely different level of photography, exemplified in Lloyd Wolf's portrait of Achmed Osman, or Duy Tran's image of the Oriental Supermarket.

I would invite the reader to see the photographs in this book as many individual fragments forming a rich mosaic. Through this mosaic, the Columbia Pike Documentary Project delivers a unique and consistent narrative of place and people living in proximity, along one of Arlington's main east-west thoroughfares.

Which is why, to me, this book is story-telling at its best. Beyond simply appreciating the beauty of the photographs, readers are encouraged to compose their own narrative tapestry.

Diversity

Fragments are produced by the shattering of other forms, just as questions are born when comfortable certainty is challenged or broken apart. Like all great images, the photographs in this book raise questions. Who is this person? Who are these people? Where are they coming from? Why are they here? Are they staying or leaving? And why?

In the same way, great art doesn't allow quick or easy answers: Is "The Pike" beautiful or ugly? Does it have a character or is it a soulless suburban thoroughfare? Is there a past worth preserving? Is there a future worth pursuing? And who gets to decide? Who owns this place anyway?

As an immigrant, I moved (several times in my life) from one territory to another. Thus I can relate to the concept of disruption, of shattering, and the ensuing trajectories of flight. In fact, I see these trajectories and my own experience represented, in all their possible dimensions, in the Project's work.

There are many cultural, economic, ethnic, political, or religious reasons why a person chooses to move away from one place and go to another. The Pike is constantly changing with the arrival of new people, and its longtime residents seem to fit seamlessly in this environment of transitions. Diversity on the Pike includes them. It would be impossible without them.

It is often said that Arlington is a "transient place." This is not only a statement about demographic movement. It also says a lot about the core character of our hometown. "Transient places" are open territories where boundaries or exclusive territorial ownership are of lesser importance. Before our eyes, this documentary project opens both "Columbia Pikes:" the destination and the place of origin, where people have arrived from elsewhere and move elsewhere; and where something of their souls, their essence remains.

Community belonging is not coded anymore solely on territorial attributes. Instead, quality of life, safety, peace, civic pride, fairness, democracy, mutual respect, social equality, solidarity, and a culture of moving forward together define the relationship of longtime residents as well as newcomers to a place. *Living Diversity* is in many ways about the strength of this relationship. The five photographers capture Columbia Pike as a state of mind and an attitude before they record it as a territory.

Beyond that, the Project's photographs reflect the amazing fact that people of all possible origins live here, together, in mixed communities and perfectly peacefully. This is not a product of chance but the result of deliberately keeping our community an open and welcoming place.

Takis Karantonis
Executive Director of the Columbia Pike
Revitalization Organization.

DUY TRAN

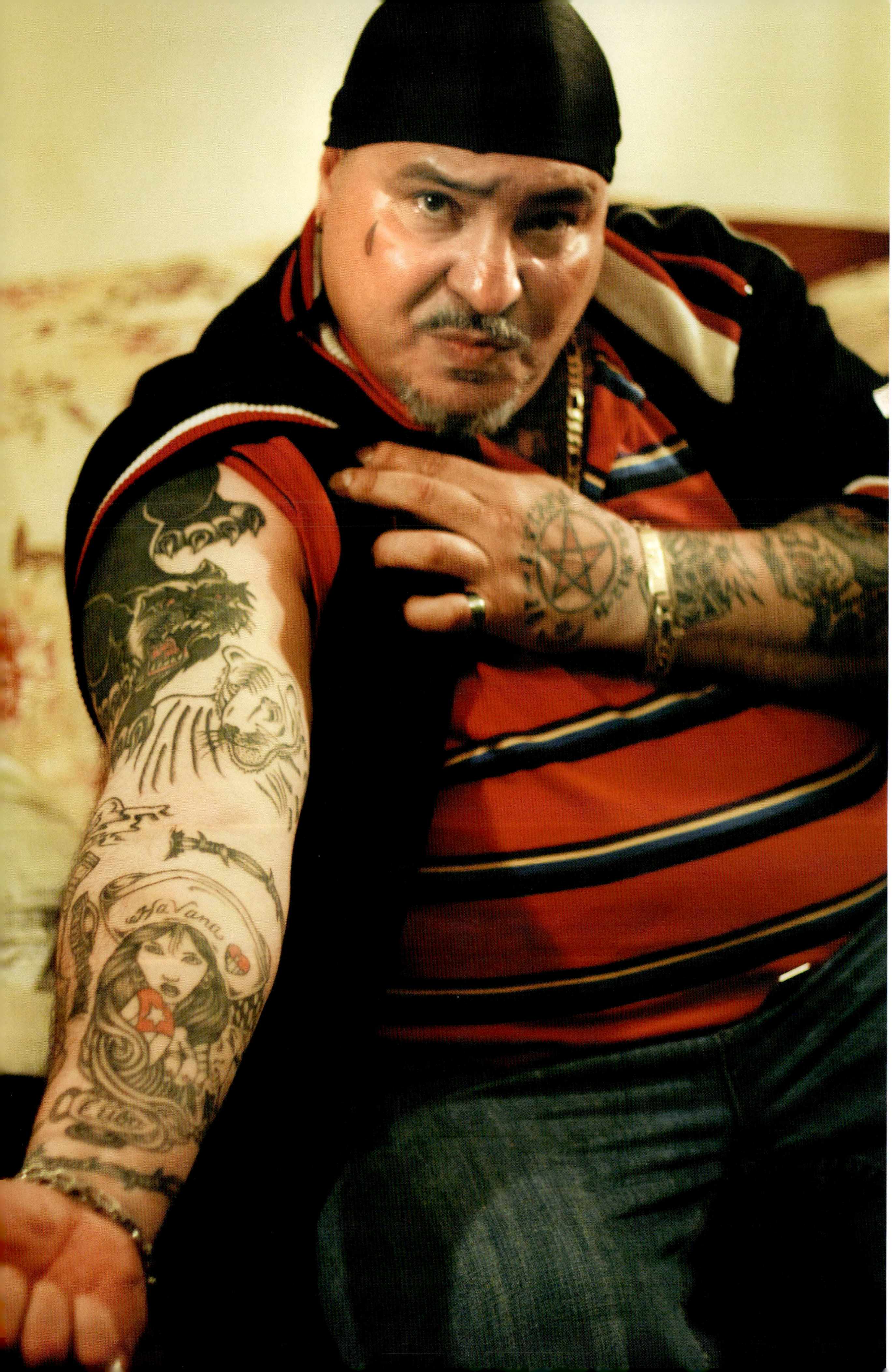
Havana

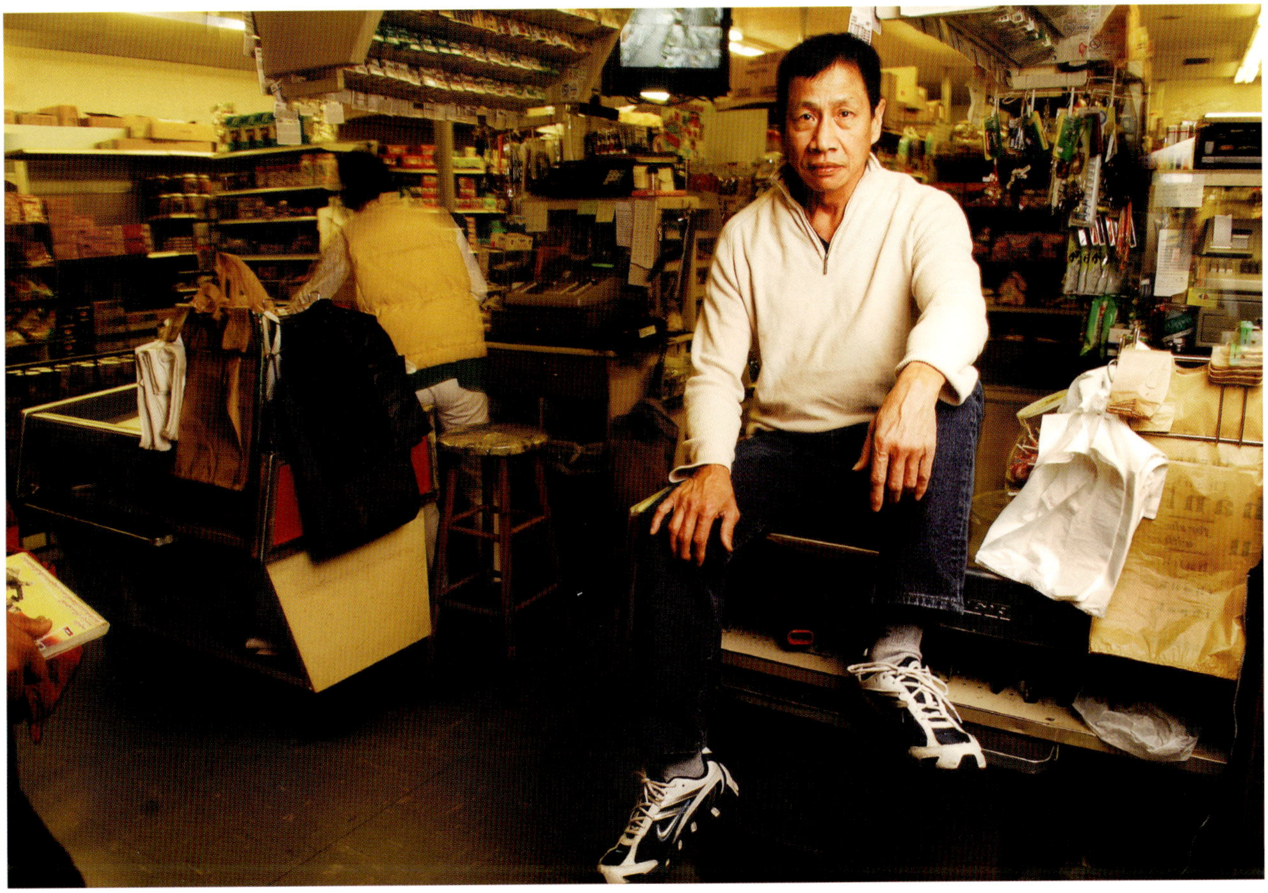

« Emilio Vasquez

Meng K. Taing, Oriental Supermarket, 5100 Columbia Pike

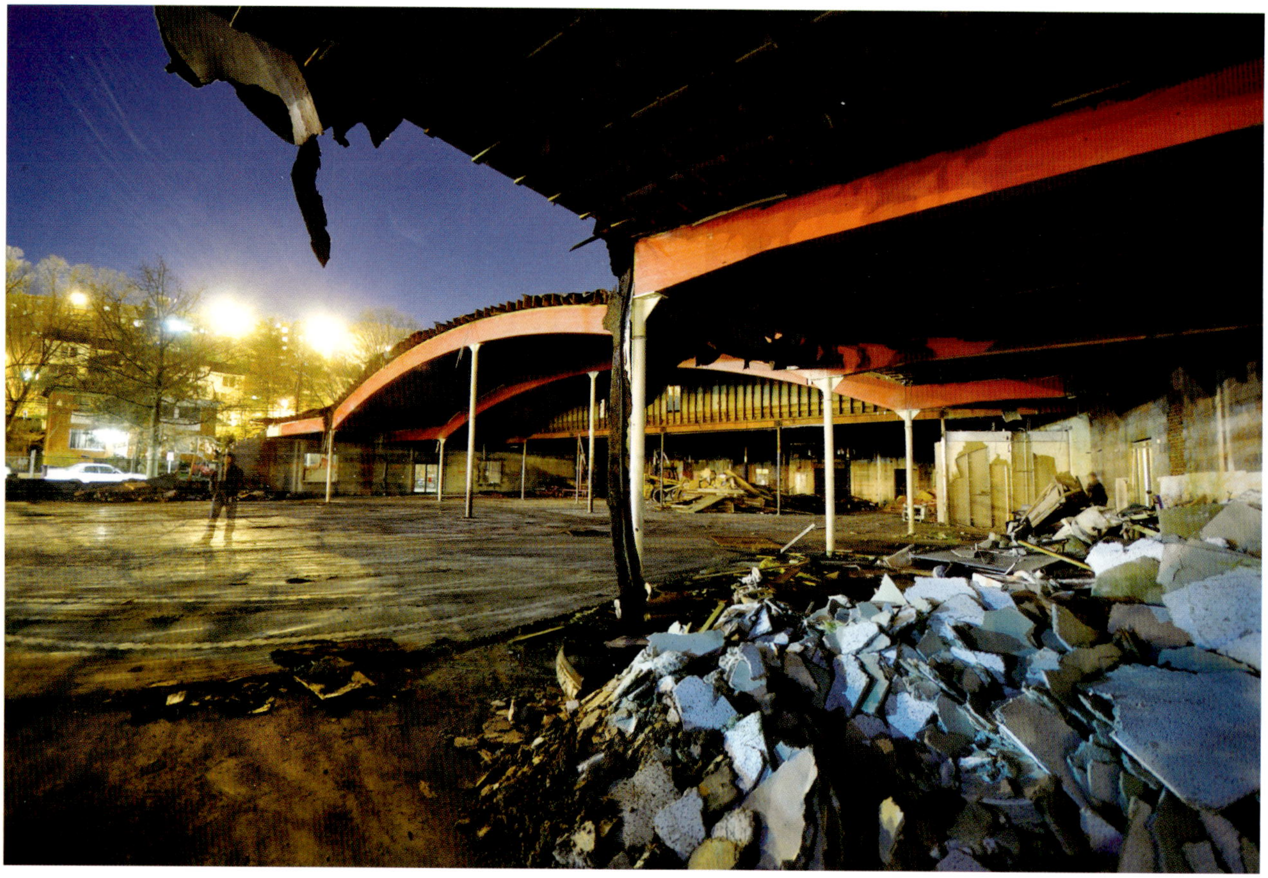

Demolition of the old Arlington Mill Community Center (self portrait)

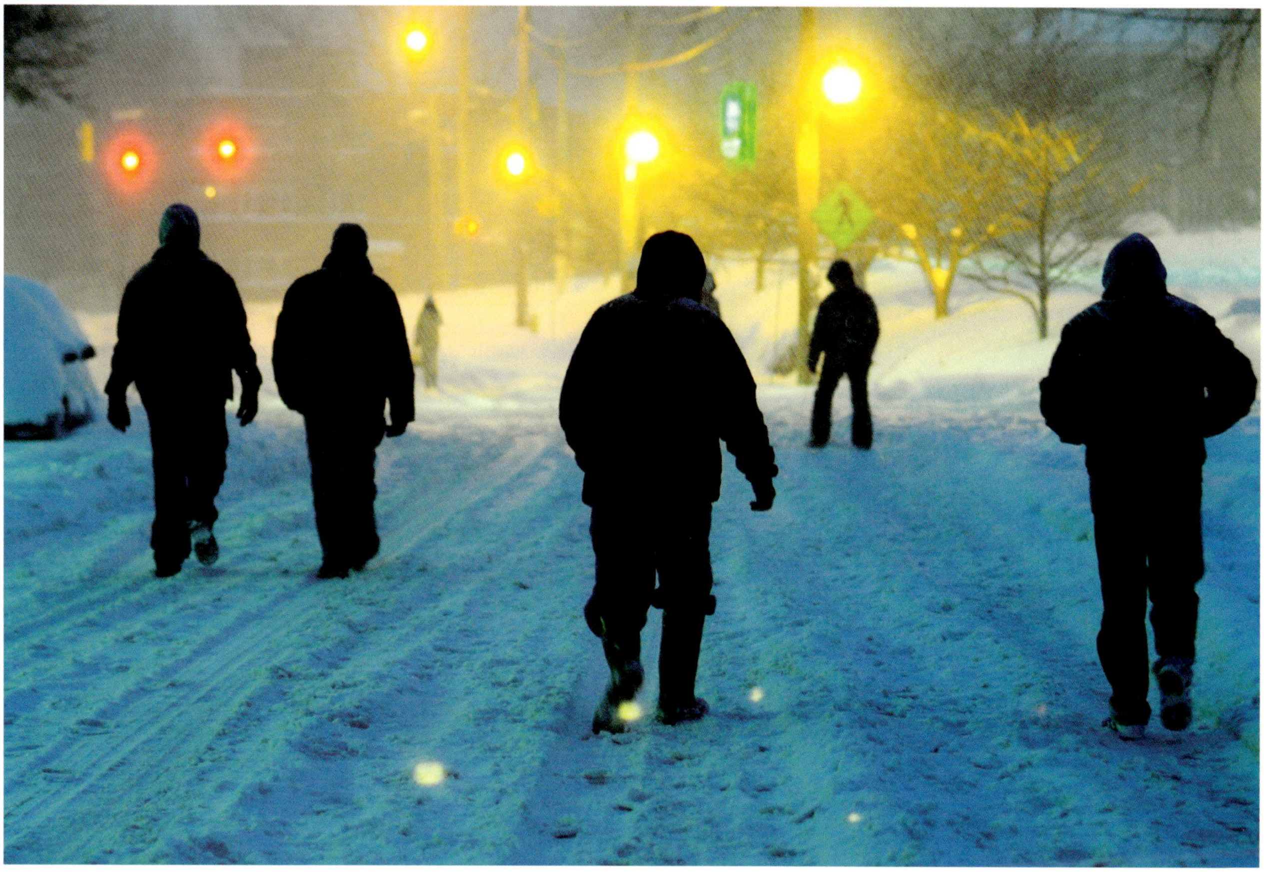

Night scene after heavy snowfall

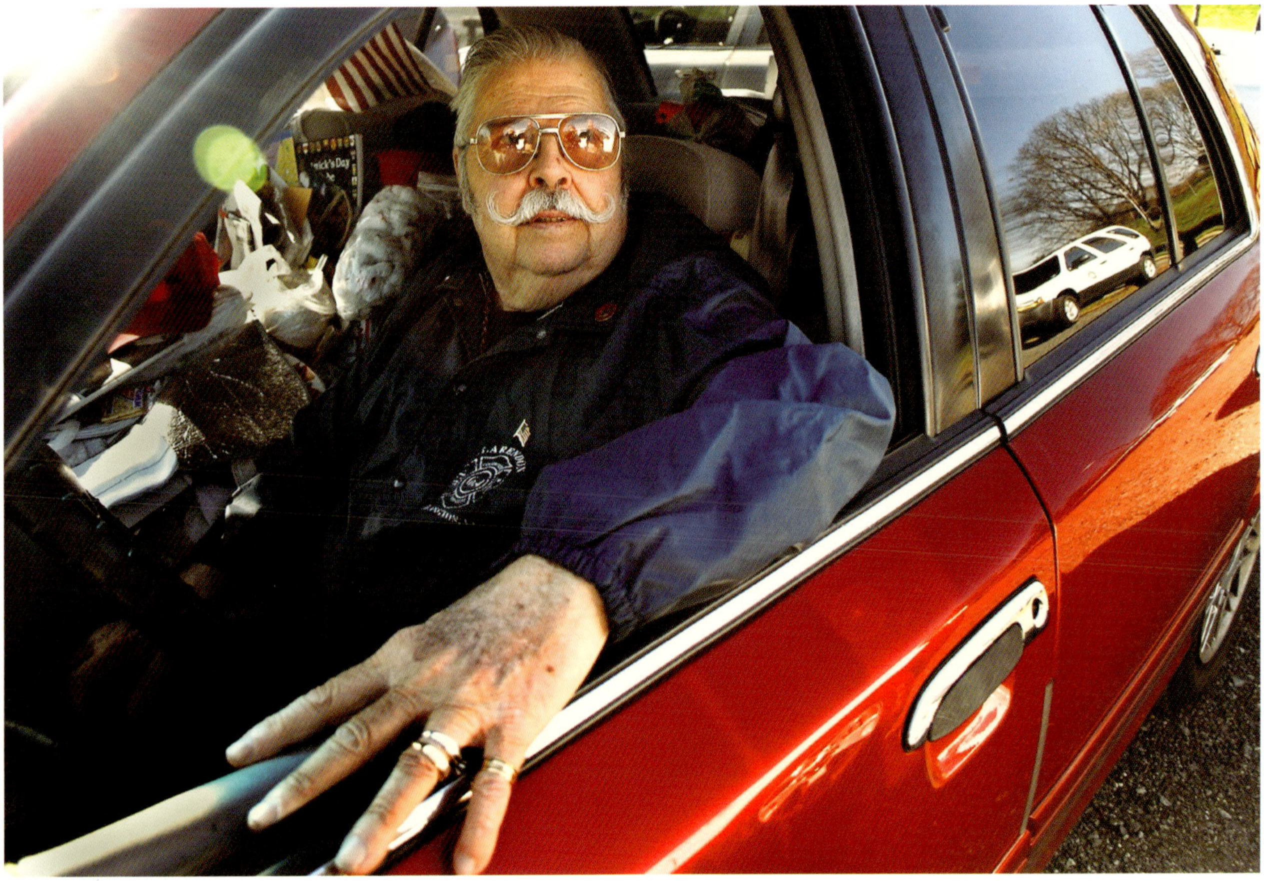

Frank Higgins; Arlington Volunteer Fire Department

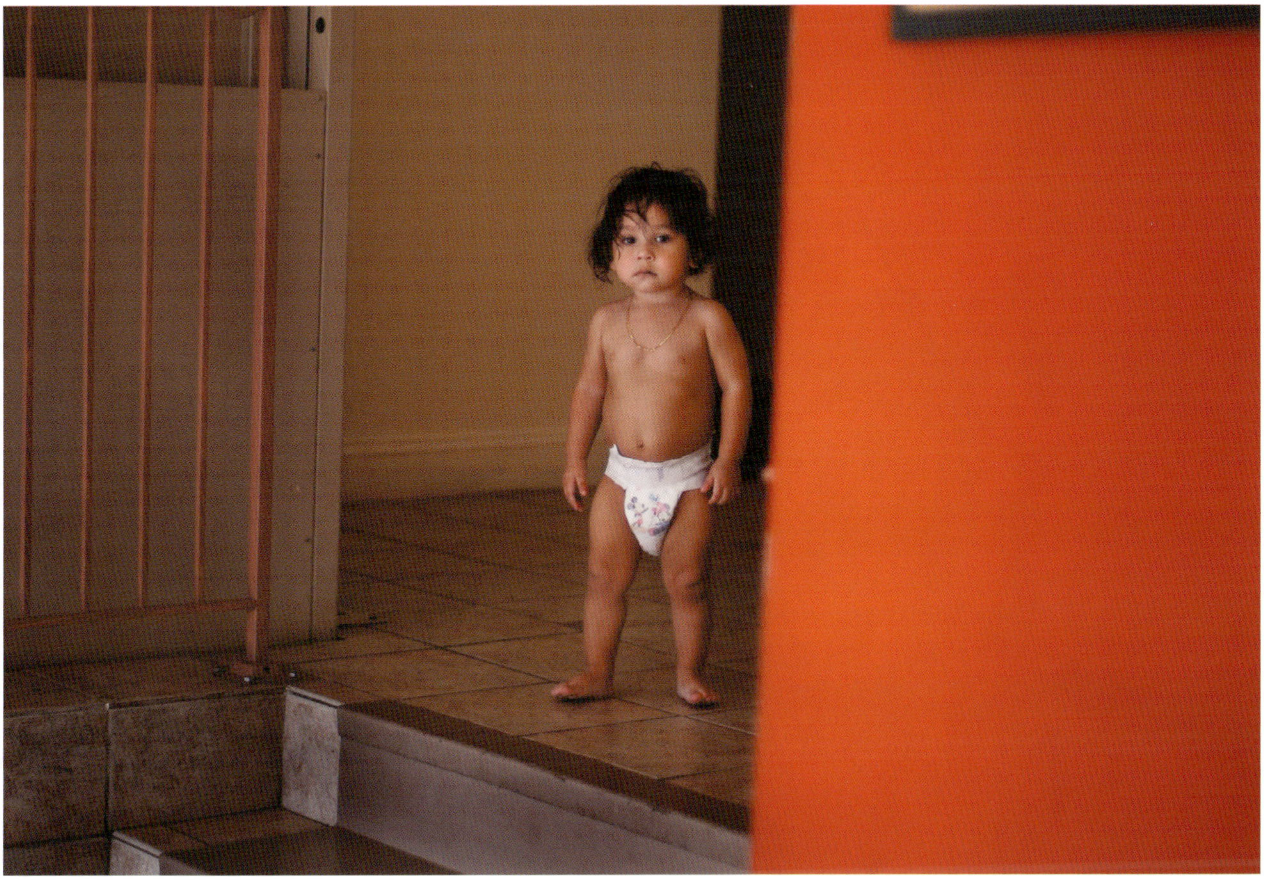

Infant, Columbia Heights West

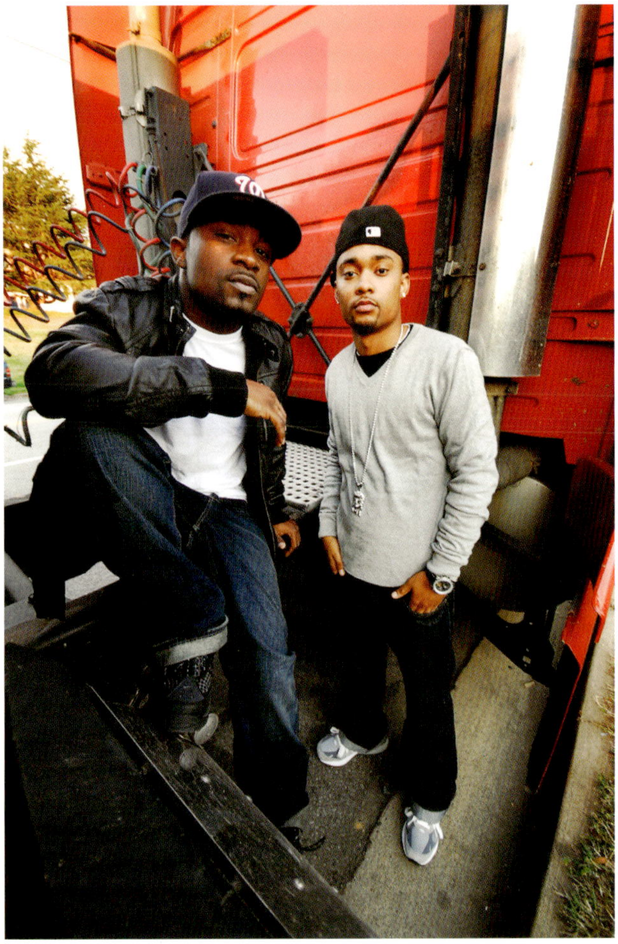

Aldwin Jones (left) and friend

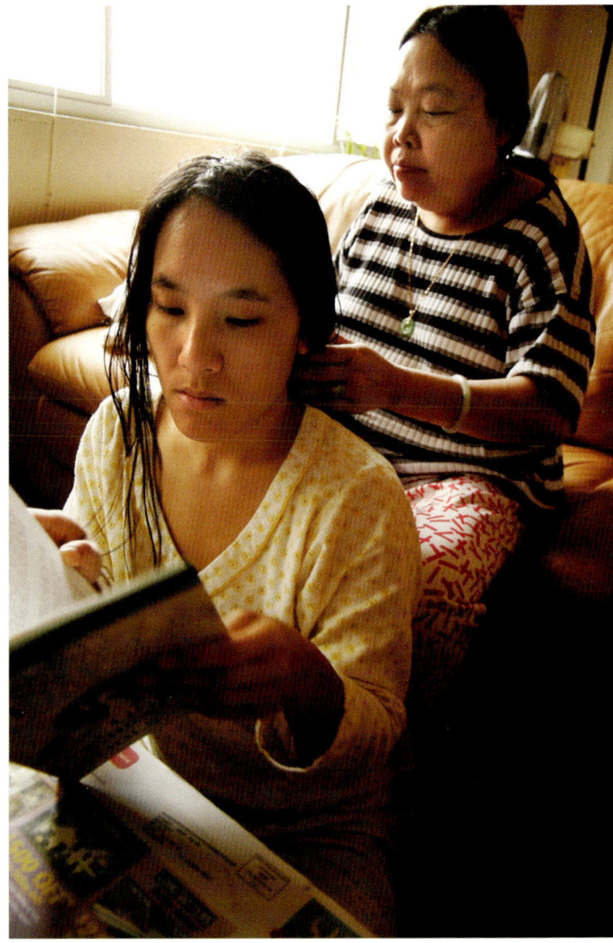

Daisy Lung and her mother, Kinh Tran

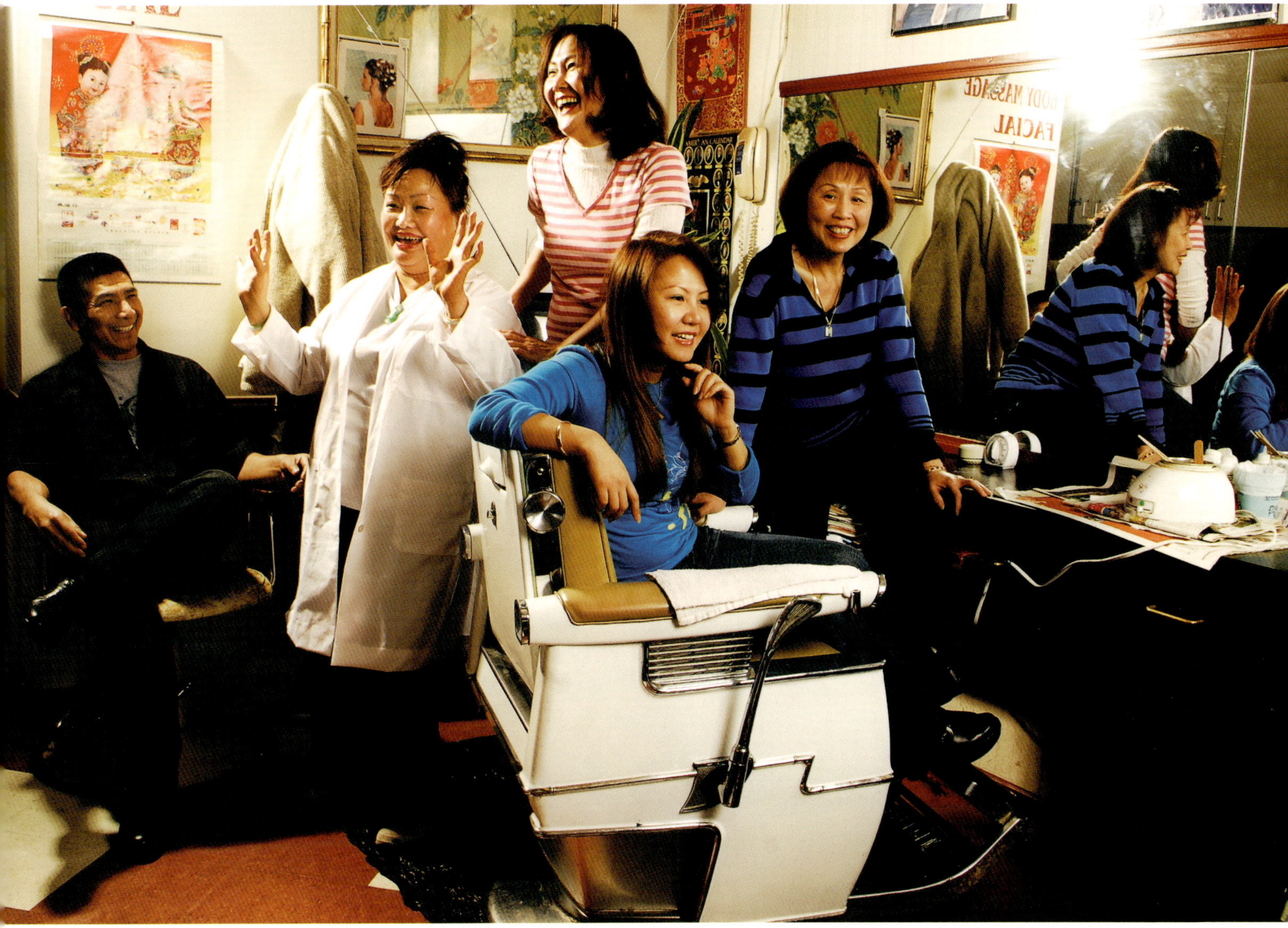

Owner and employees of the International Barbershop;

Huong K Hoang, Sirinapa Srinuan, Jeanine Phoung, Hue So Huynh, 5035 Columbia Pike

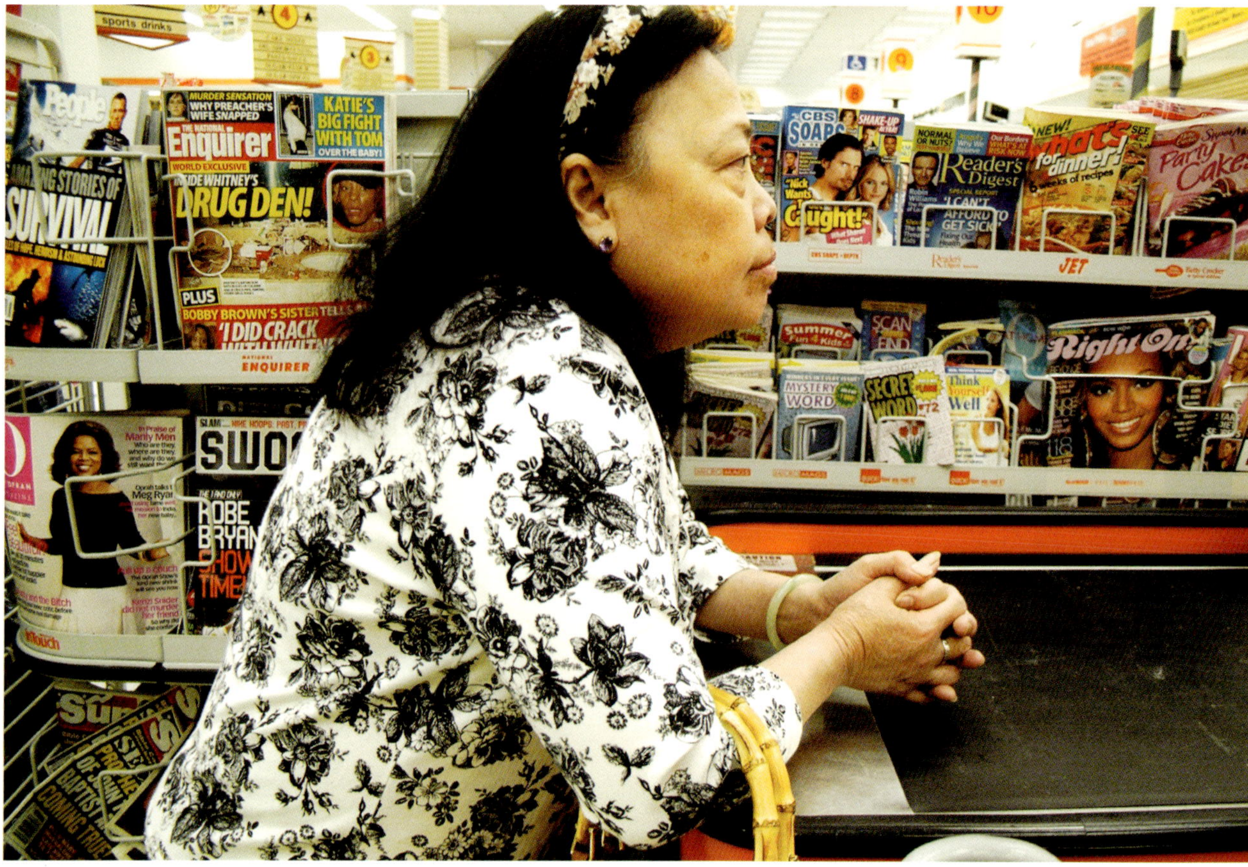
sports drinks
People
SURVIVAL
MURDER SENSATION
WHY PREACHER'S WIFE SNAPPED
Enquirer
KATIE'S BIG FIGHT WITH TOM
OVER THE BABY!
WORLD EXCLUSIVE
DRUG DEN!
PLUS
BOBBY BROWN'S SISTER TELLS
'I DID CRACK
ENQUIRER
CBS SOAPS
SHAKE-UP
Caught!
Reader's Digest
NEW!
What's for dinner?
Party Cakes
JET
SCAN
MYSTERY WORD
SECRET WORD
Think Yourself Well
Right On!
In Praise of Manly Men

Kinh Tran

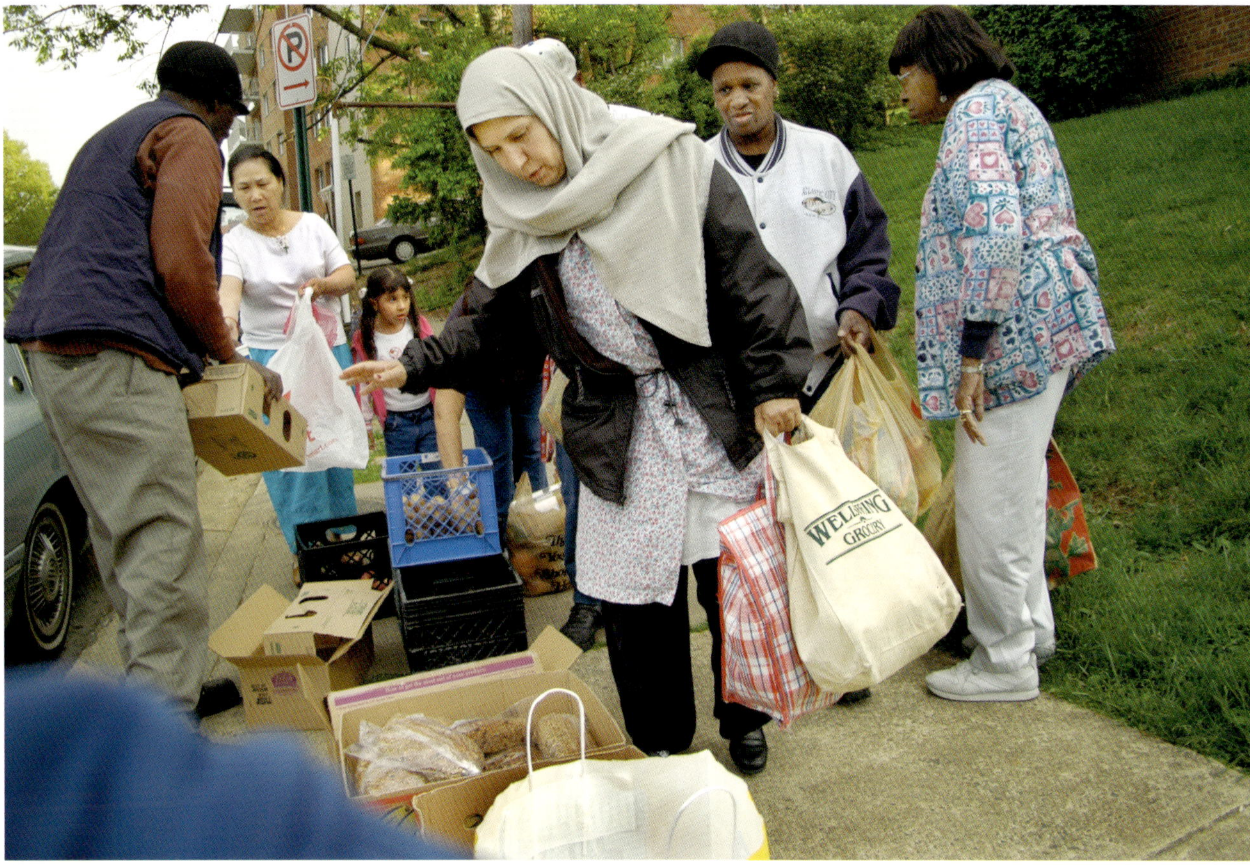

Columbia Heights West

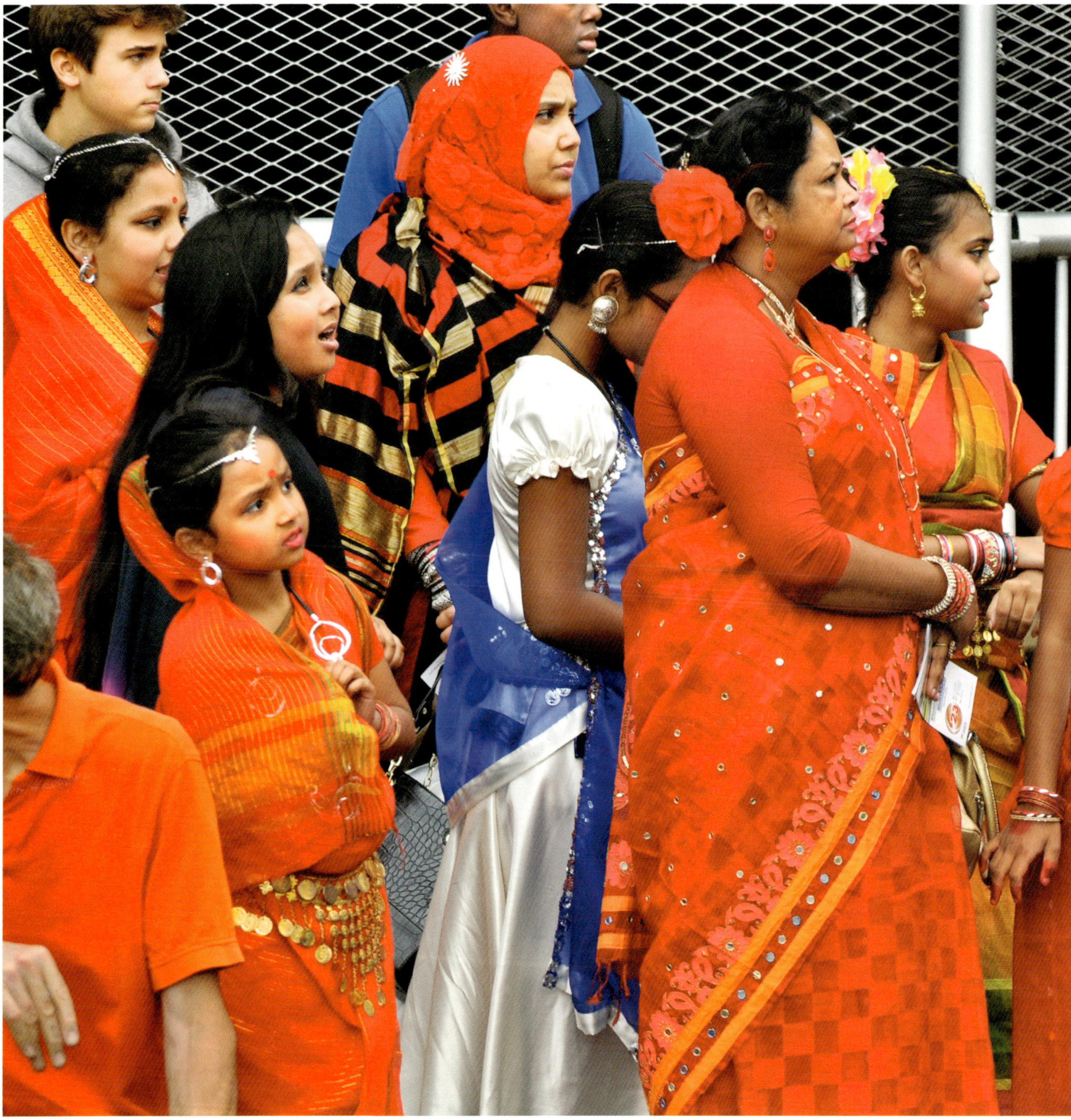

Prio Bangla Festival

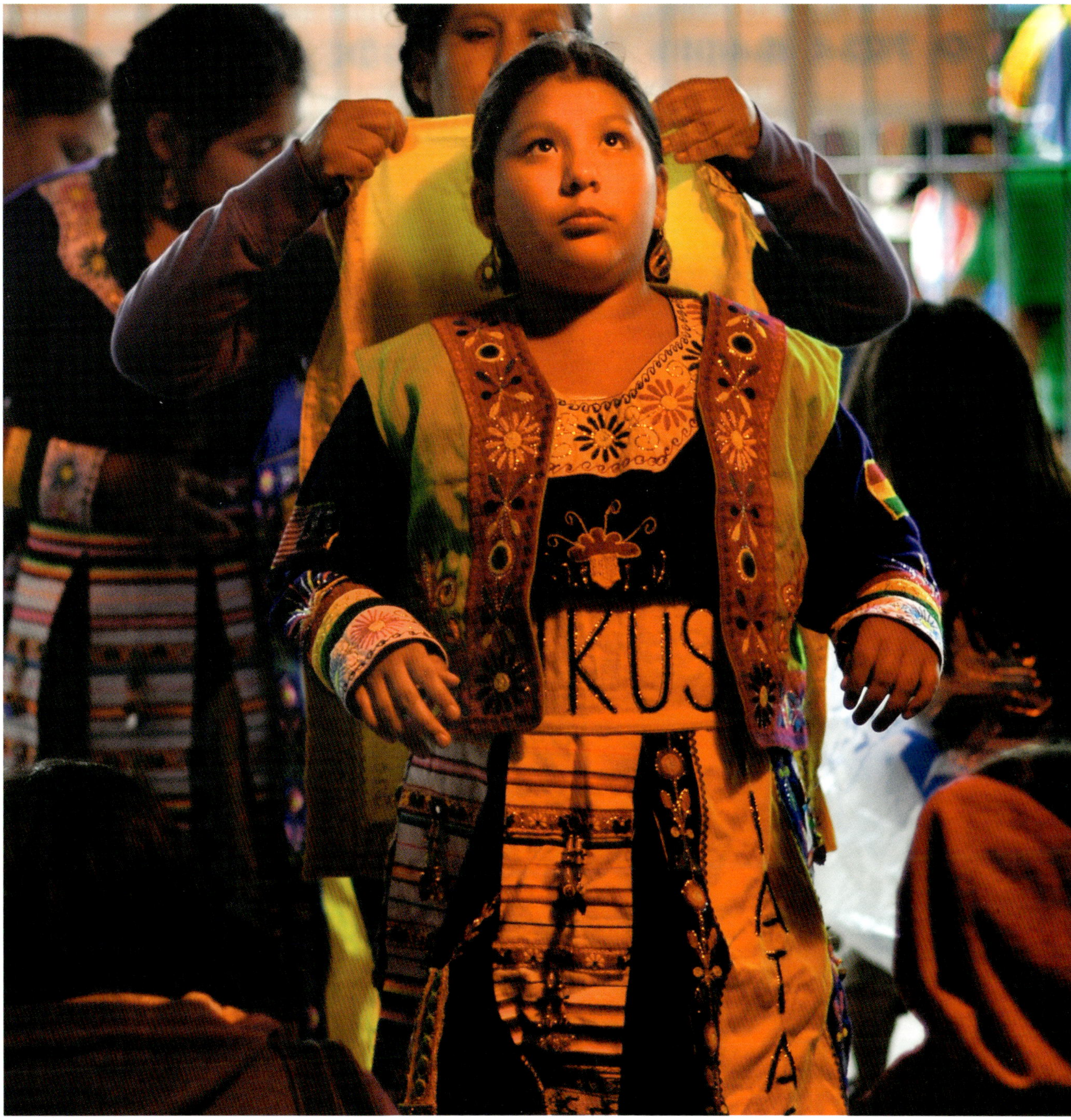

Prio Bangla Festival

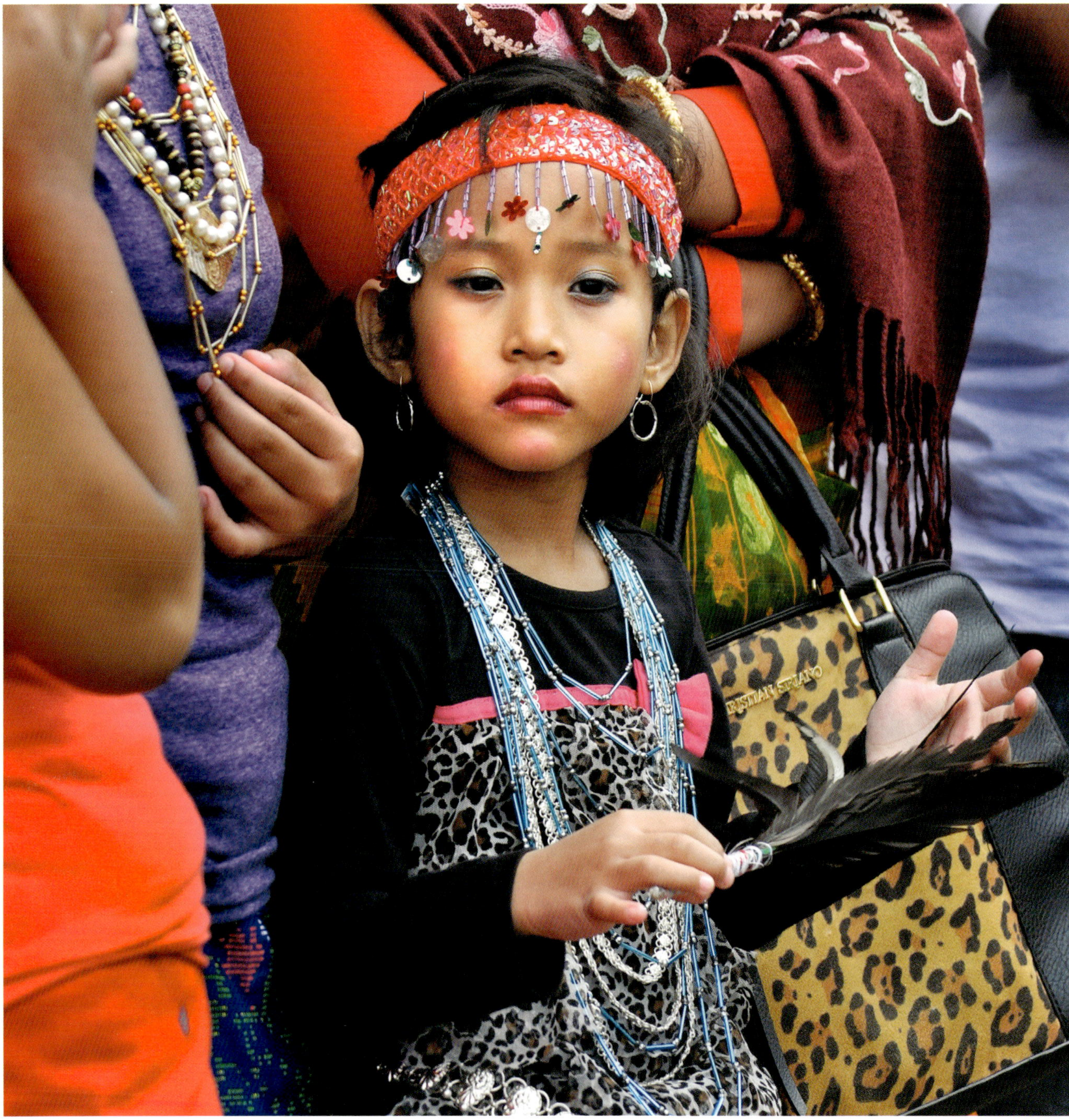

Prio Bangla Festival

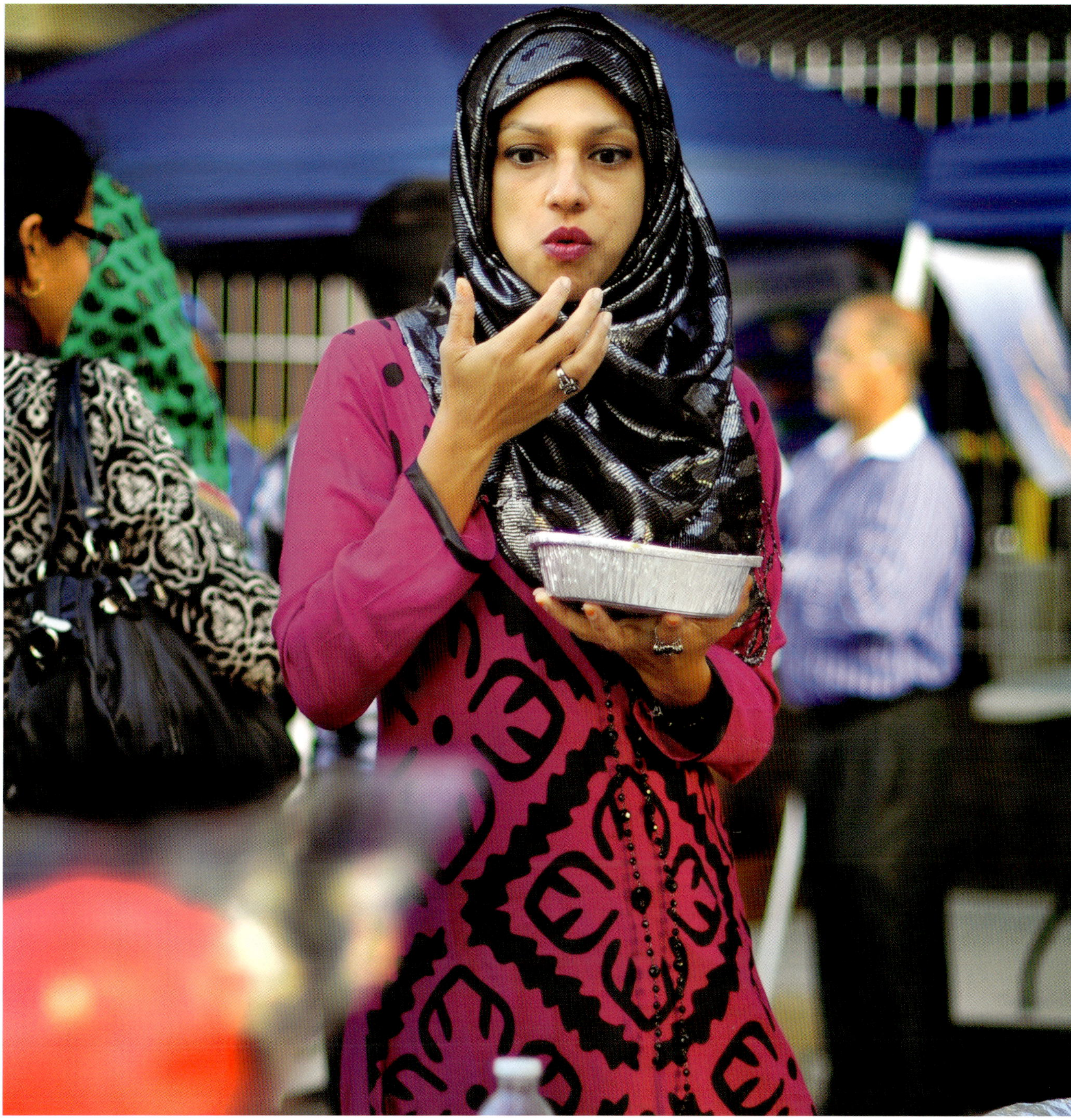

Prio Bangla Festival

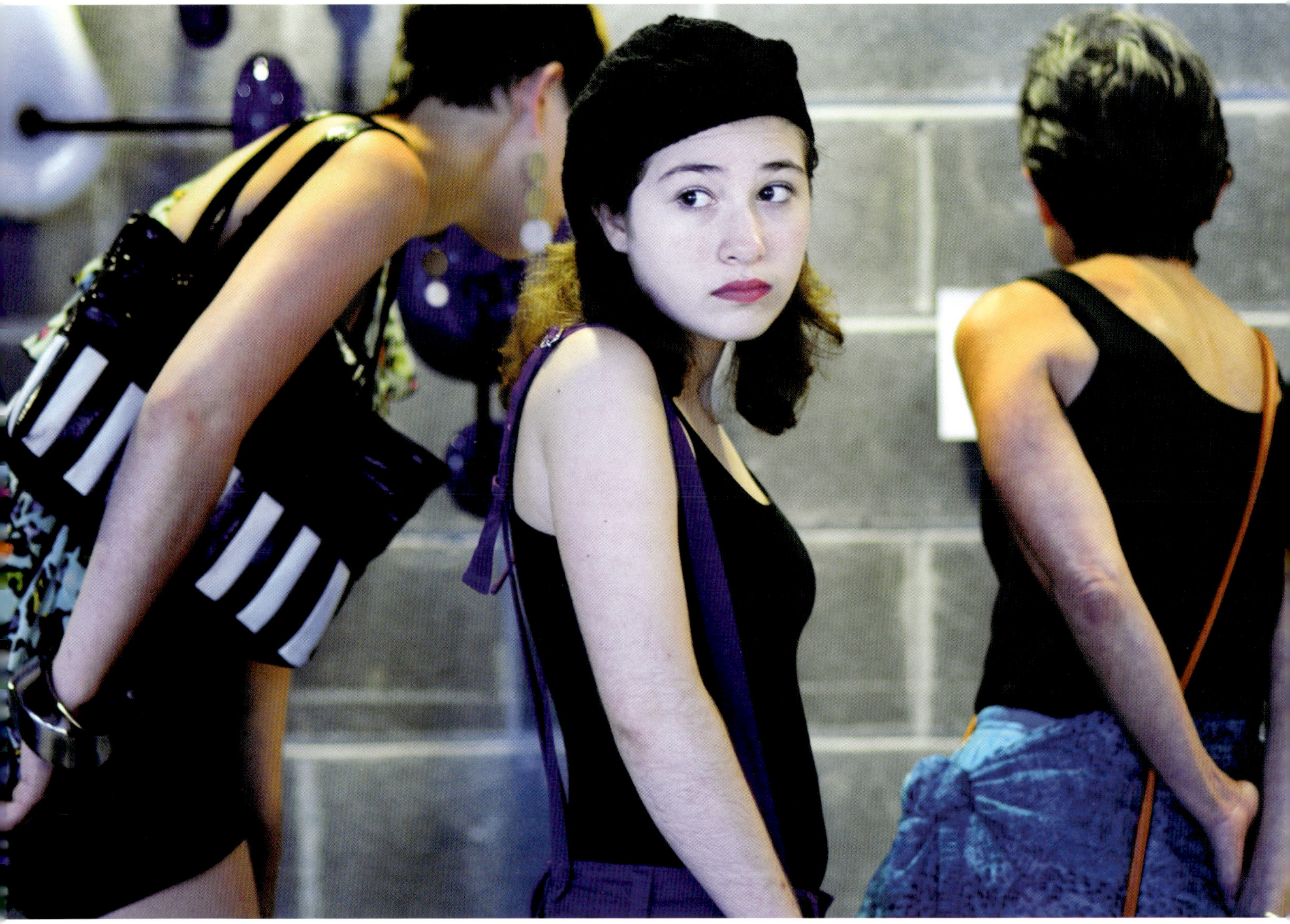

Zip Code Show, Art Outlet event at the Halstead, Columbia Pike and South Walter Reed Drive

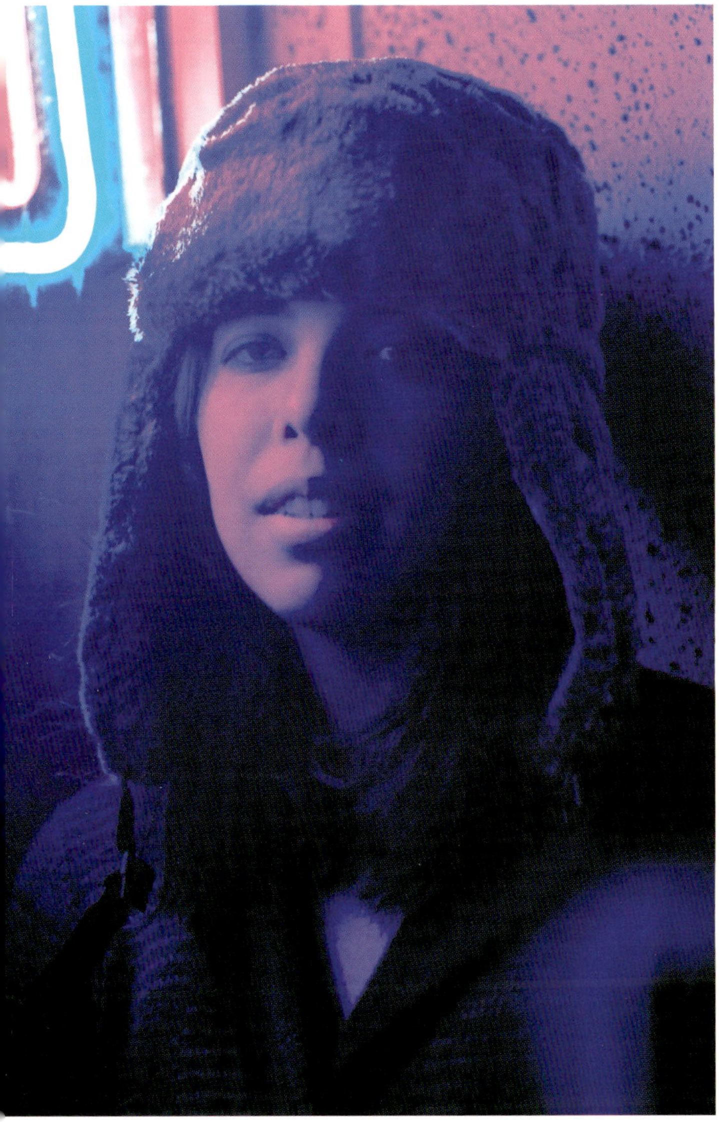

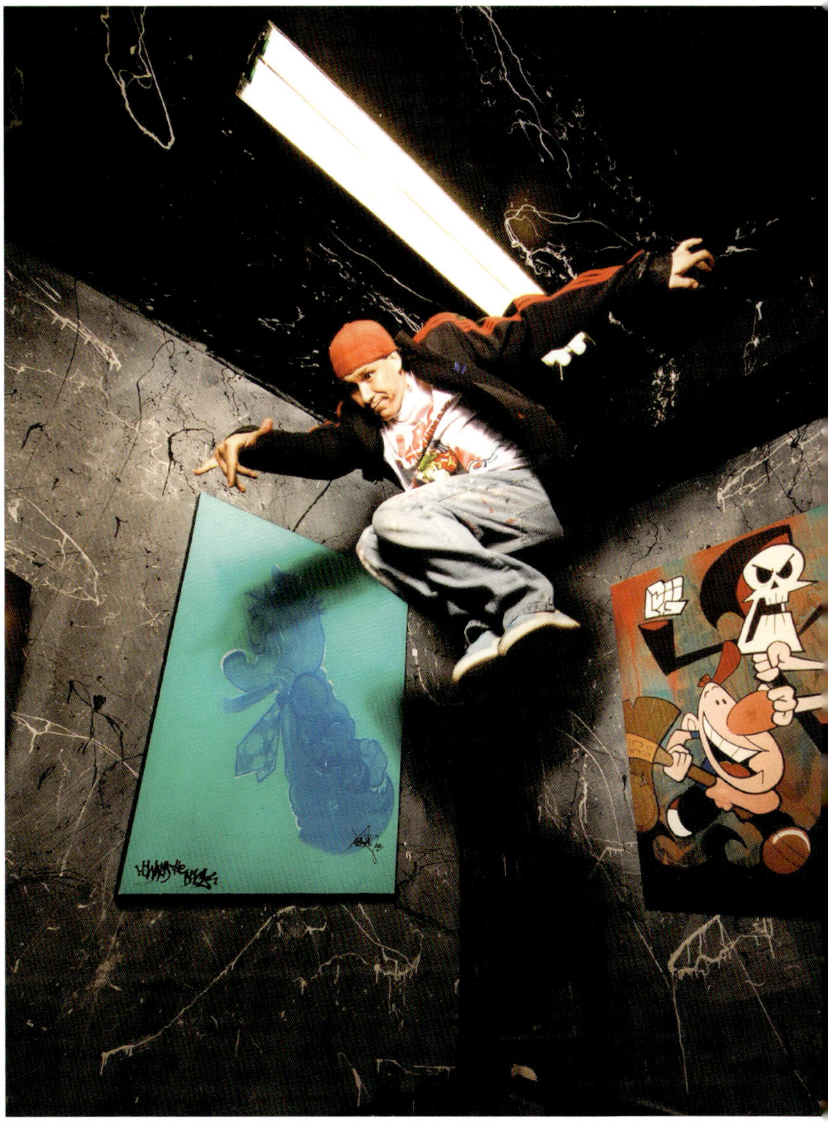

Allie Alvarado

JaziRock (Kevin Ervin), 3213 Columbia Pike

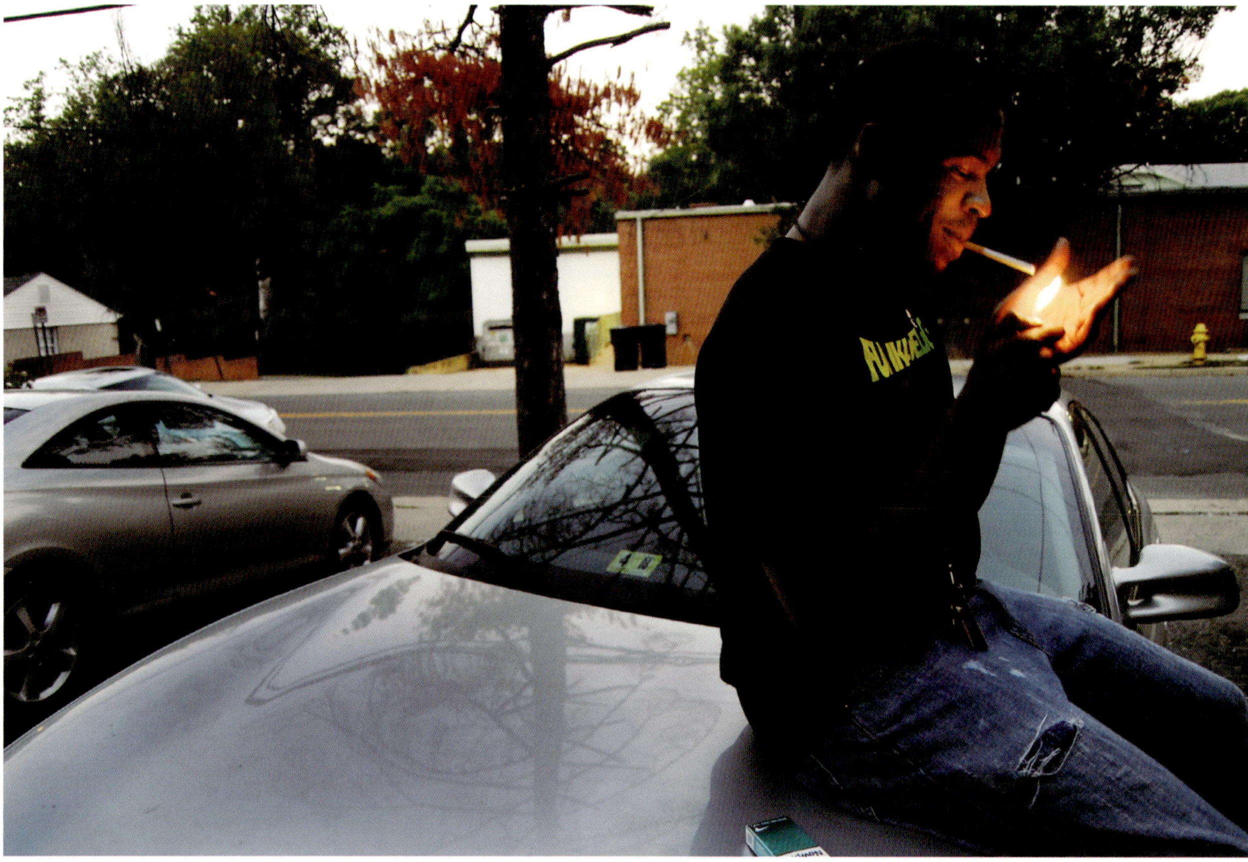

Shawn McGhee

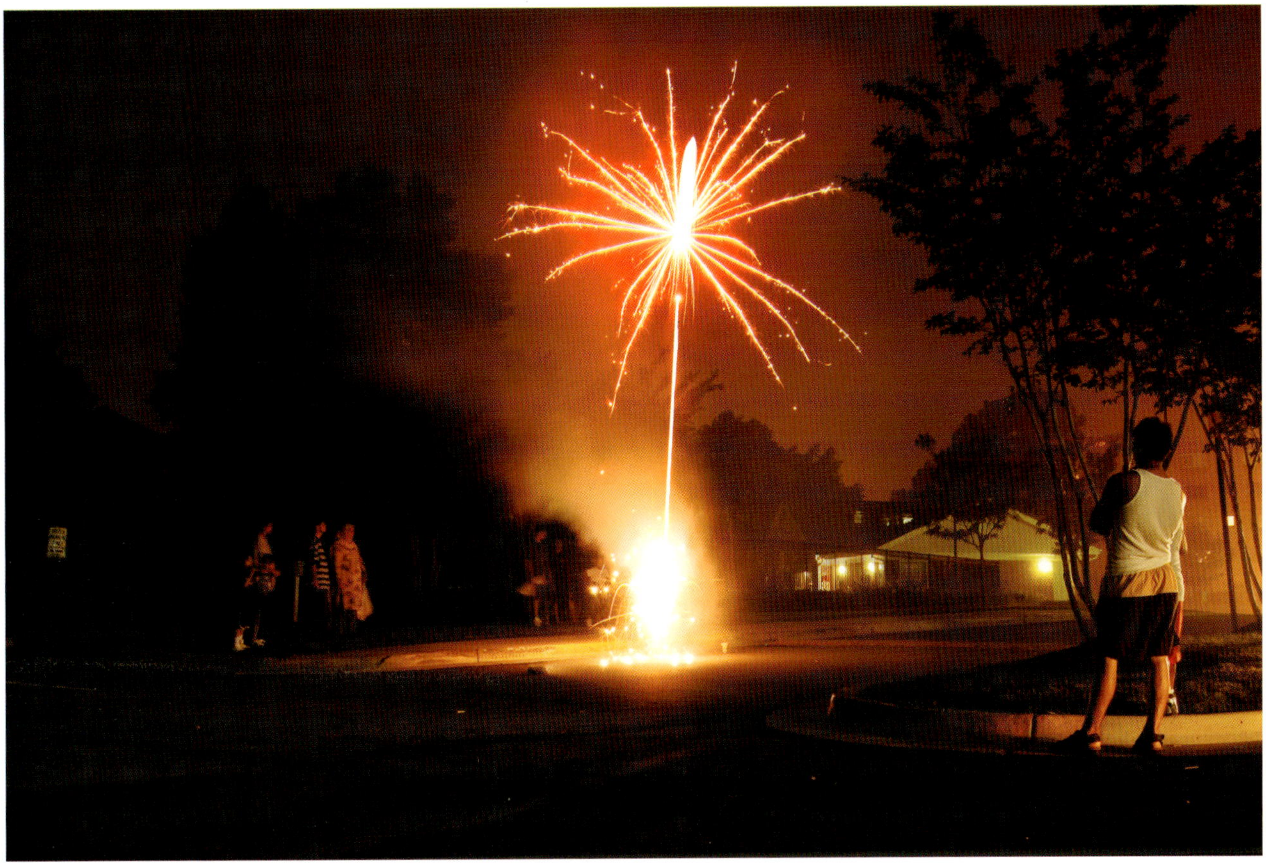

Fourth of July, Columbia Heights West

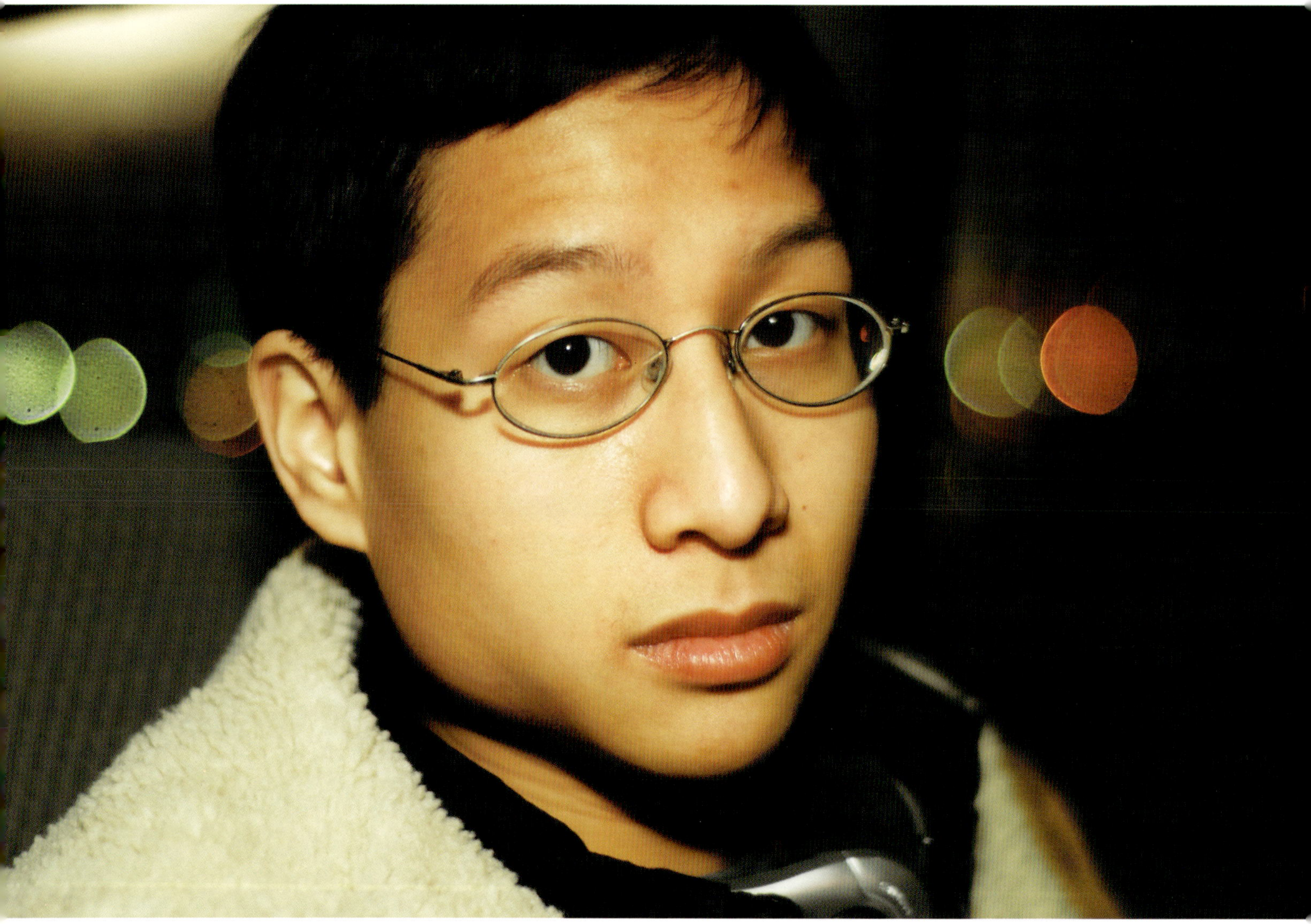

Chau Tran

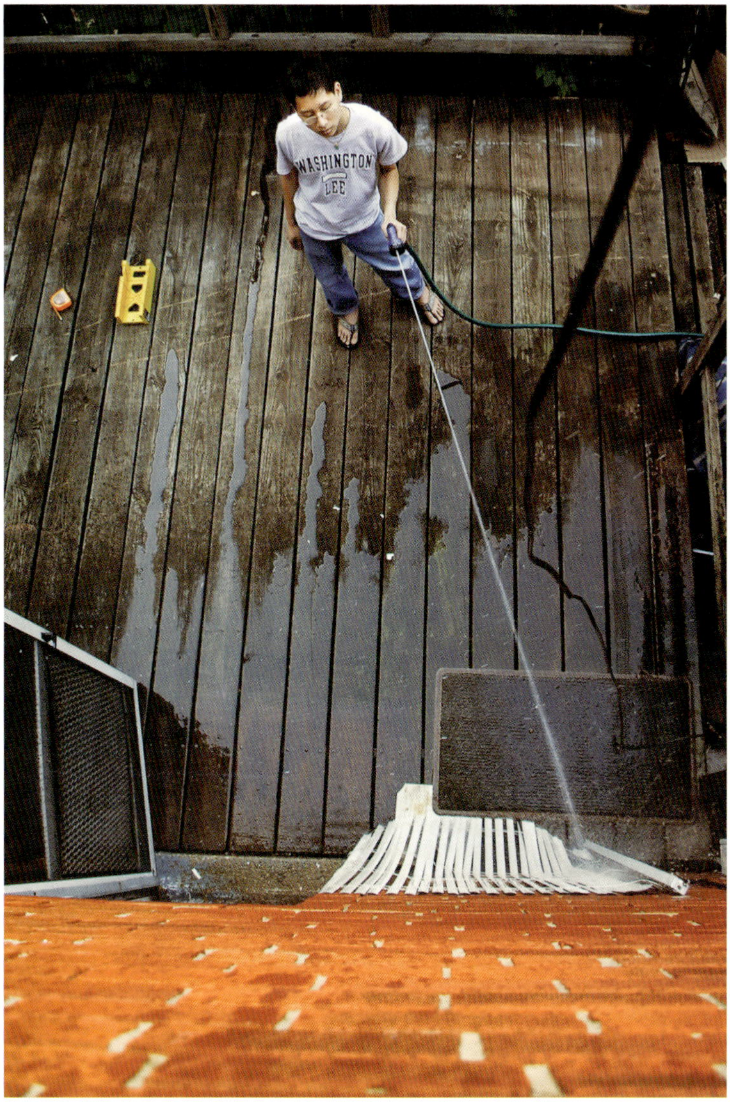

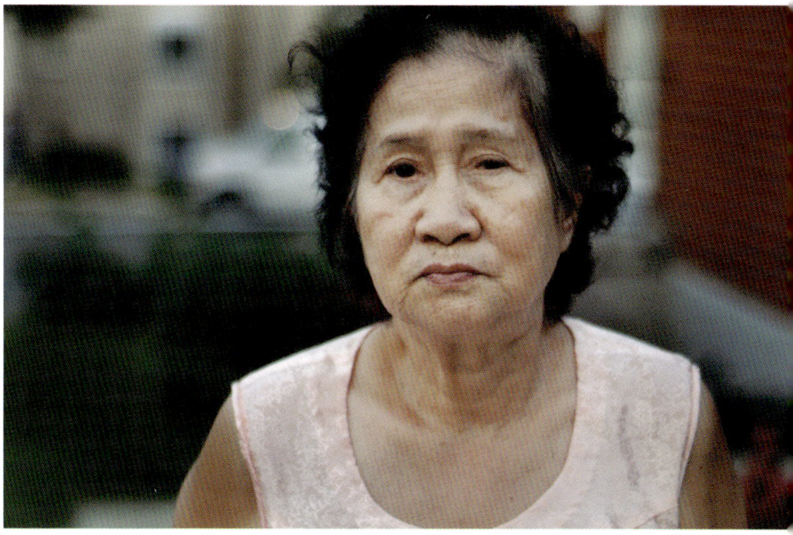

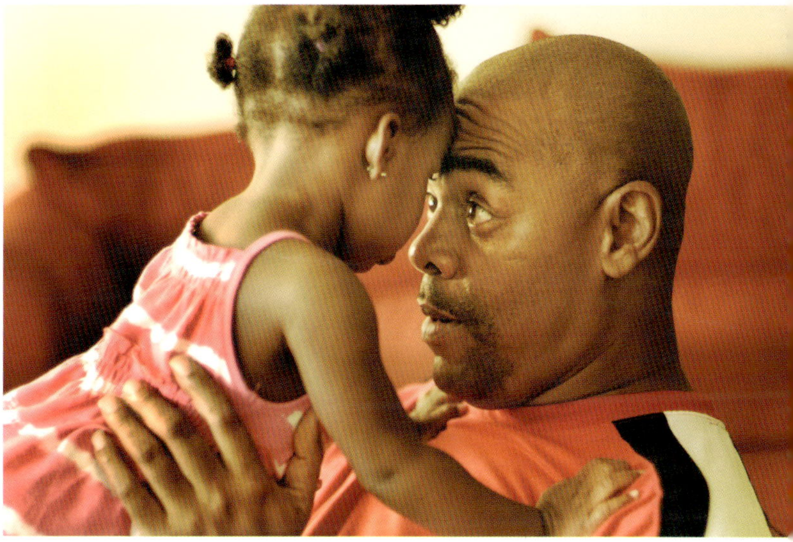

Chau Tran

Bay Nguyen (top)

Ted and niece (bottom)

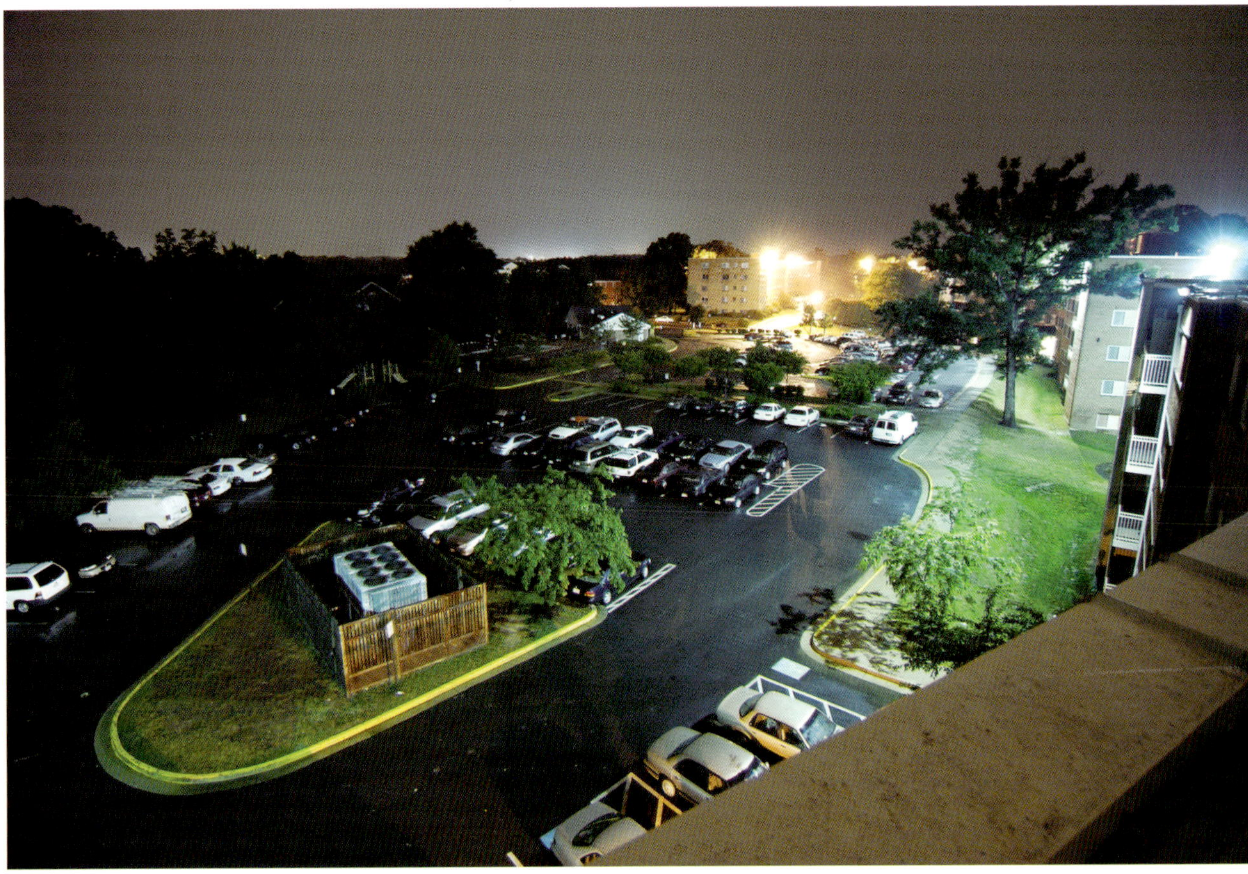

Parking lot at night, 5100 South Eighth Road. Columbia Heights West

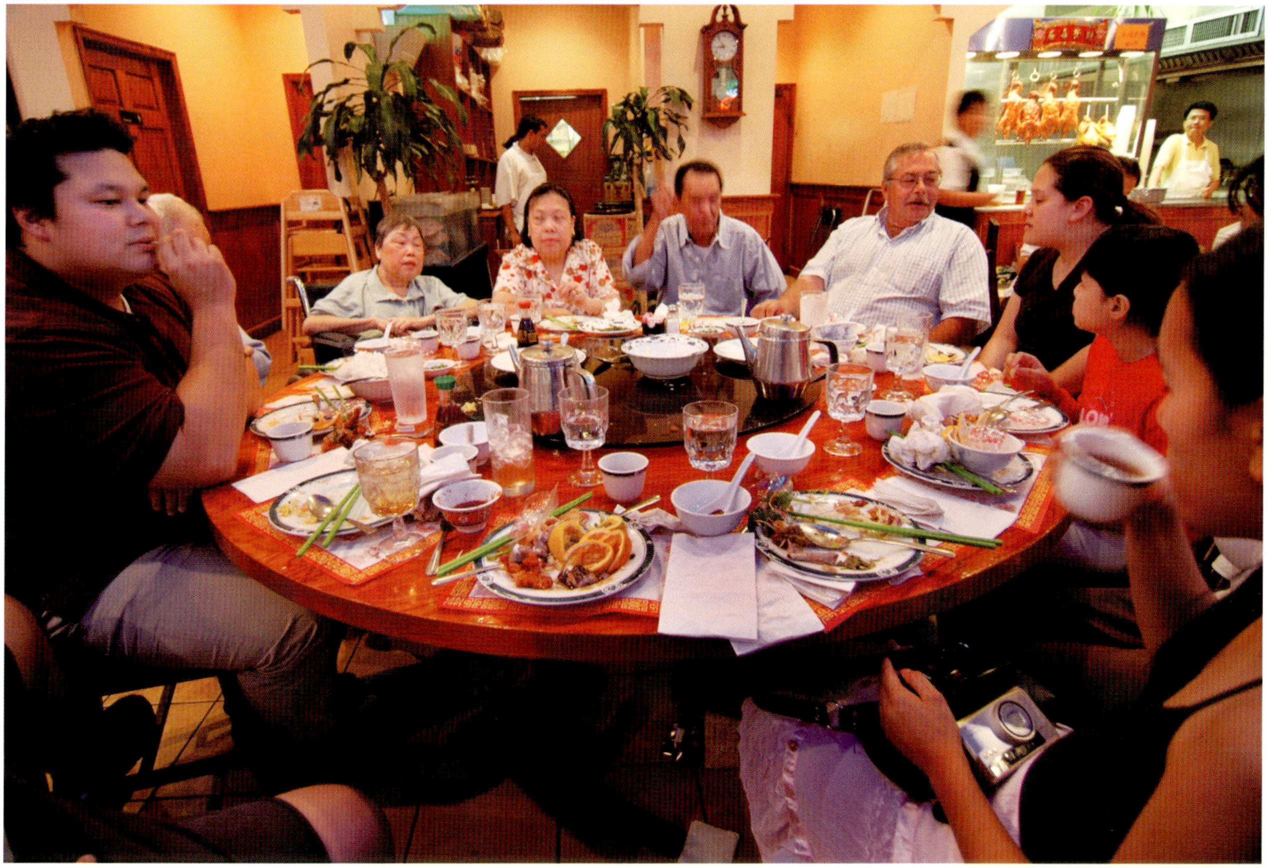

Andrew Chamaj, Yen Ngo, Kinh Tran, W. Tran, Jim Chamaj, Karen Chamaj, Nhi Tran, Daisy Lung
at Full Kee Restaurant, 5830 Columbia Pike

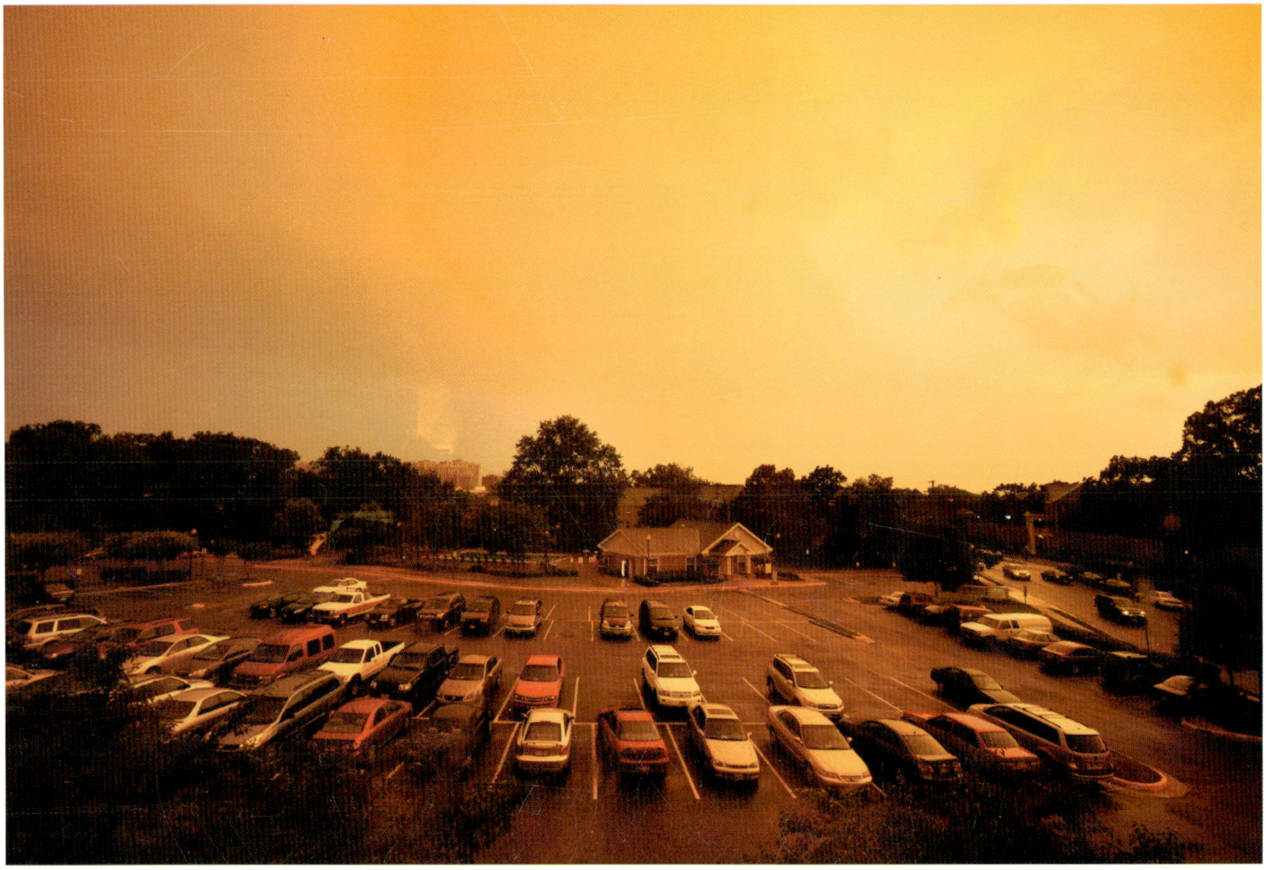

Parking lot at sunset, Columbia Heights West

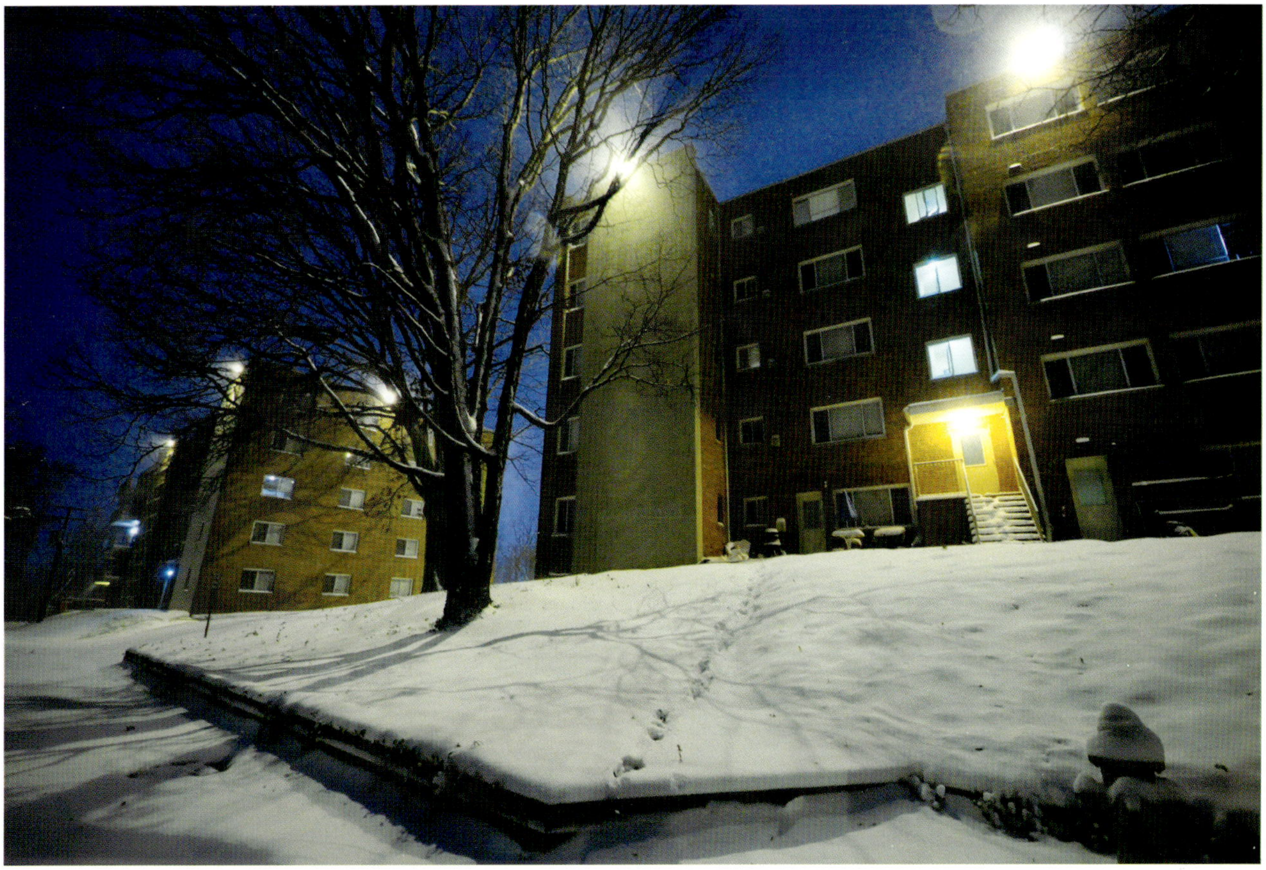

Columbia Heights West after a snowstorm

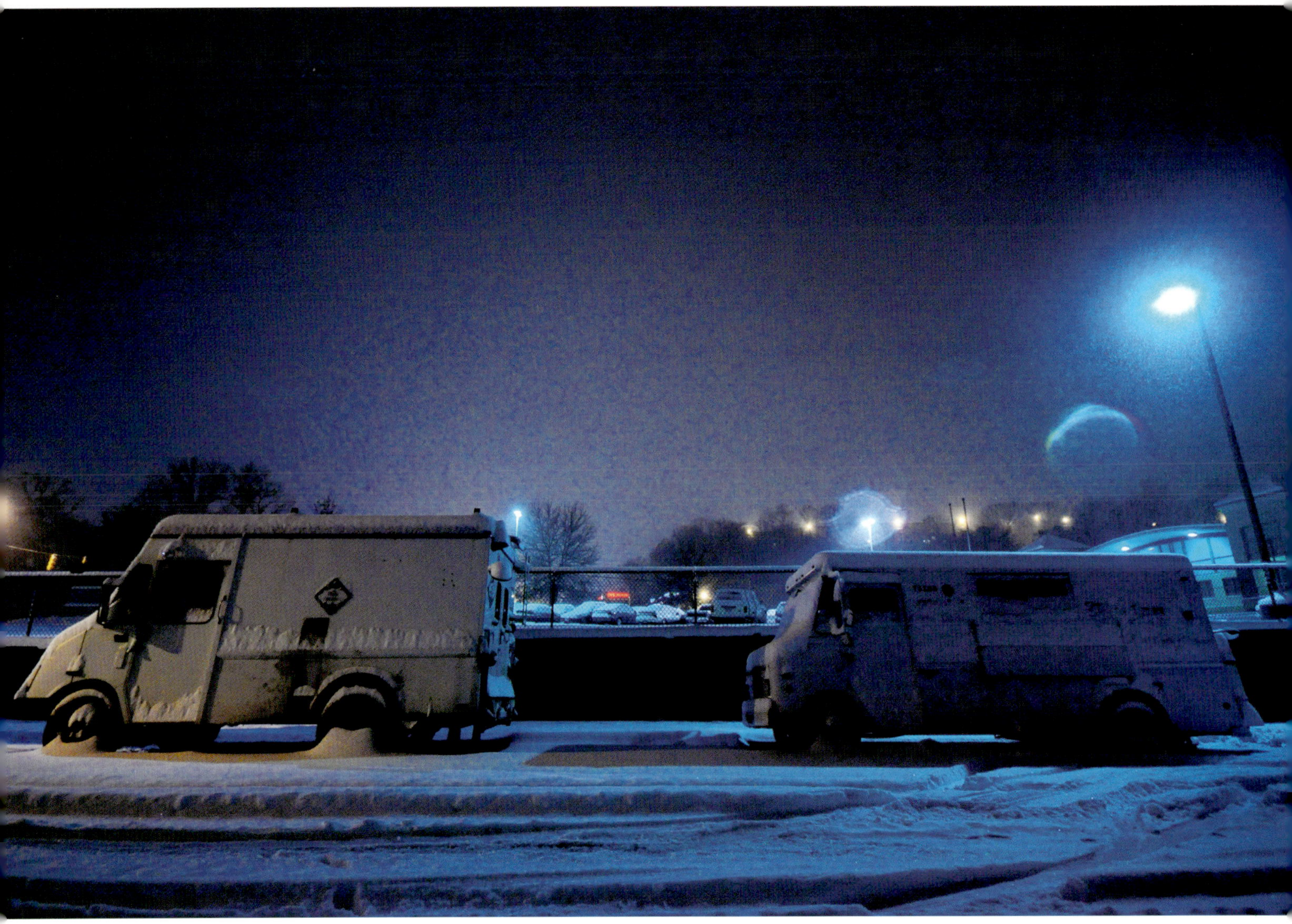

Columbia Heights West after a snowstorm

LLOYD WOLF

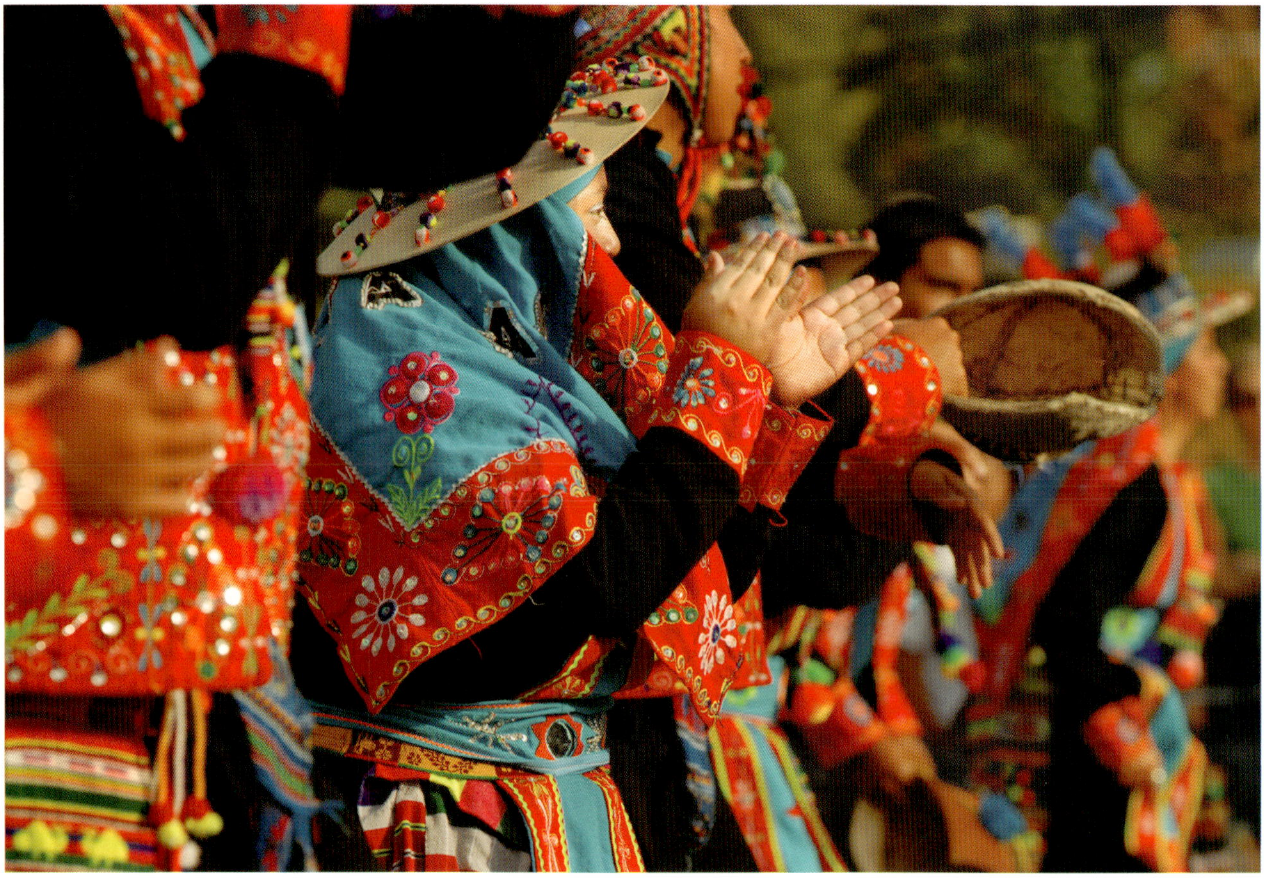

Bolivian dancers, Taste of the Pike Festival

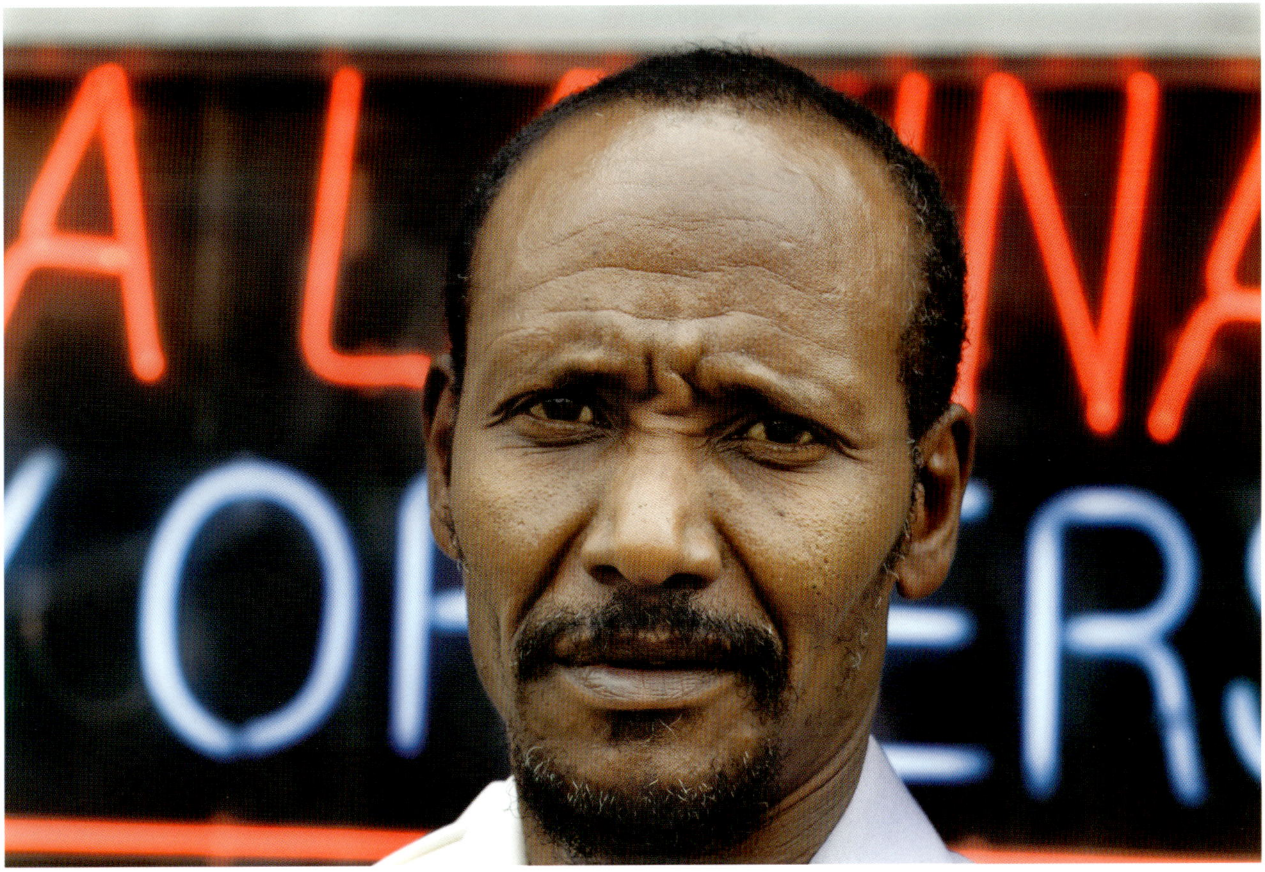

African man, 4700 block of Columbia Pike

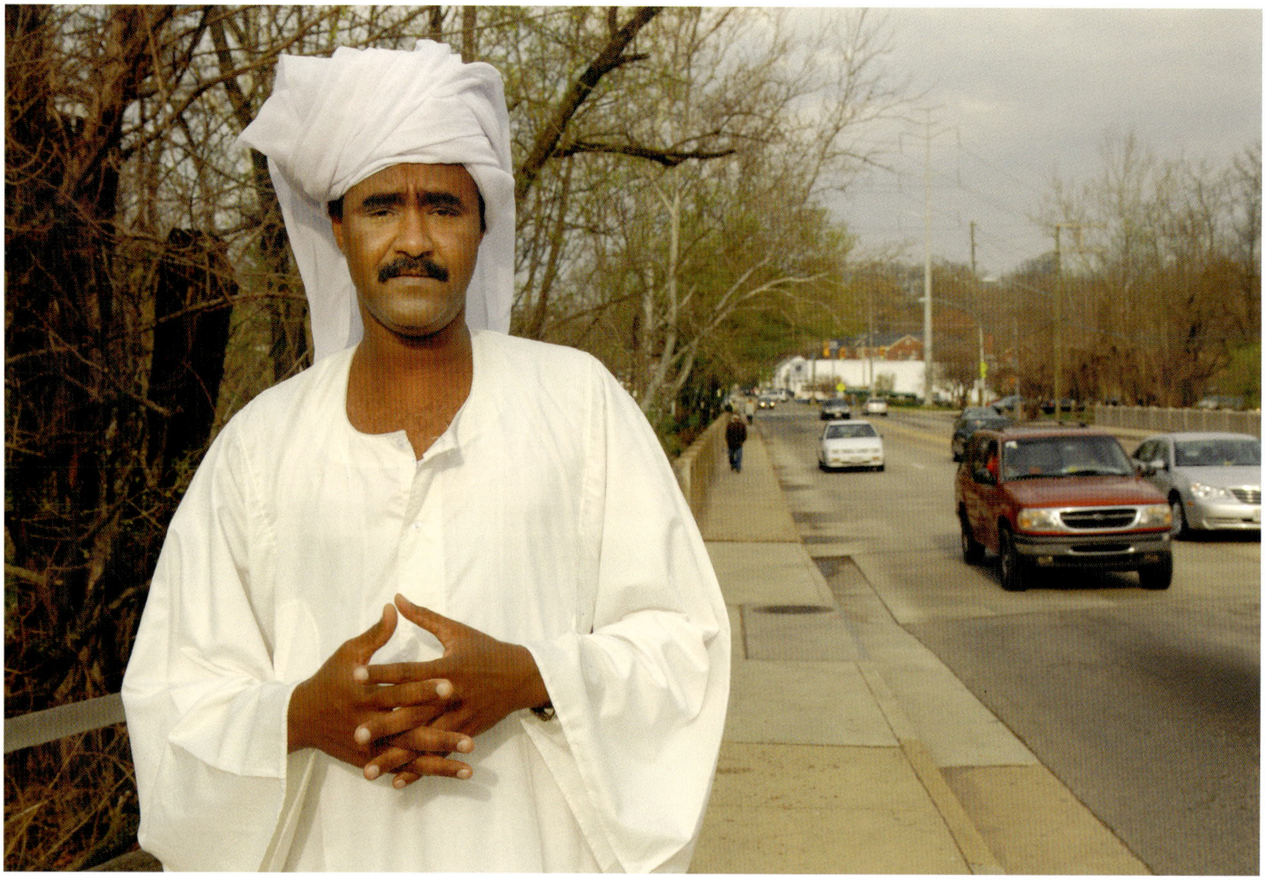

Achmed Osman

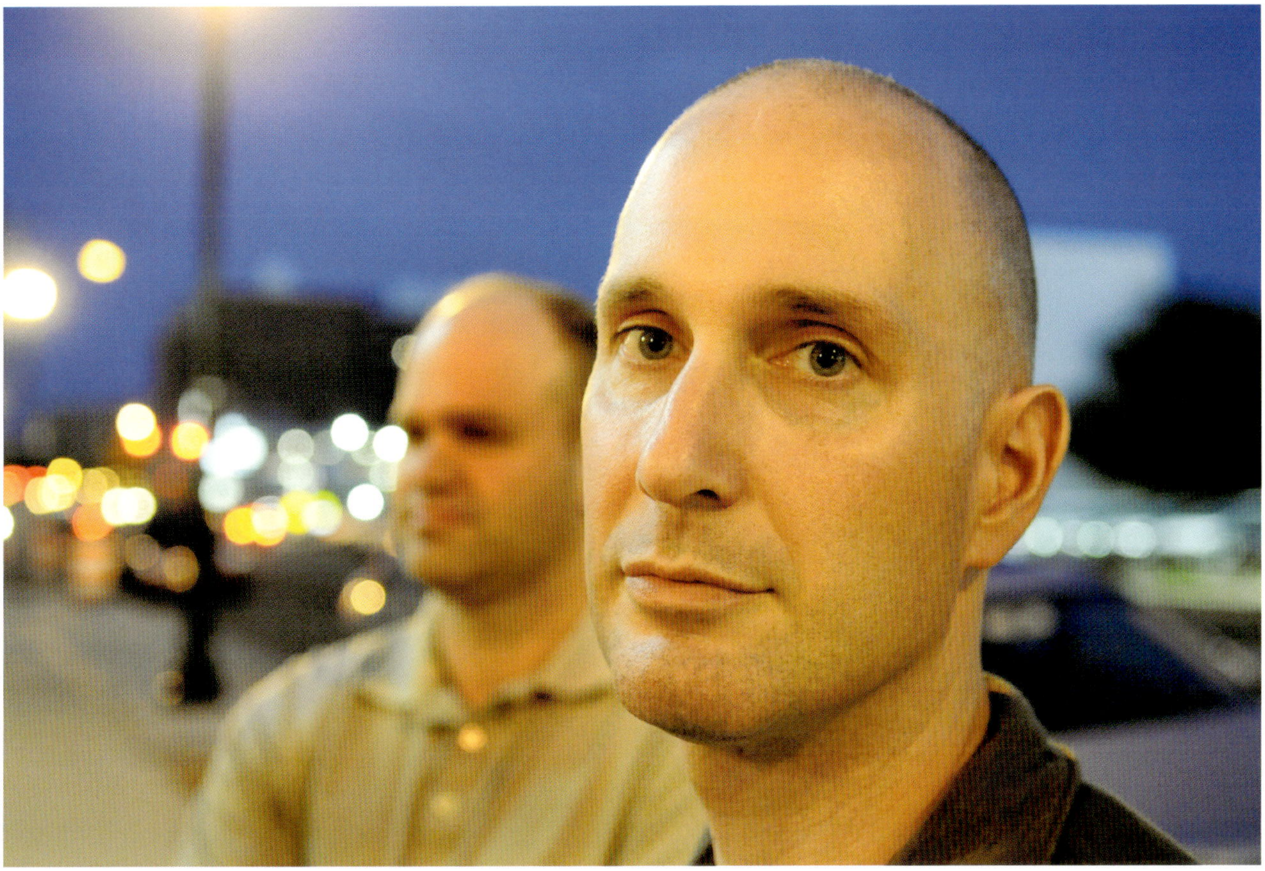

Mike Morgan, Art Outlet event

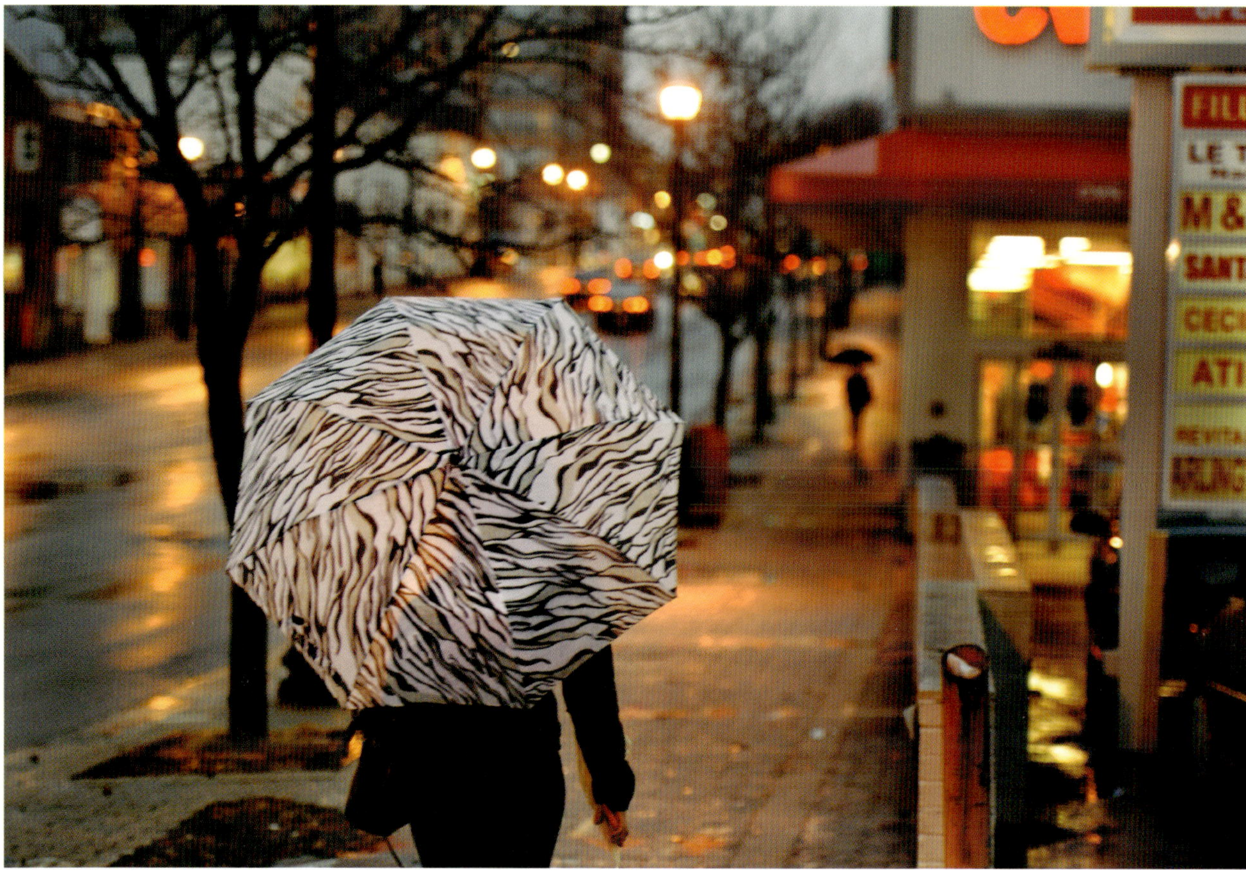

Night, 2600 block of Columbia Pike

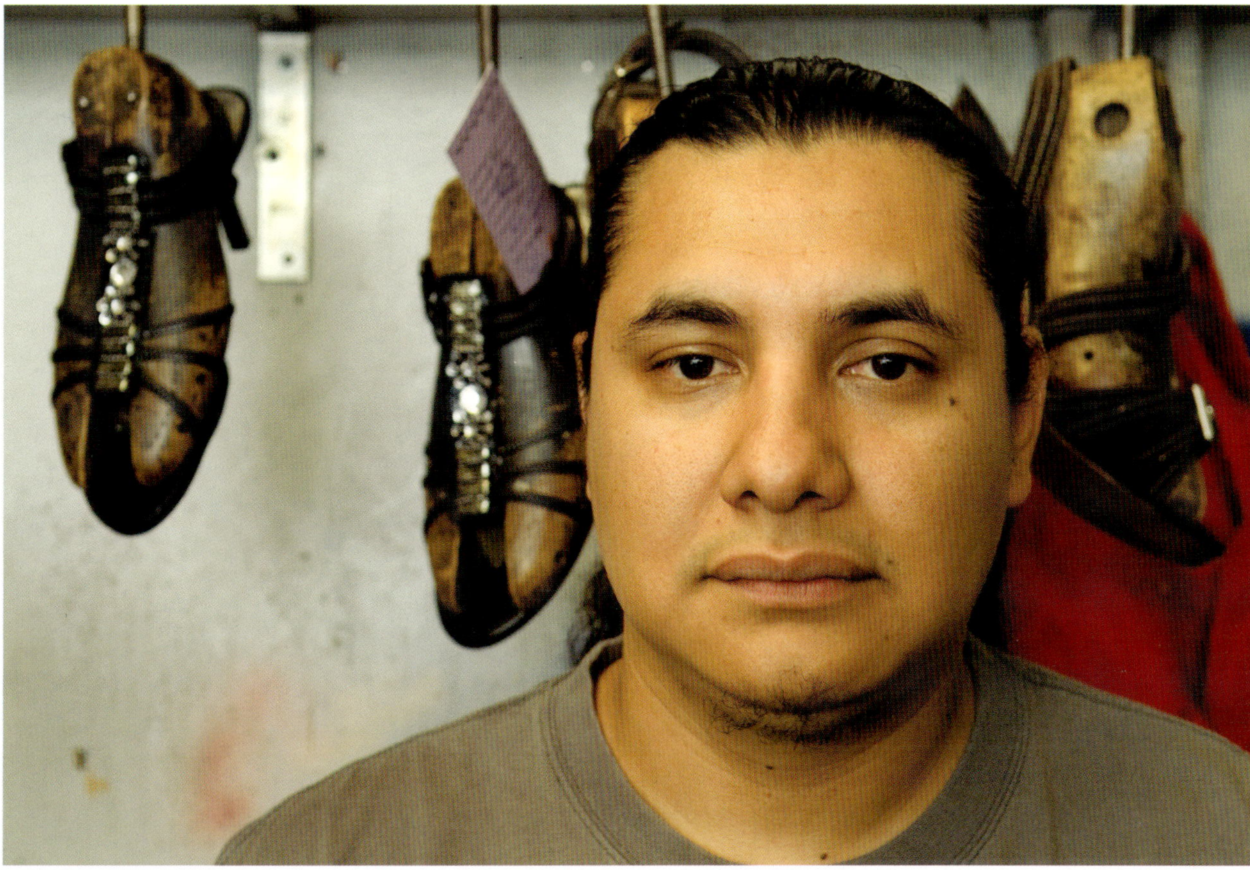

William Alfara, Domenick's Shoe Repair

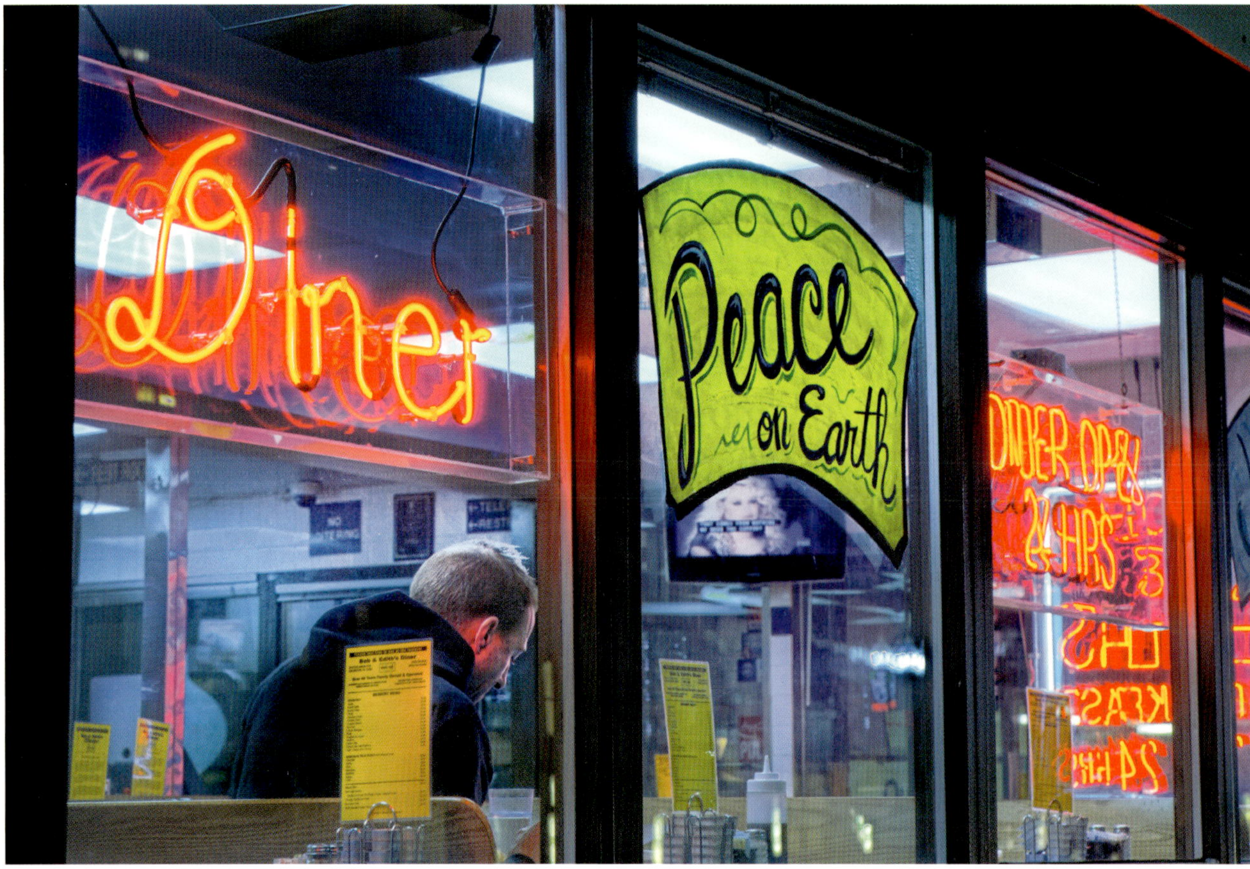

Yuletide, Bob and Edith's Diner, 2310 Columbia Pike

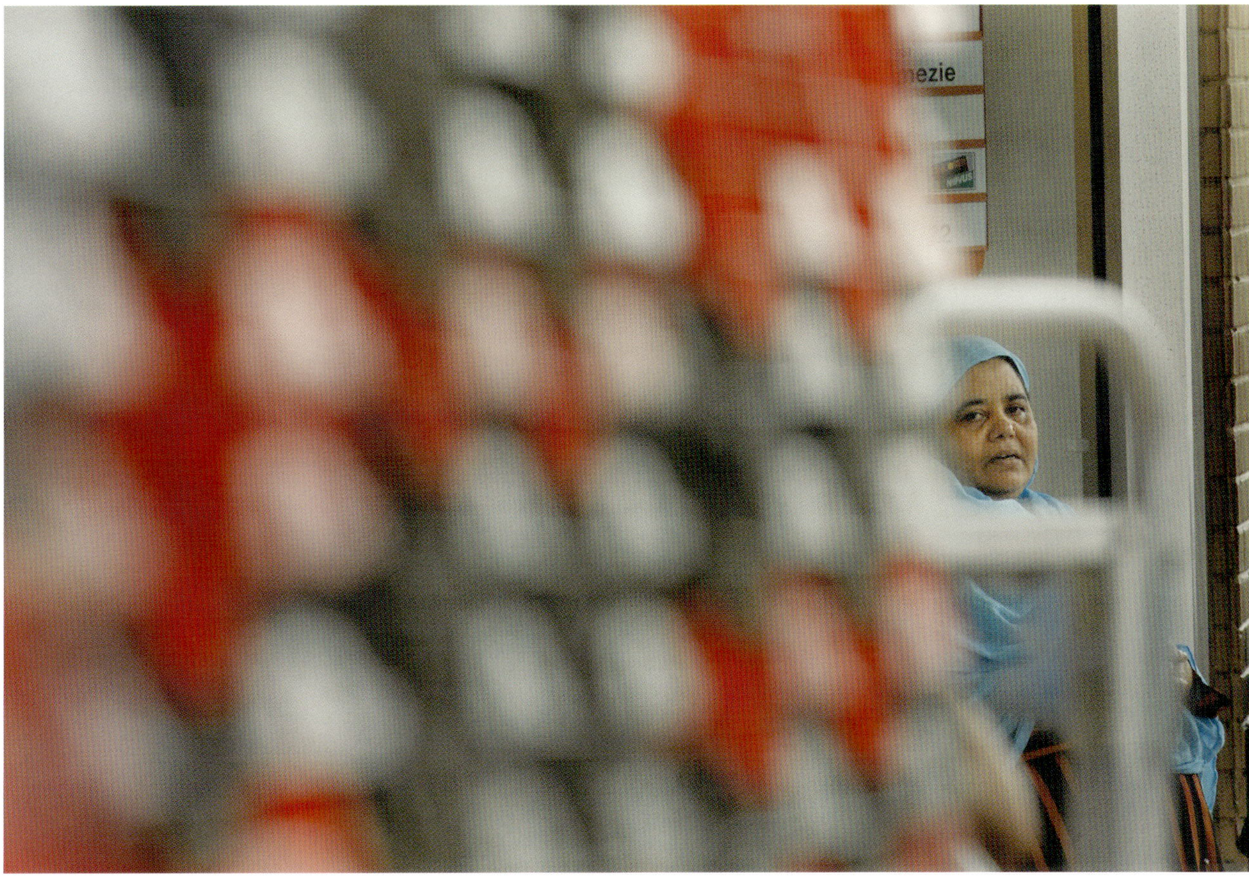

Columbia Pike Plaza Shopping Center

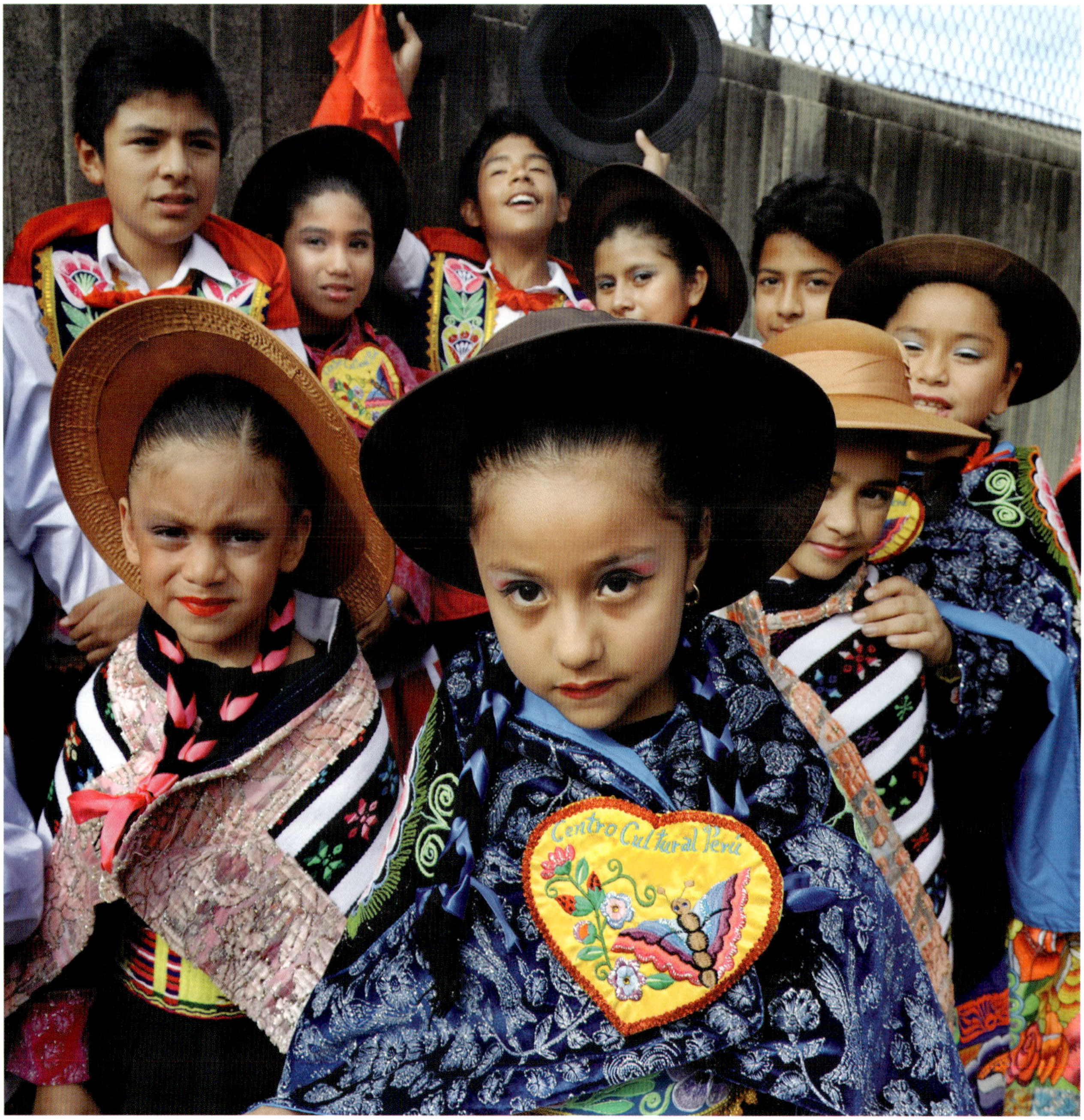

South American dancers, Prio Bangla Festival

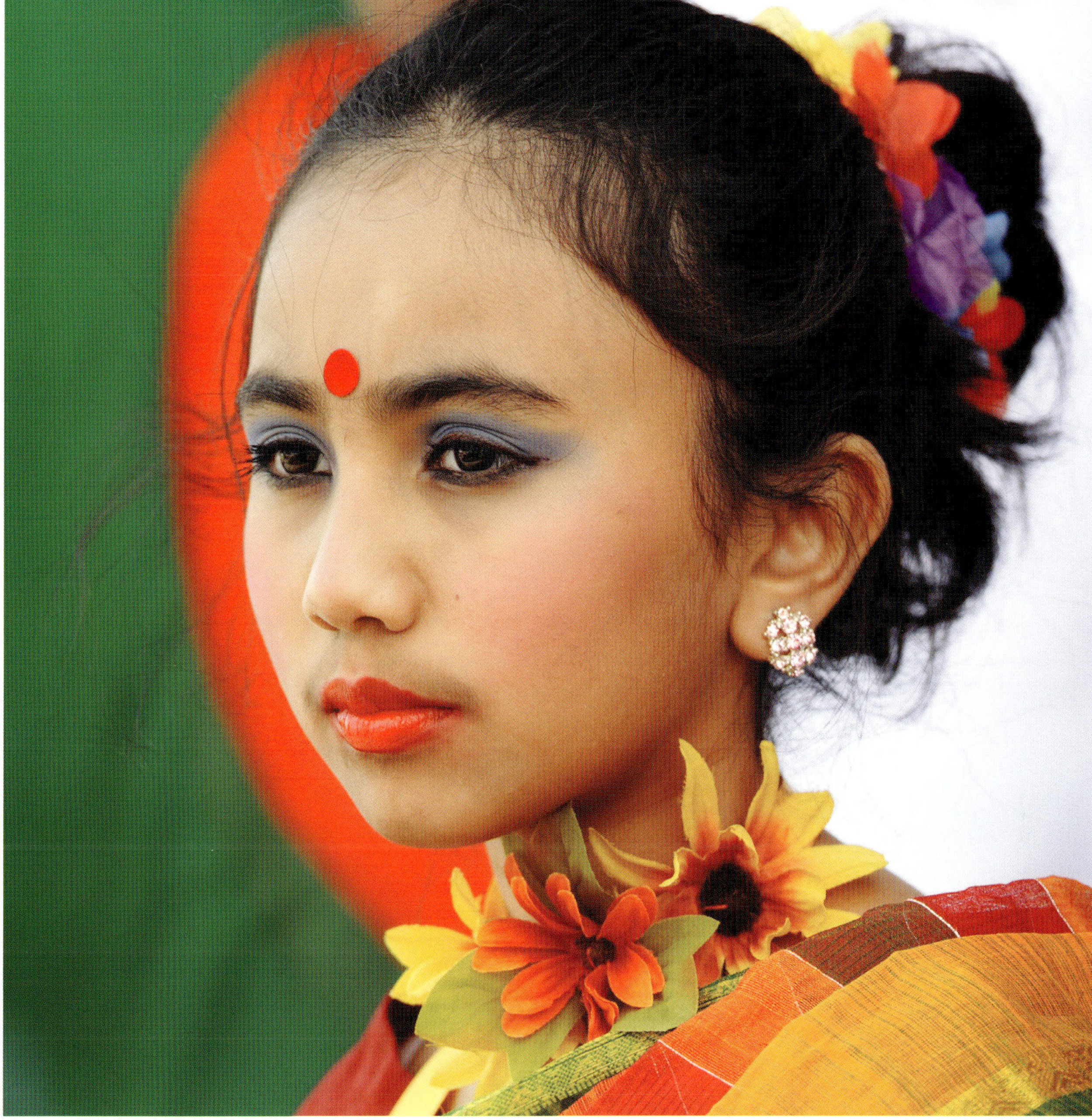

Bangladeshi dancer, Prio Bangla Festival

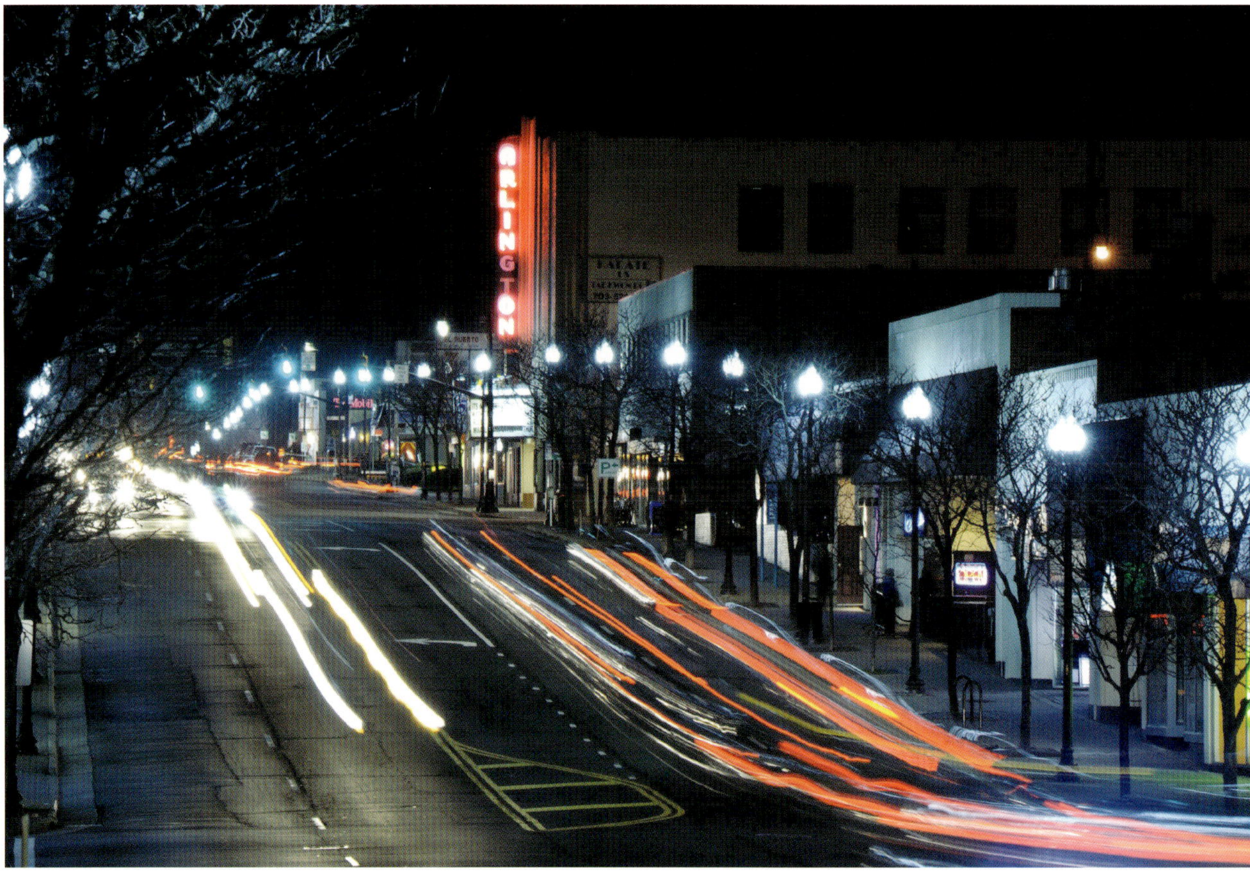

2600 and 2700 block of Columbia Pike at night

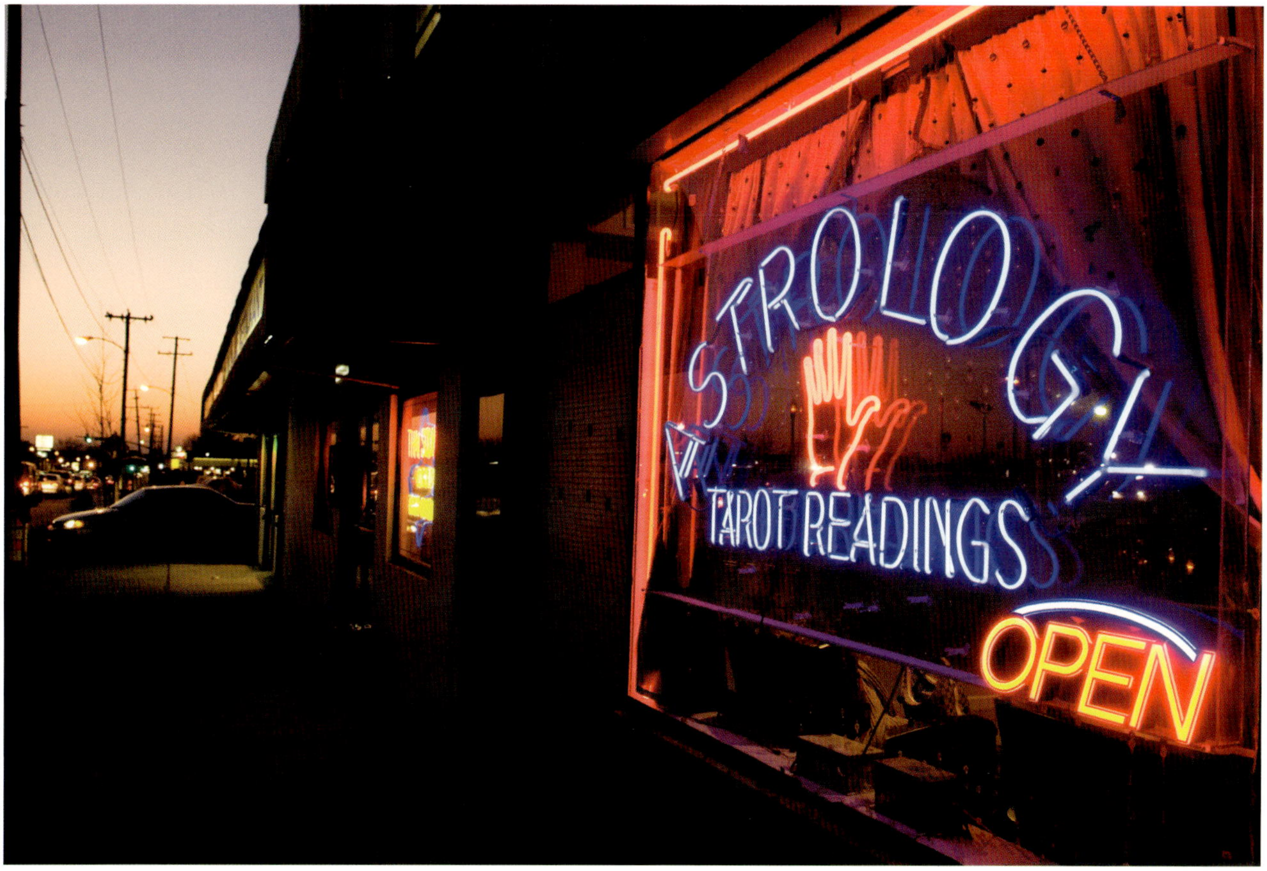

Astrologer, 3200 block of Columbia Pike

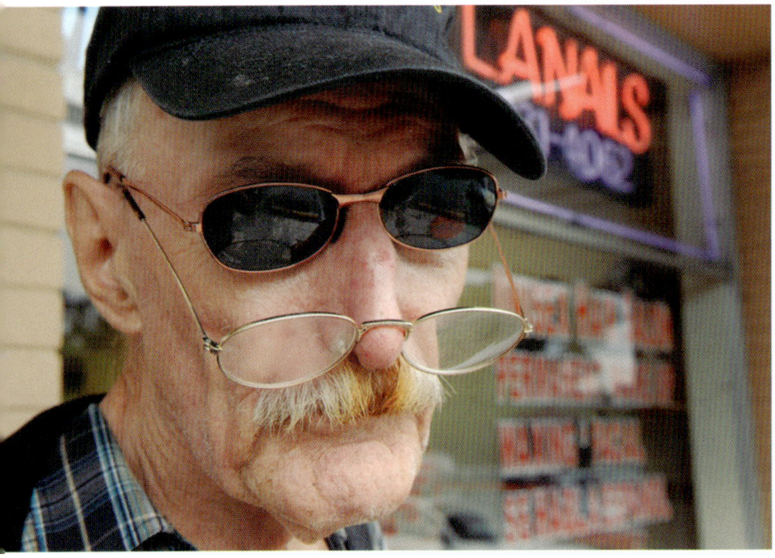

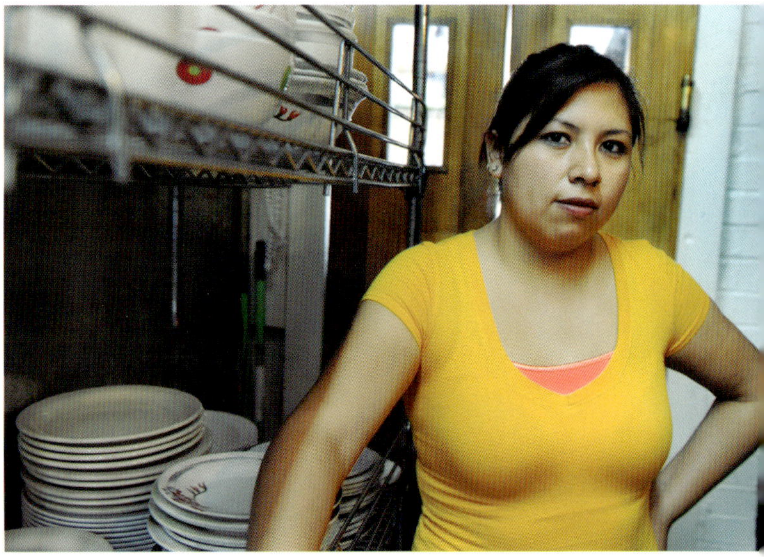

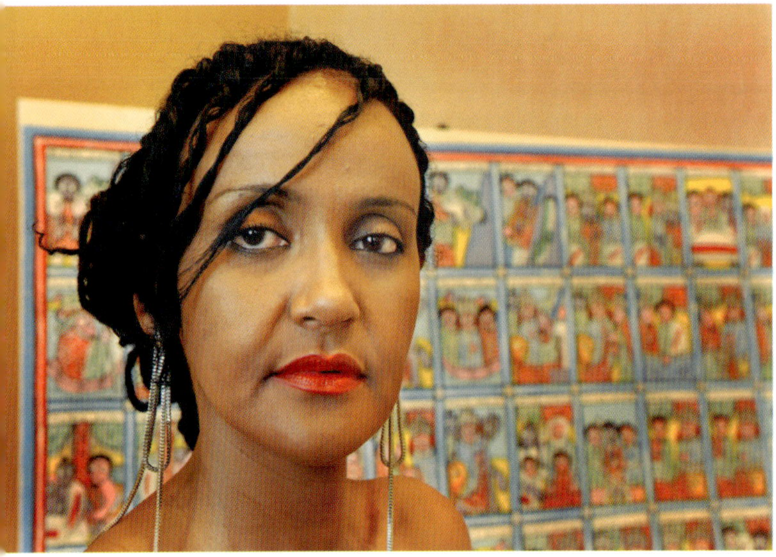

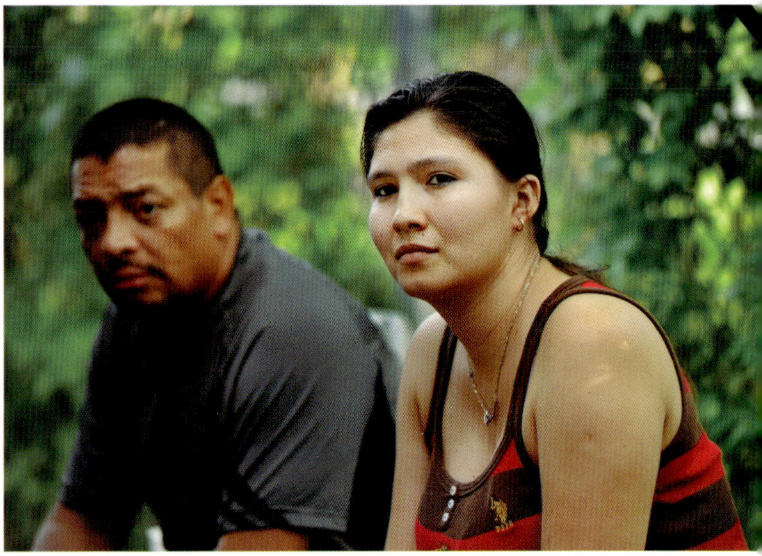

Clint Hanover

El Pike Restaurant staff

Ethiopian woman, Ethiopian Community Development Council Gala

Residents, Buchanan Gardens

Prio Bangla Festival ››

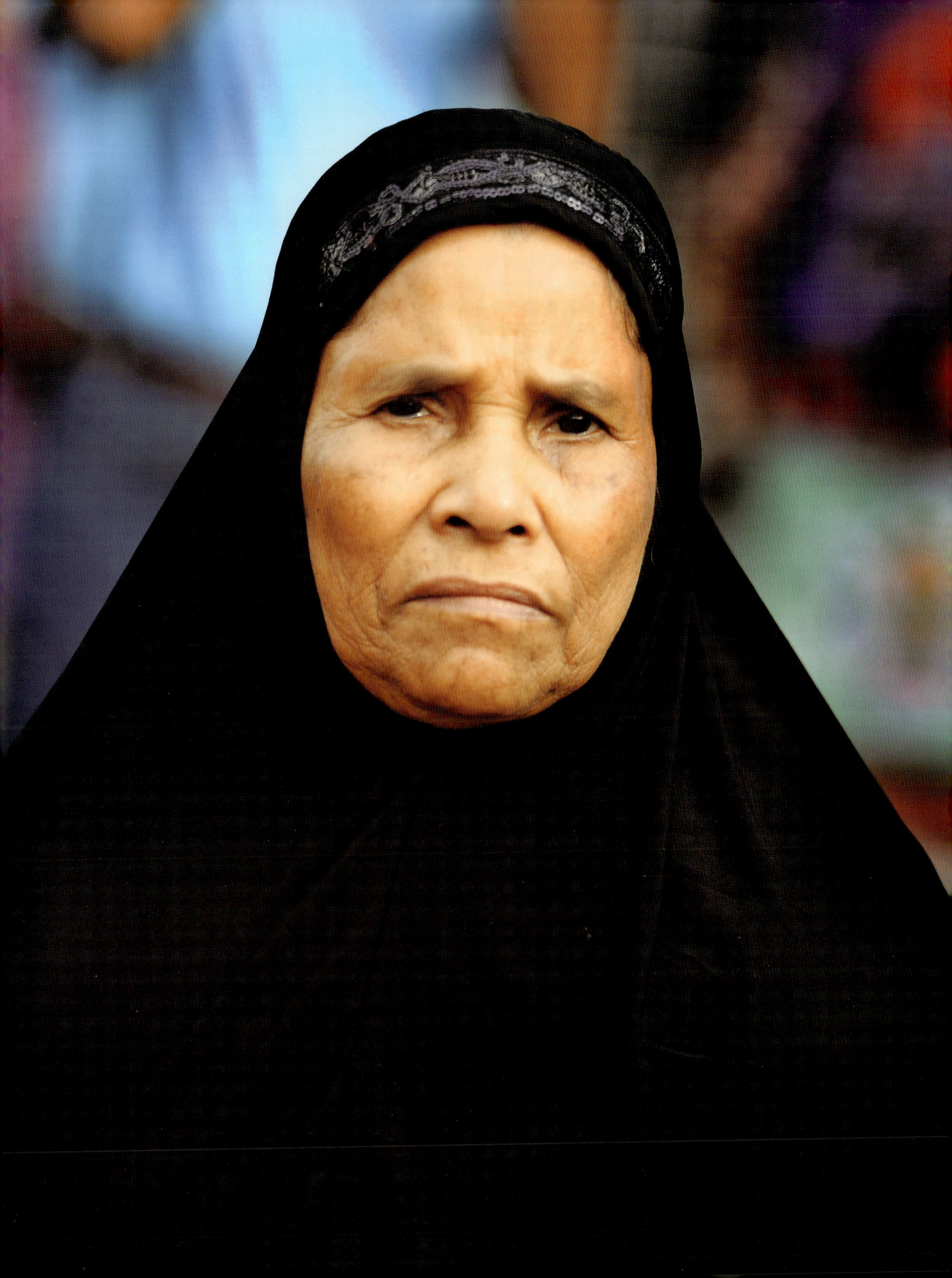

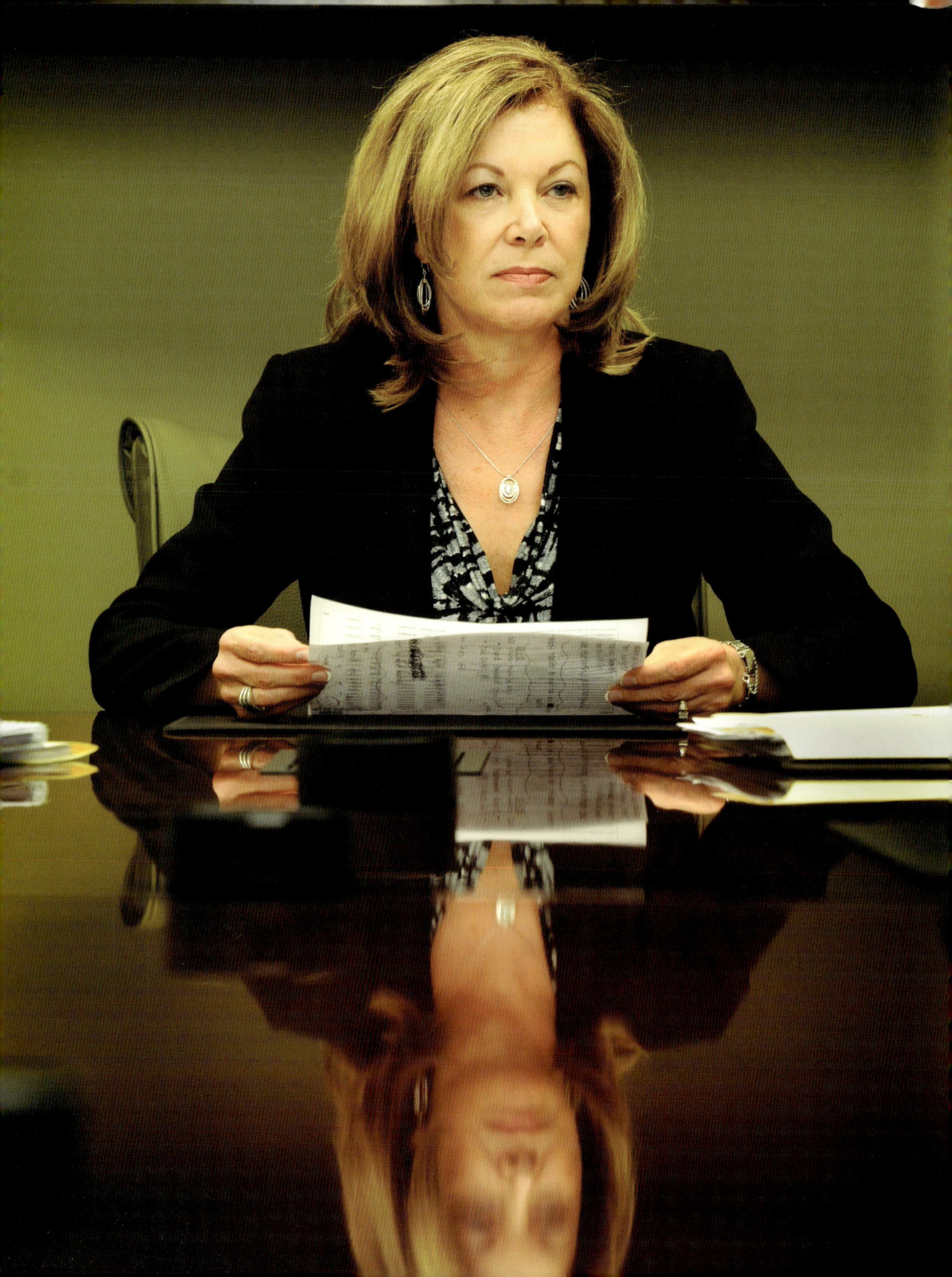

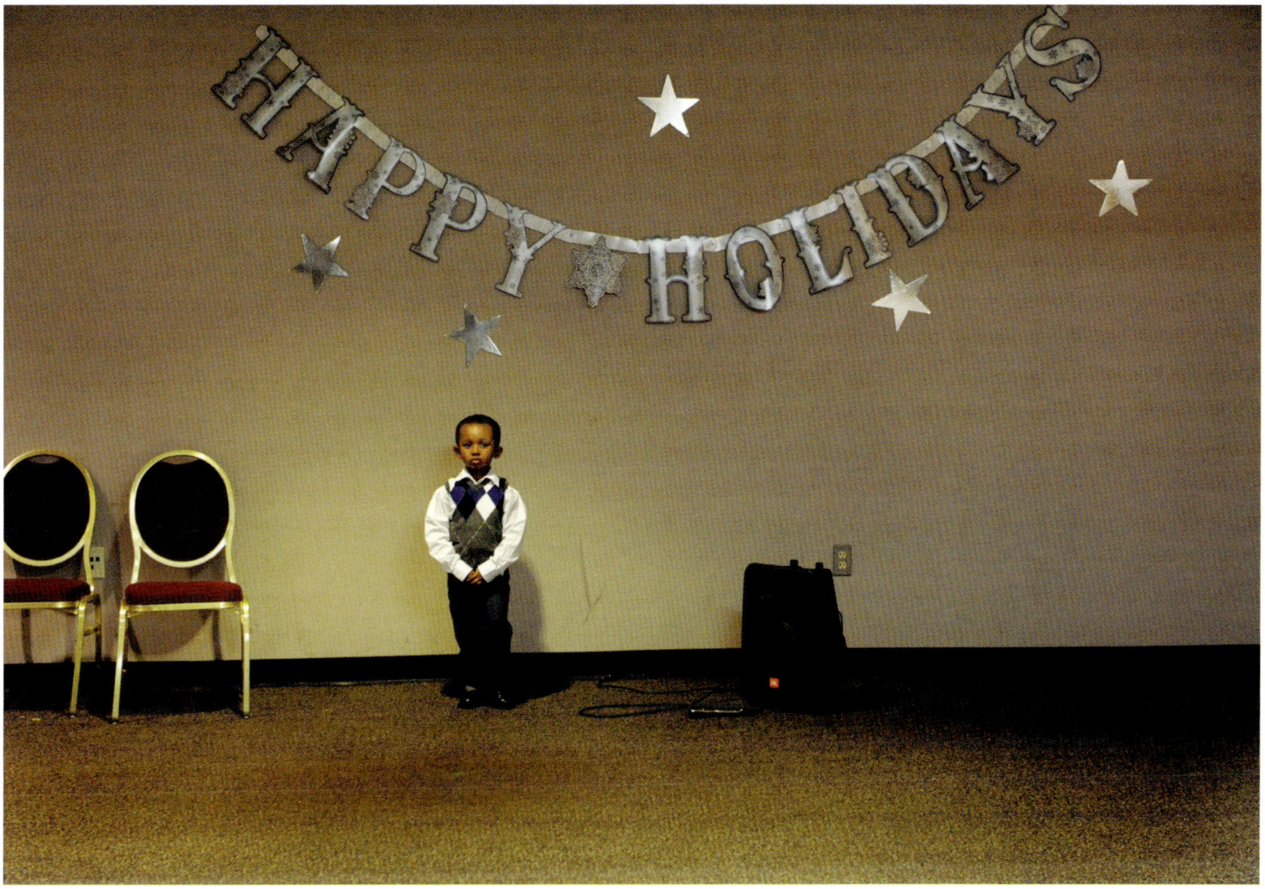

Christmas Party, Ethiopian Community Development Council's Office

‹‹ Brenda Turner, CEO of the Arlington Federal Credit Union

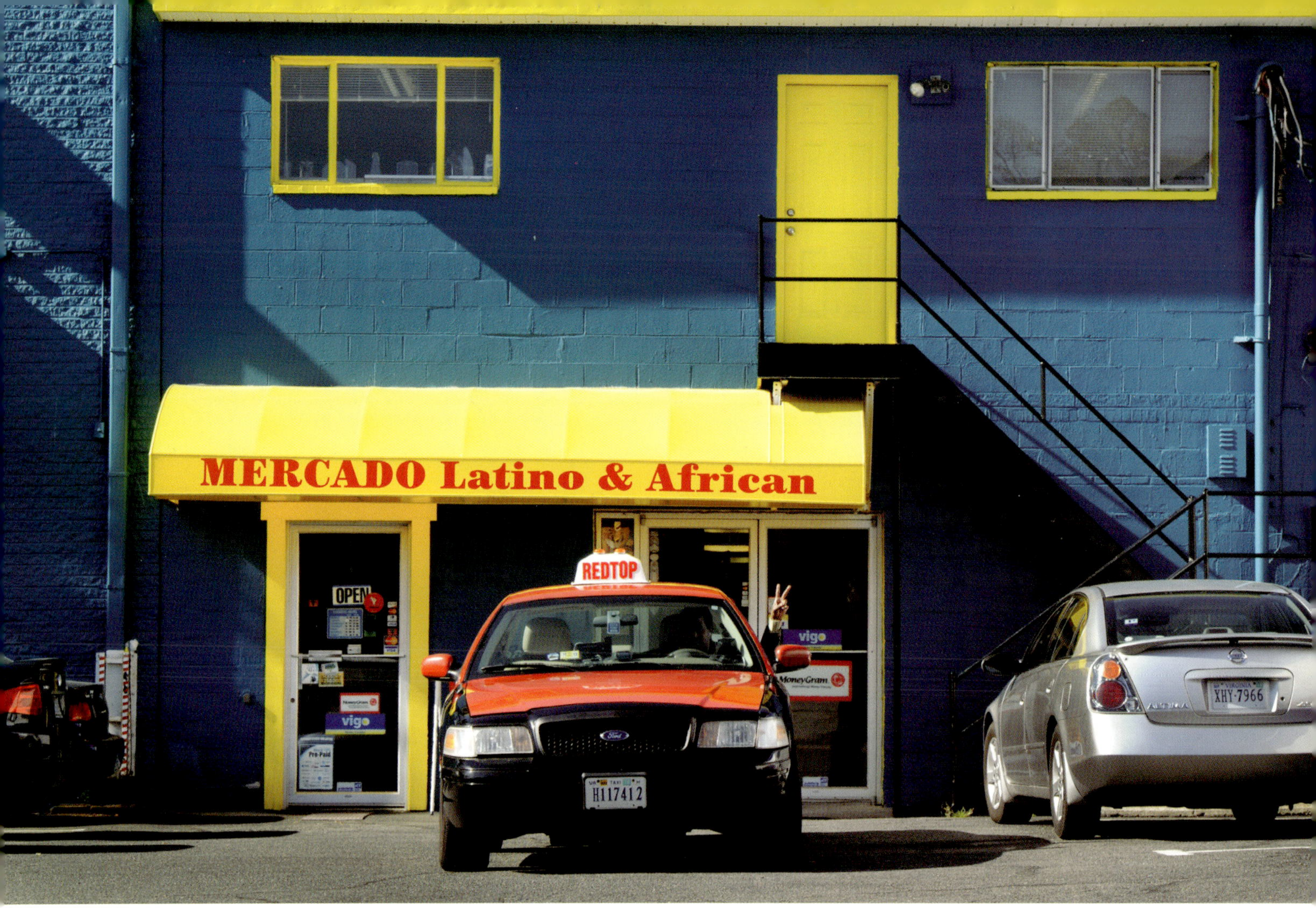

Mercado Latino and African, 4800 block of Columbia Pike

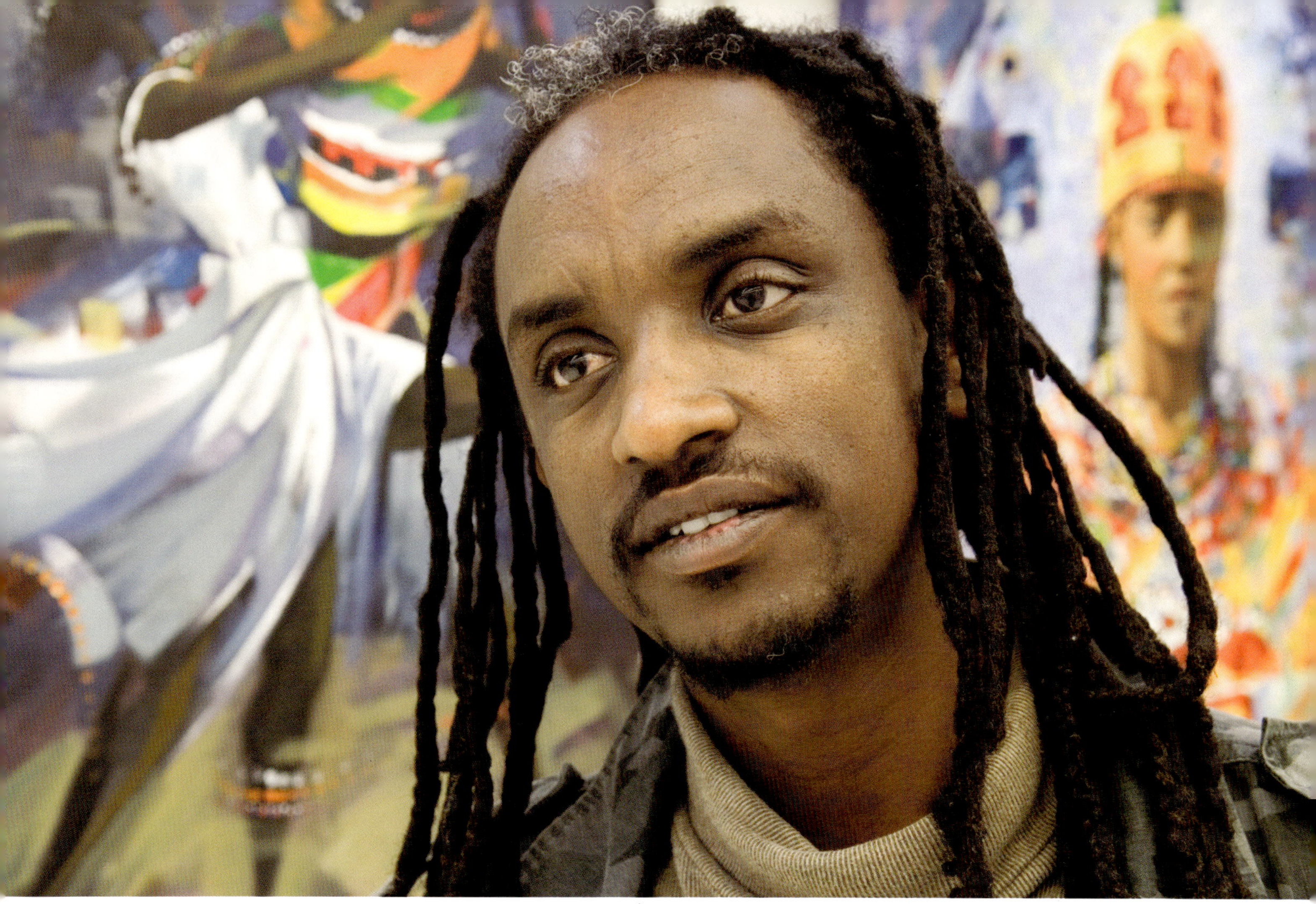

I was born and grow up in Wadlo, the northern part of Ethiopia. After that I went to Addis Ababa and joined to the art school. I am now enrolled in Howard University's masters art program.

My father was the governor in Wollo Province. The Communist Mengistu regime put him in prison for 13 years. When I came to the US he was still in the prison. And as soon as he came out, I tried to help him get out of Ethiopia. The government they announce his name on the TV and the radio and they say we need you to go back in the prison, so that was terrible. One of my sisters called me to tell me. I was shocked, so we tried to take help him get out from the country. They escaped to Nairobi, and eventually the UN and American government approved his case and he was able to come here. He got a job a part-time job in a clothes store, selling clothes.

Columbia Pike has a diversity and is also convenient for transport. That's why we decided to come to Arlington. Arlington community service is really good. It helped us process my family things, like house hunting, all that kind of service,

All my sisters they are living back home in Ethiopia. Recently I lost one, my closest sister. I miss her.

Mekbib Gebertsadik

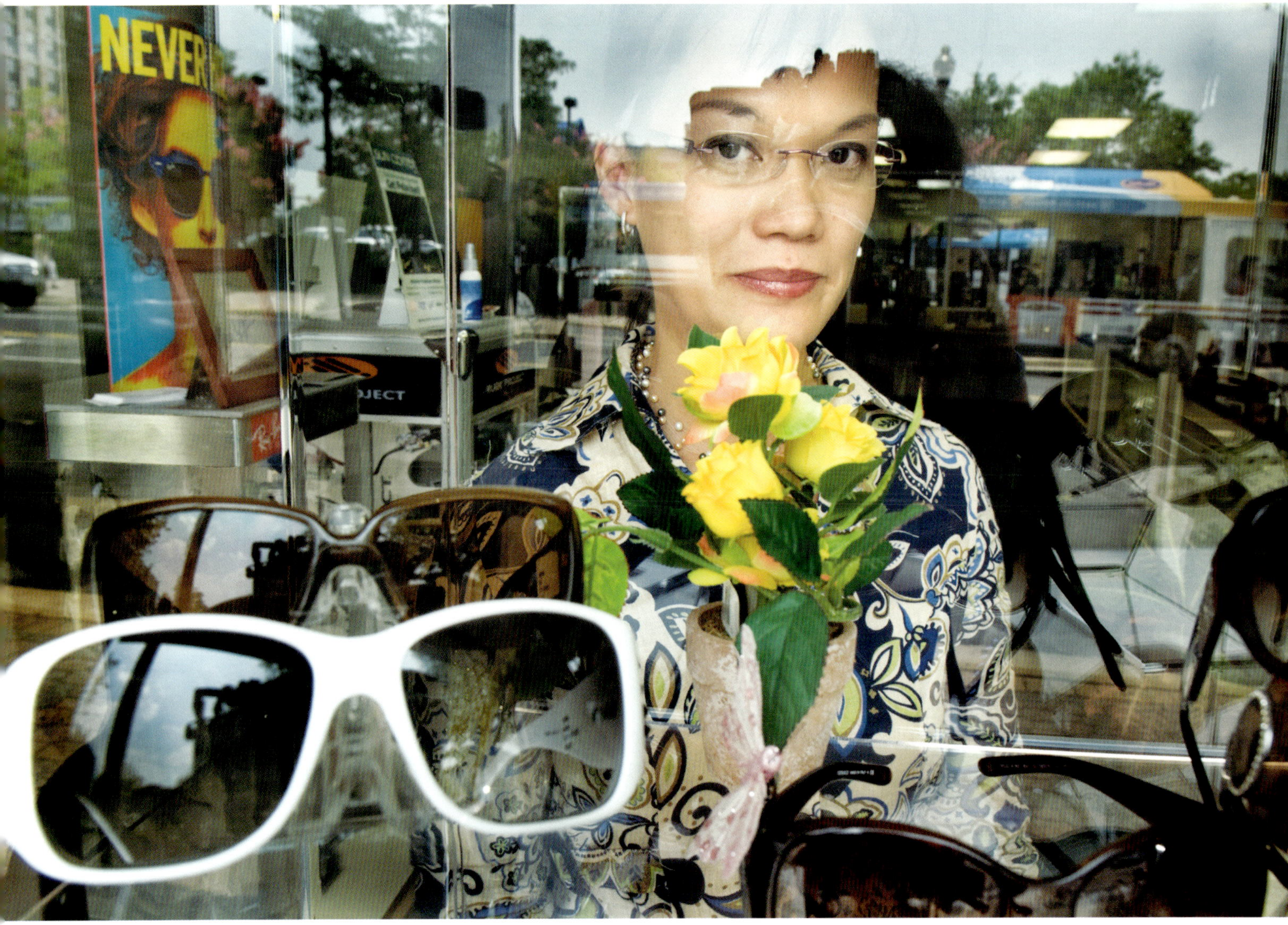

Dr. Linh Hoang-Braley, O.D. Eye Site Optometrists,

2800 block of Columbia Pike

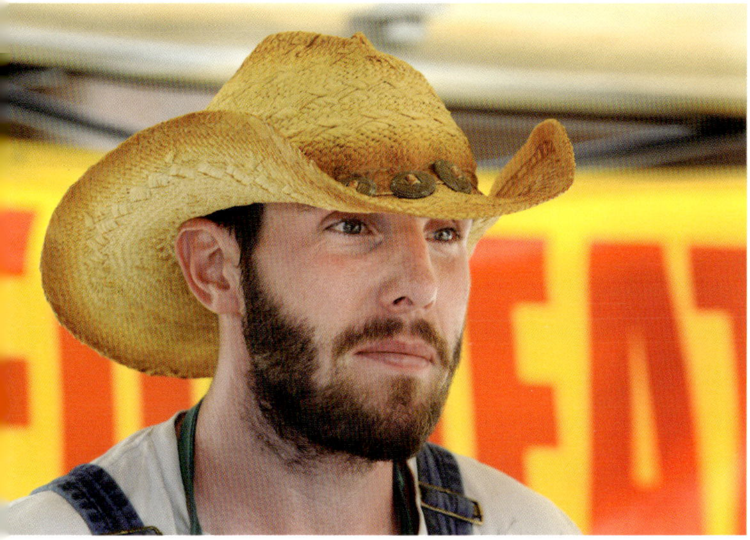

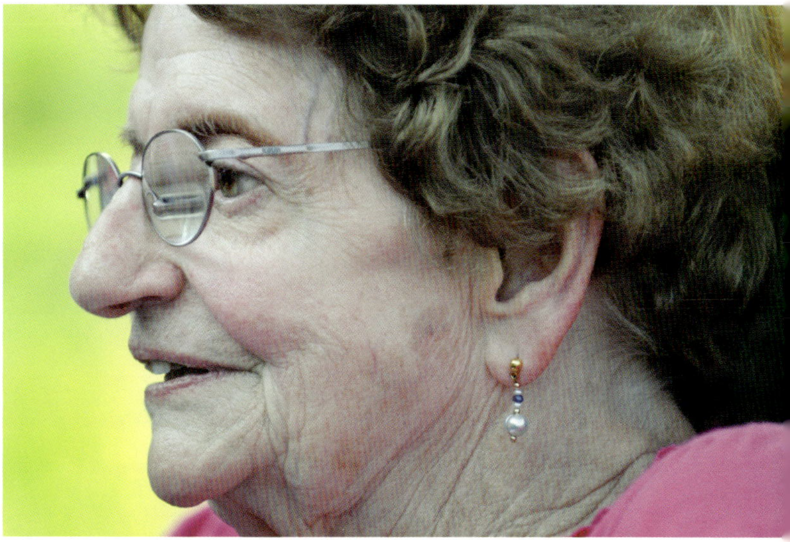

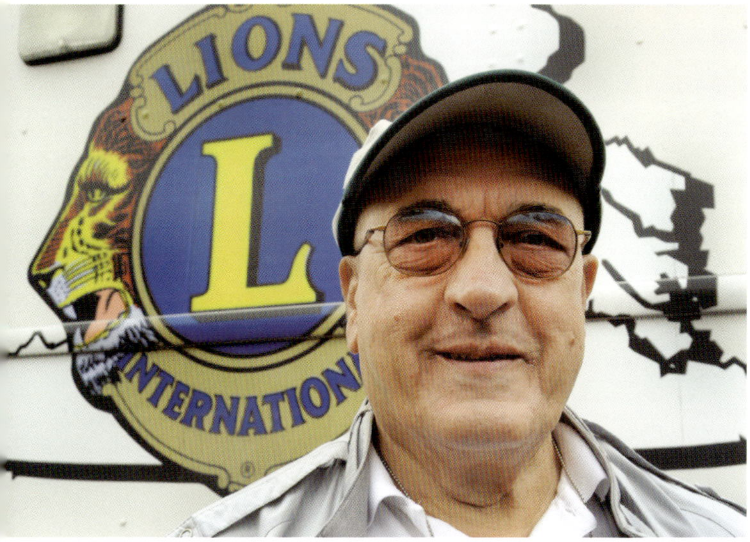

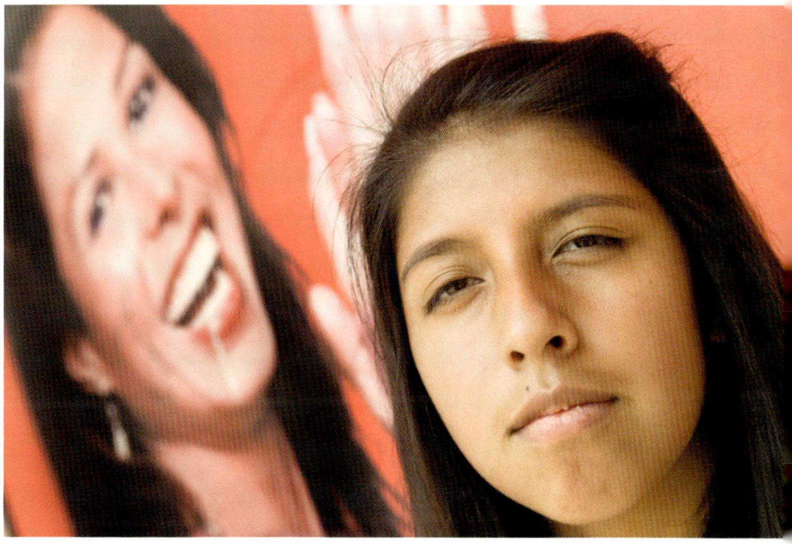

Vendor, Columbia Pike Farmers Market

Maria G. Flores, Flores-Gambino

45th Annual Memorial Day Picnic

Lions Cub Volunteer, Columbia Grove Health Fair

Melissa Vasquez

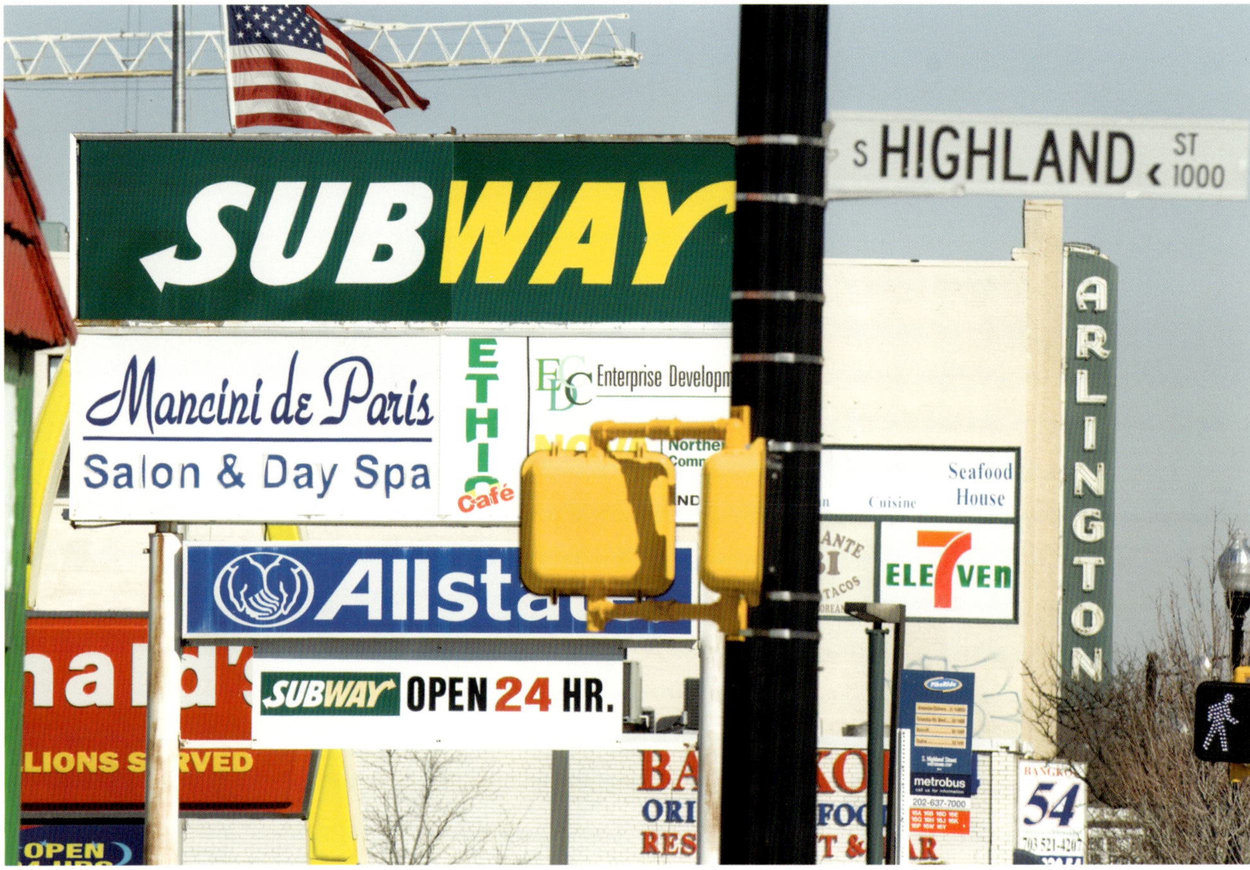

Columbia Pike at South Highland Street

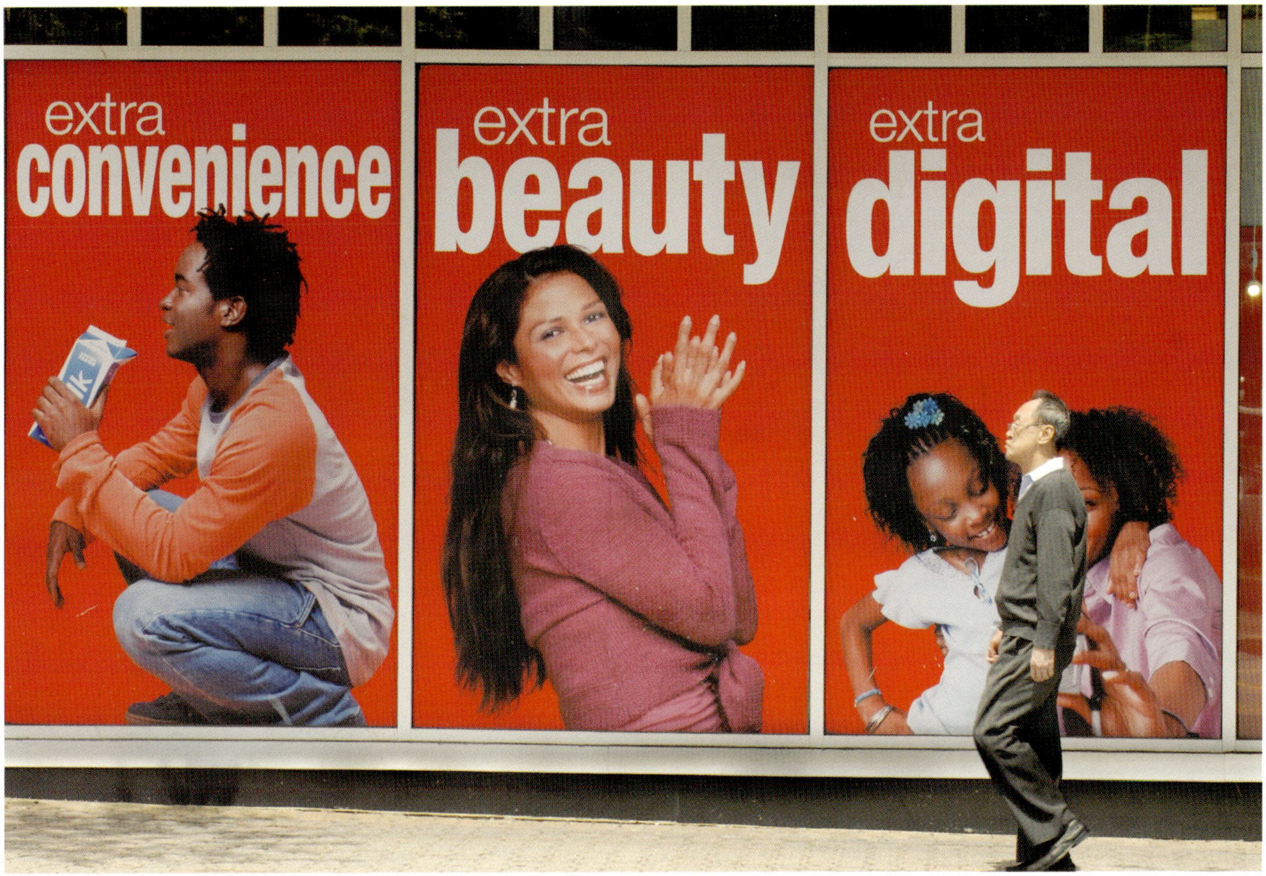

2600 block of Columbia Pike

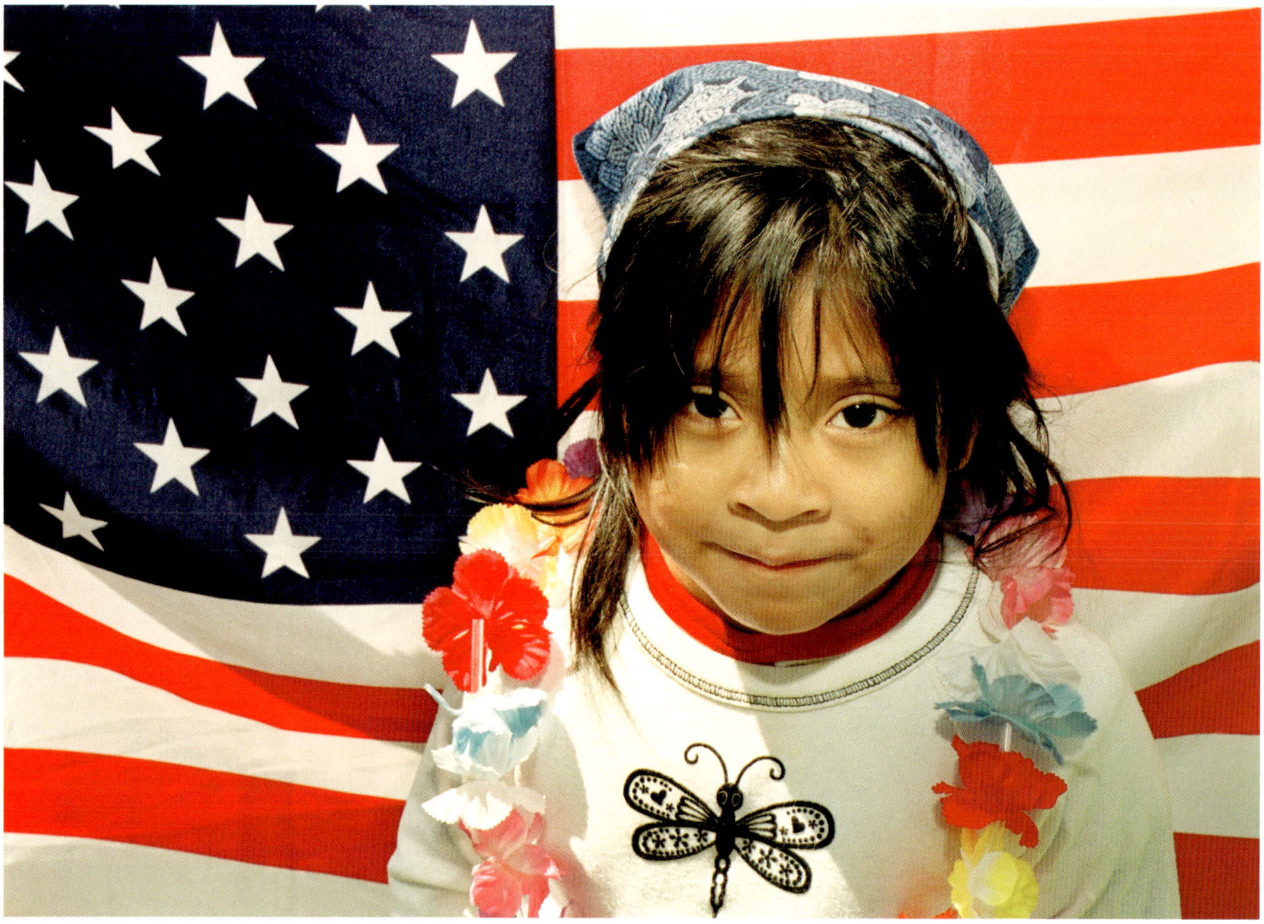

Central American Girl, Columbia Heights West Festival

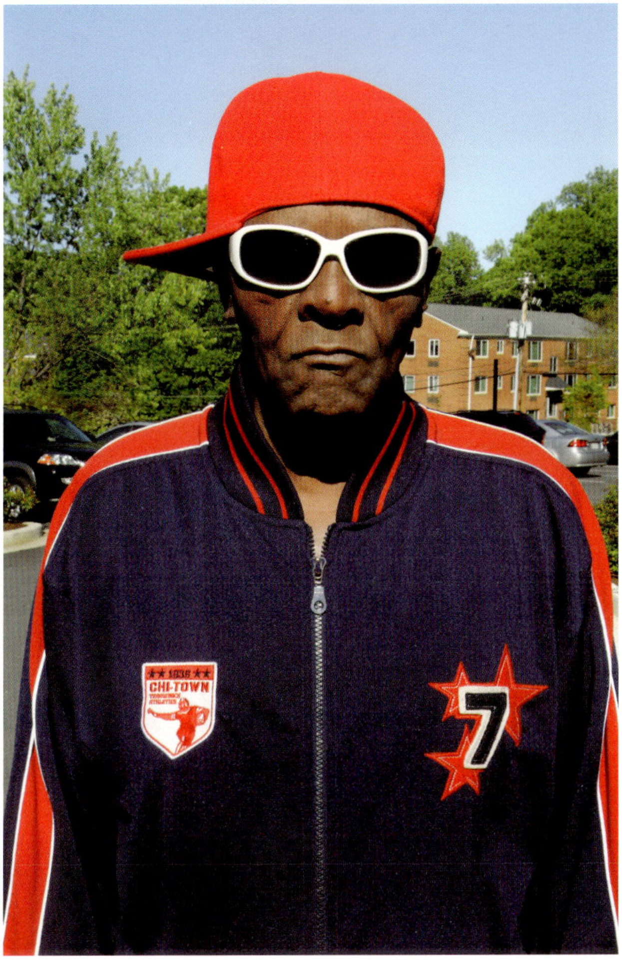

Columbia Grove Health Fair

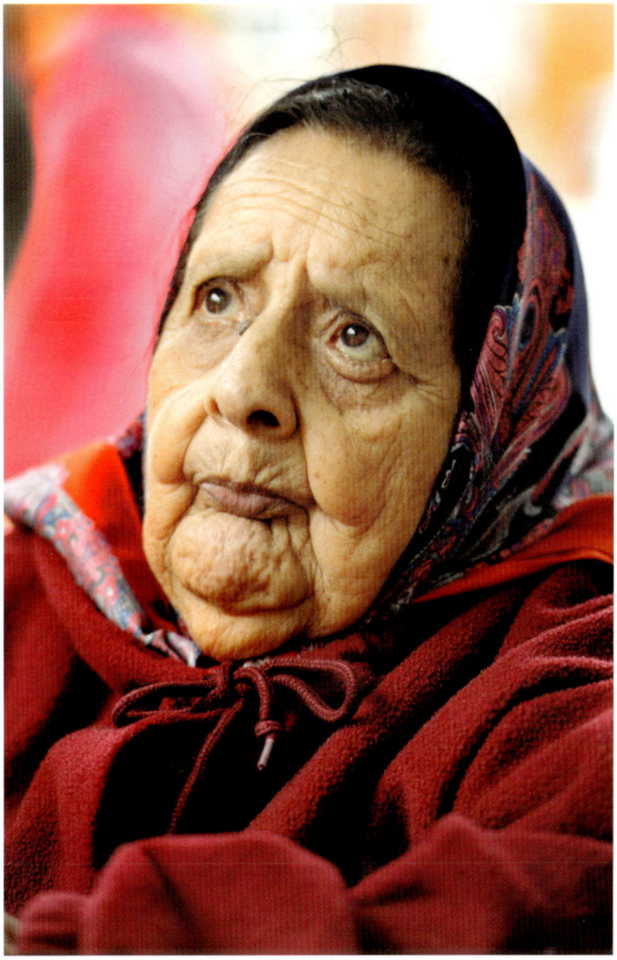

Columbia Grove Health Fair

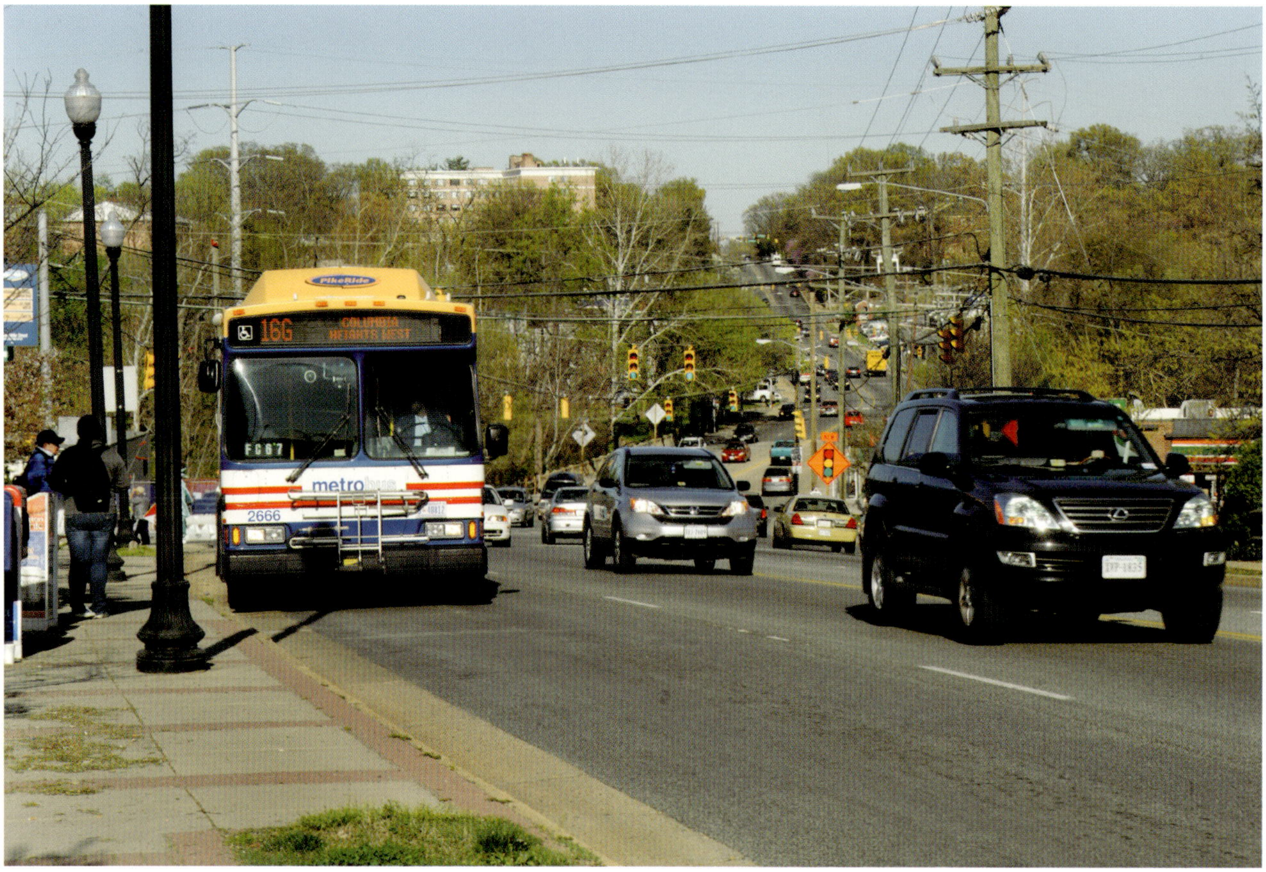

5000 block of Columbia Pike (looking east)

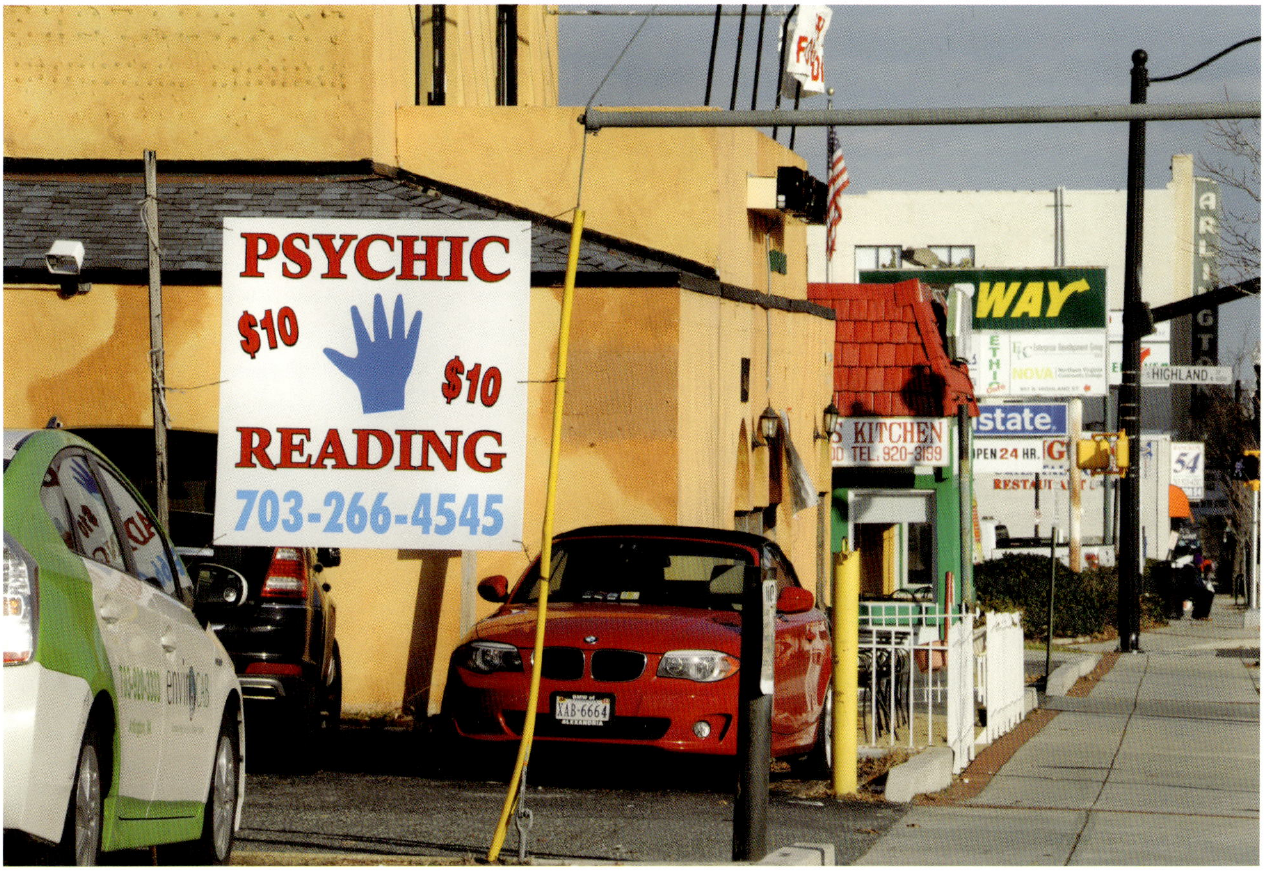

3100 block of Columbia Pike

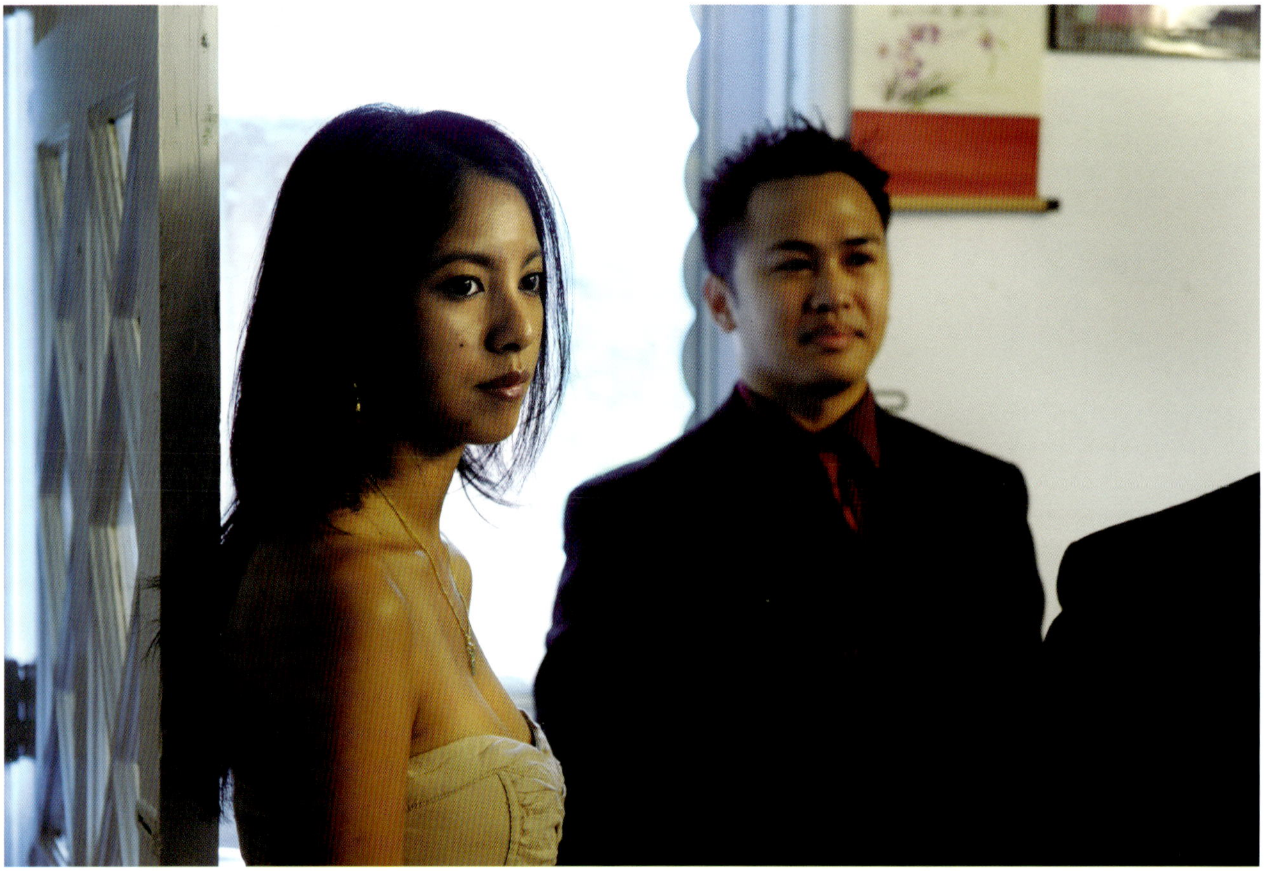

Guests at the Tran-Lung wedding

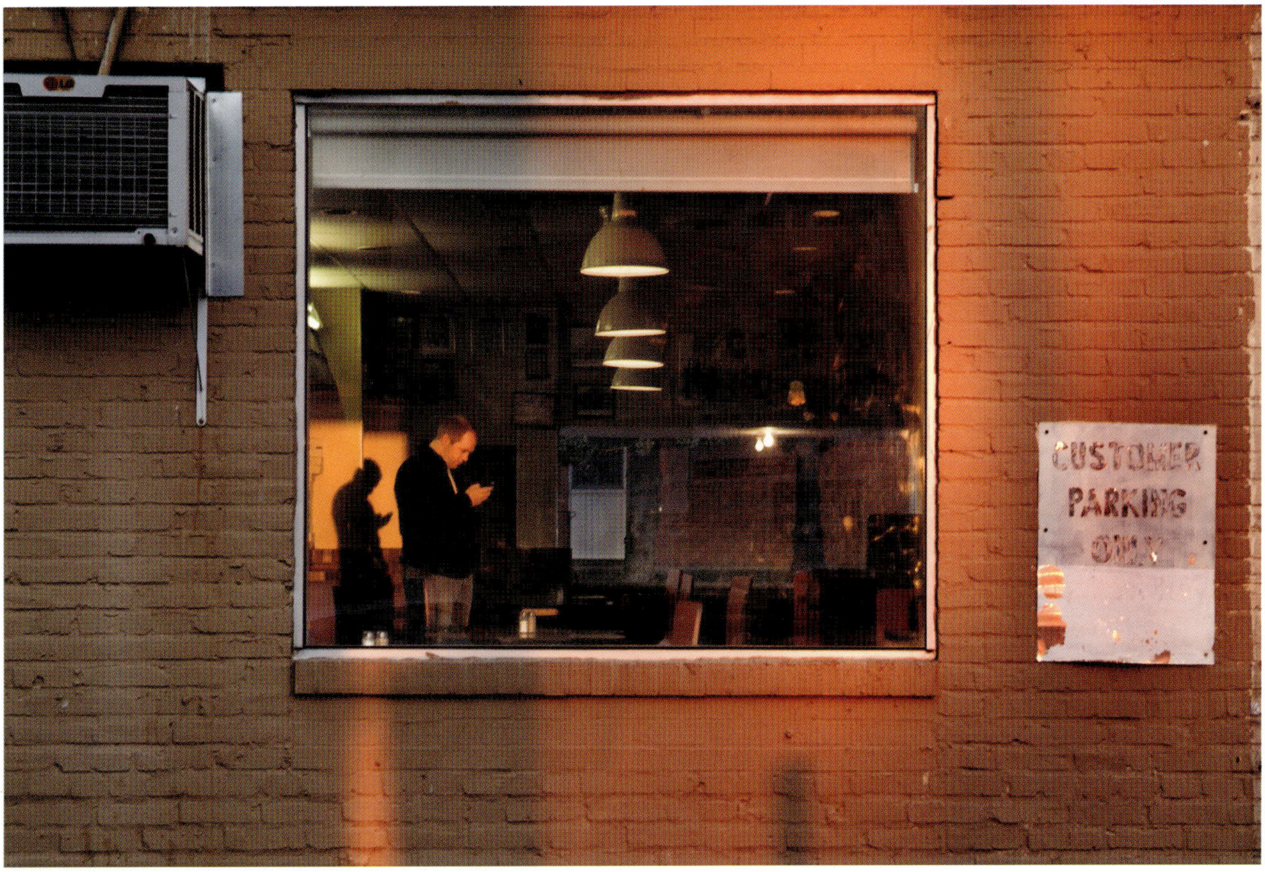

Side Window, The Broiler Restaurant, 3601 Columbia Pike

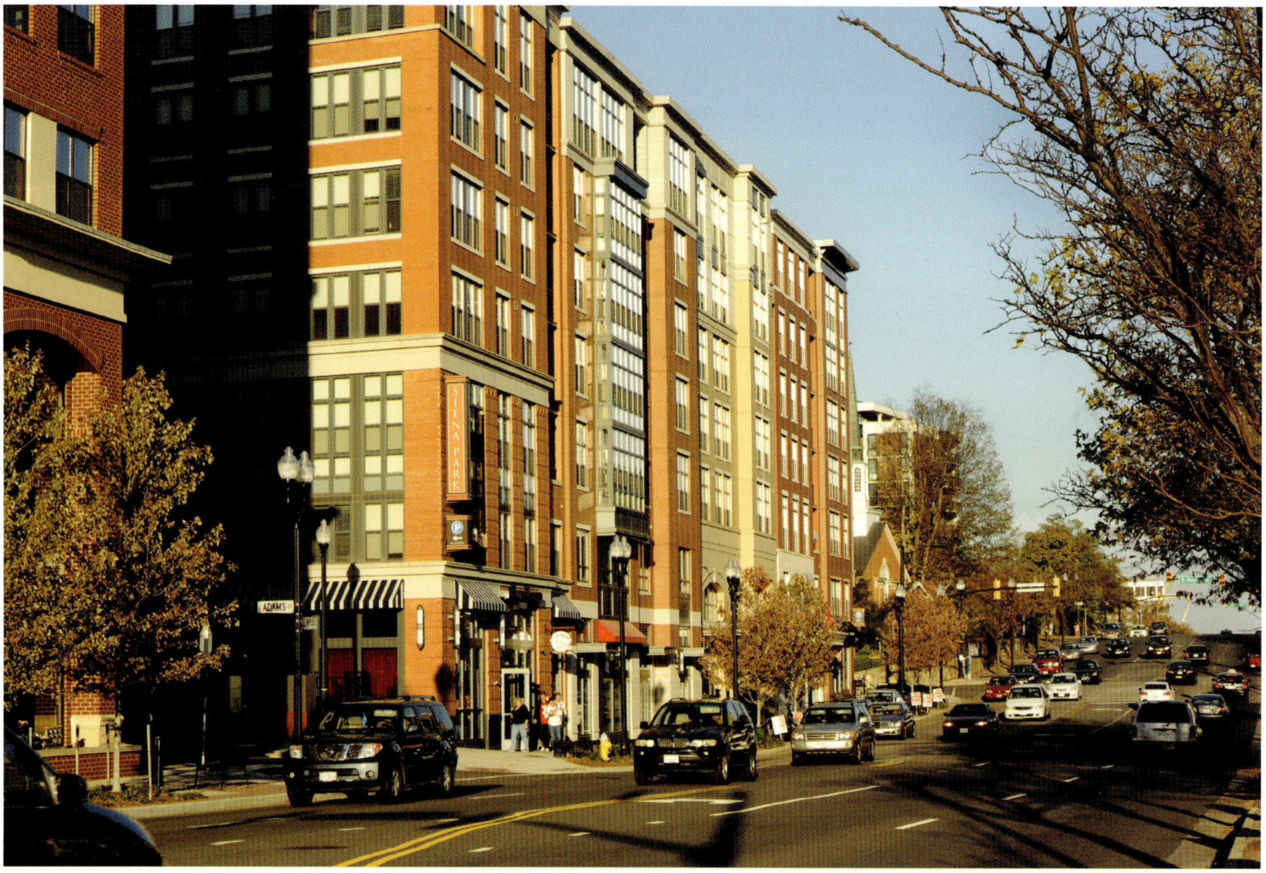

Penrose Square and Siena Apartments, 2400 block of Columbia Pike

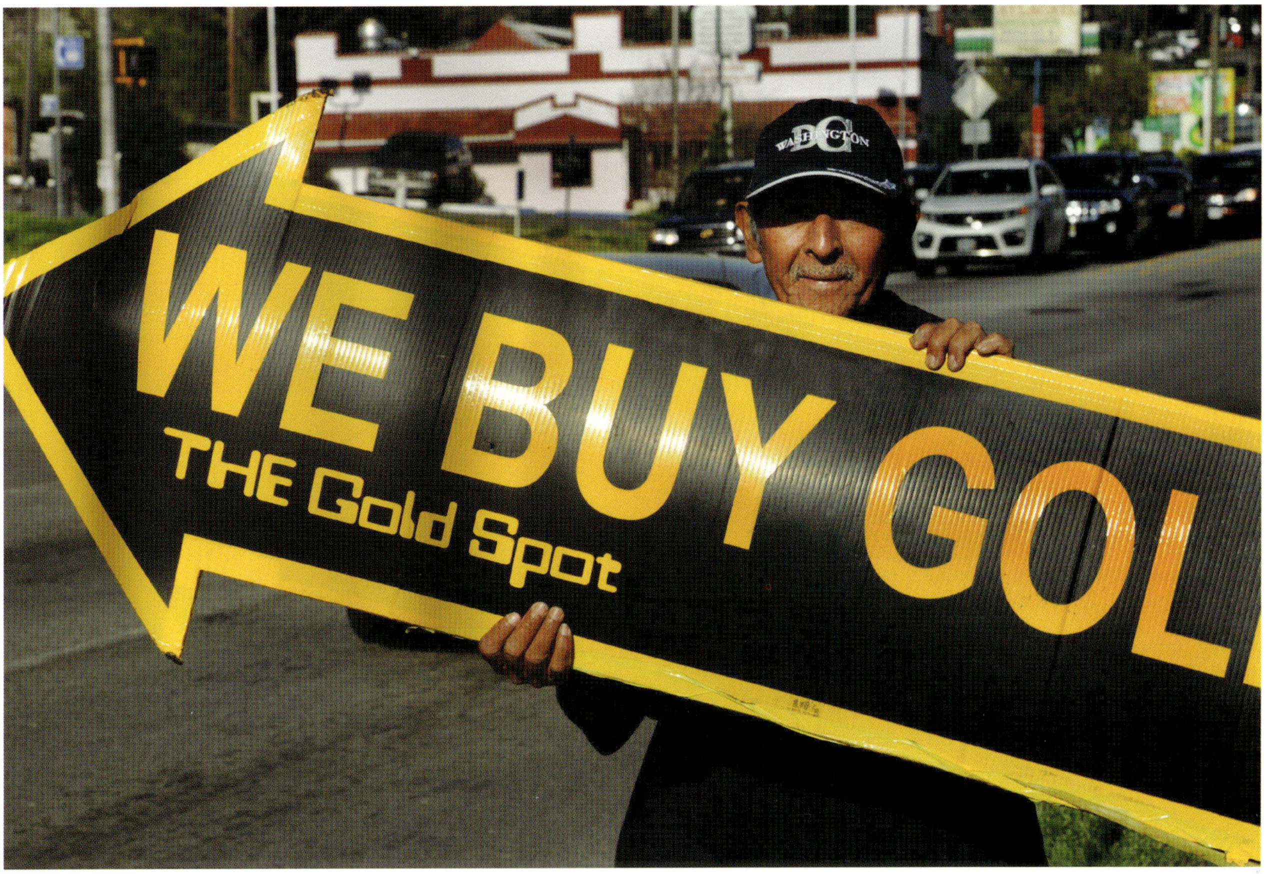

Man with gold advertising sign, 4800 block of Columbia Pike

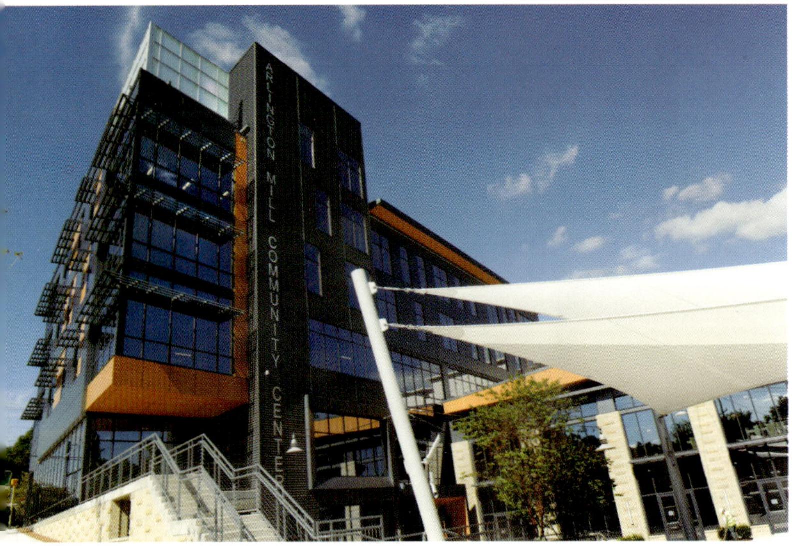

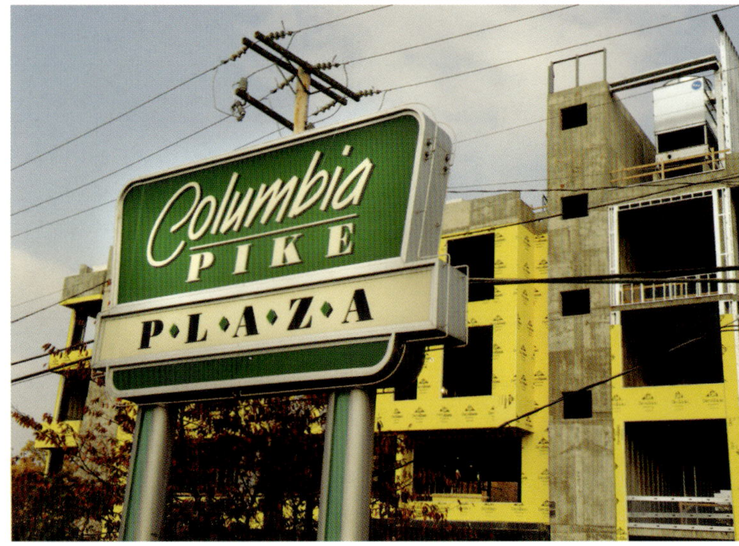

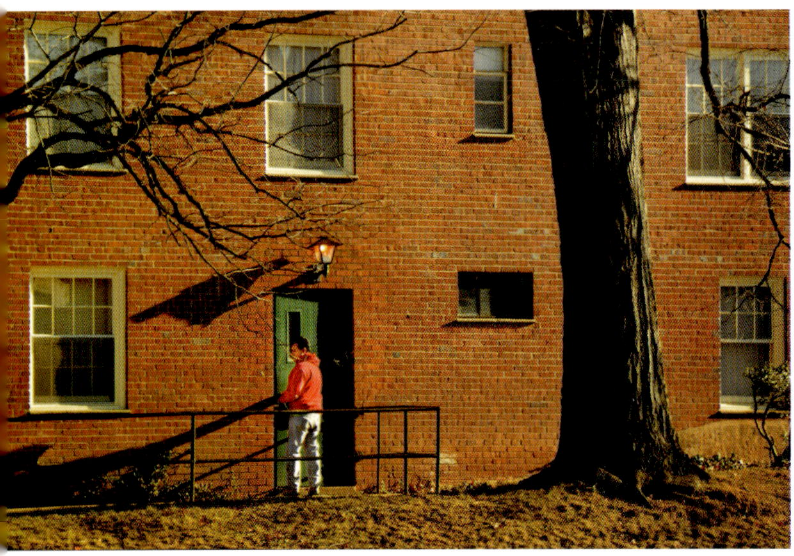

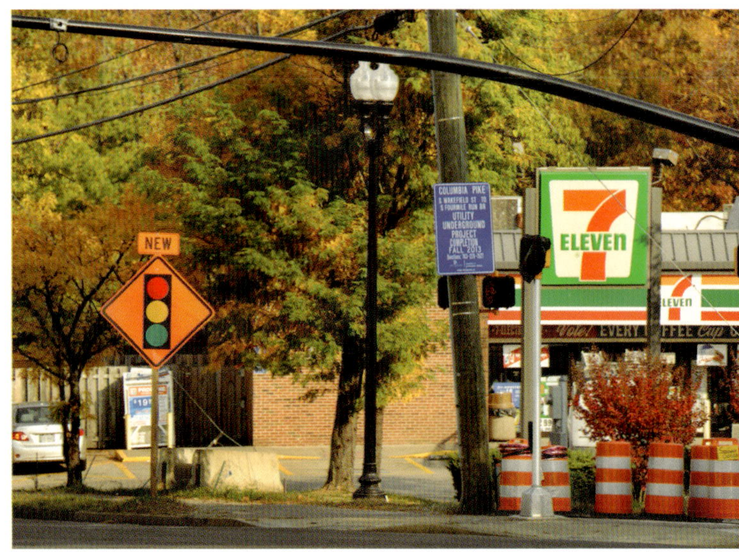

Arlington Mill Community Center, Columbia Pike at South Dinwiddie Street

4600 block of Columbia Pike

Columbia Pike Plaza with Arlington Mill Community Center Construction

4900 block of Columbia Pike

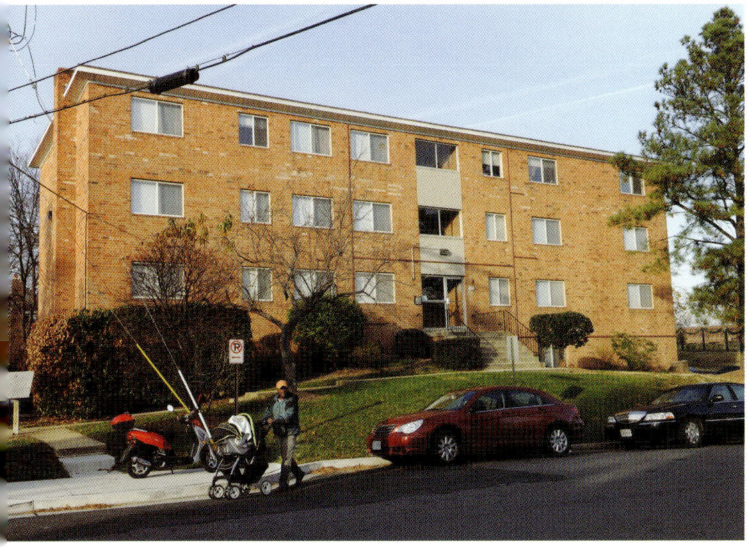

Apartments in Penrose Neighborhood

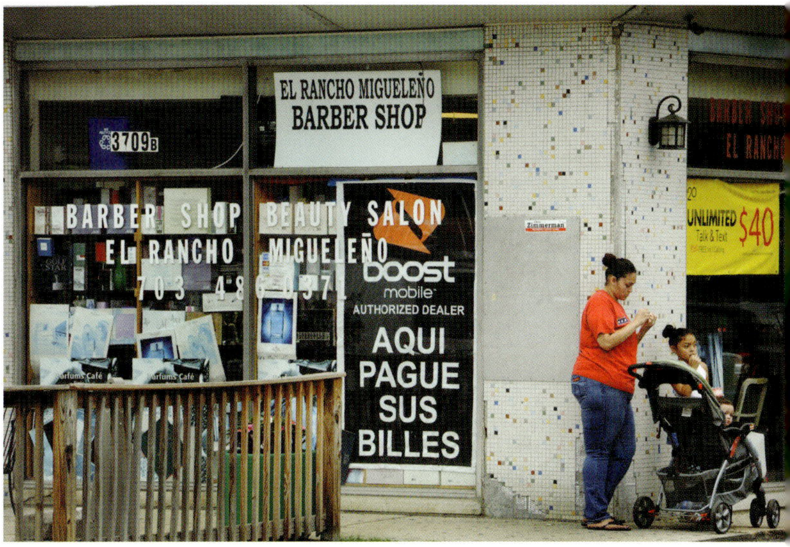

3700 block of Columbia Pike

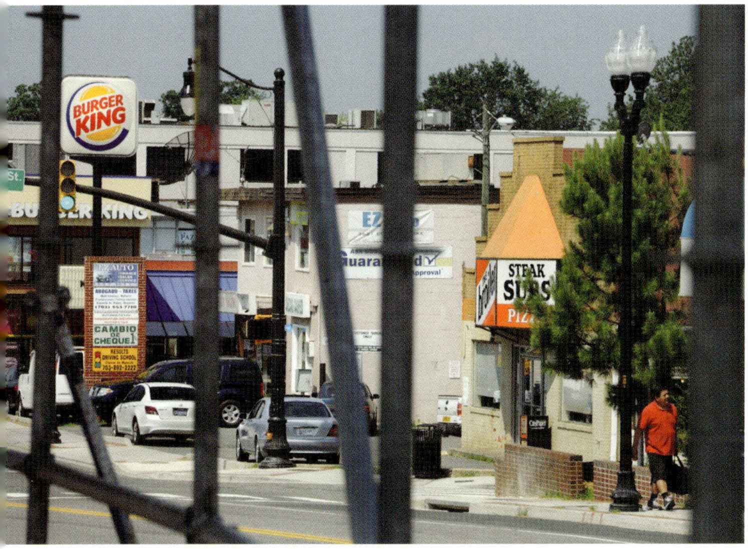

Columbia Pike, looking west from South Glebe Road

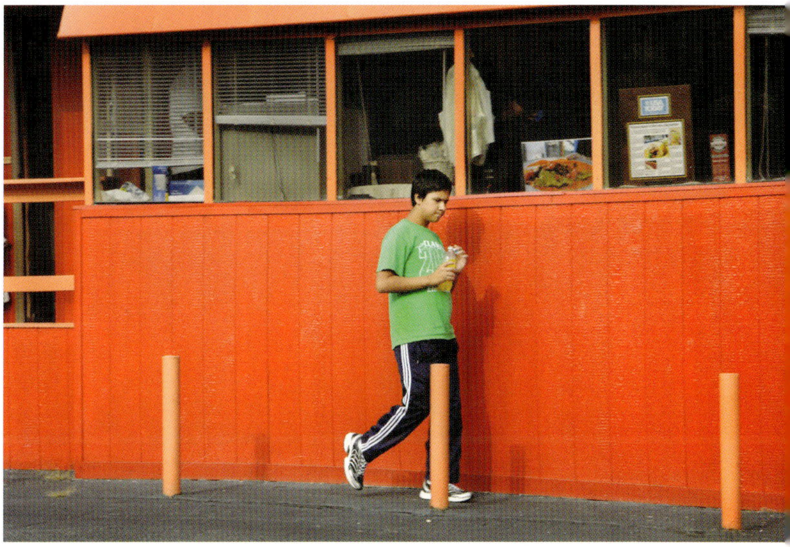

Pedro and Vinny's Burritos, 2599 Columbia Pike

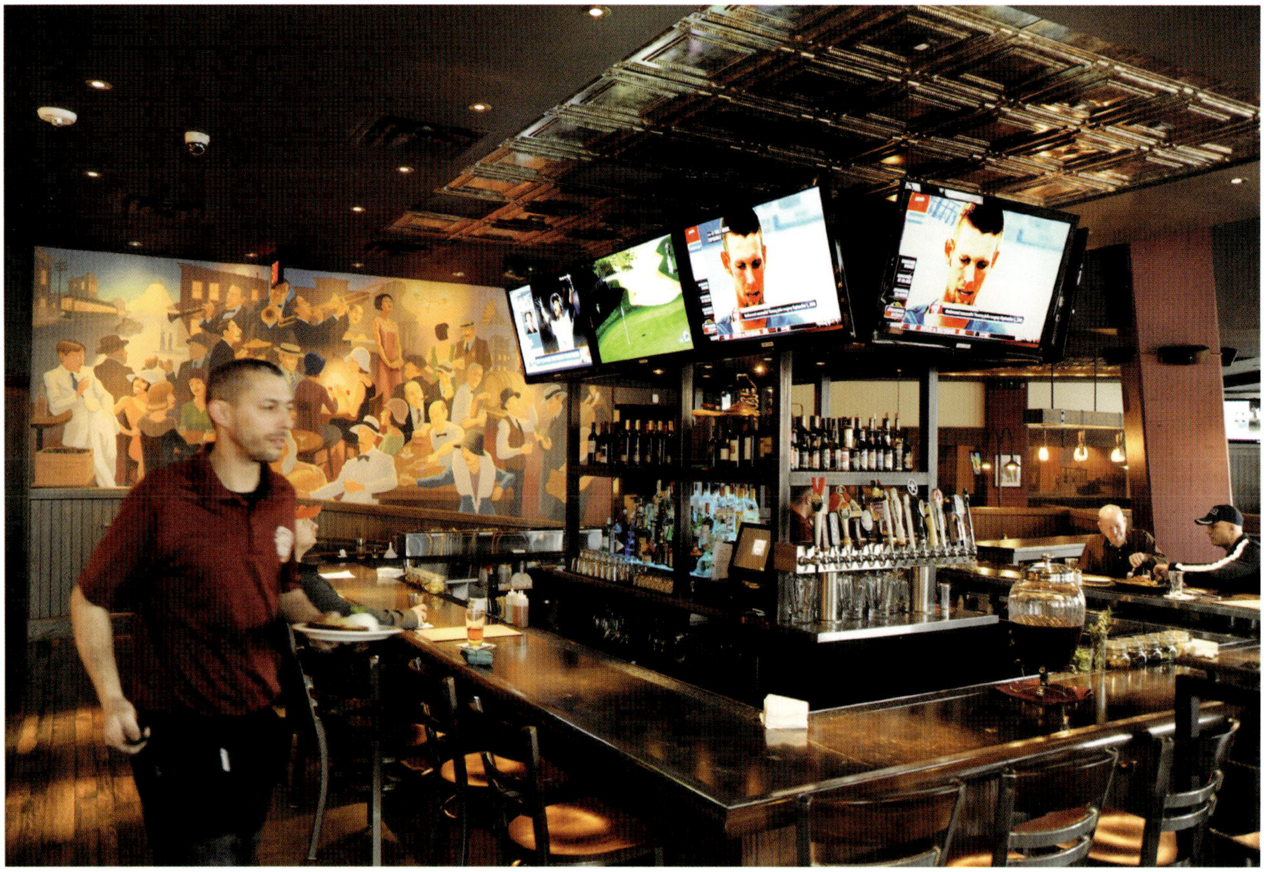

William Jeffery's Tavern, 2301 Columbia Pike

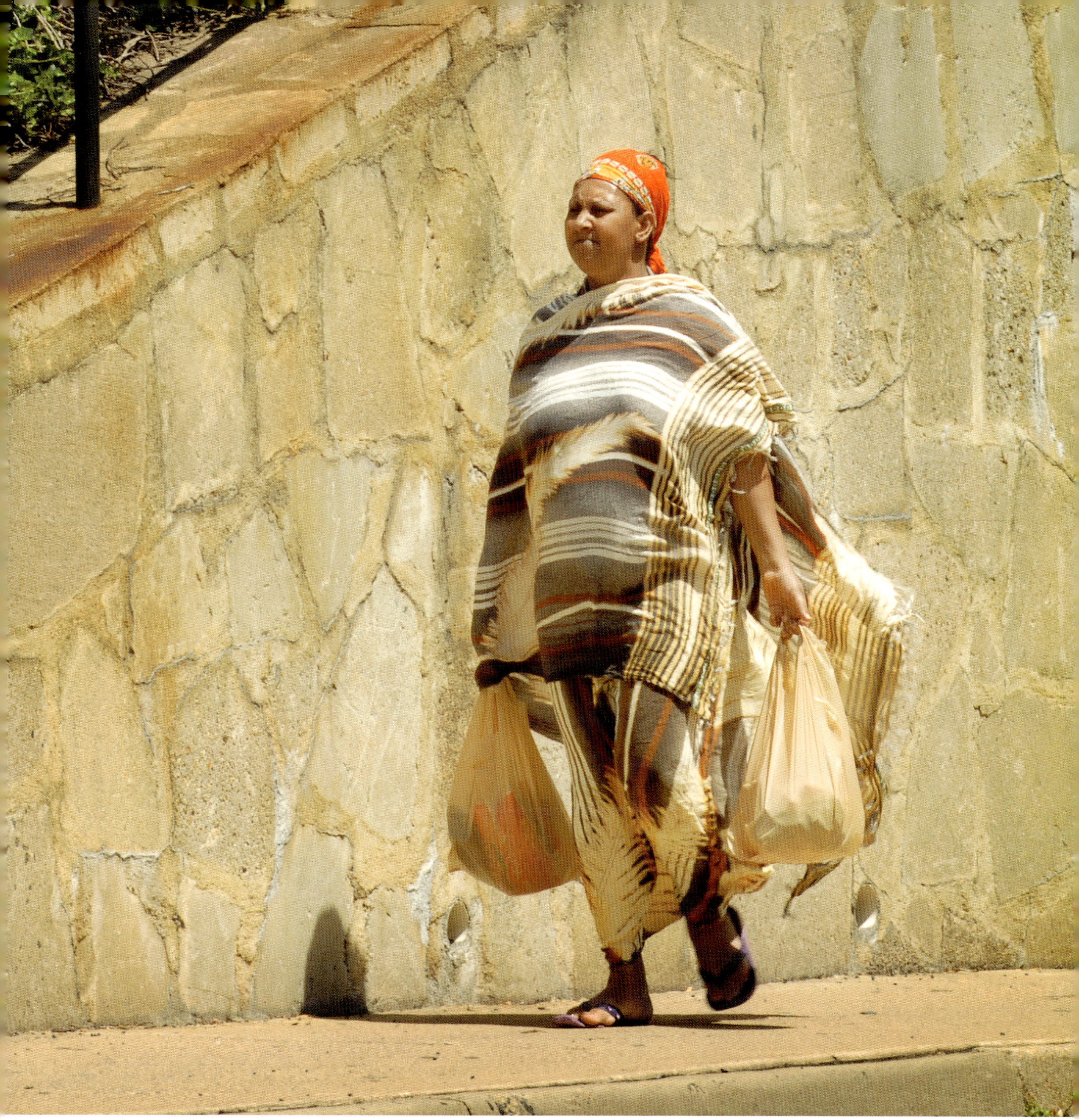

Woman, 5300 block of Columbia Pike

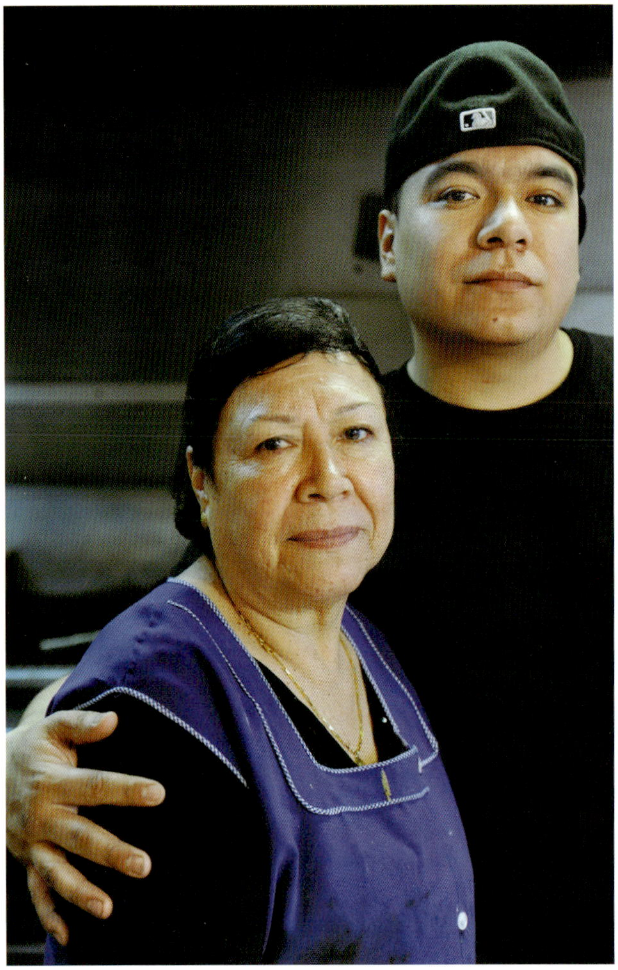

Owner Roger Coroneo, with his mother, Yolanda; Pedro and Vinny's Burritos

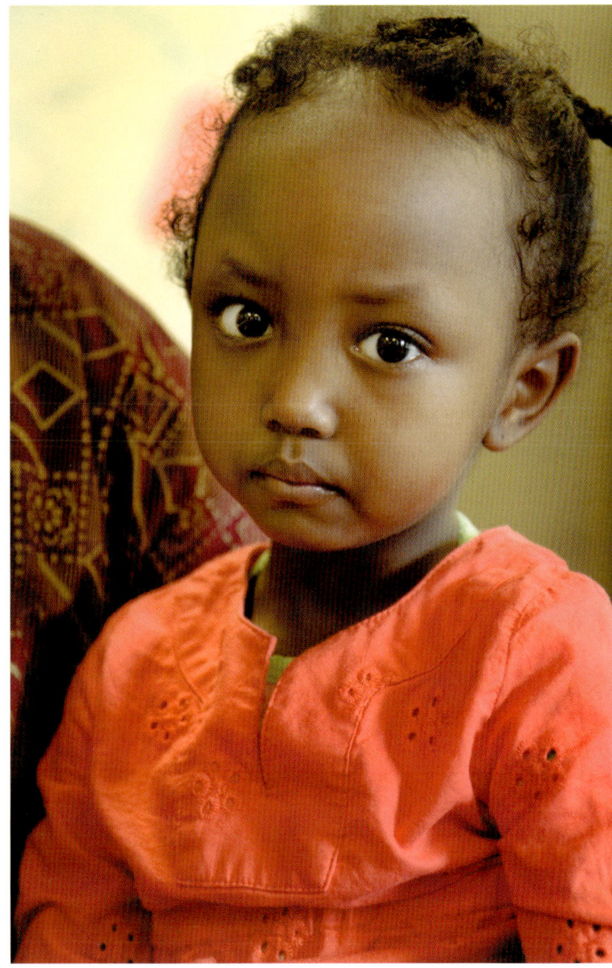

Meryam Mohammed

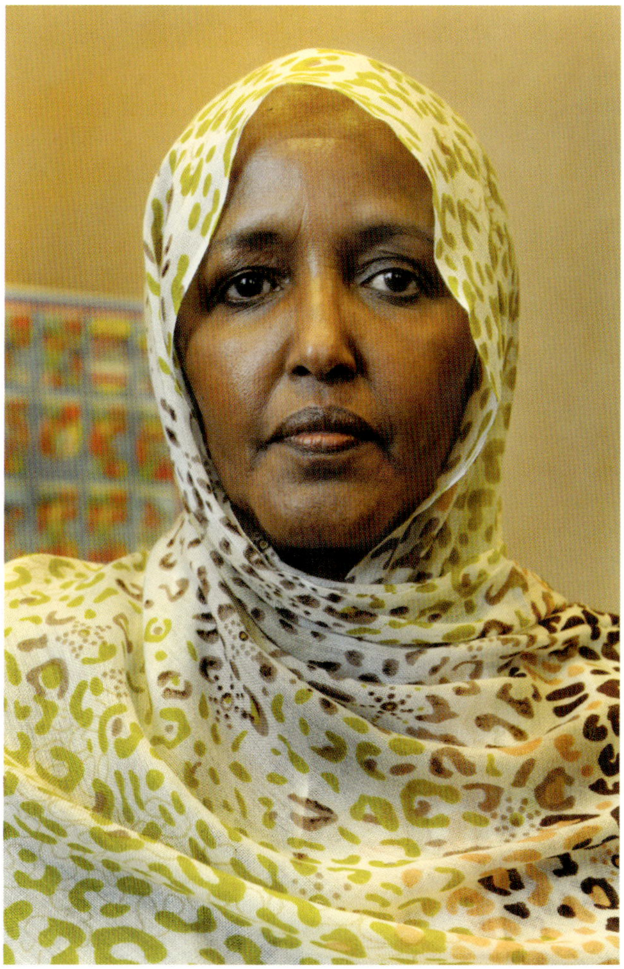

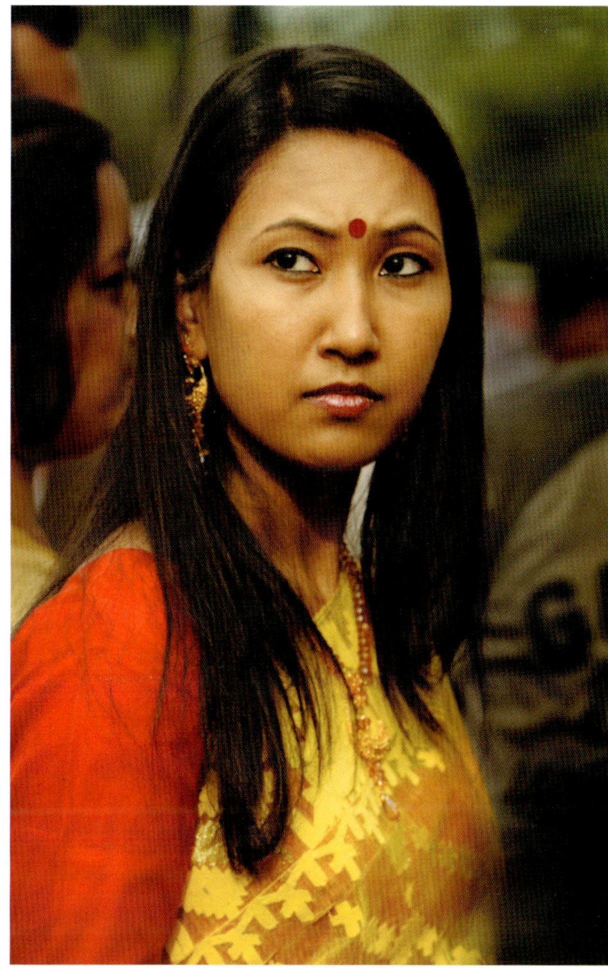

Woman, Ethiopian Community Development Council Event

Woman, Prio Bangla Festival

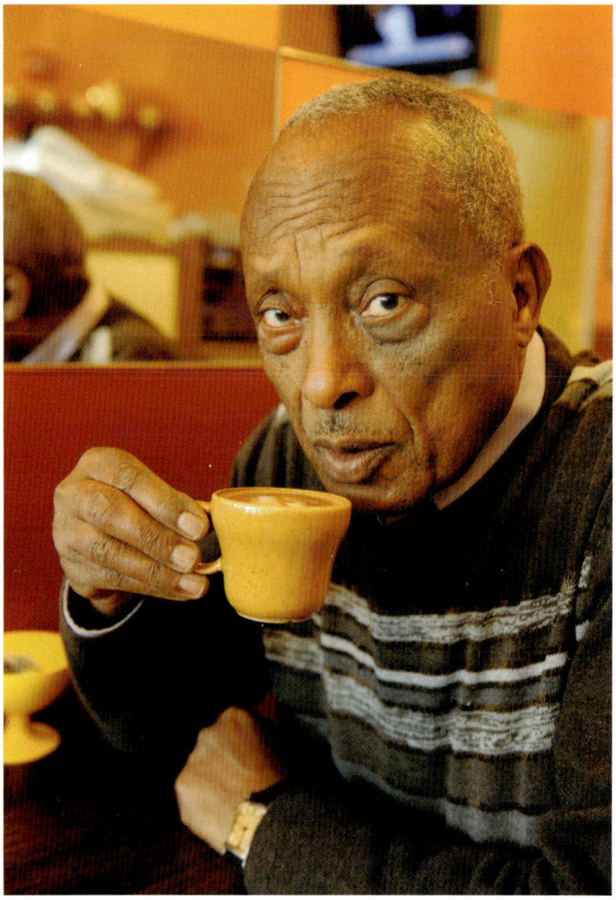

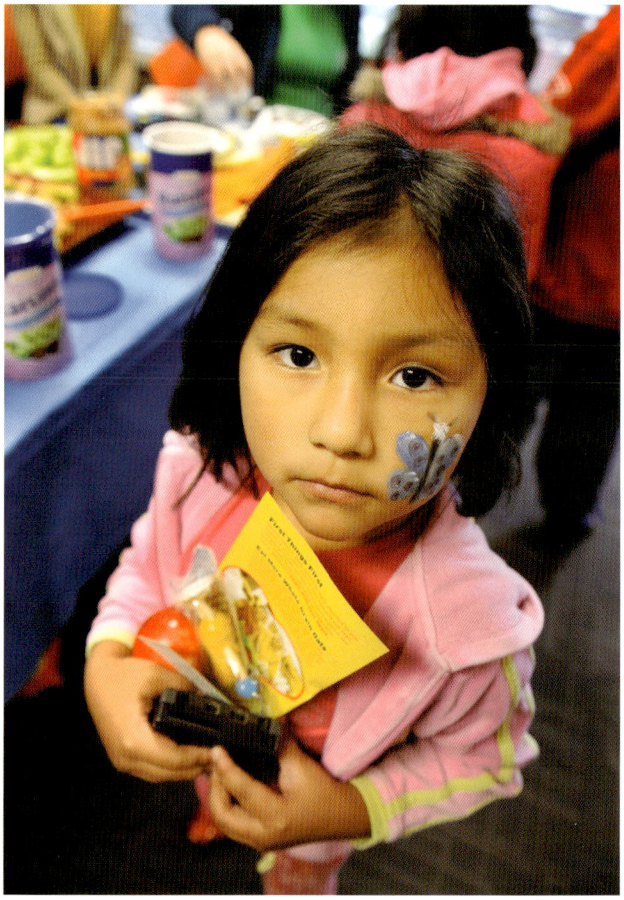

Abraham Yohannes Haile at Ethio Café, 3045A Columbia Pike

Columbia Gardens Health Fair

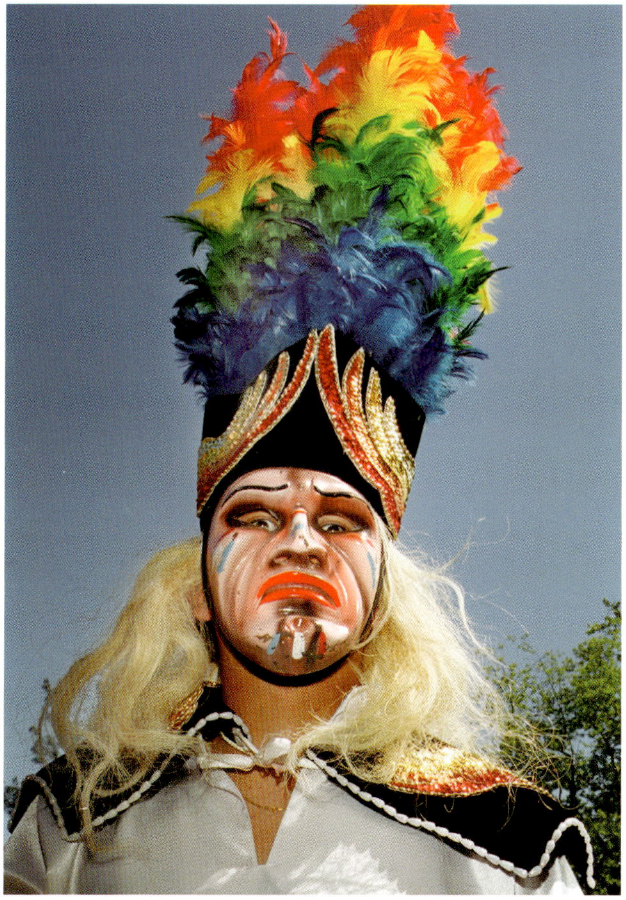

Bolivian Dancer, Columbia Heights West Festival

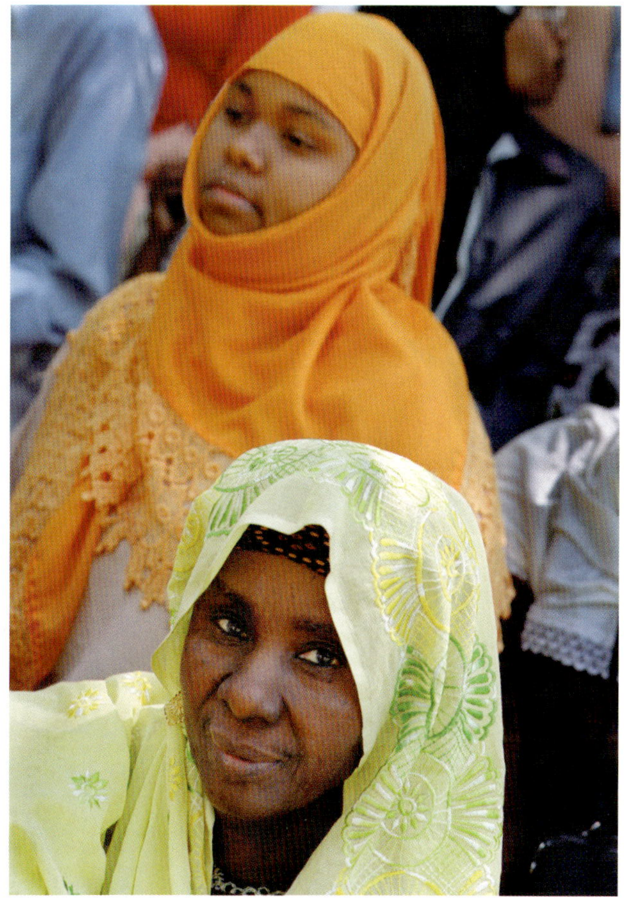

Somali Women, Columbia Heights West Festival

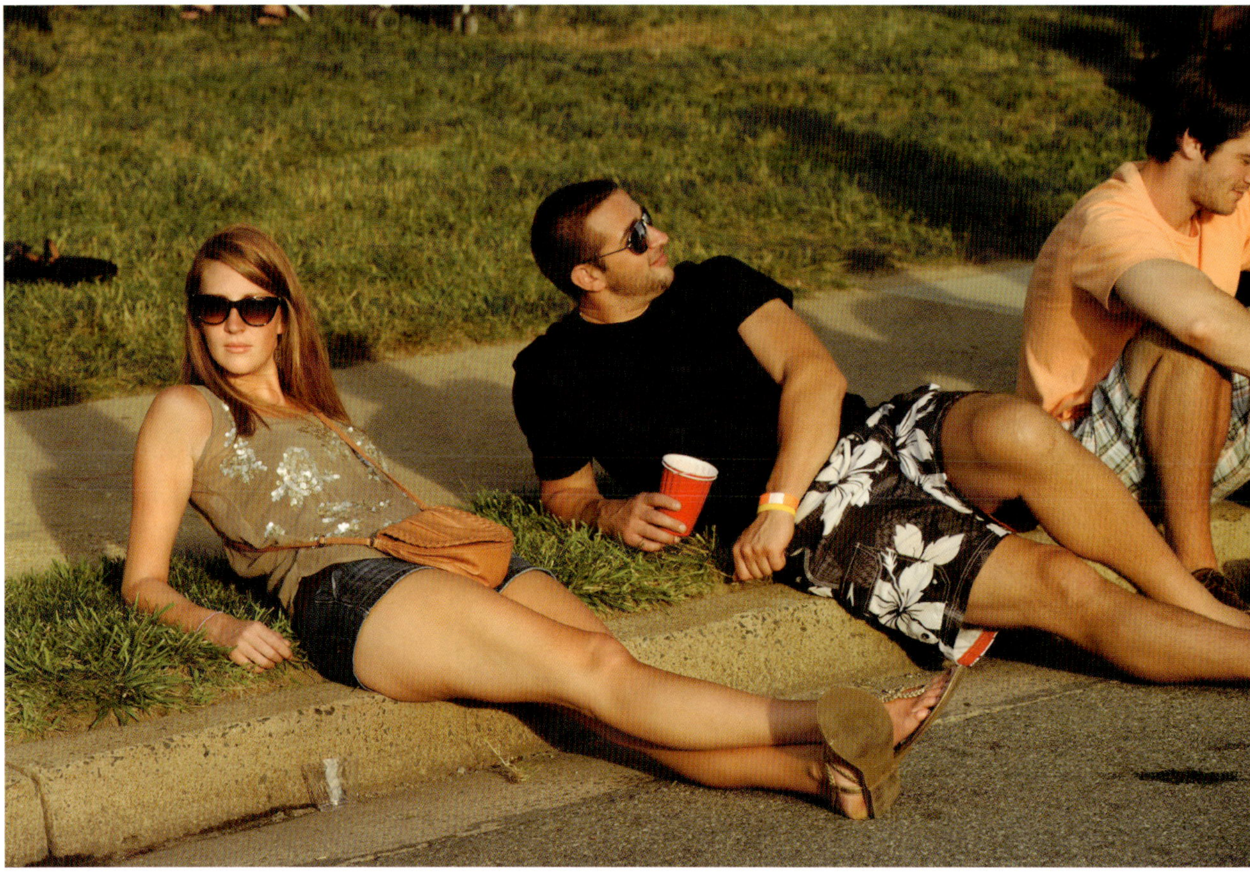

Columbia Pike Blues Festival

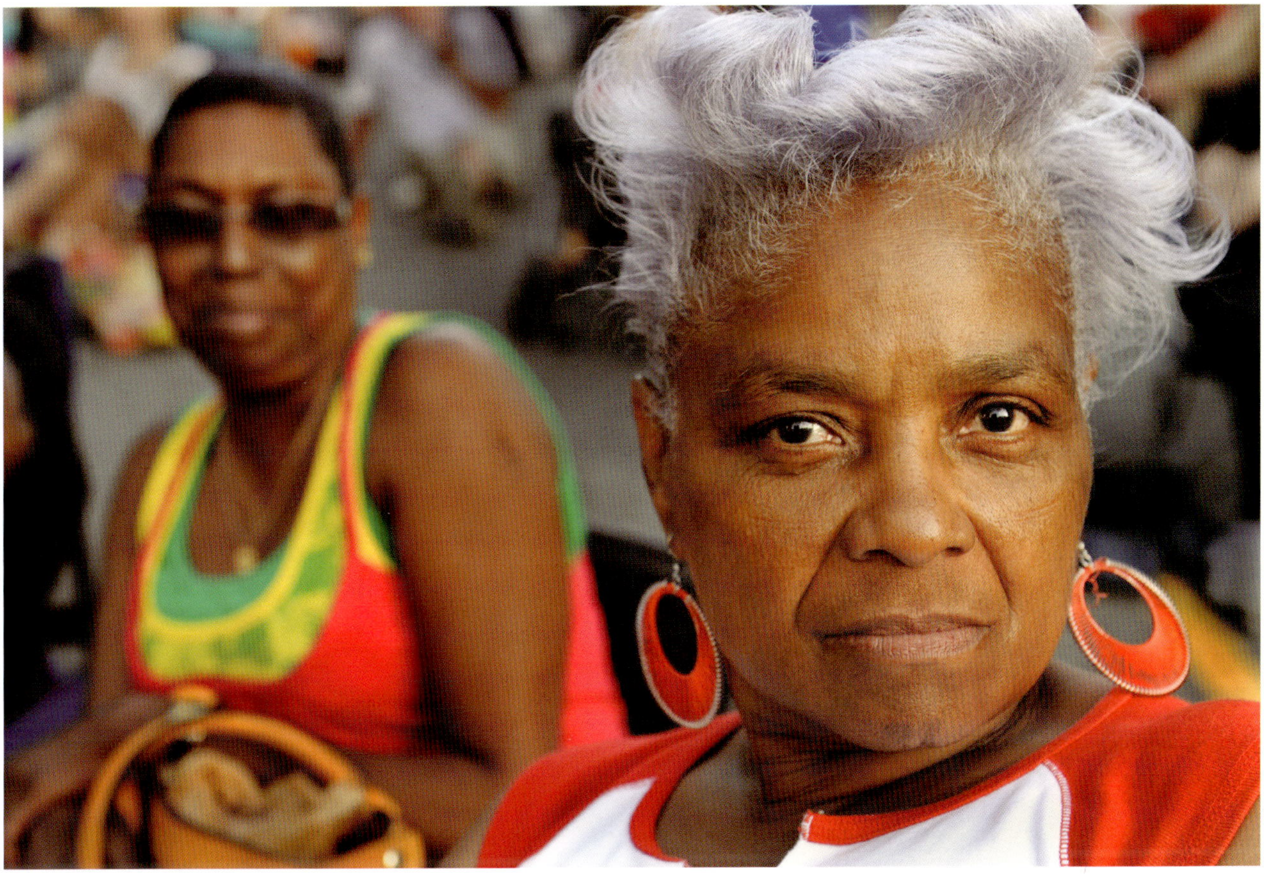

Columbia Pike Blues Festival

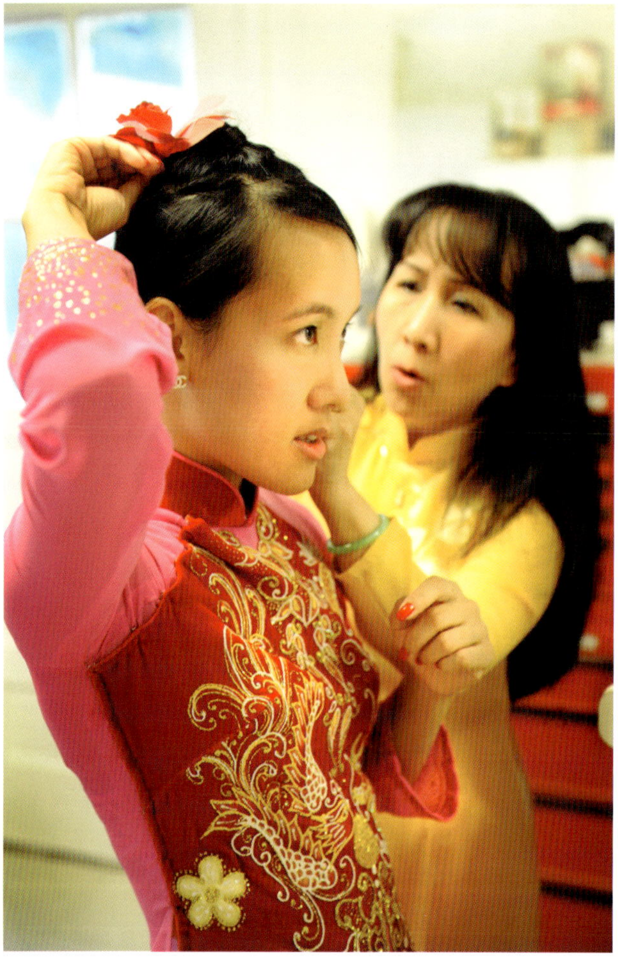

Daisy Lung with her mother in-law, Mrs. Tran, at her wedding

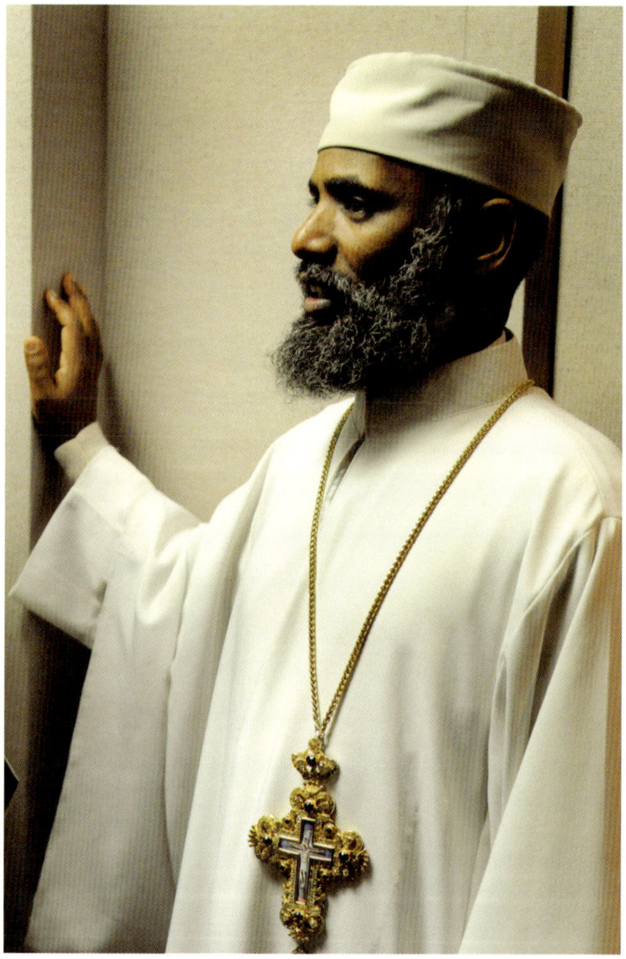

Coptic Priest, Ethiopian Christmas Celebration

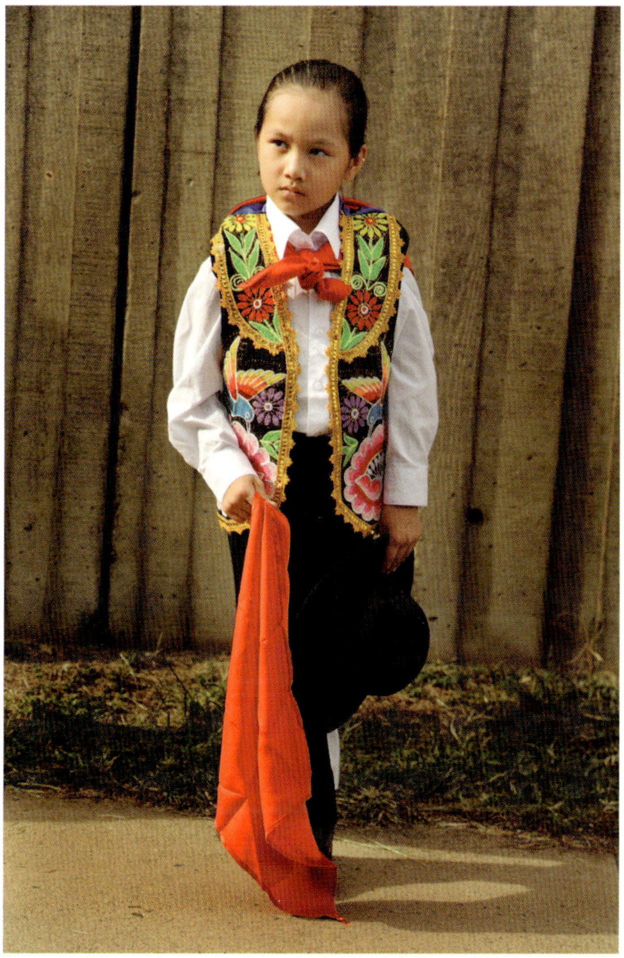

Central American Dancer, Prio Bangla Festival

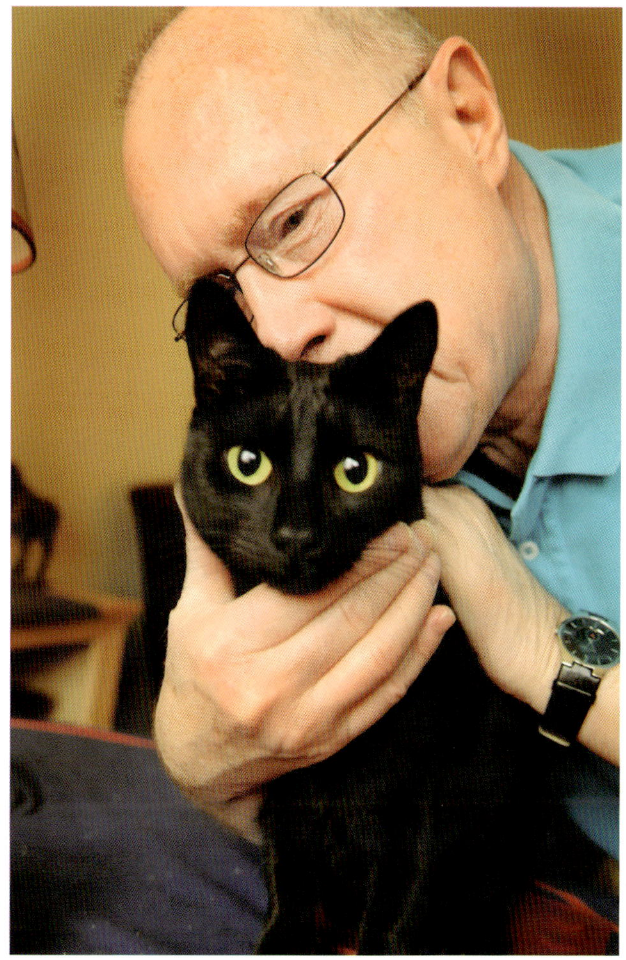

Jim McCaskill

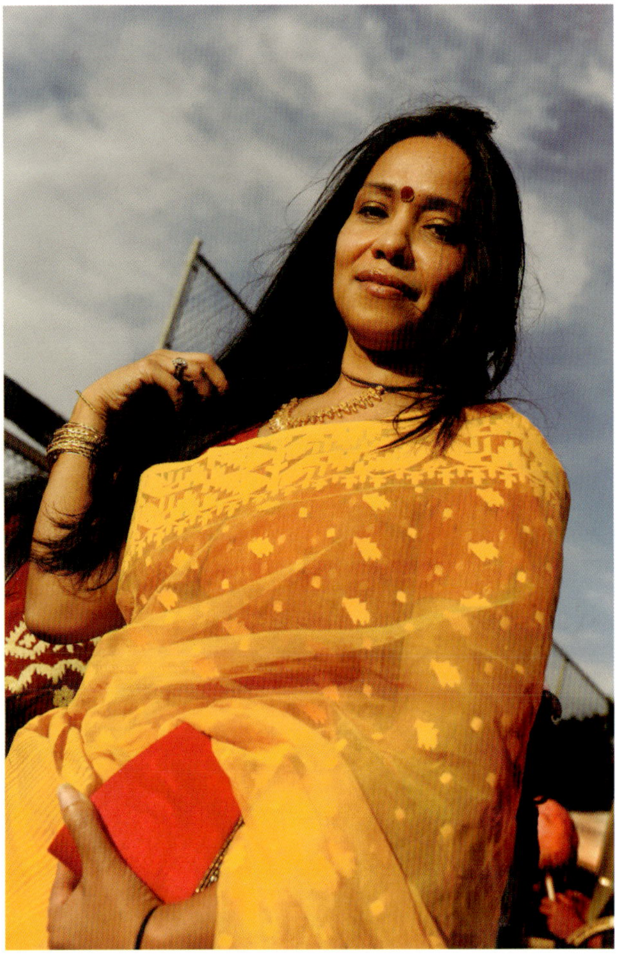

Prio Bangla Festival

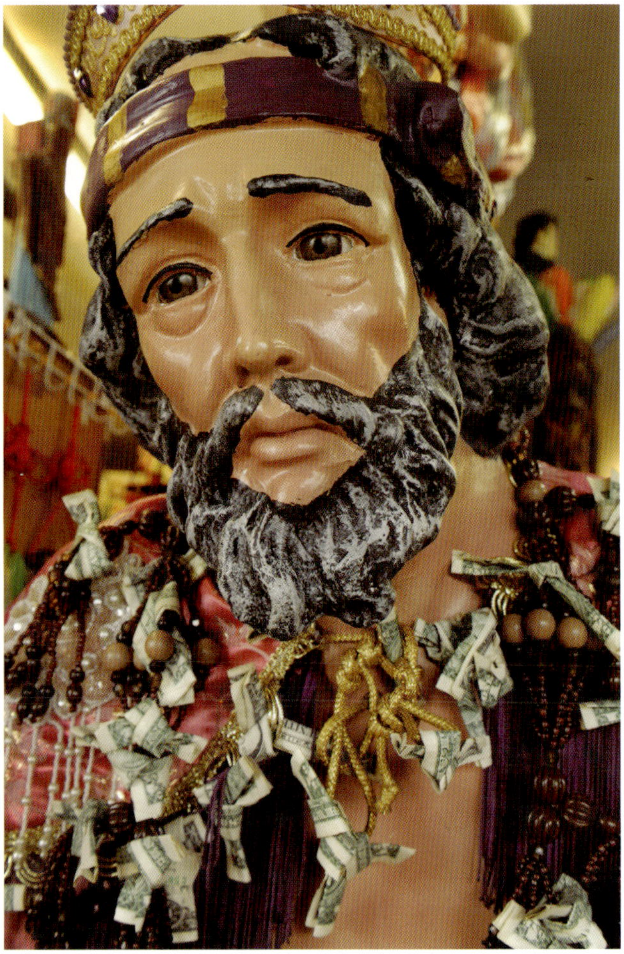

Botanica Boricua, 2634 Columbia Pike

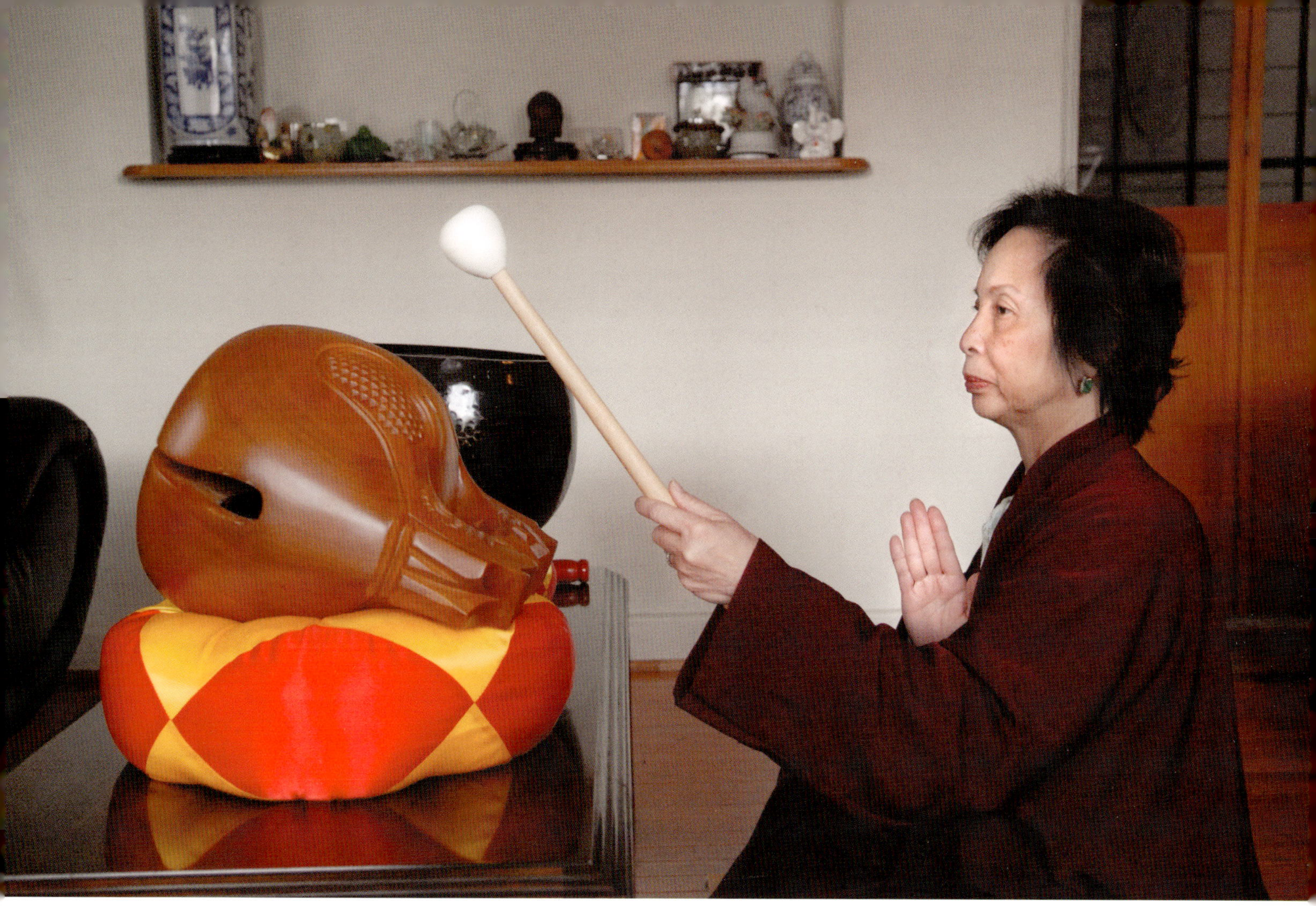

I was a boat person. I came to the United States from Vietnam in 1979. I was 27. I came to Arlington two weeks after I arrived in the United States. The only family I knew was in the same boat with me.

My uncle got me out of the country. Six days, five nights on the boat. Our food and water began to run out after the fourth day, but we don' have other problems, like fishing boats attacking us, like other boat people..

I start my life here with nothing, only $50. I met my husband here and married, and I have one daughter. She grew up in Arlington, and she was a very good student. Trinh went to UVA and graduated in Systems Engineering, and minored in Biology.

I was lucky to escape from Vietnam. I have freedom here. I can learn and to work at whatever career I like. I have the chance to move up in my life. This is my second country.

I am Buddhist..... Buddhists believe in Buddha, and Catholics believe in God, in Jesus Christ. Do the right thing, the good thing, try to love and help other people. For me, God or Buddha or Jesus Christ are the same. They are the highest person, who teaches us to do the right thing. I sit meditation, I pray... Doing the right thing is important.

Kim-Hanh T. Nguyen

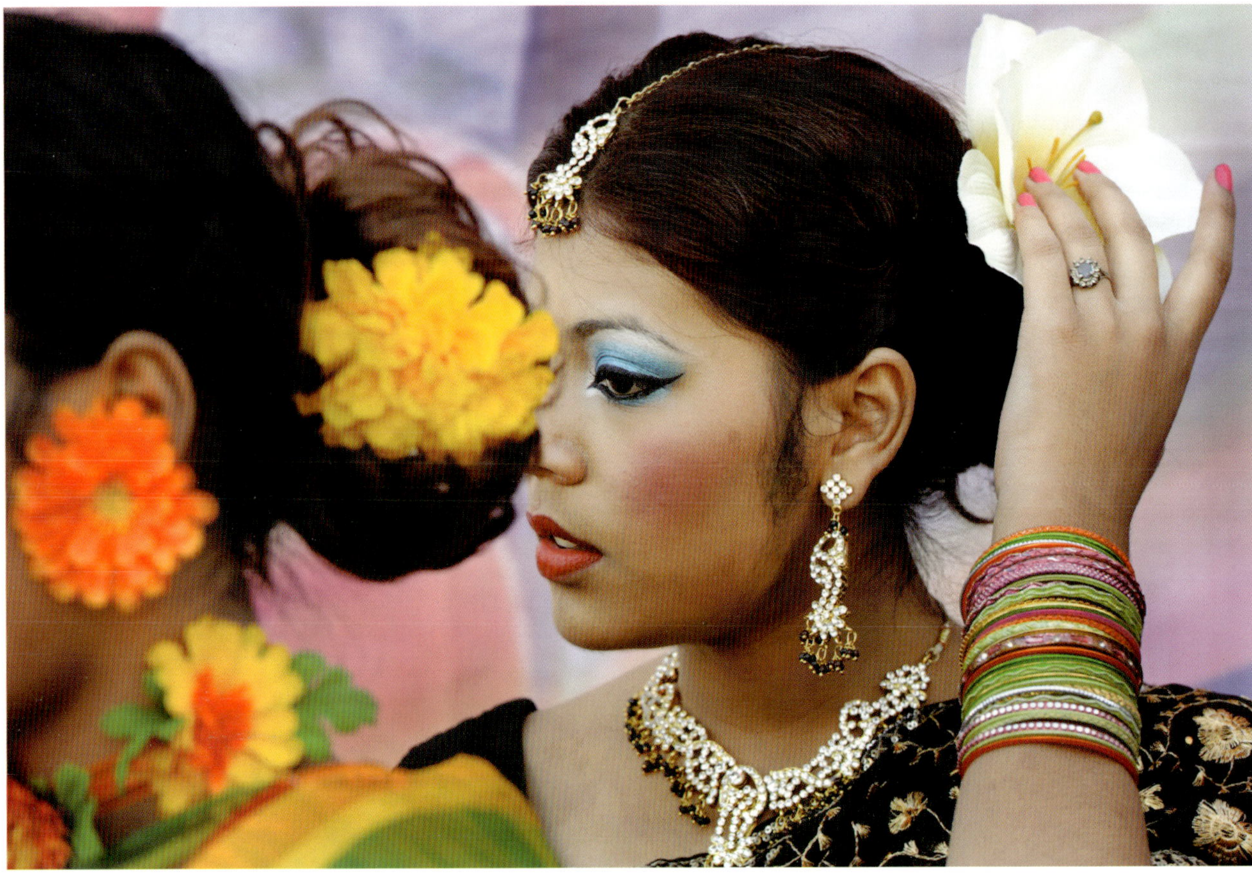

Dancers, Prio Bangla Festival

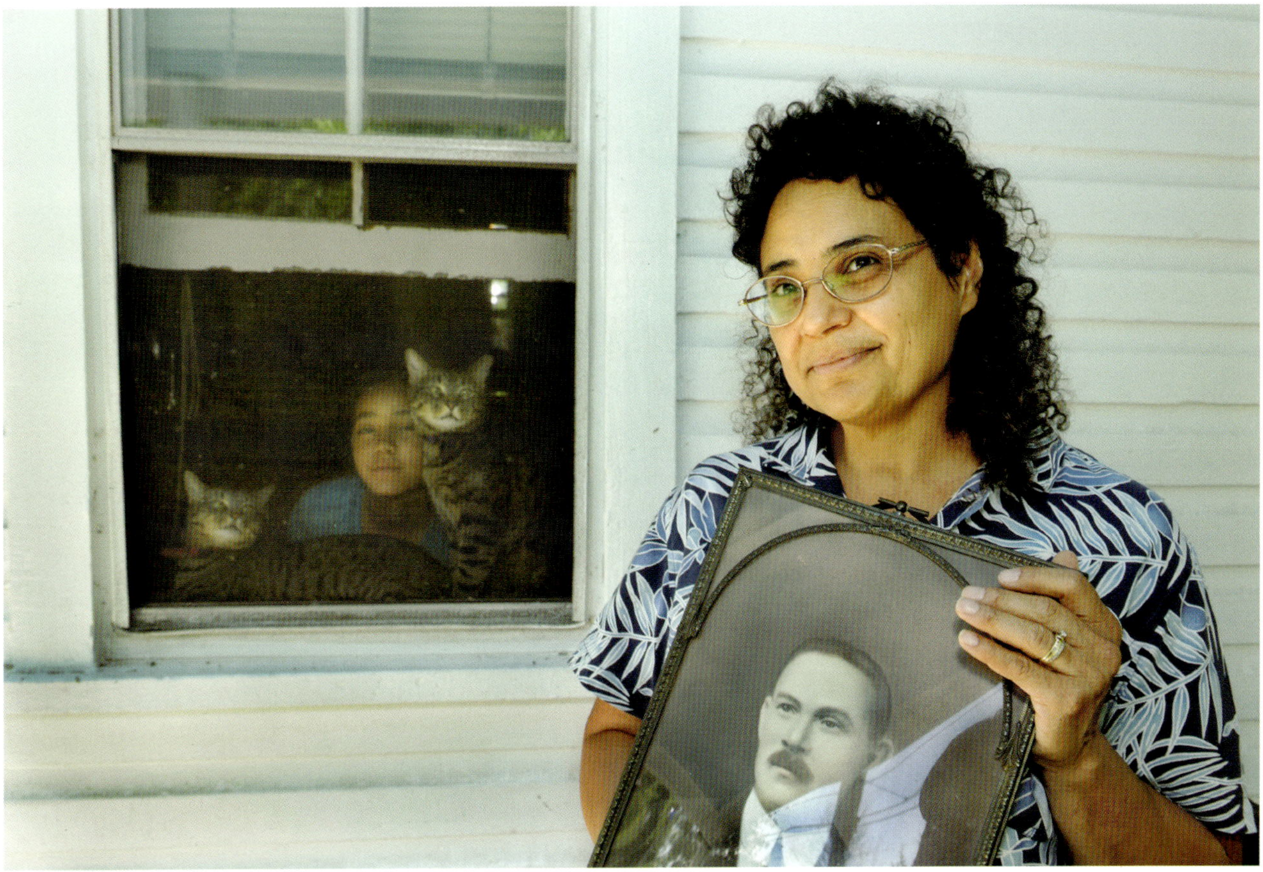

Cathleen "Catie" Drew is a museum education director, and the grandniece of the pioneering African-American physician, Dr. Charles R. Drew.

My great-grandfather, Richard Thomas Drew, was living in Washington. He and my great-grandmother Nora, had four children, Charles, Elsie, Joseph, and Nora. Elsie died from tuberculosis and my great-grandfather blamed it on the bad air of Foggy Bottom, which was rife with "fever 'n' ague."

He looked around for some good "country" property and in 1920 purchased a home in Arlington, in one of the few African-American neighborhoods, the Butler-Holmes Subdivision. They raised their family there. The neighborhood has since seen major changes.

Because my dad was in the Air Force, we moved all over. This house in Arlington was my home base. I was married at the house to my husband, Wayne Botts. Our children, Jordan, Sarah and Adam, are the 5th generation of the Drew family to live here.

I started the big gardens at the house. This year we grew tomatoes, cucumbers, eggplant, peppers, squashes, carrots, pole beans, beets, turnips, kale, collards, broccoli, cauliflower, lettuce, cabbage, blueberries, blackberries, strawberries, asparagus, echinacea, basil, rosemary, cilantro, parsley, sweet and white potatoes, and onions. We consume most of it ourselves, and give some away.

My kids grew up with diversity. They have friends from across the spectrum; I couldn't pronounce all of their names at first! There were more non-American names than American in their school. Arab, Russian, Korean, Latino, Chinese. They don't seem to notice differences in background, which is good. People should be taken as who they are. I'm a scientist and an educator... that's the way it should be I believe.

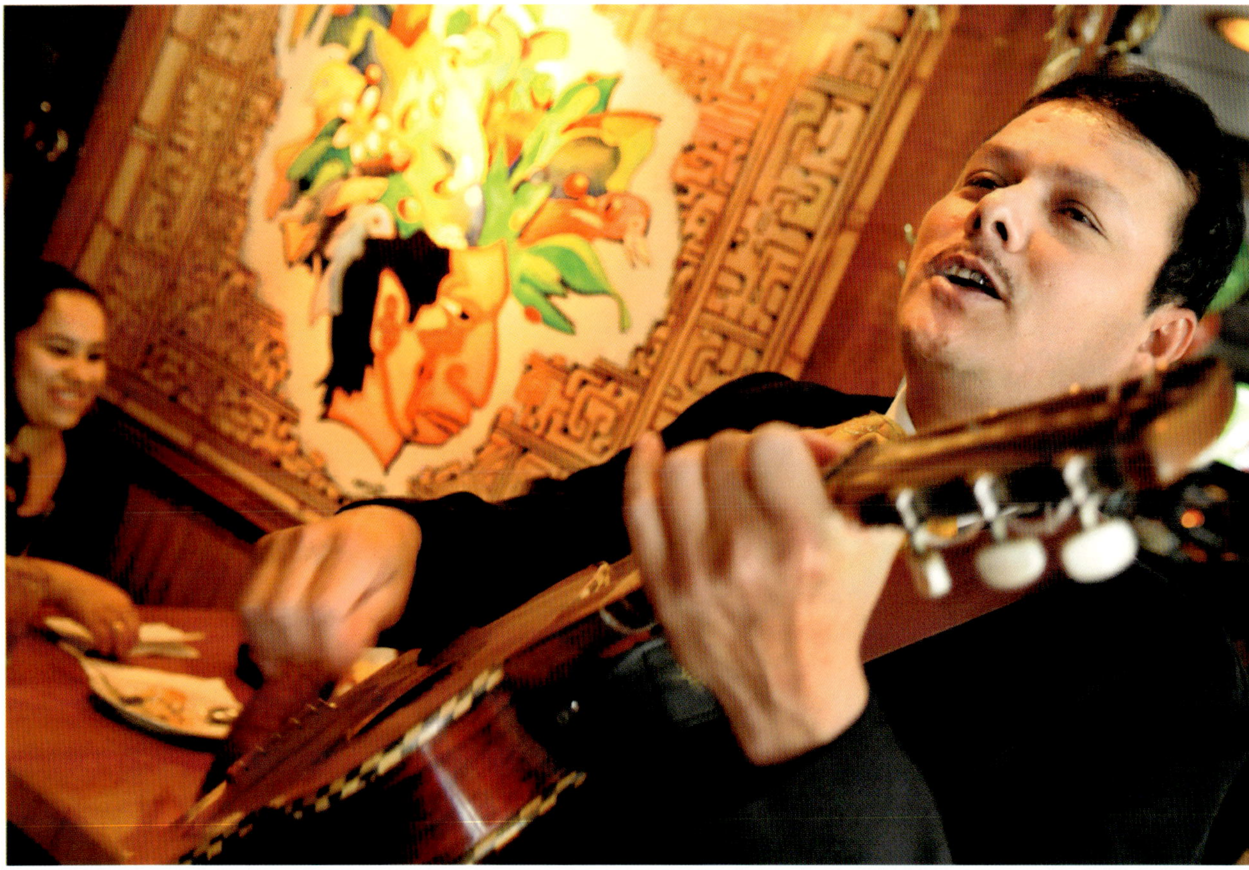

Mariachi band, Abi's Restaurante, 3005 Columbia Pike

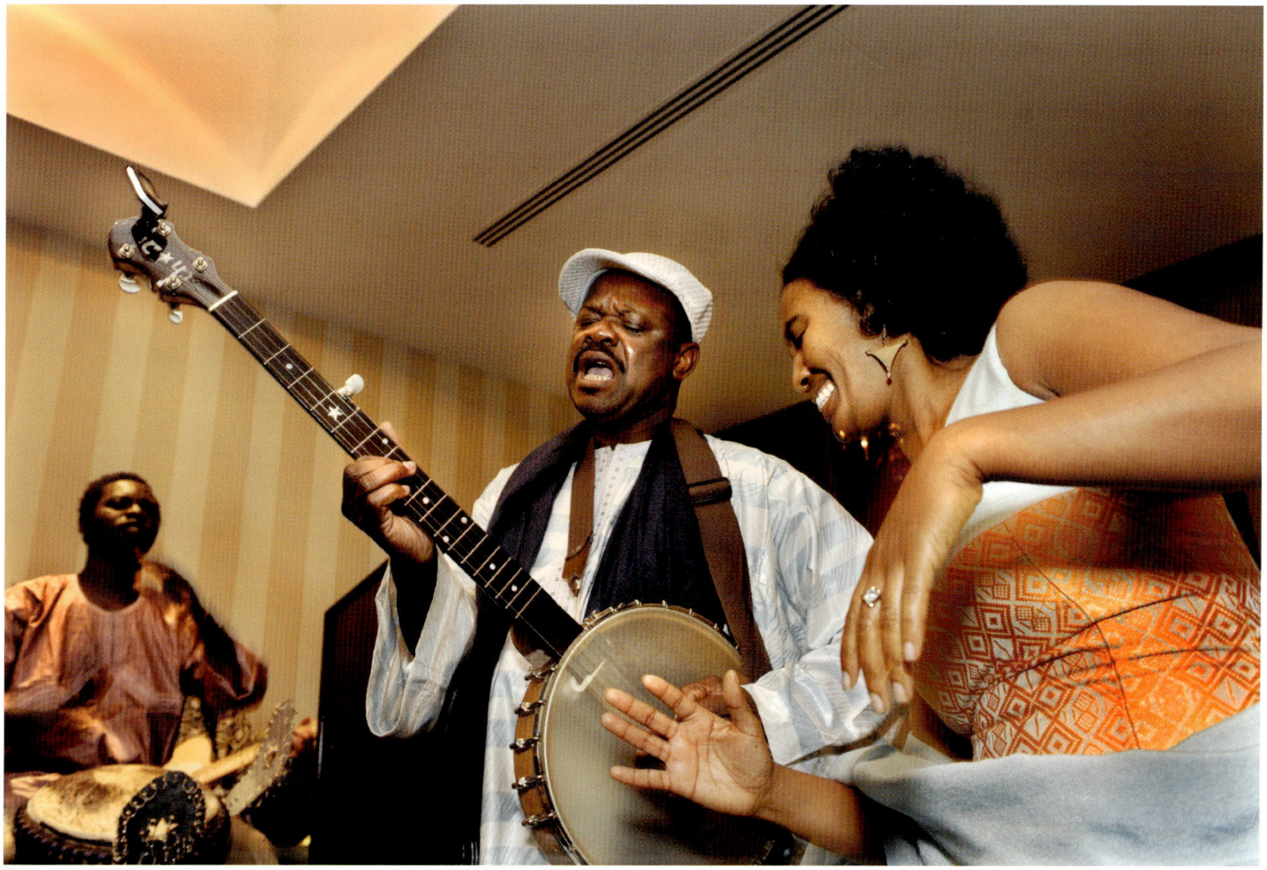

Cheick Hamala's Griot Street Band, at Ethiopian Community Development Council Gala

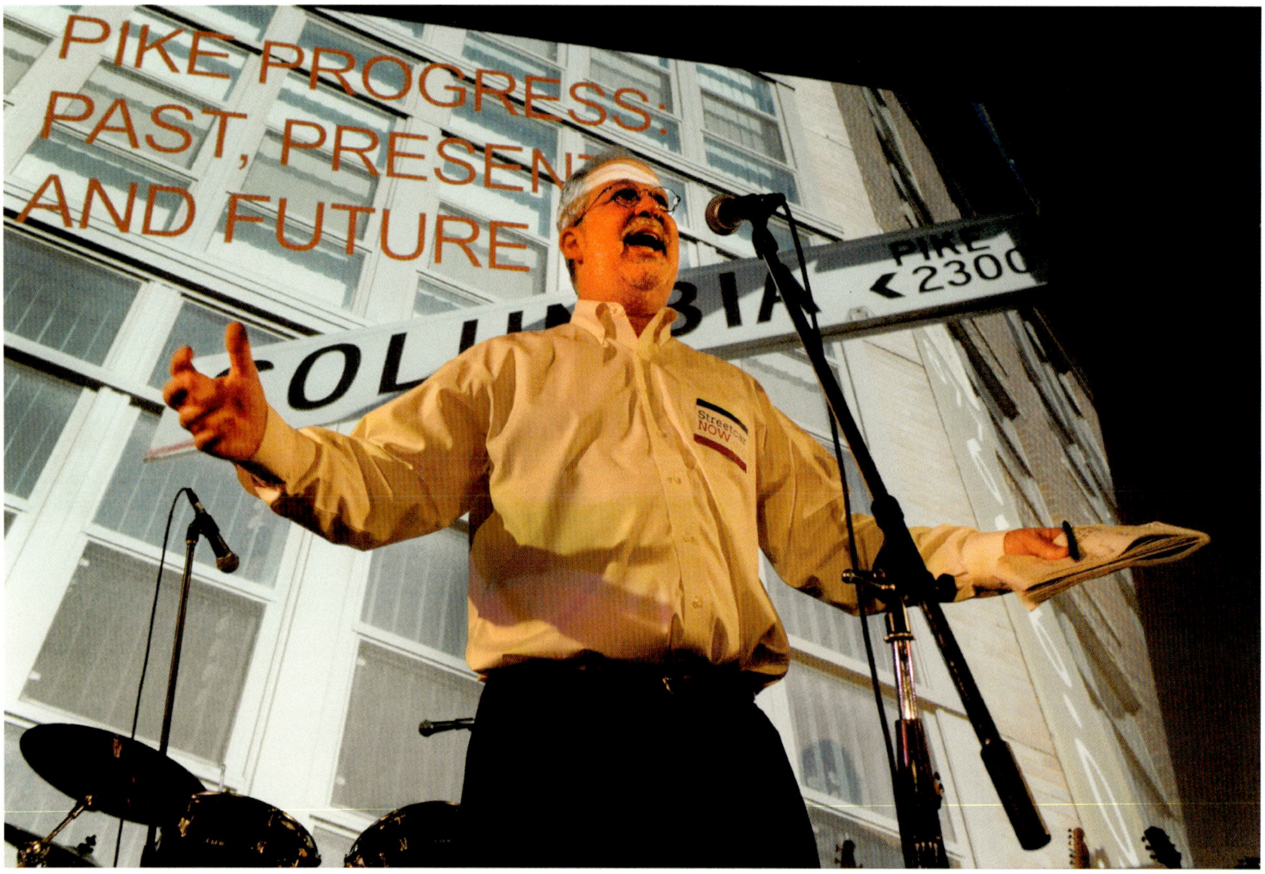

John Snyder, Arlington Streetcar Now Event, Arlington Cinema and Drafthouse, 2903 Columbia Pike

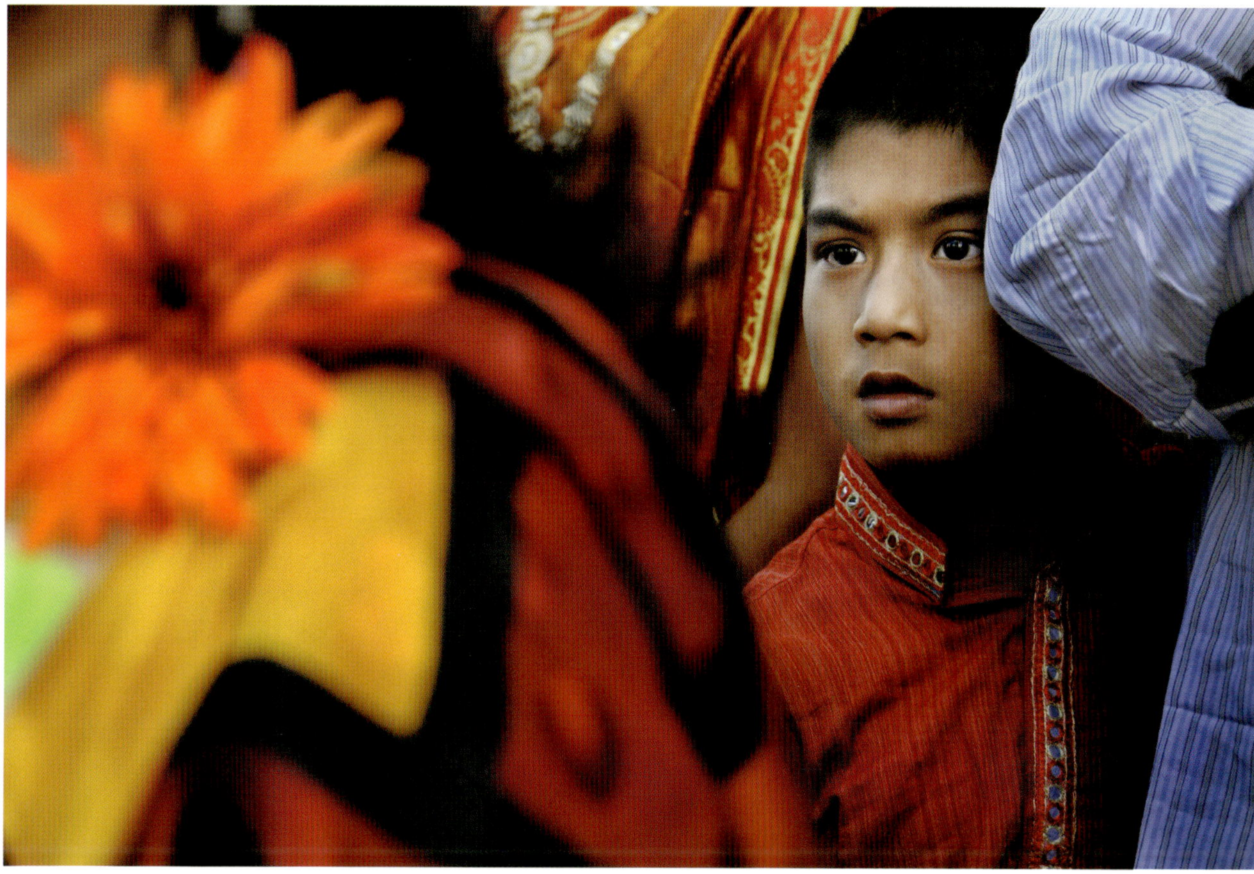

Boy, Prio Bangla Festival

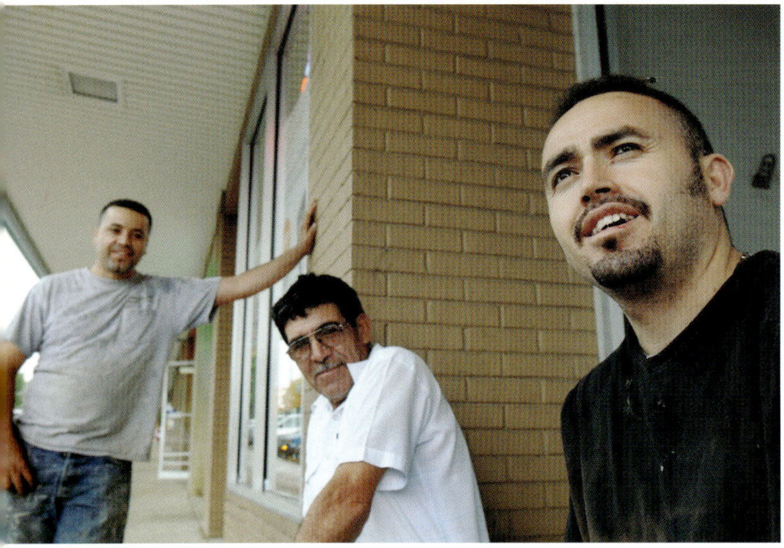

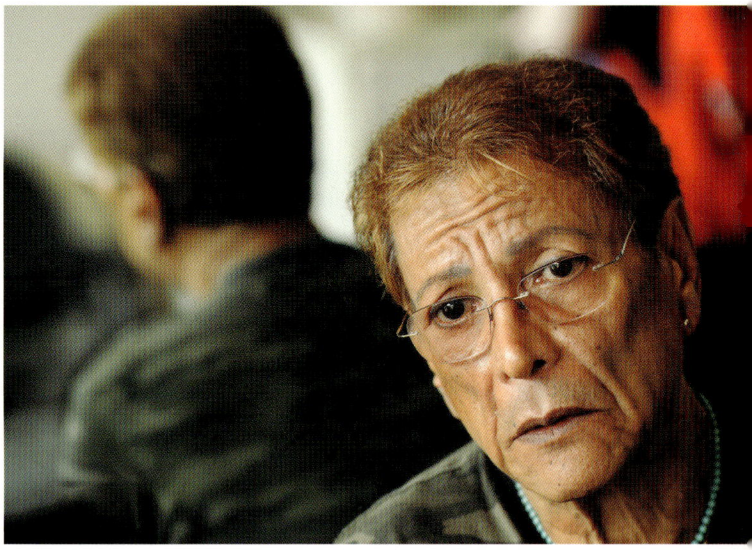

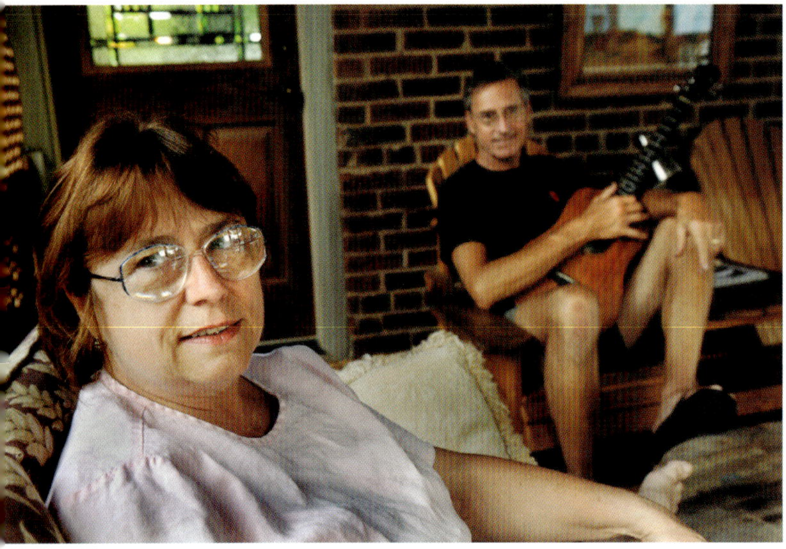

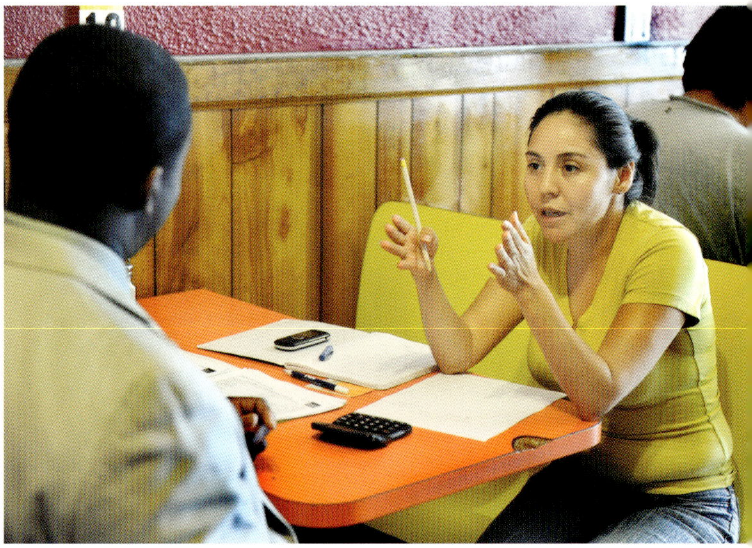

Friends, Columbia Pike Plaza

Moroccan stylist, Beauty Fair Salon, 4105 Columbia Pike

Juanita and Don Zientara

El Pike Restaurant, 4111 Columbia Pike

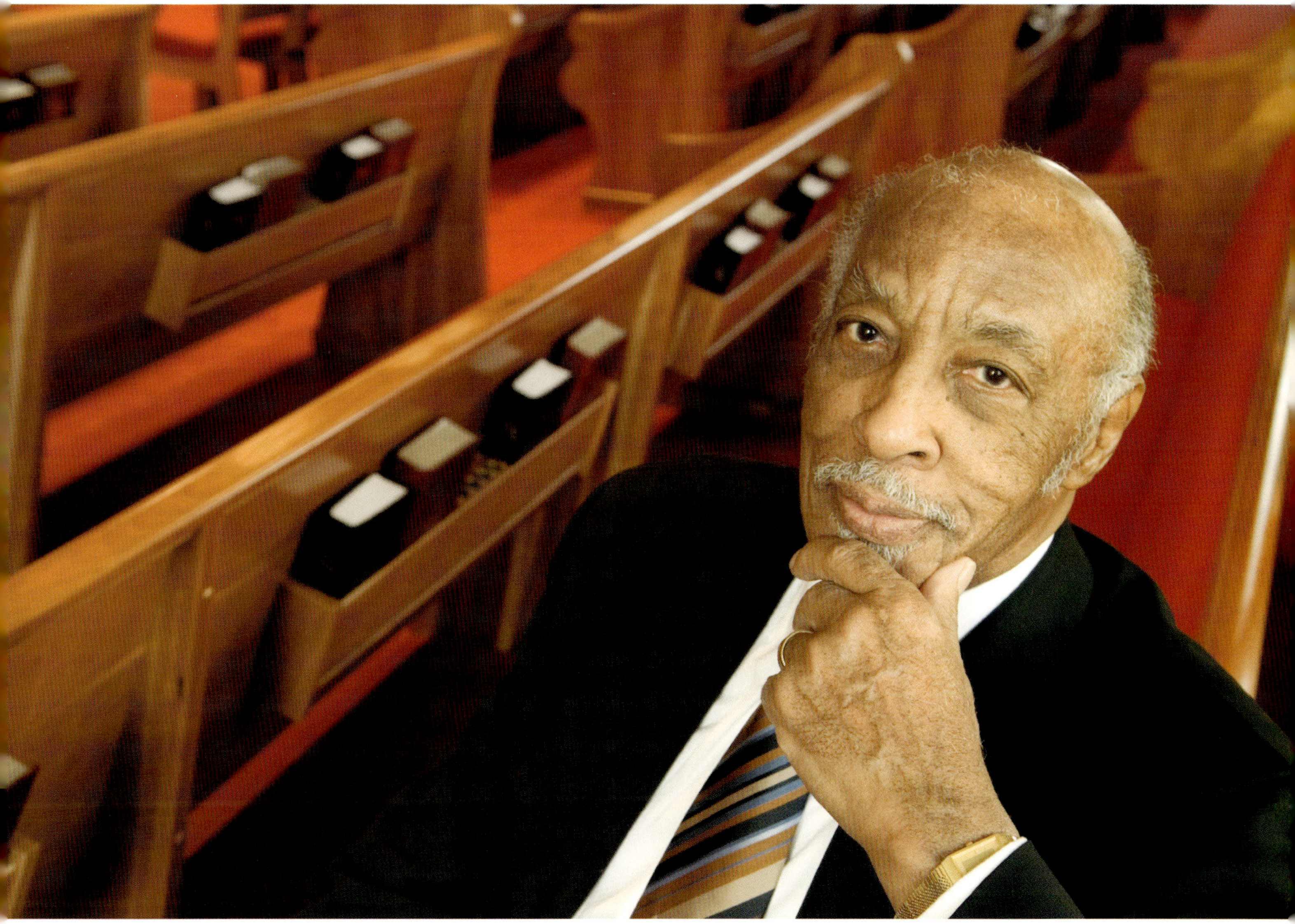

We have people from five different countries from Africa who are members here at St. John's Church. We have them from Ghana, we have them from Liberia, Zambia, Sudan. Over time we've had Hispanics, Caucasians, who are members here now, a Russian family, Lithuanians, who were members here,

The exciting thing here is to be in this area with this ethnic background of cultural ministry, and be able to translate that same ministry to those people and to see all of us come together and be one with a variety of backgrounds. And yet have the same gospel and the same ministry. It has been exciting - that has been the most exciting thing about it for me.

So, my hope is to see, first of all, affordable housing, and then to see the church move to the point where it can bring together the urban, the suburban, the ethnic background of all people into one worshiping and social environment where we can interact, develop and grow together.

Pastor John Nicholas, St. John's Church, 1905 Columbia Pike

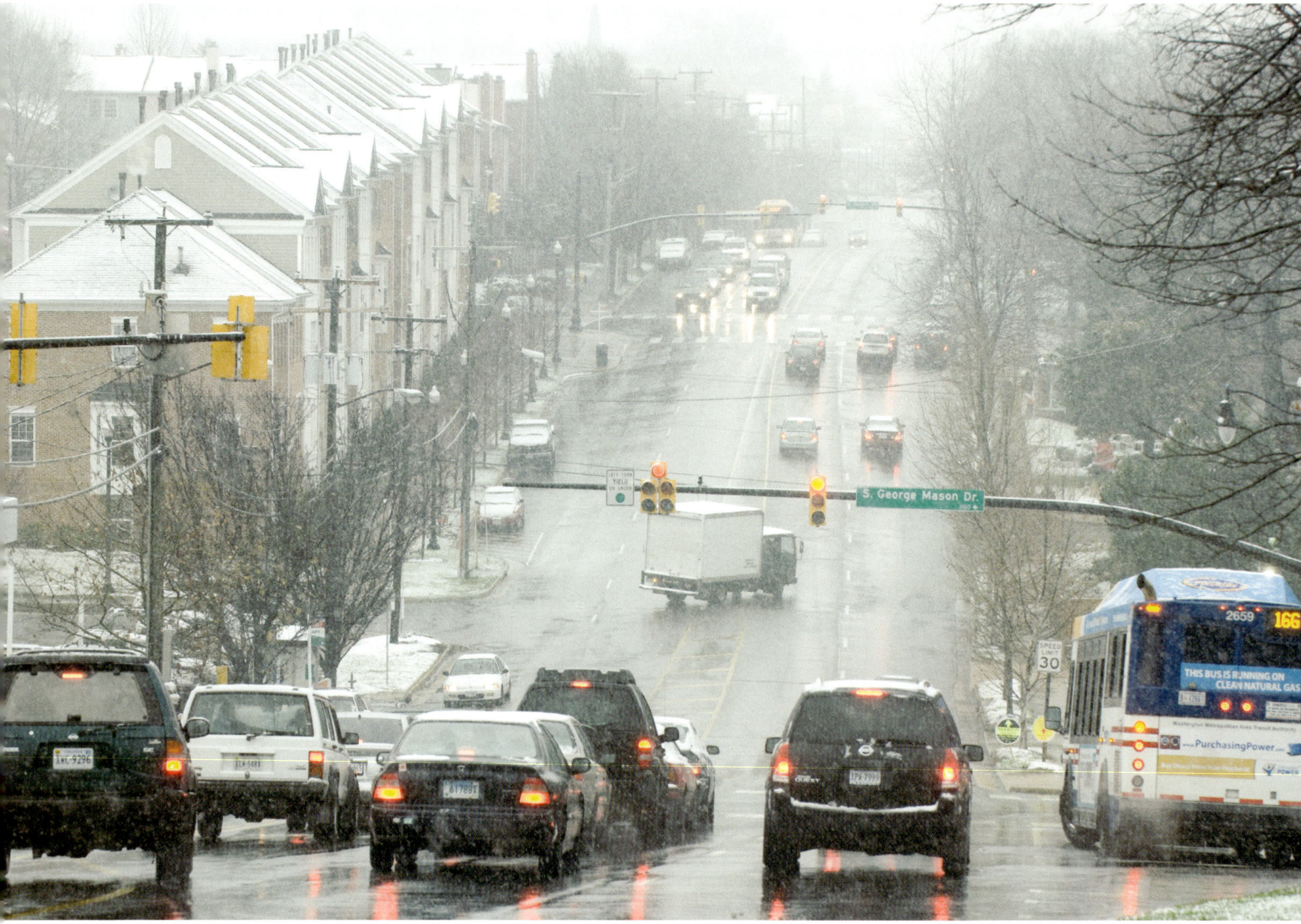

Columbia Pike at South George Mason Drive (Eastern View)

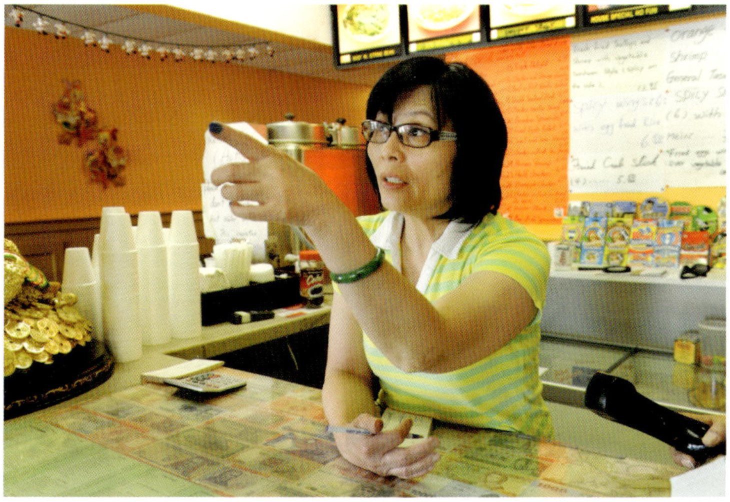

Jing Wei Maria, Mrs. Chens Kitchen restaurant,

3101 Columbia Pike

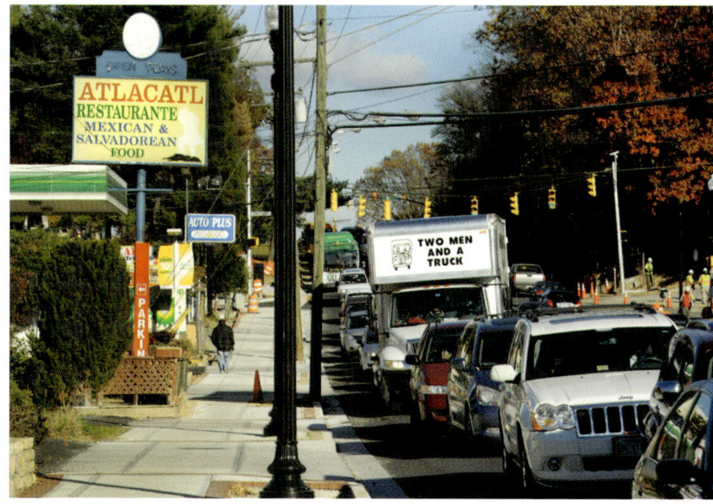

4700 block of Columbia Pike

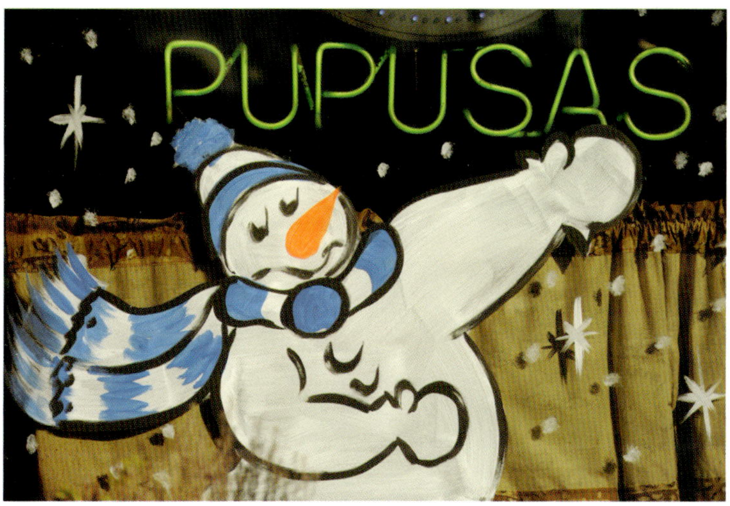

Holiday Decoration, Atlcatl Restaurant, 4701 Columbia Pike

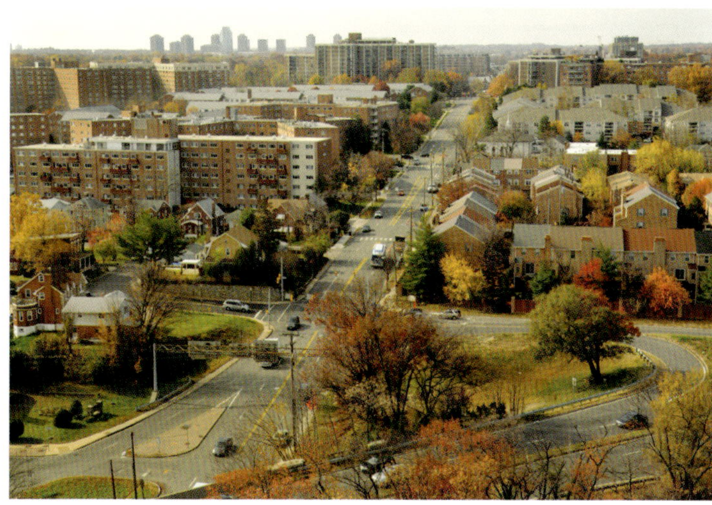

Eastern end of Columbia Pike (Western View)

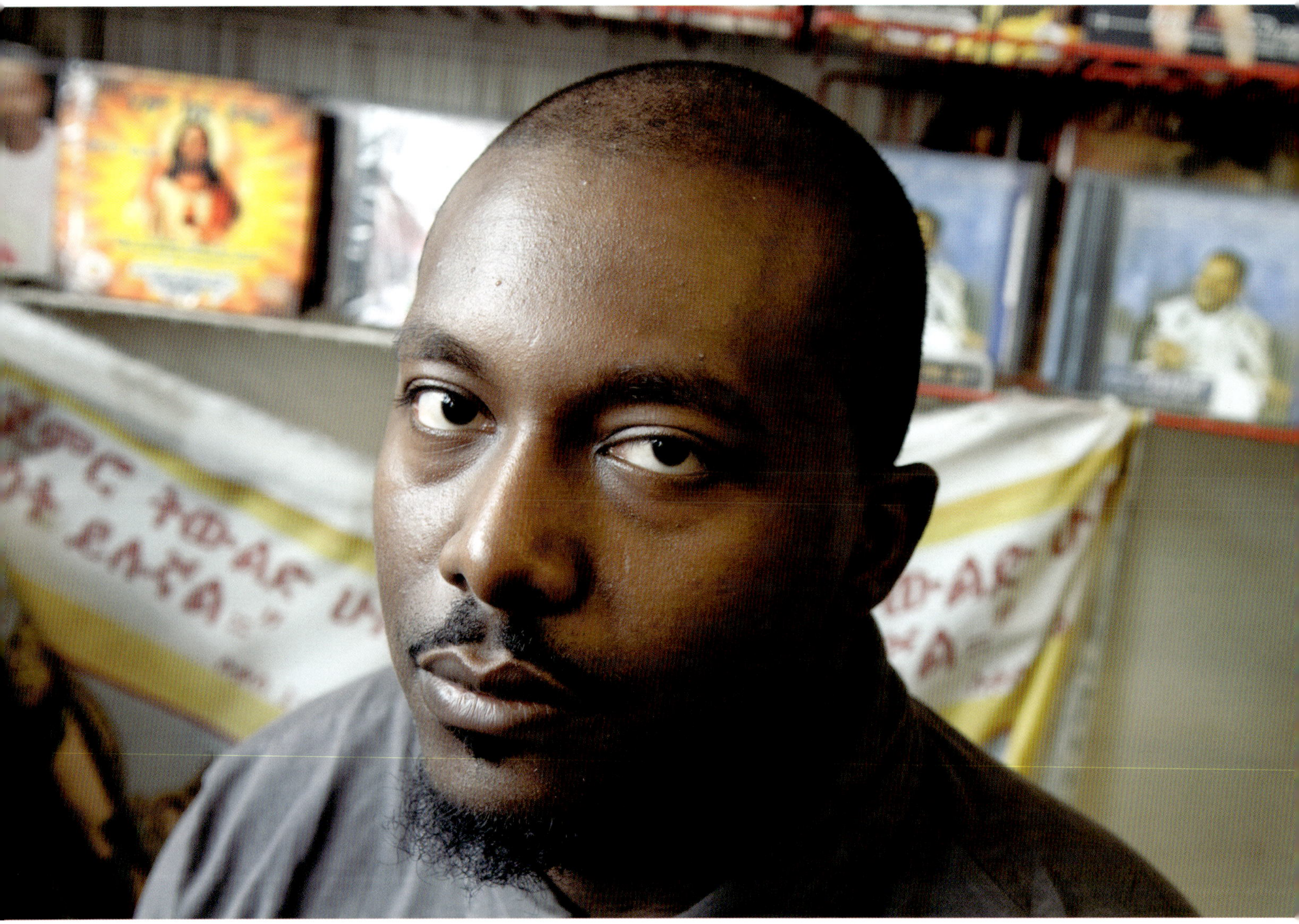

Binyam Geb, of Lideta Gebeya store, 2630 Columbia Pike

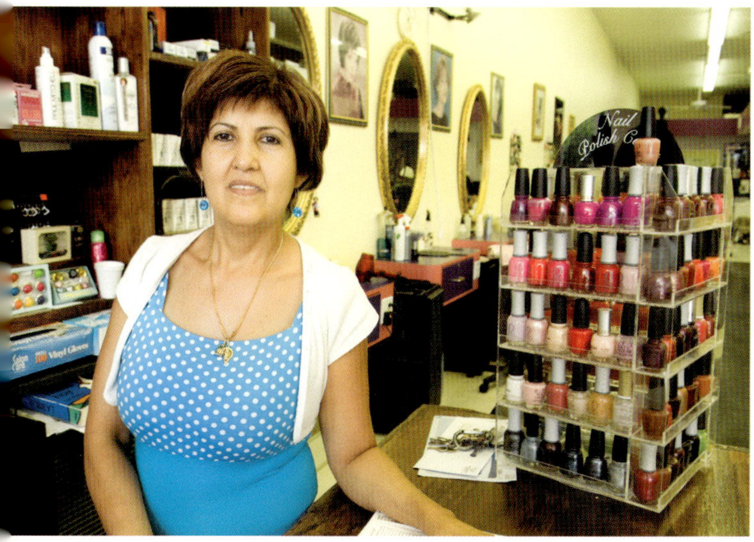

Vicky Sanchez, La Touche Day Spa, 2615 Columbia Pike

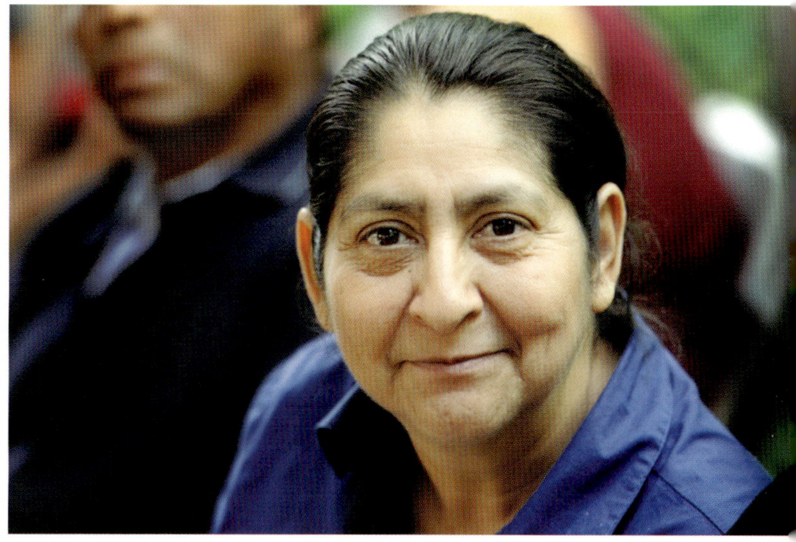

Woman, Buchanan Gardens

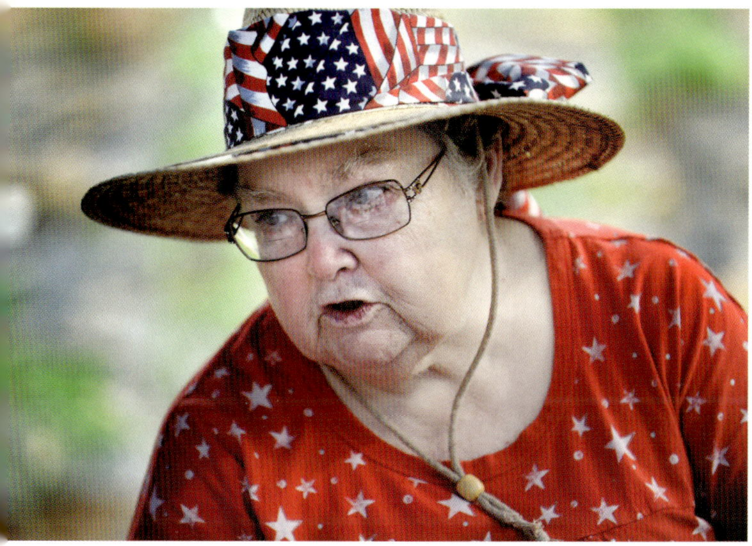

Woman, Flores-Gambino Memorial Day Picnic

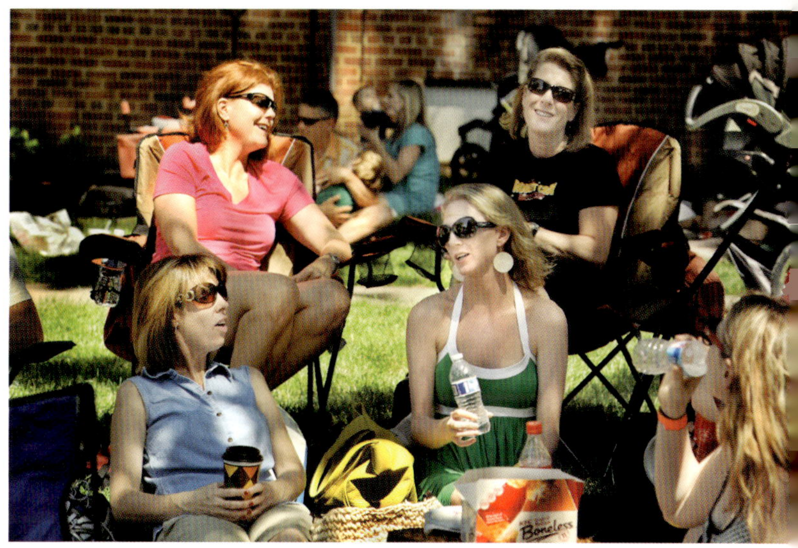

Columbia Pike Blues Festival

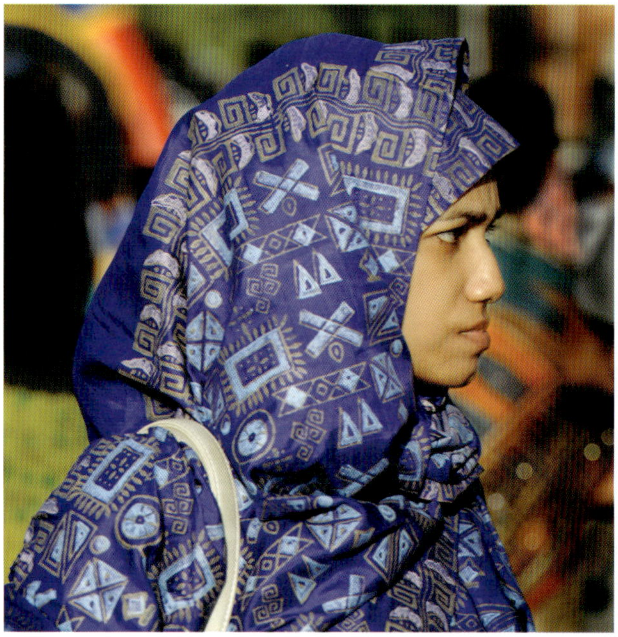

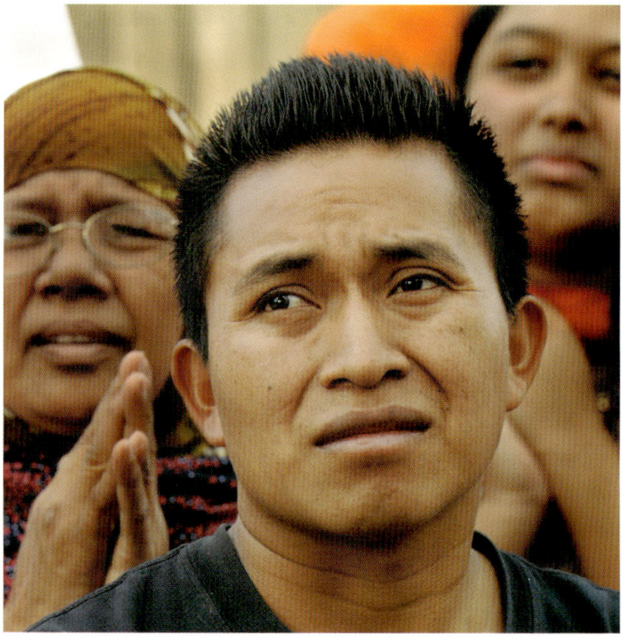

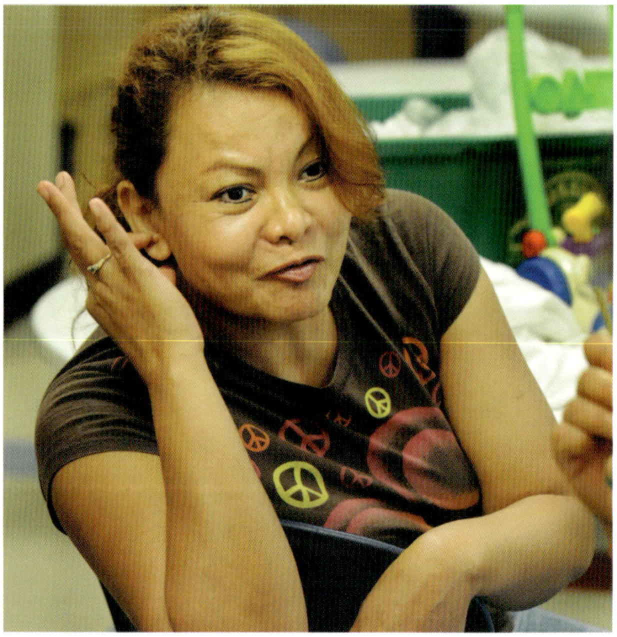

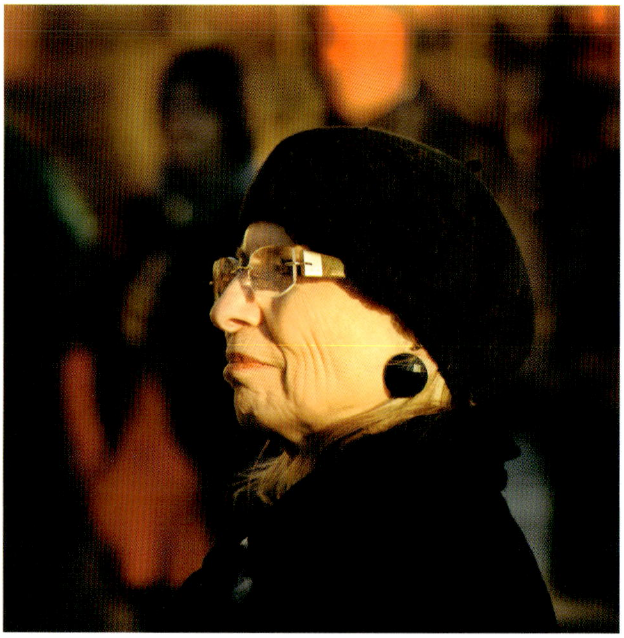

Prio Bangla Festival

Prio Bangla Festival

Harvey Hall community arts class

Woman at sculpture unveiling, Penrose Square

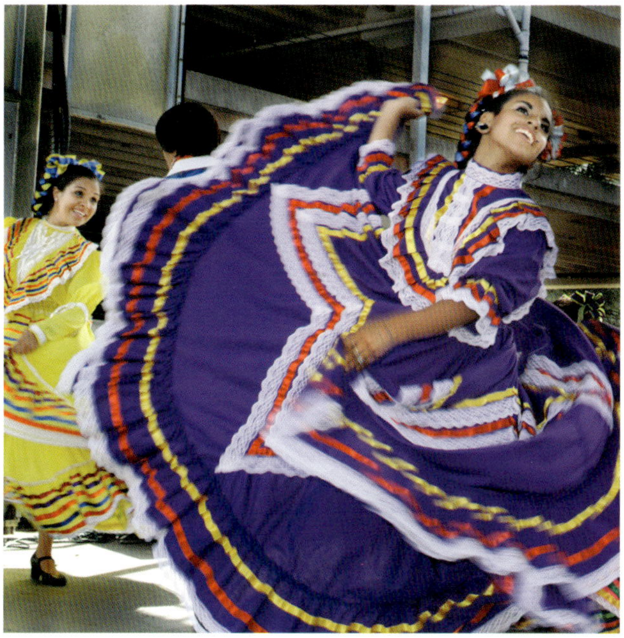

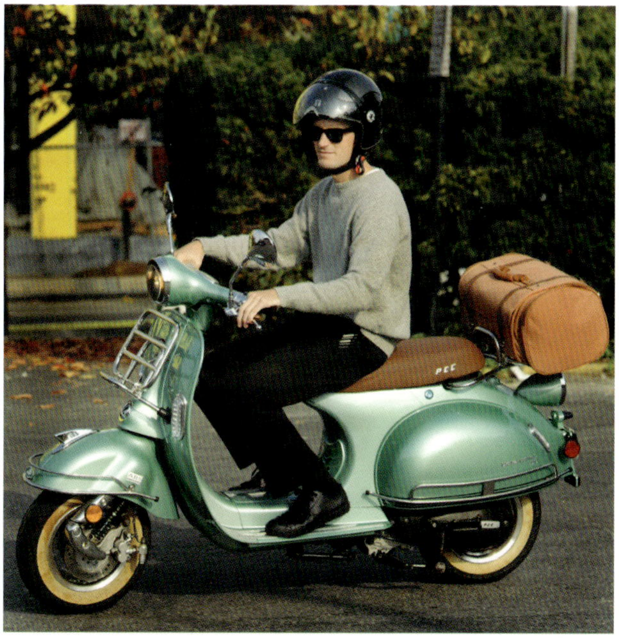

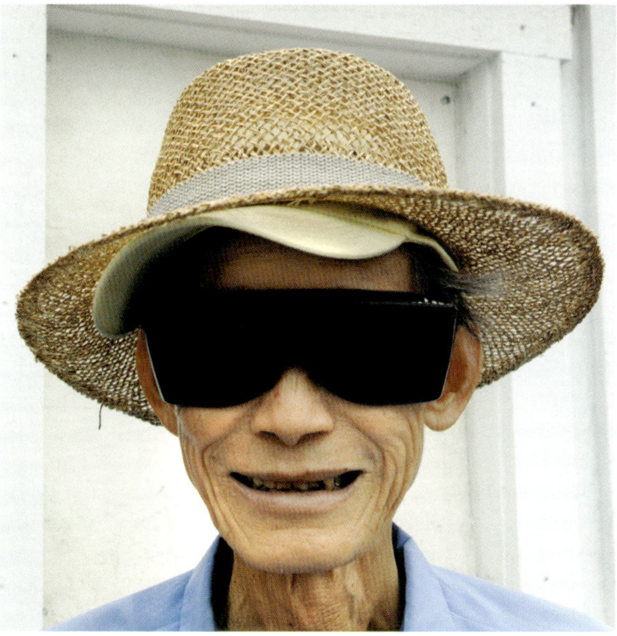

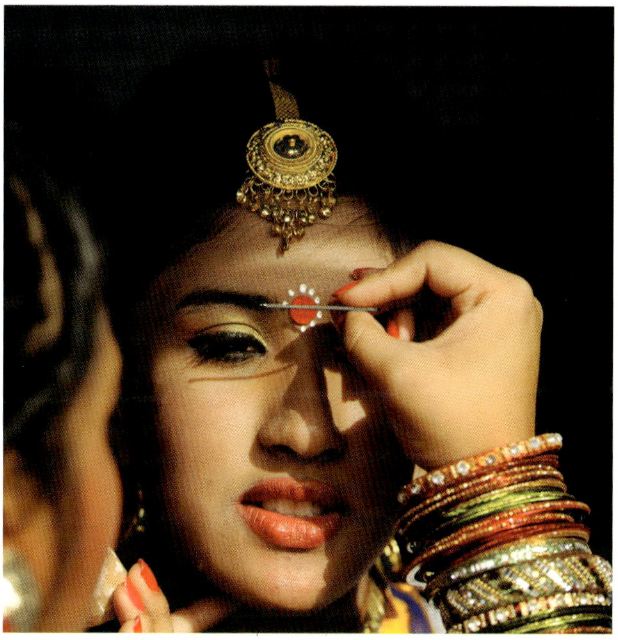

Mexican Dancers, Prio Bangla Festival

Scooter, Columbia Pike Plaza

Mr. Buu, Fillmore Center, 2800 block of Columbia Pike

Bangladeshi Dancers, Prio Bangla Festival

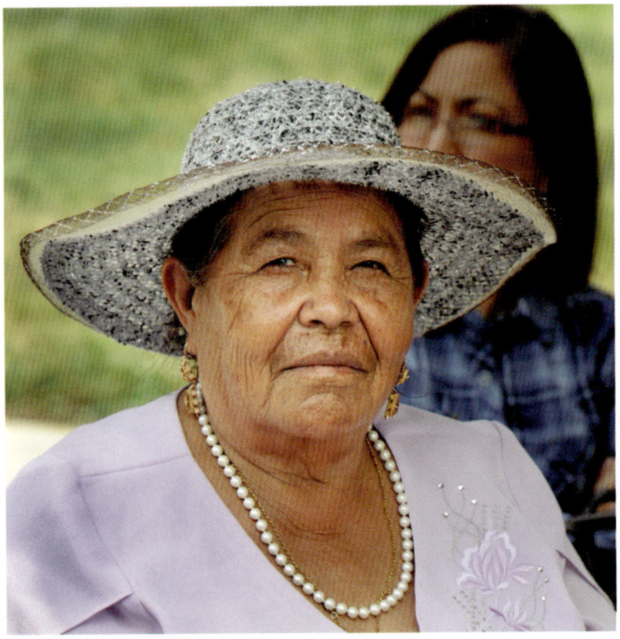
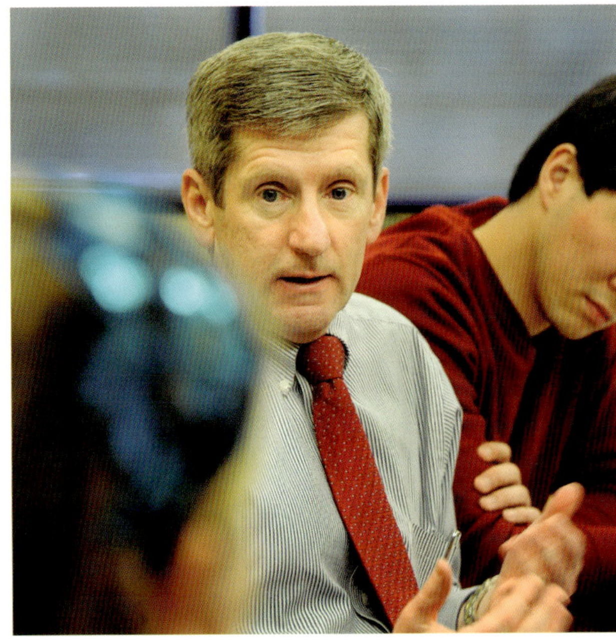
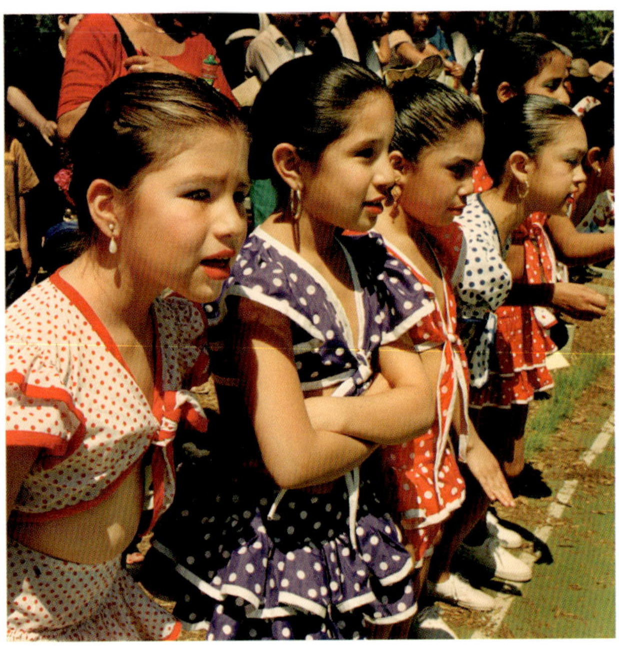
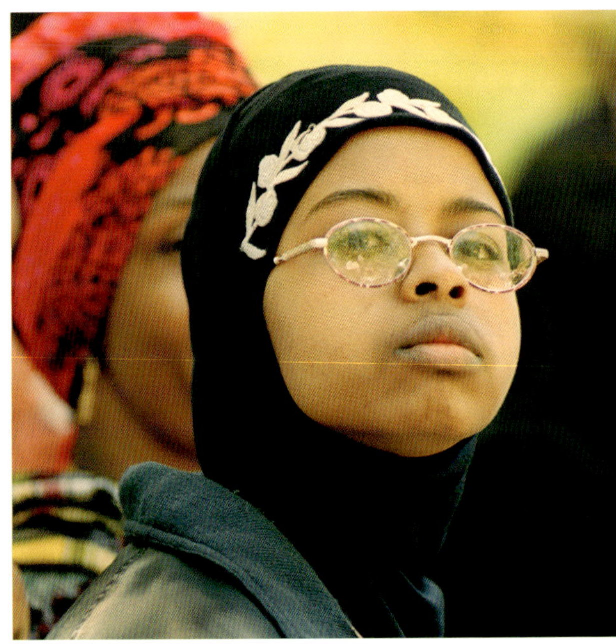

Woman, Flores-Gambino Memorial Day Picnic

Meeting, Arlington Federal Credit Union

Dancers, Columbia Heights West Festival

Somali Girl, Columbia Heights West Festival

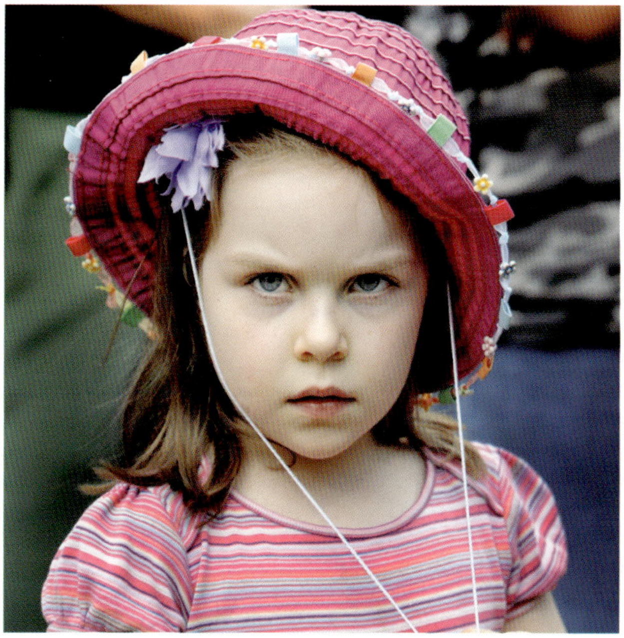

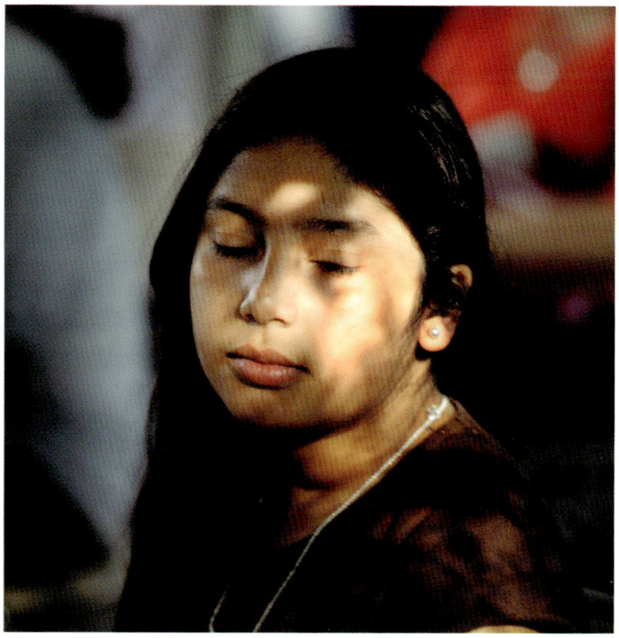

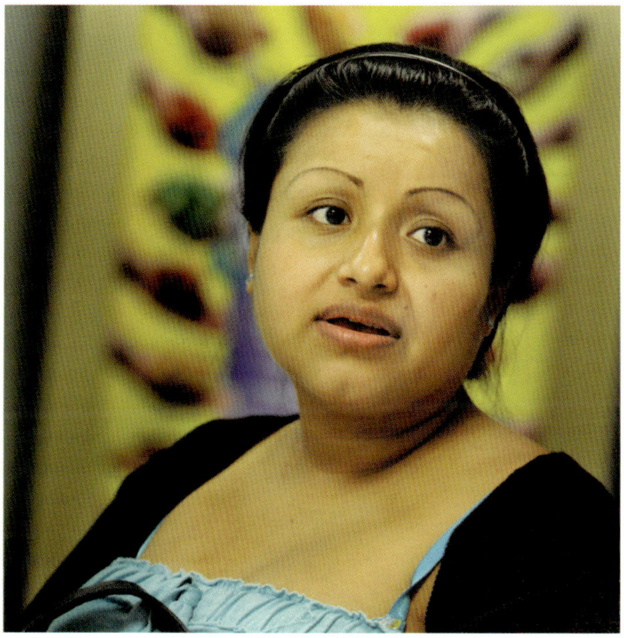

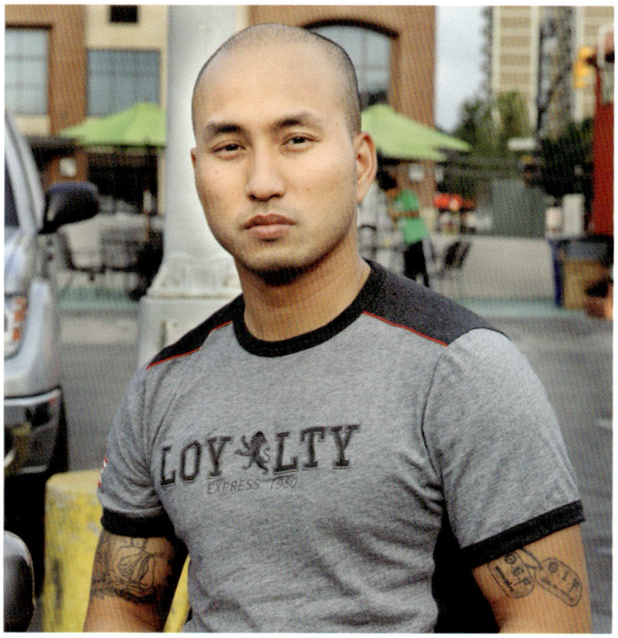

Girl, Columbia Pike

Girl, Columbia Pike

Harvey Hall community arts class

Man, Penrose Square

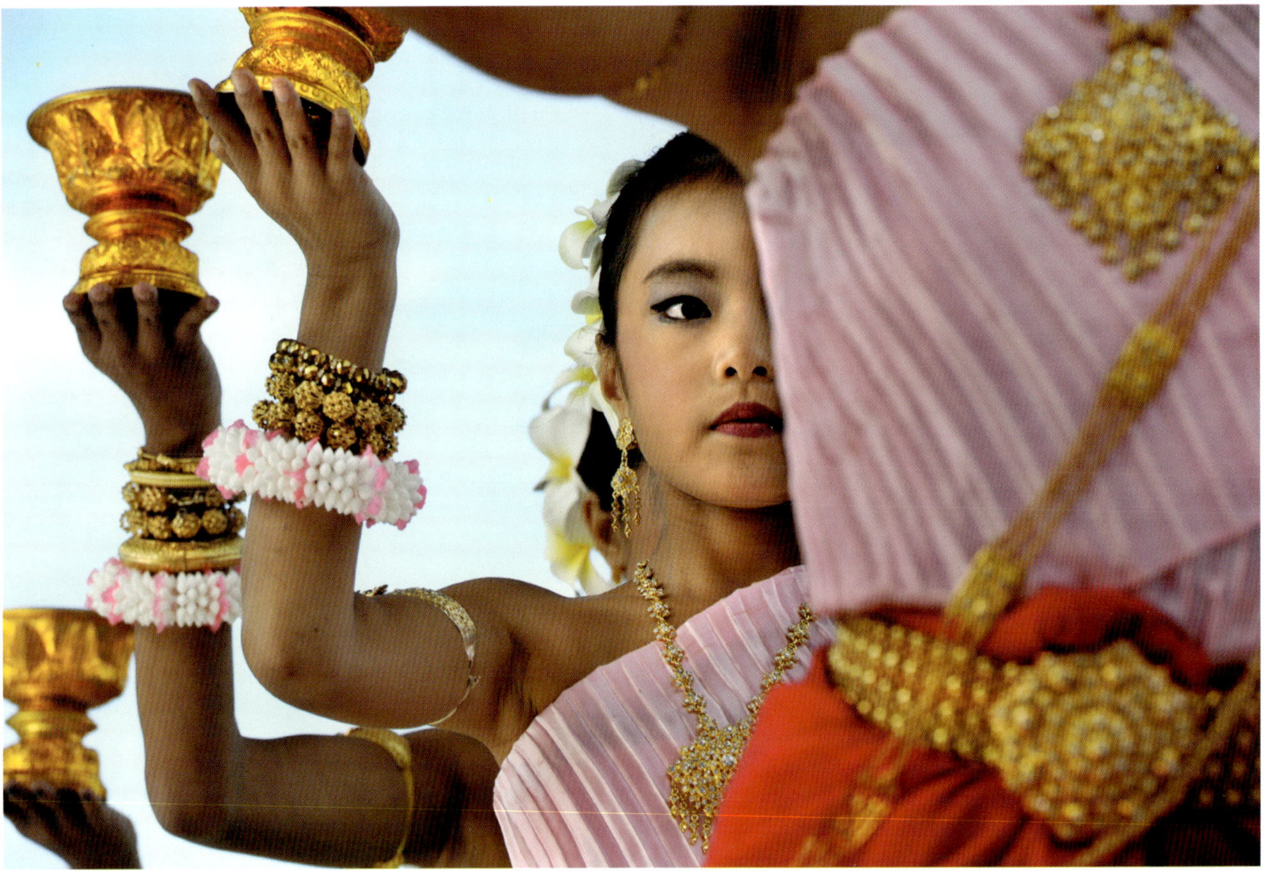

Cambodian Dancers, Prio Bangla Festival

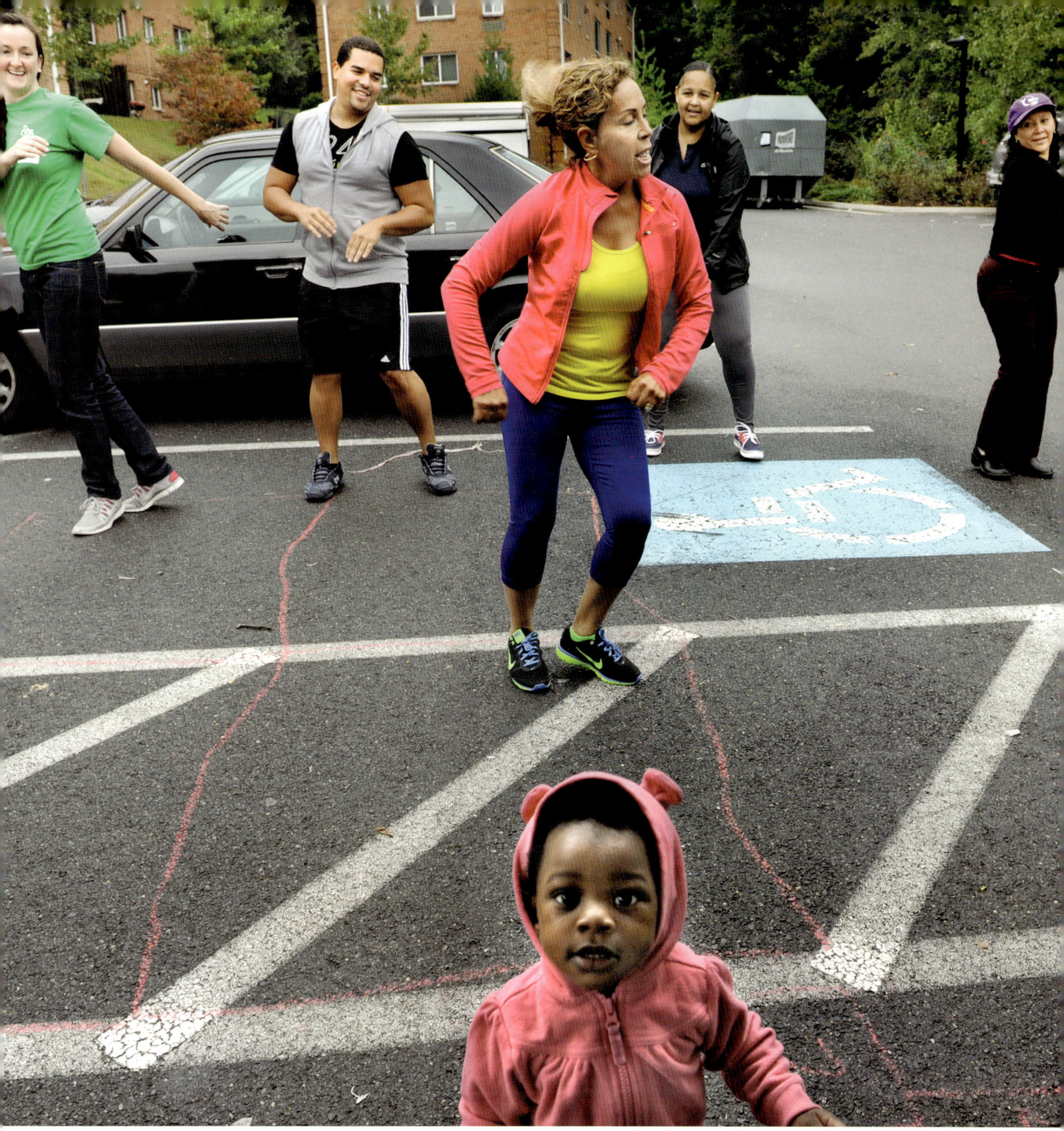

Exercise Demonstration. Columbia Grove Health Fair

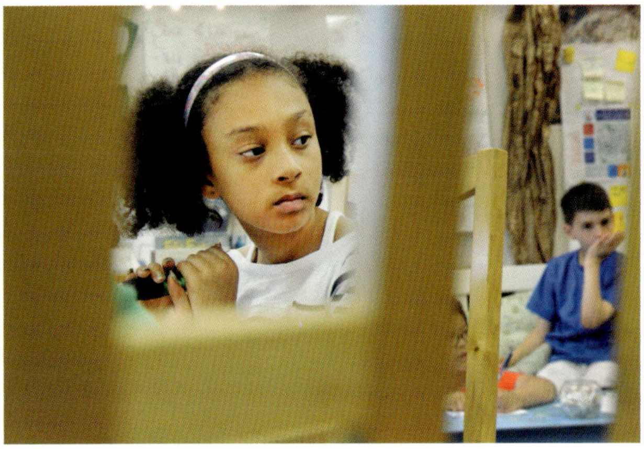

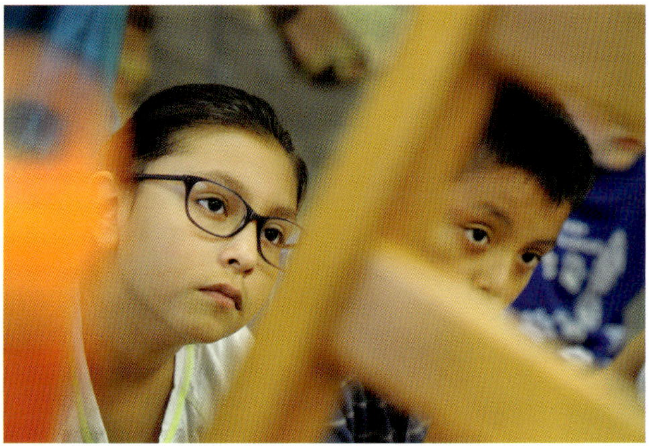

Carson Stadler

There are lots of languages in my class. I know some Hawaiian, because my mother is native Hawaiian. I also know some French from learning it in school. I also take Spanish.

I want to be in the armed forces when I grow up. I would rather be in battle and have bad experiences than have the USA turned into some kind of a slave country.

Columbia Pike is a bit unusual, but really special, because it's so diverse. It's not like many other places in the world. Most kids get along. Some don't play with one each other, but they mostly don't get angry with each other, too.

When I visit another family's house, I've had things other than I usually eat, depending on their culture. One of my mom's friends is from India. They have different rice, different spices, different meats, and they wear different clothing. I think that's where I got interested in spicy food.

Columbia Pike might seem sort of dirty if you walk just along the Pike, but if you get off the main street a block or so, to the parks and nearby, it's pretty nice. You meet all kinds of interesting people and new traditions.

Estee Ruiz

I am half Mexican and half Italian. My dad is from Texas and my mom is from Connecticut.

I am the only girl on my soccer team. My team is called "The Revolutionaries," but we call ourselves the "Revs." We tied for first place in our league. I like to play offense. I can really kick well, but I need to work on my skills as a goalie, dealing with all those balls and people coming from every direction at once.

The kids I know are from many different backgrounds, and we're a really connected community. Because we have to work together, it pushes us together. We play it out as teams in class; we do chorales for example.

My grandma is Italian, and she showed me how to make sweetbread, which is kind of like a cake. We also eat fajitas and empanadas. I like tacos best, I'll eat like seven of them! When I eat a food that's new to me, it makes my stomach sparkle.

Columbia Pike is kind of different. Many people come from different countries. One boy in my class didn't know any English at the beginning of the year. My friend Grayson is from Indonesia. Our community has lots of people from different continents. Kids here get along pretty well, no matter where they're from. If someone doesn't get along, we should try to work things out.

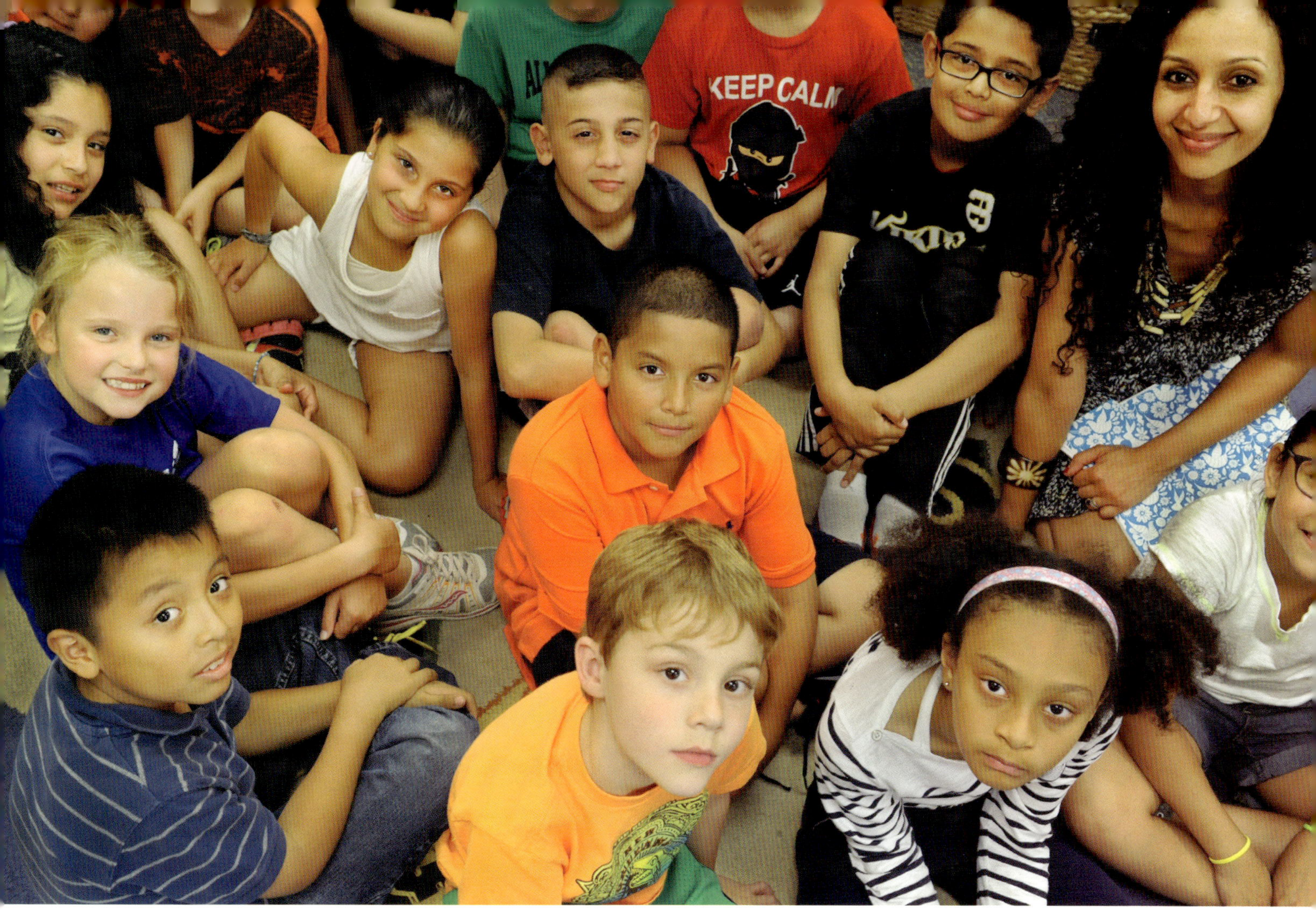

Ronan Valdesuso

My Dad came here from Cuba, my Mom is from Massachusetts. There are many Spanish people here that are not from Virginia. I don't speak Spanish. I used to know a little French from pre-K. My friend Carson is from Hawaii, Some of my friends are from El Salvador. People get along pretty well, getting together, which is good.

Today at recess I talked with Carson about the spring concert. I play xylophone in a school group called the Music Makers.

If you go looking at places and investigating them, you can learn by watching and then writing about it. You can share about the place. You can see what they're selling, how friends act, or a place to have fun. You can write about it.

Photos on this spread and following page: Third grade class, Patrick Henry School. Ms. Dahlia Constantine, teacher.

Gabriel Alfaro

I like to talk to my cousin and my friend, to read on my Kindle, and to listen to music on my laptop. Mostly I like Spanish music, all kinds. My favorite food is pico de gallo, which my grandmother and grandfather make. My Dad is from El Salvador, my grandfather is from Peru, and my Mom is from Washington, DC. My mom studies for college and she also works. She finishes all her homework on Mondays. Sometimes we study together.

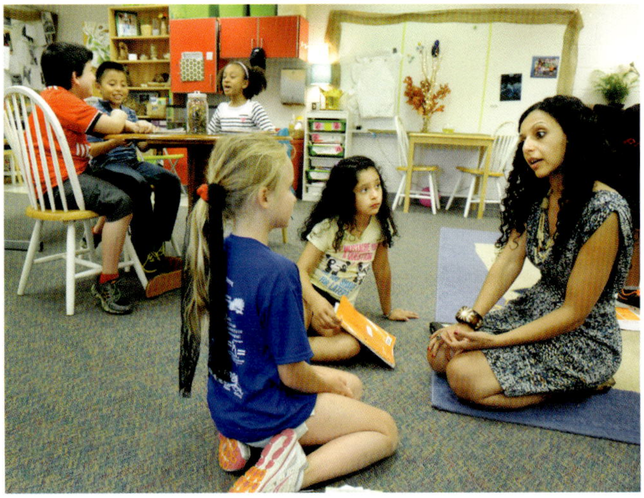

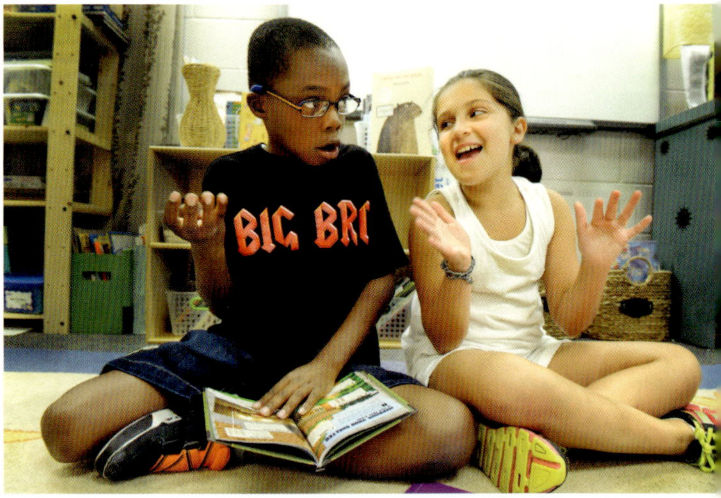

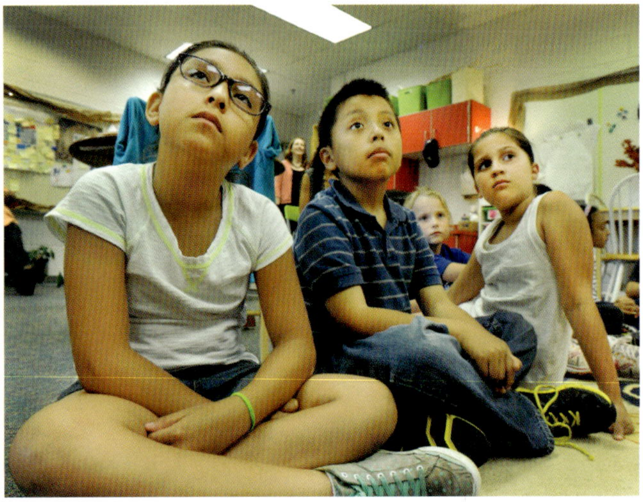

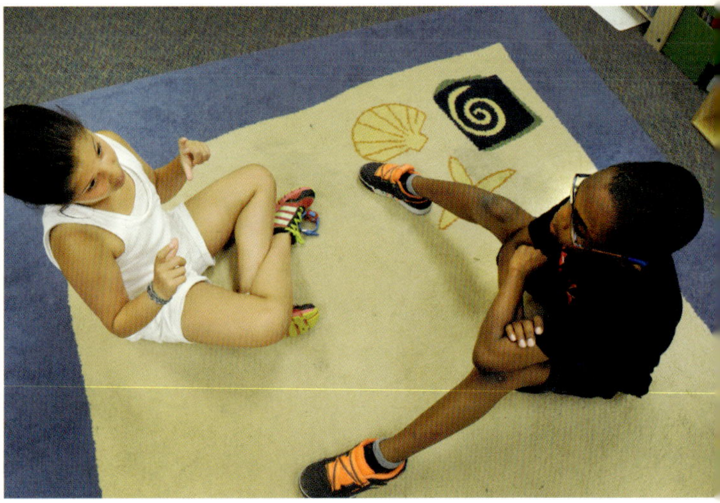

Charrod Pelham

I would tell other kids who don't know anything about Columbia Pike that it's a good area to live in. You can make lots of friends here. Some are from different backgrounds.

When I get older, I want to be a teacher. I want to teach people what I got taught. I would teach that people should not get in trouble. They should act properly, and do the right things.

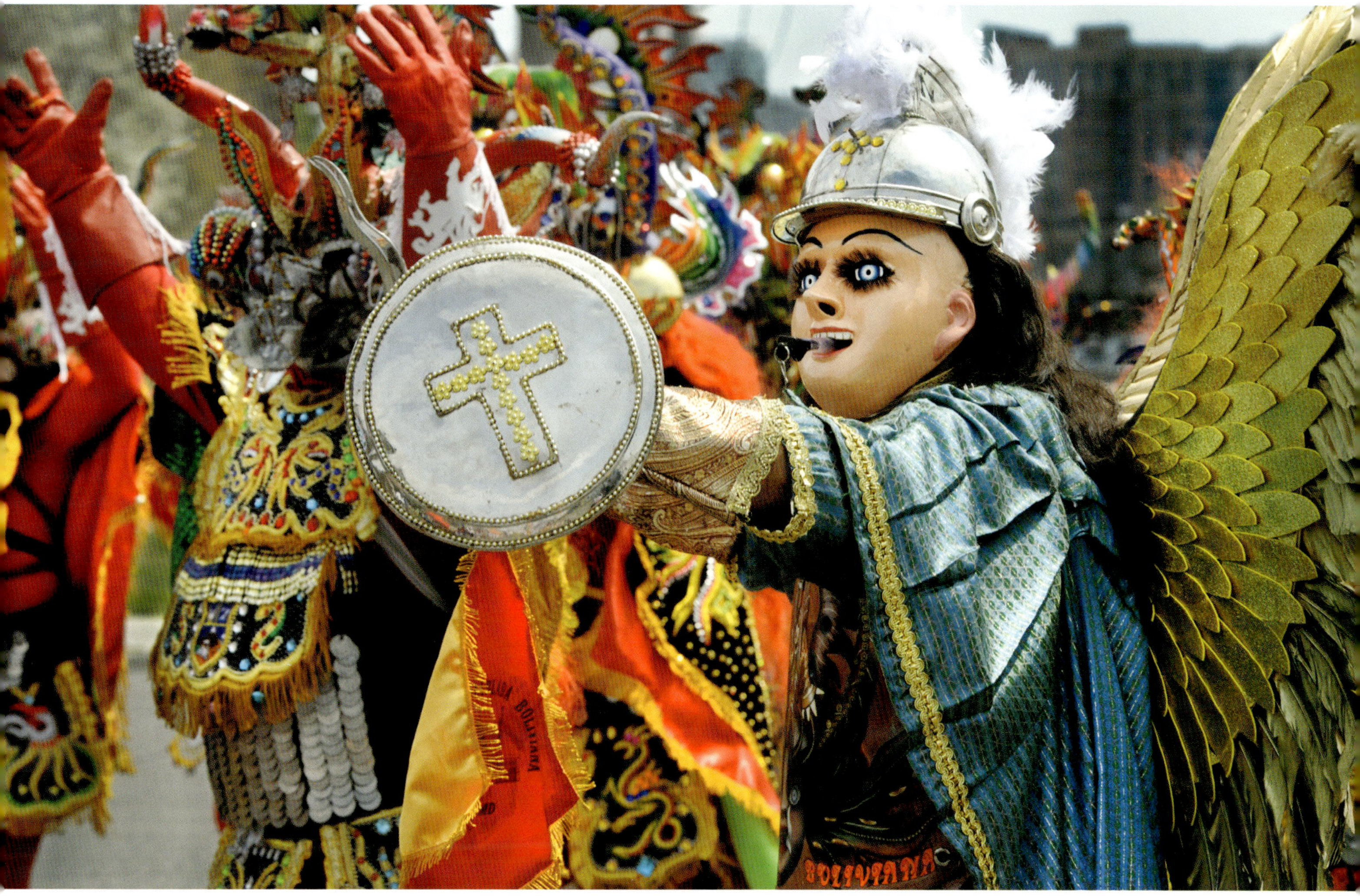

Saint George, Oruru Carnival

Oruru Carnival preparations ››

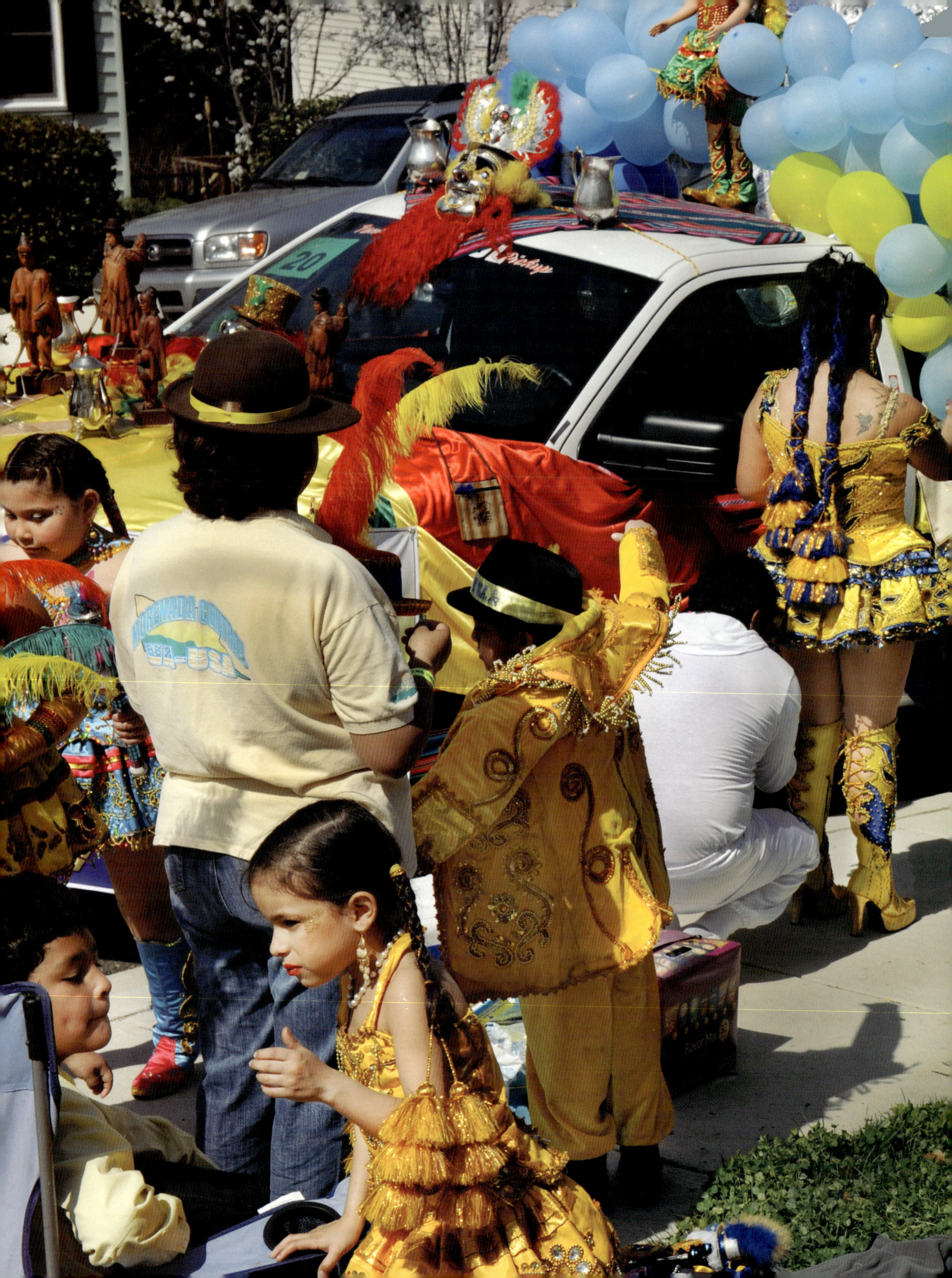
20

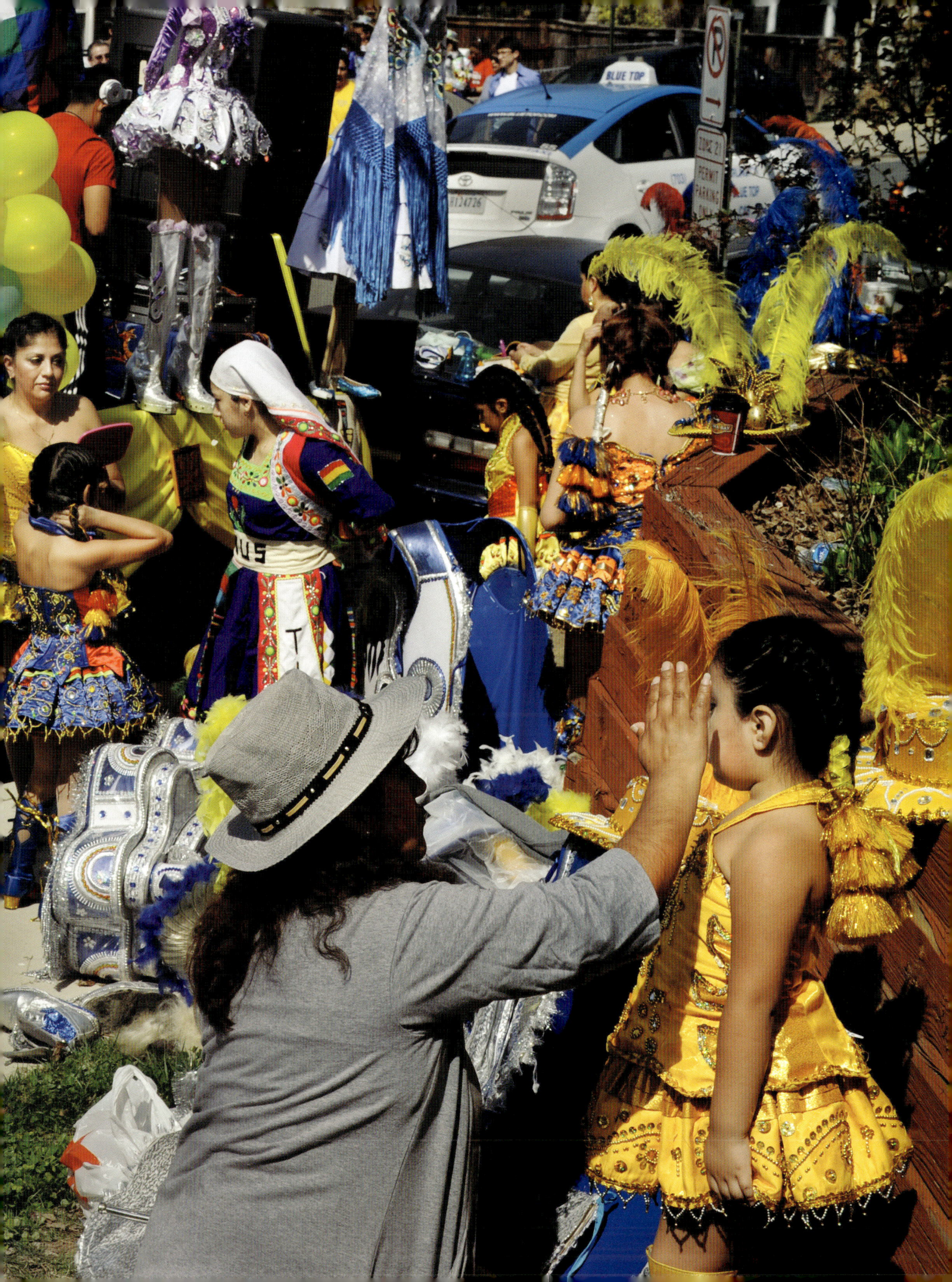
BLUE TOP

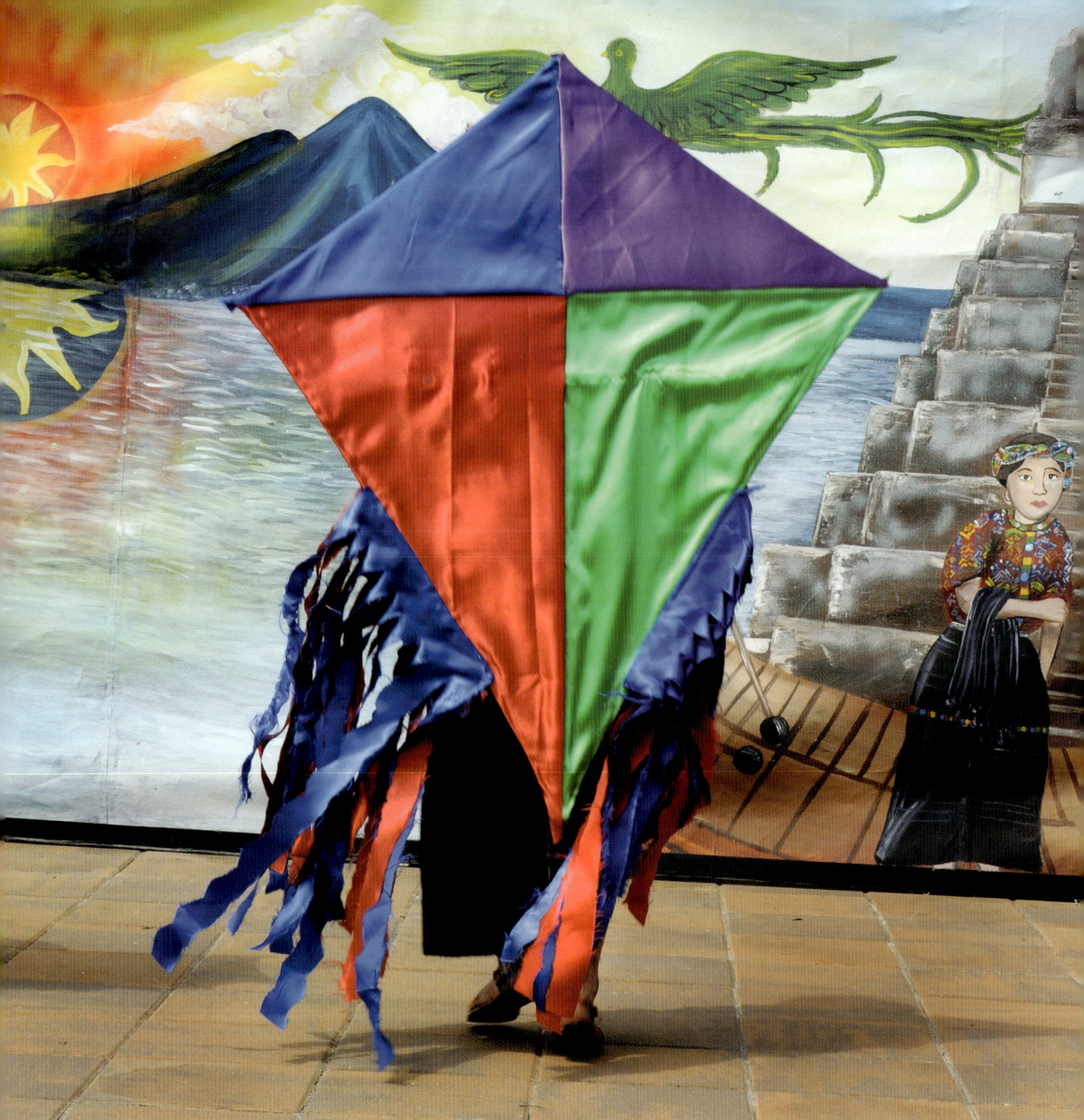

Grupo Awal, Mayan dance troupe, Latin-American Family Day

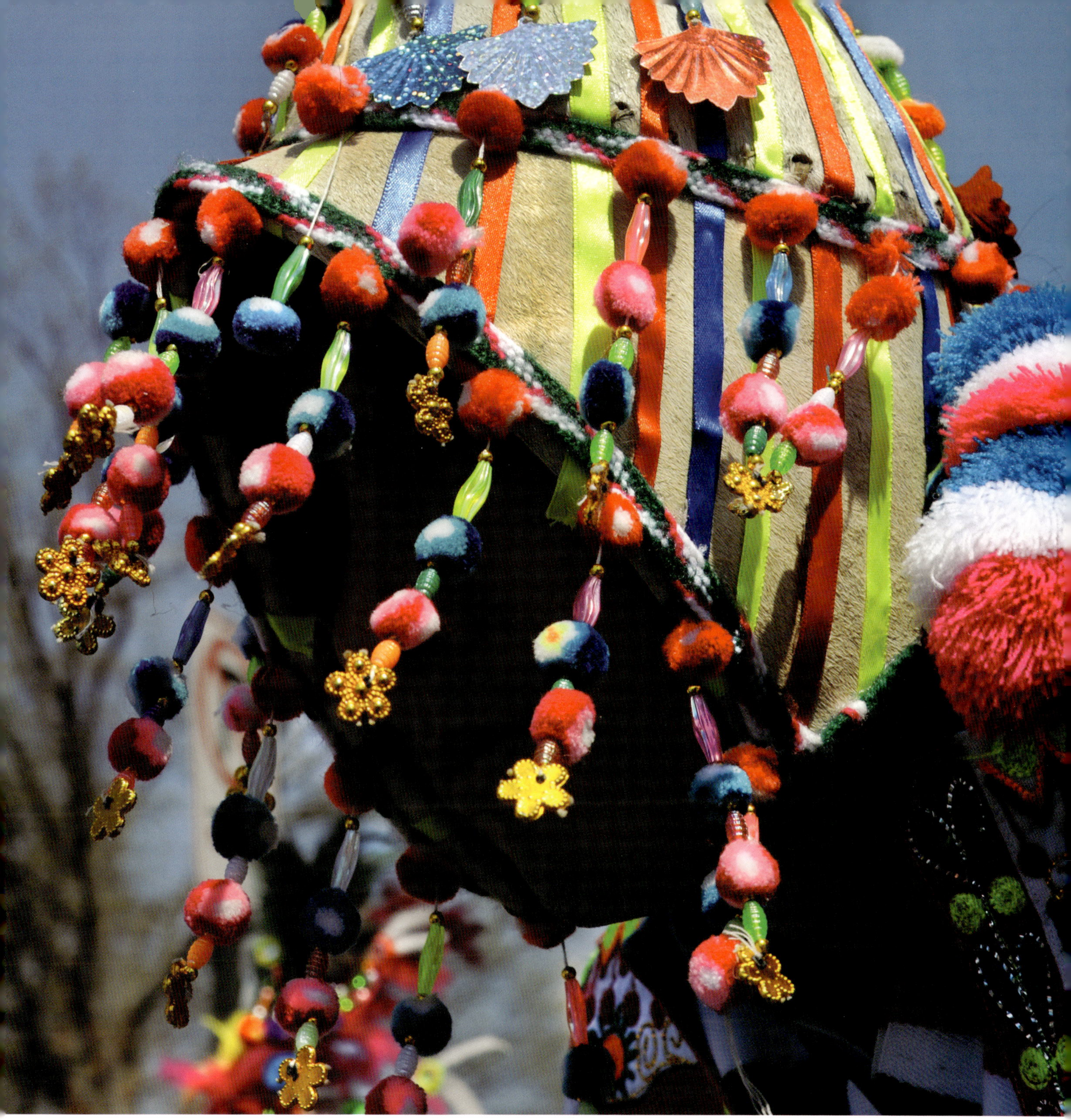

Oruru Carnival, Bolivian dancer

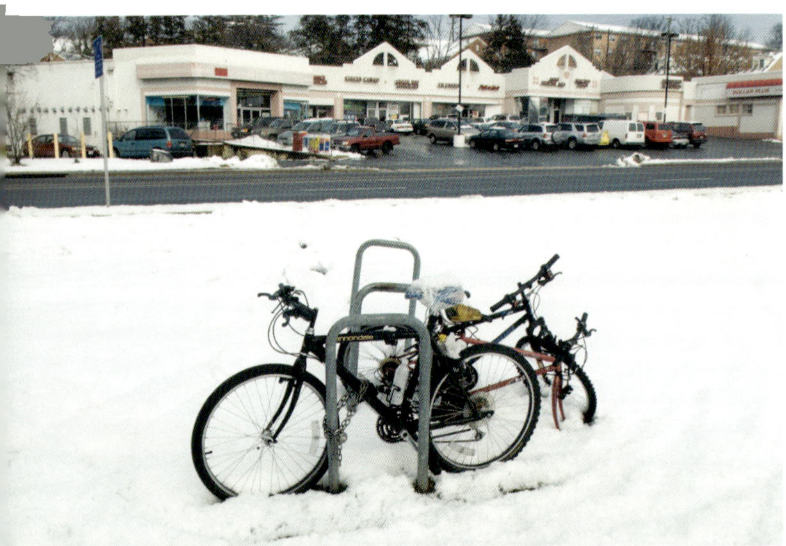

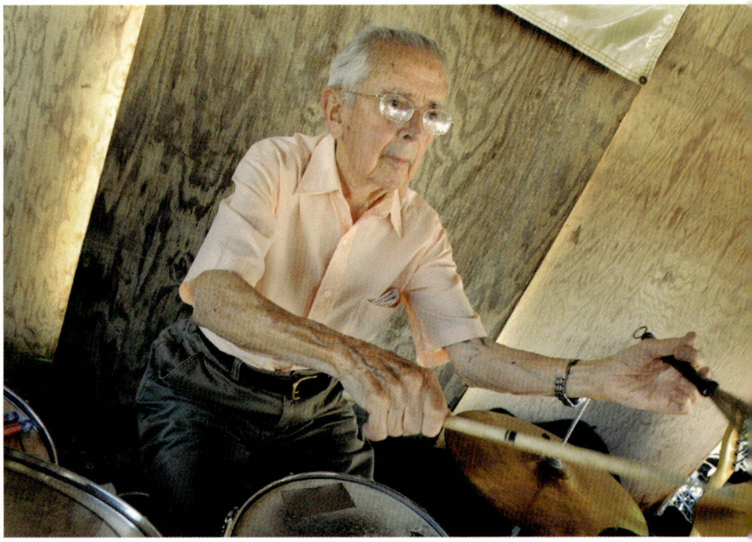

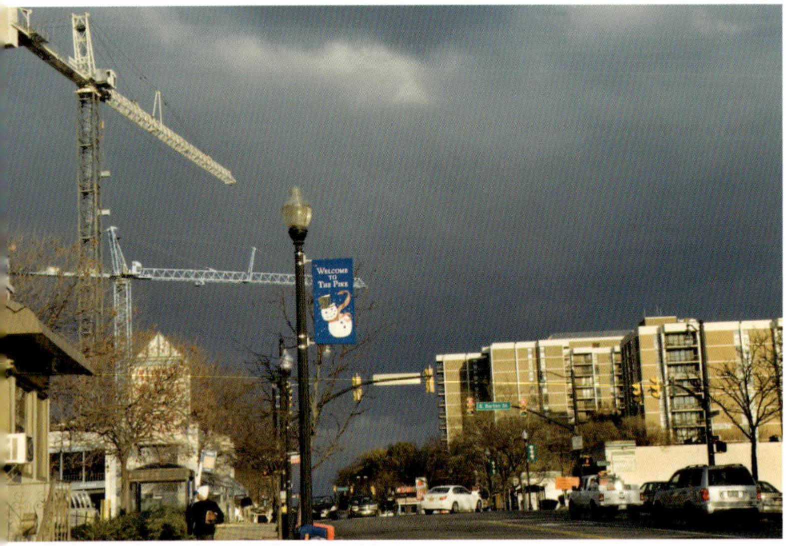

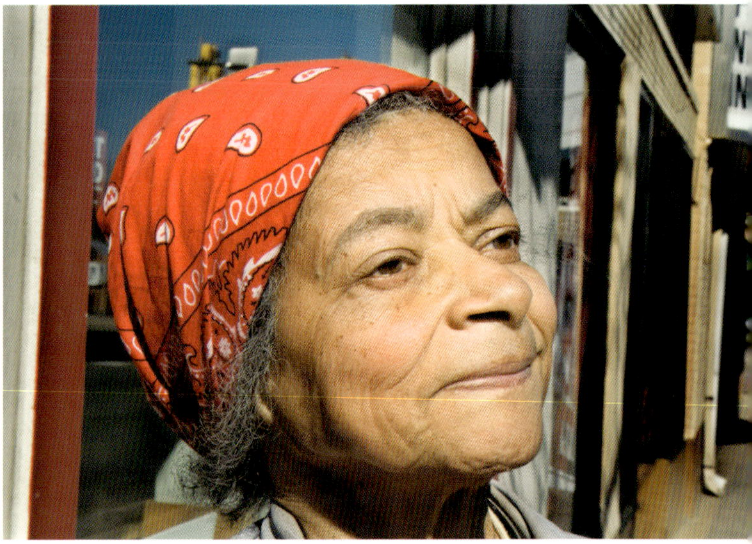

Columbia Pike at South Four Mile Run Drive

Eddie Jenkins, Flores-Gambino Memorial Day Picnic

2400 block of Columbia Pike (Eastern View)

Woman, 2900 block of Columbia Pike

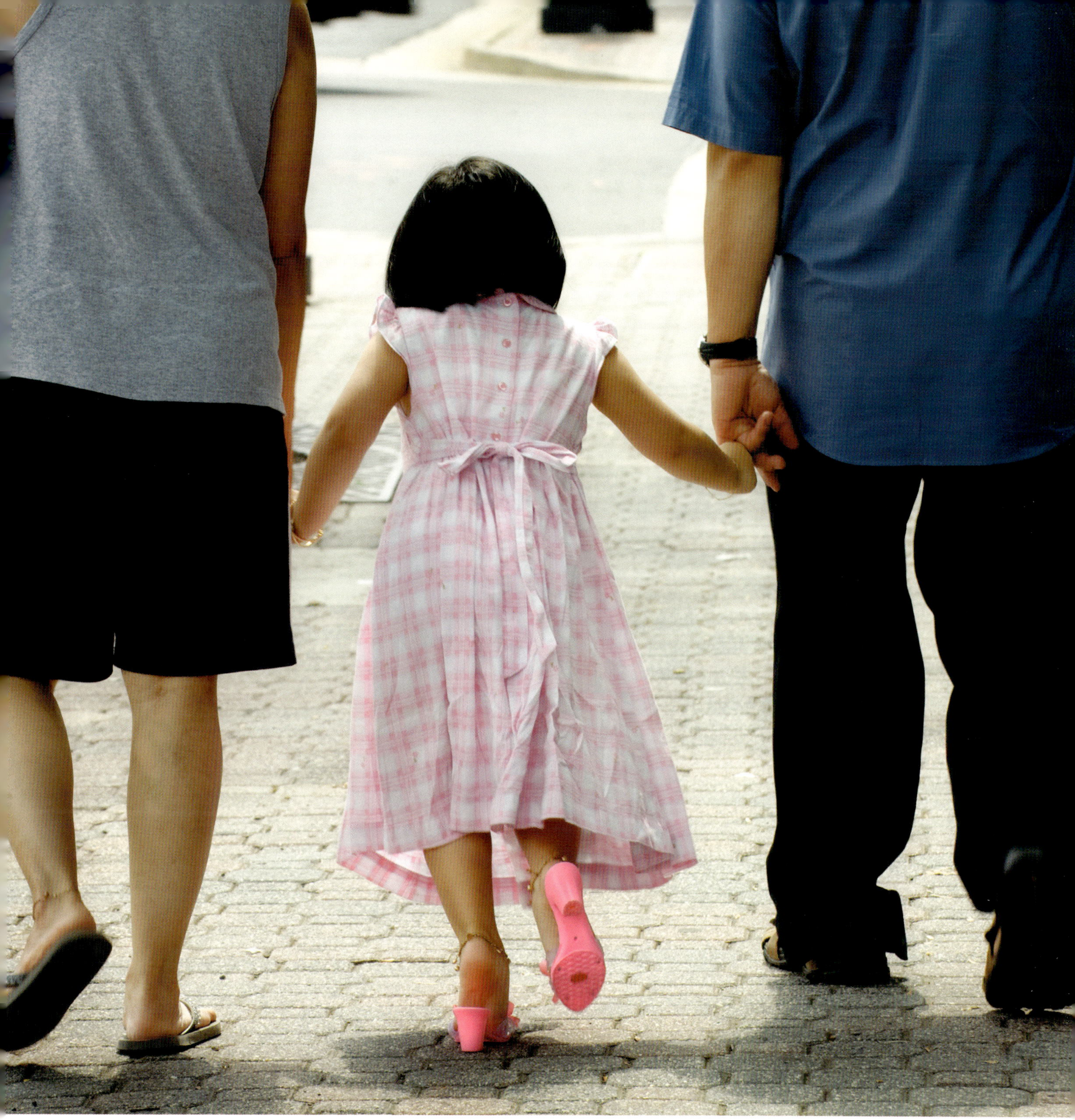

Pink Shoes

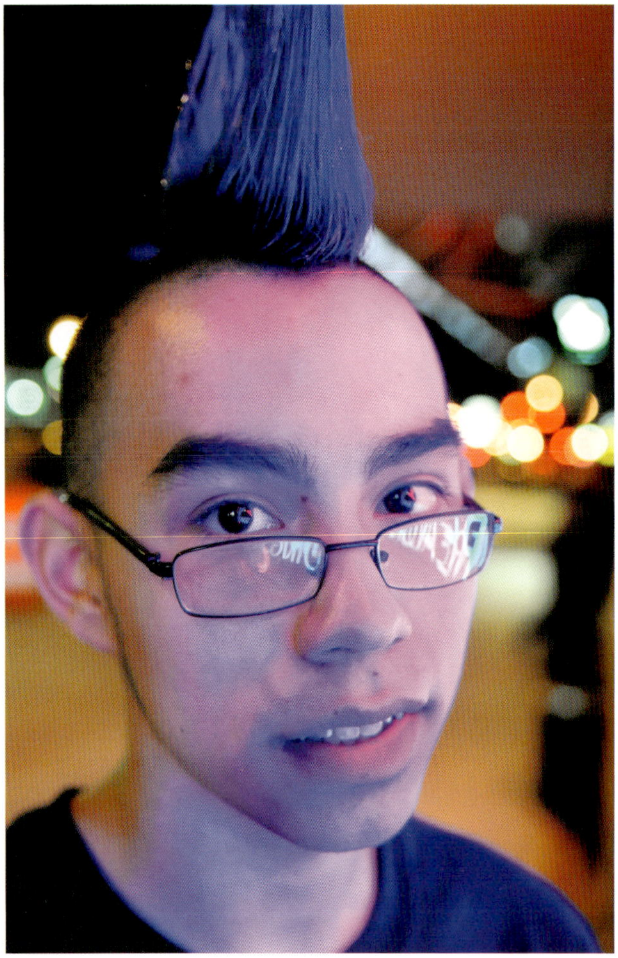

Francisco Mejia

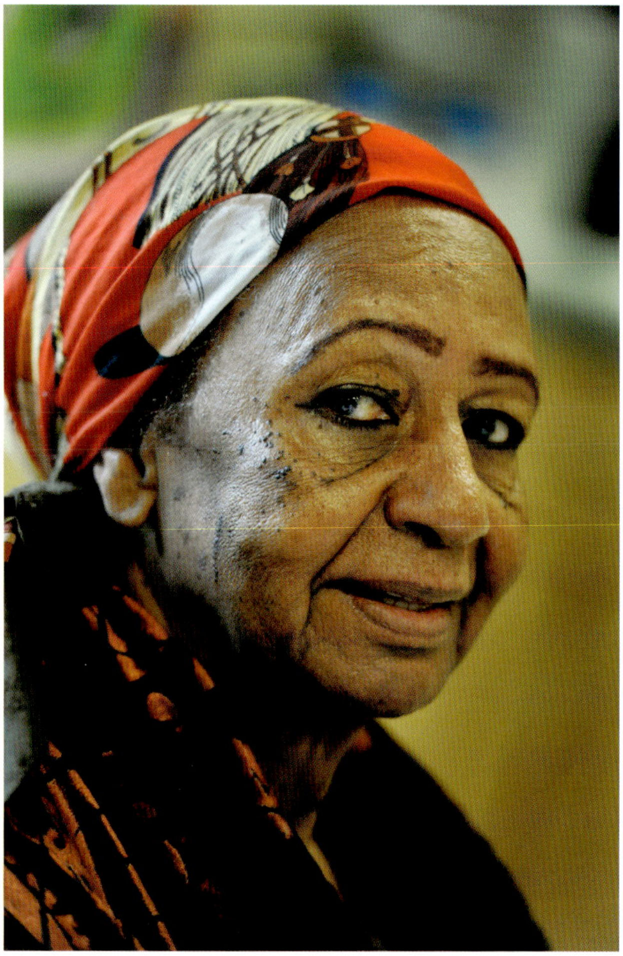

Mary Nablusi, Harvey Hall community arts class

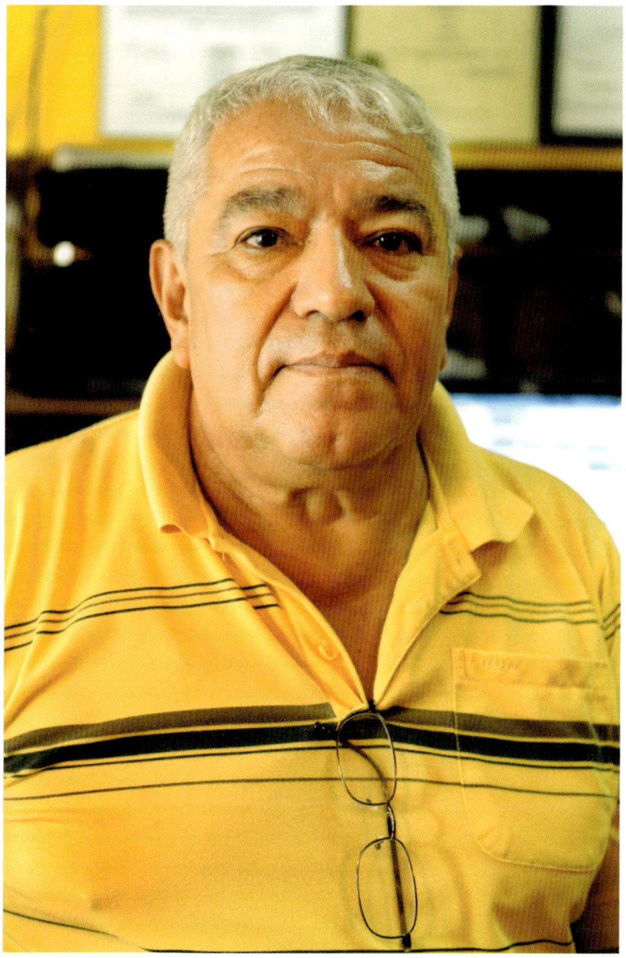

El Pike Restaurant

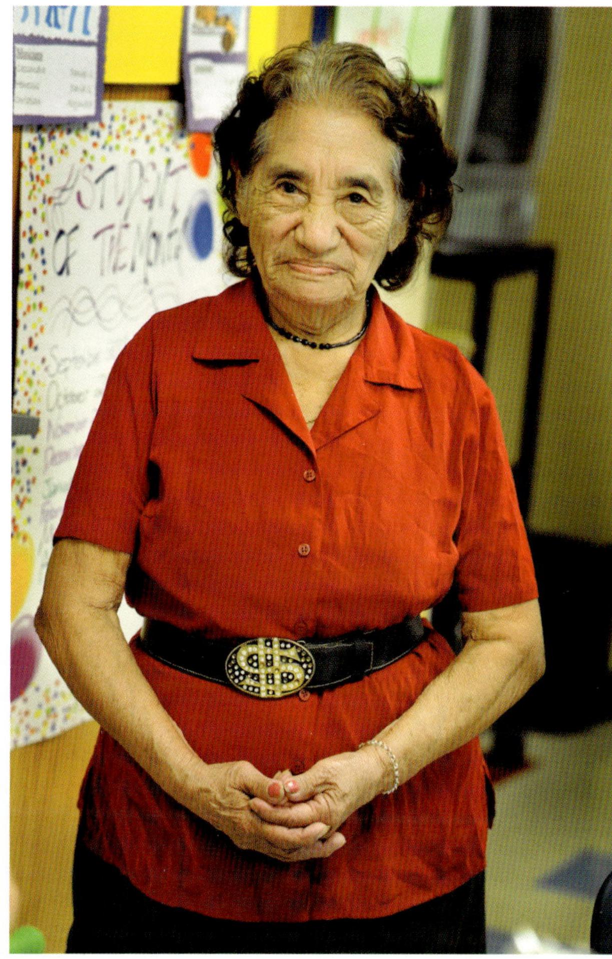

Woman, Harvey Hall community arts class

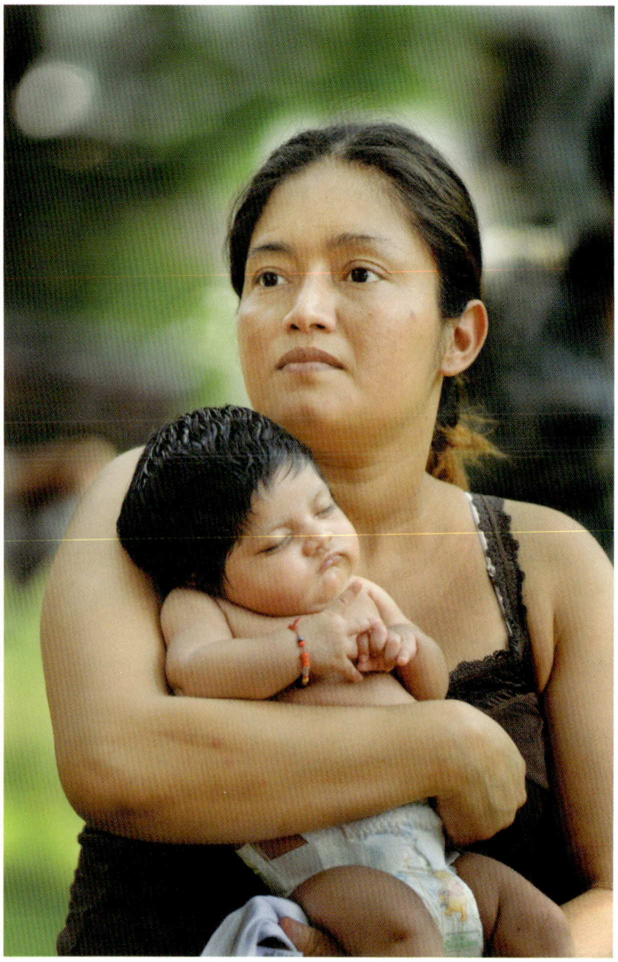

Mother And Child, Buchanan Gardens

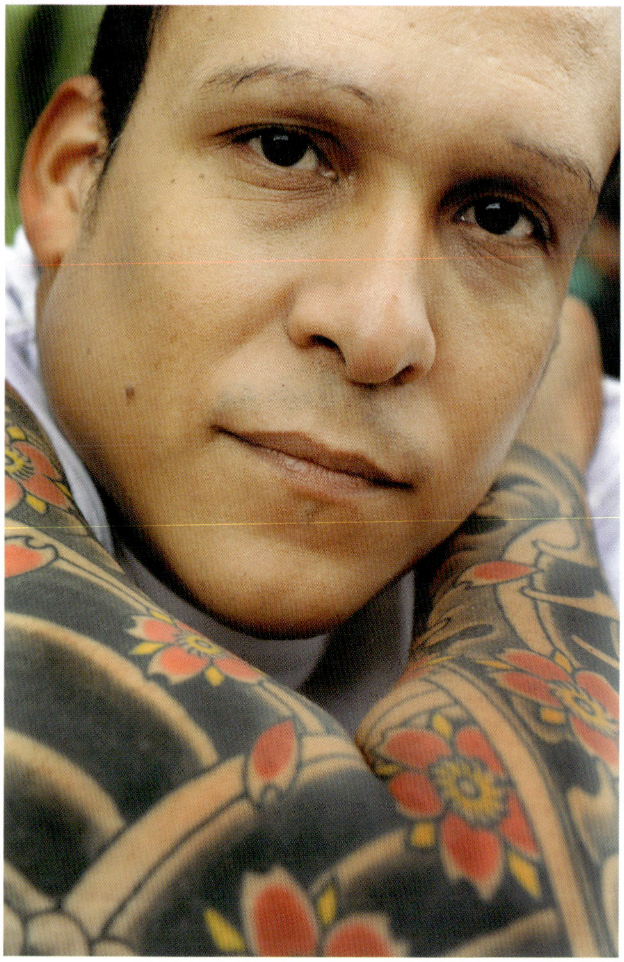

Angel Morales

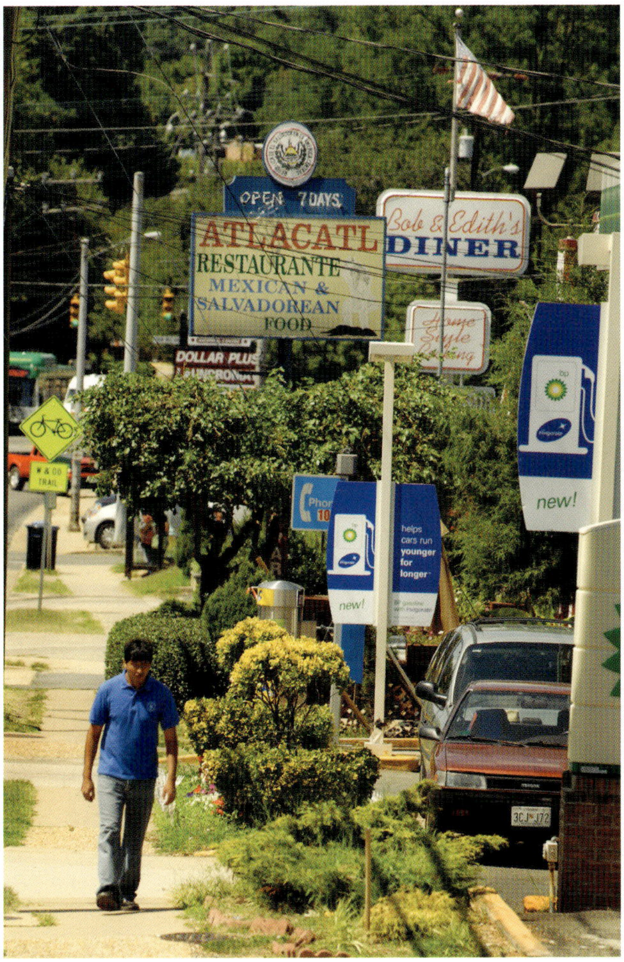

4700 block of Columbia Pike (Western View)

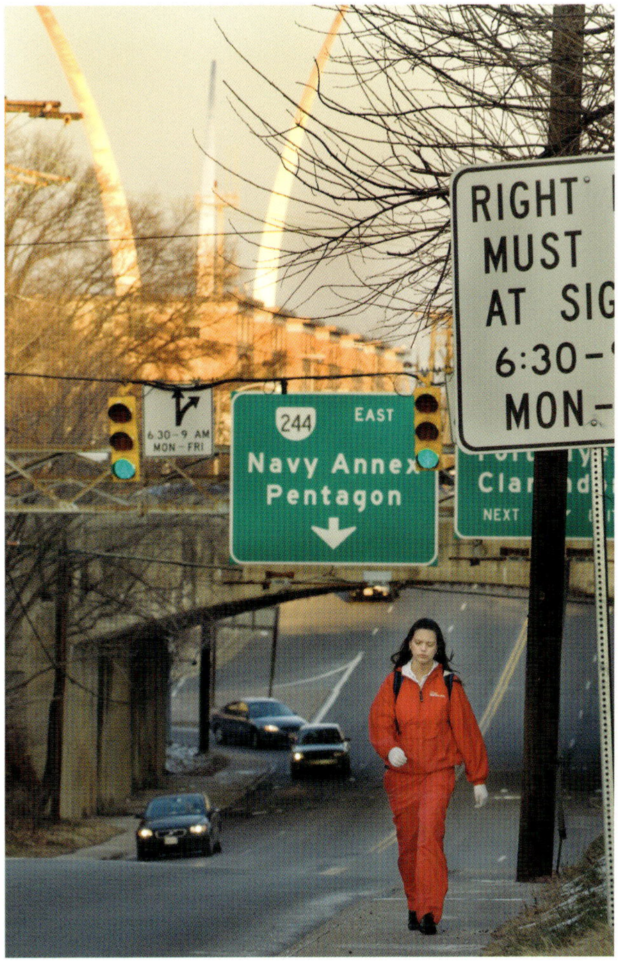

Columbia Pike and Washington Boulevard (Eastern View)

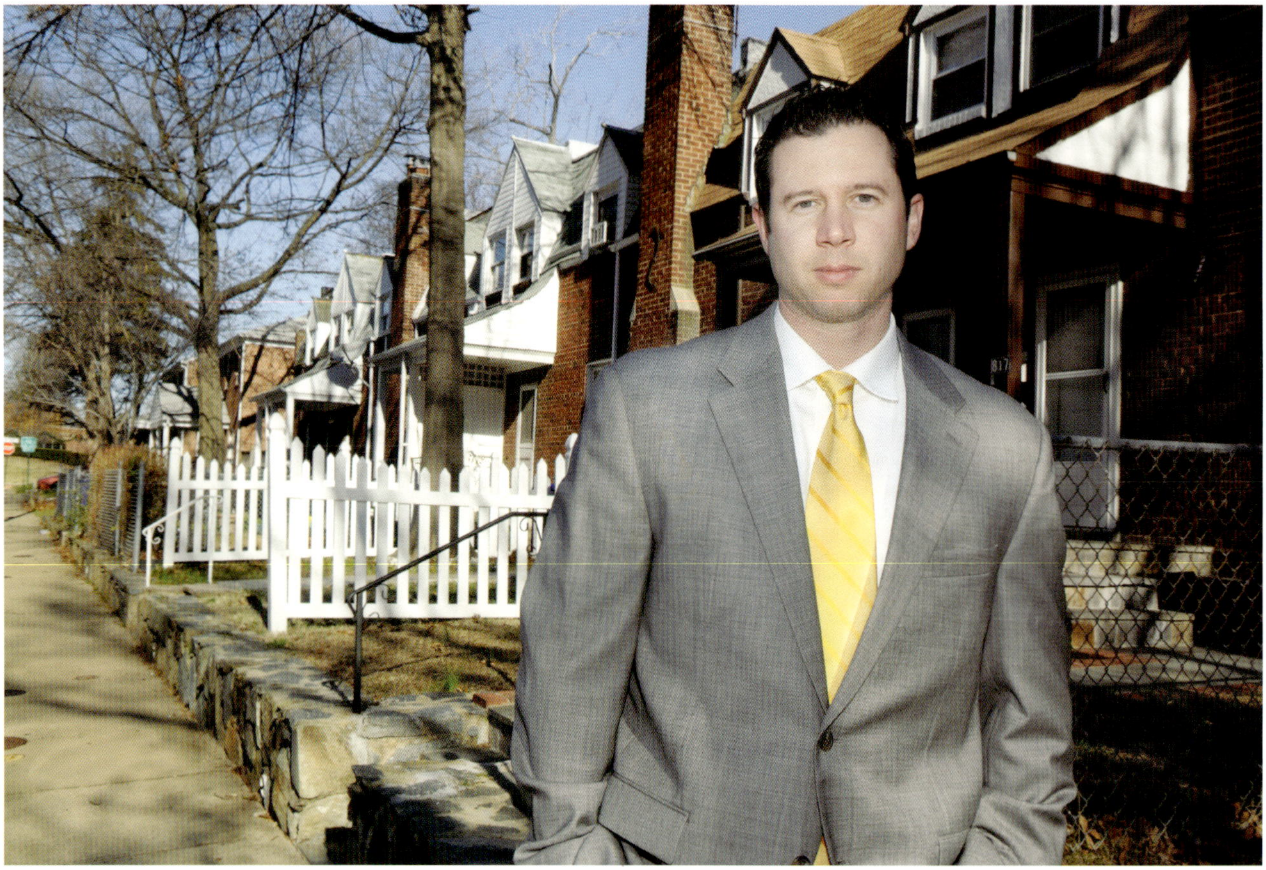

Michael Servello, Foxcroft Heights

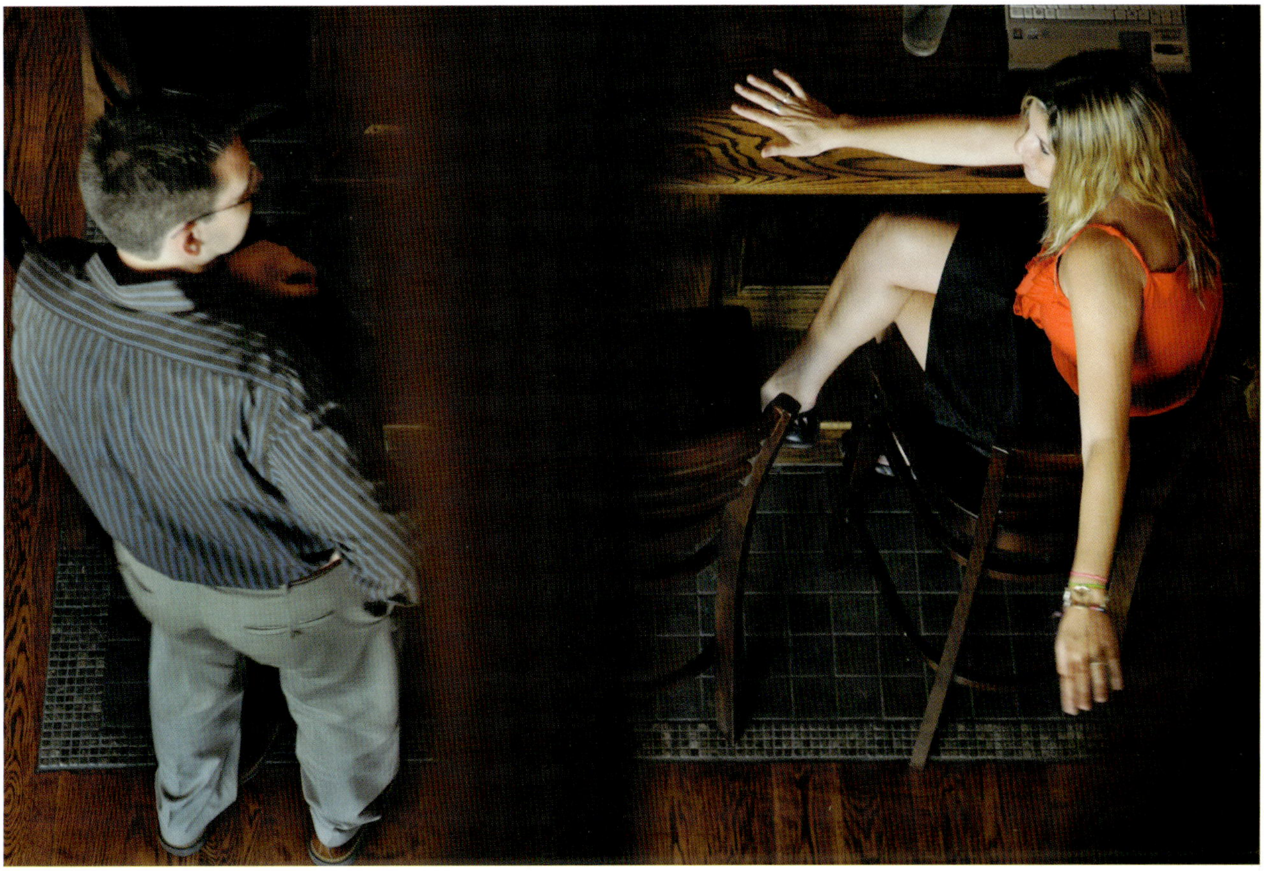

P. Brennan's Irish Pub, 2910 Columbia Pike

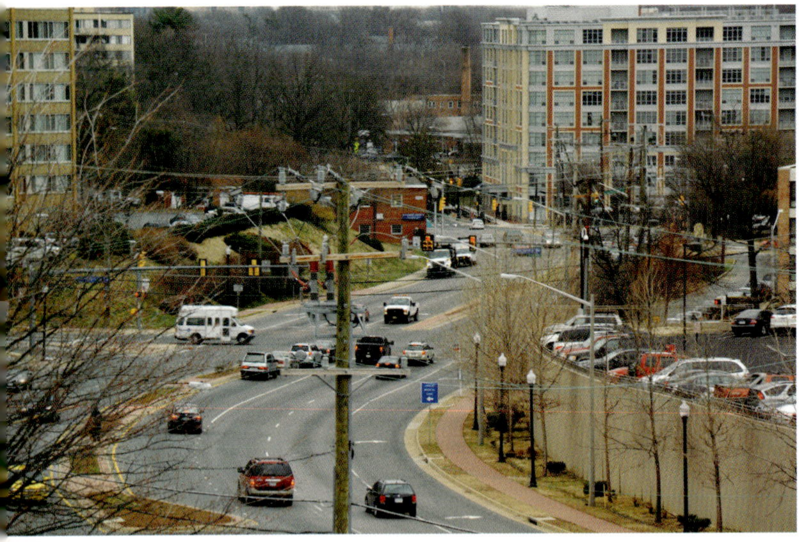

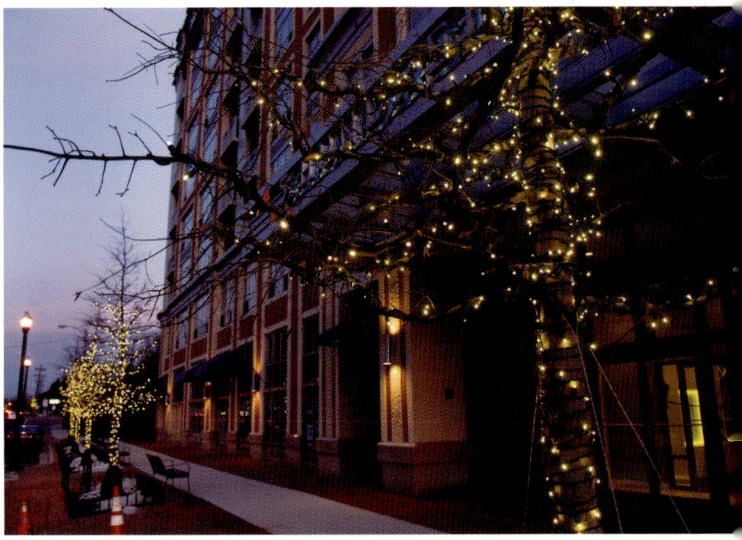

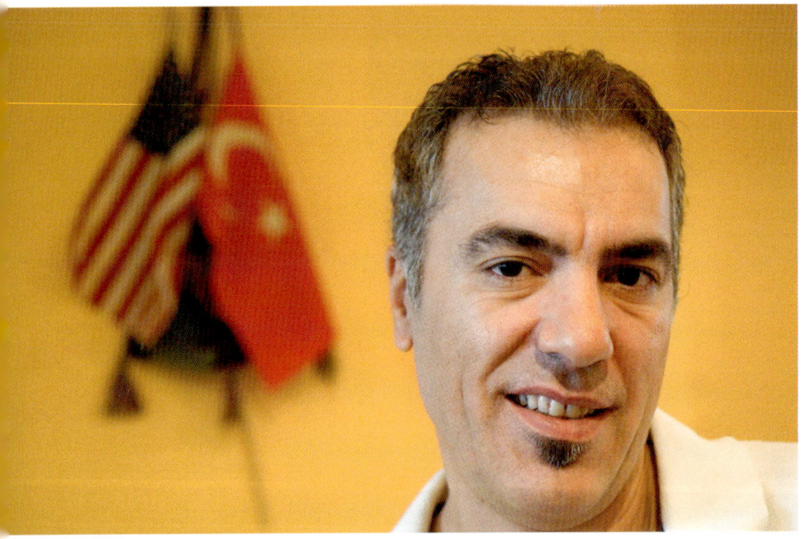

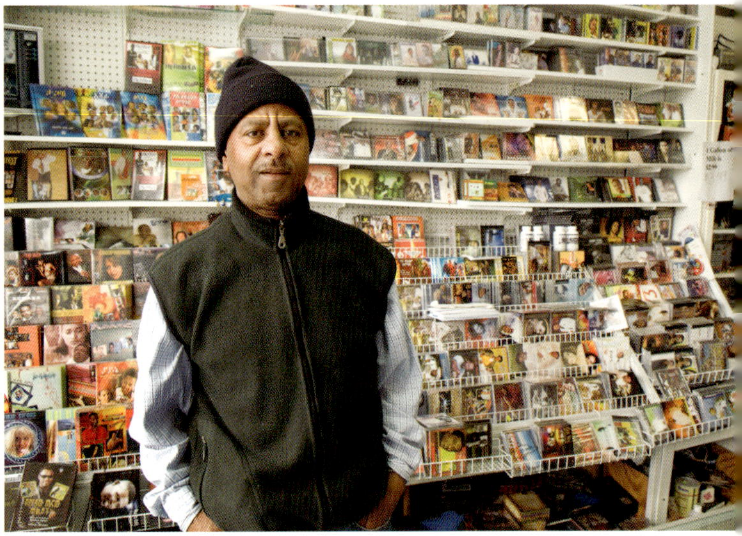

Western end of Columbia Pike in Arlington (Eastern View)

Holiday lights, 5500 Columbia Pike

Zulkuf Gezgic, Owner, Atilla's Restaurant,
2705 Columbia Pike

Mr. Muhamed, Asni Ethiopian Store,
1045 South Edgewood Street

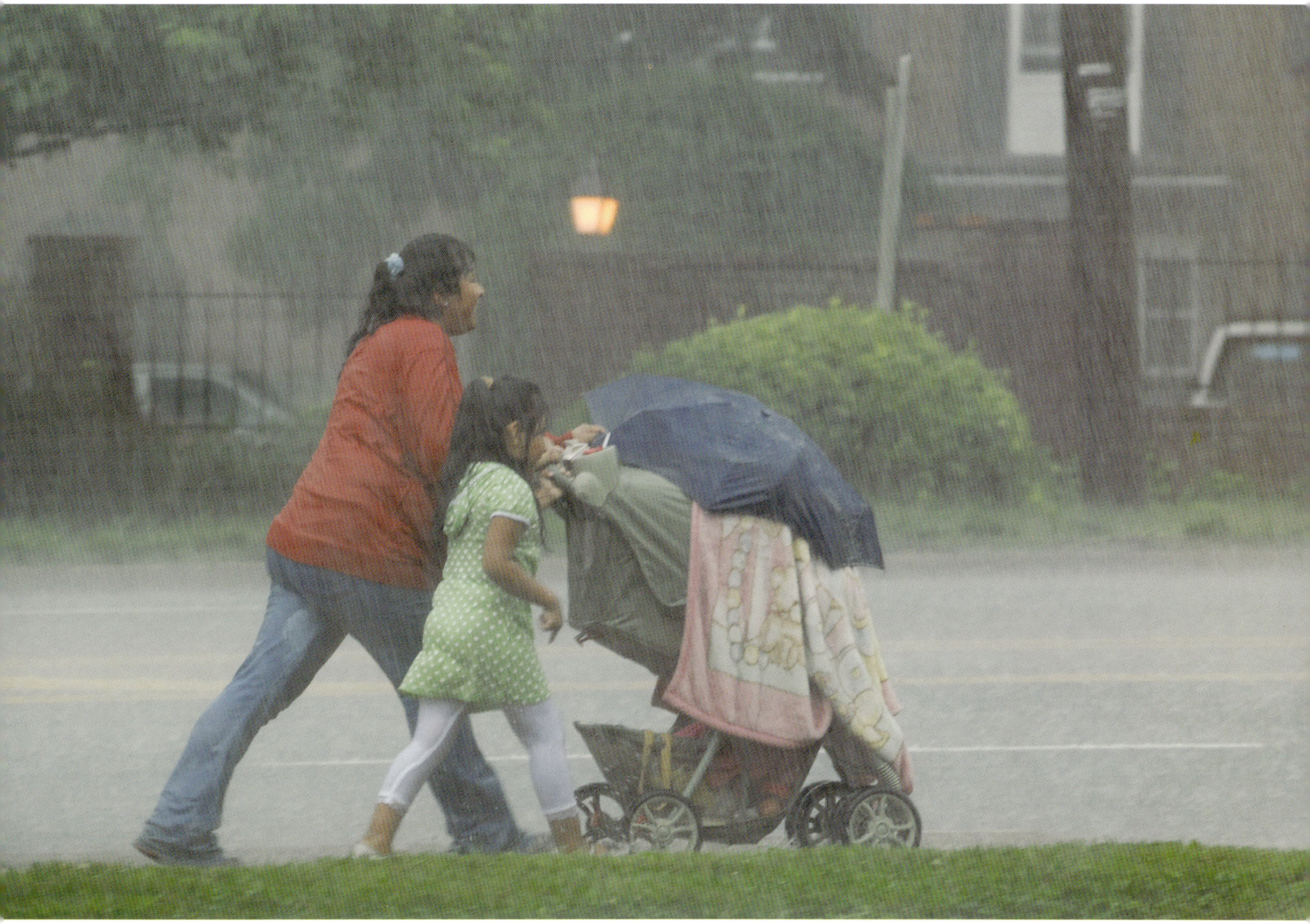

Summer rain, 5000 block of Columbia Pike

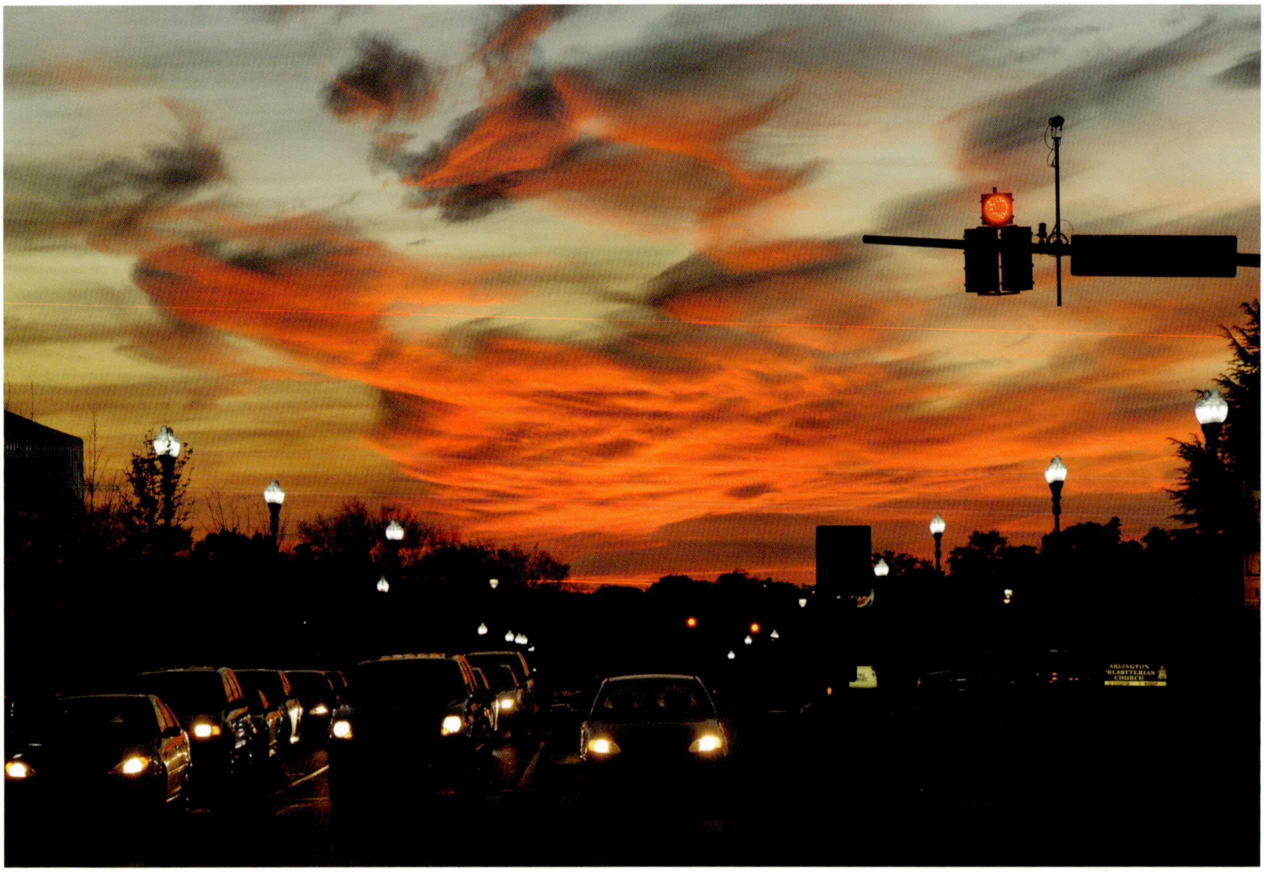

Sunset, Columbia Pike near South Glebe Road

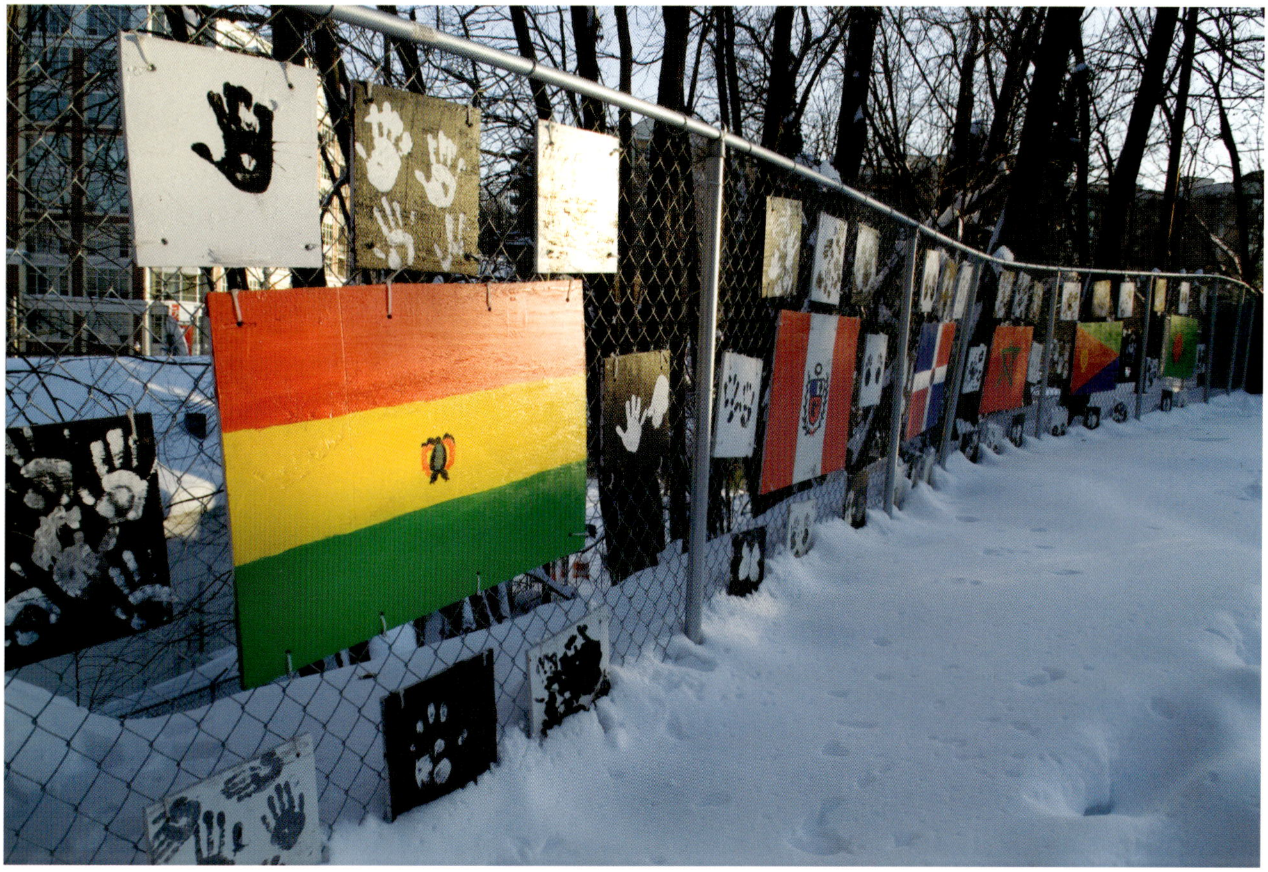

Fence behind Harvey Hall. 5400 block of Columbia Pike

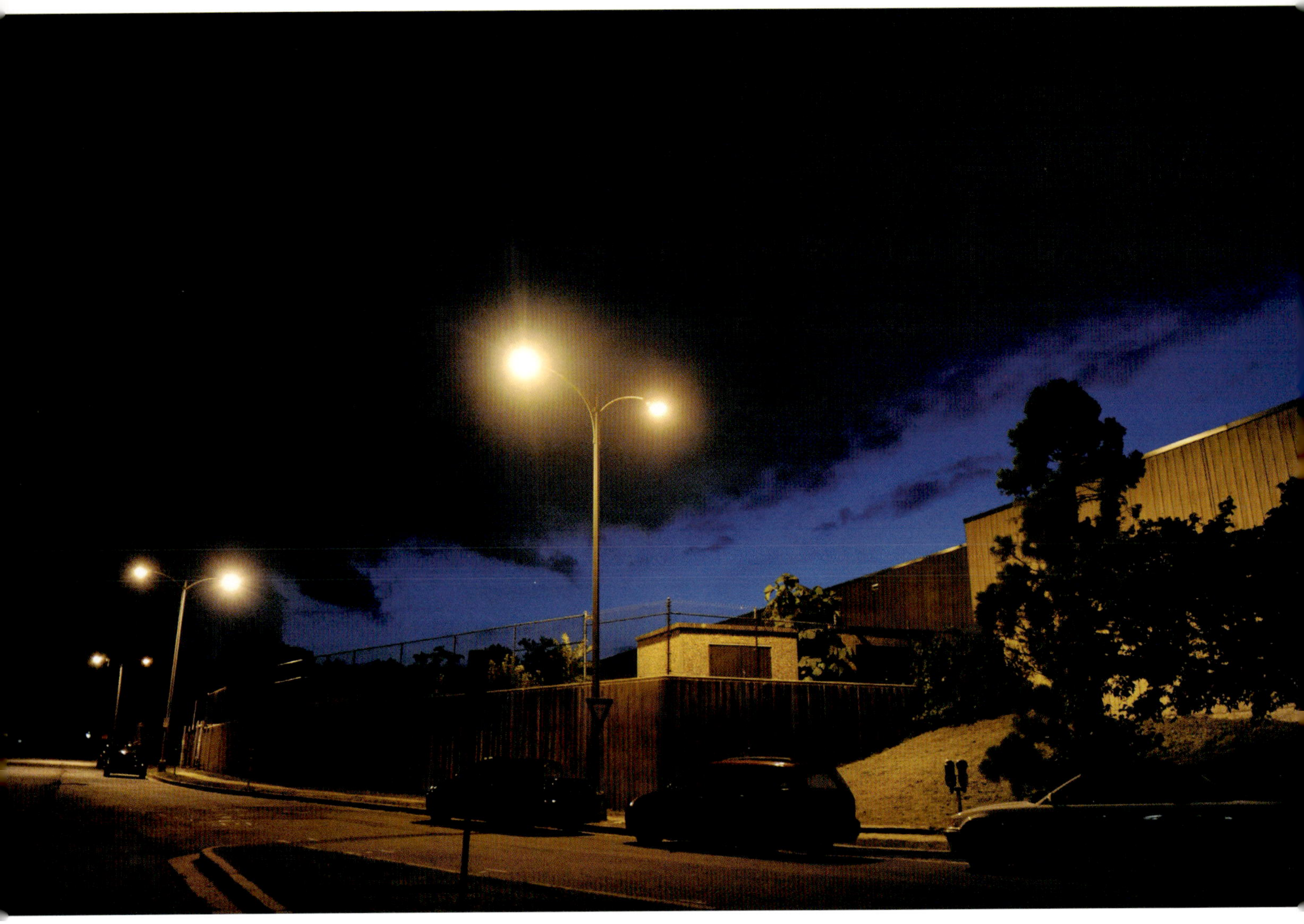

Night, 2900 block of South Ninth Street

ALEKSANDRA LAGKUEVA

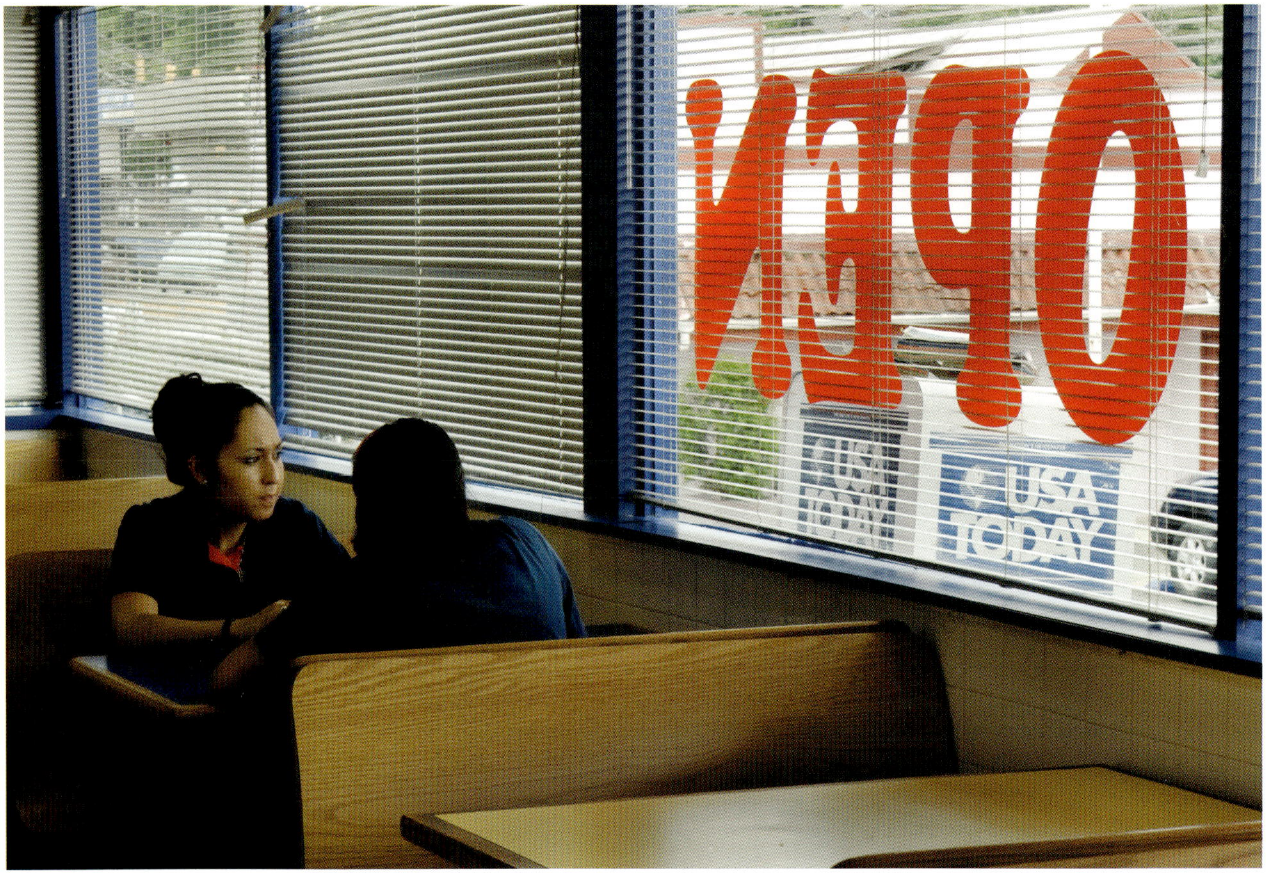

Diner, 4700 block Columbia Pike

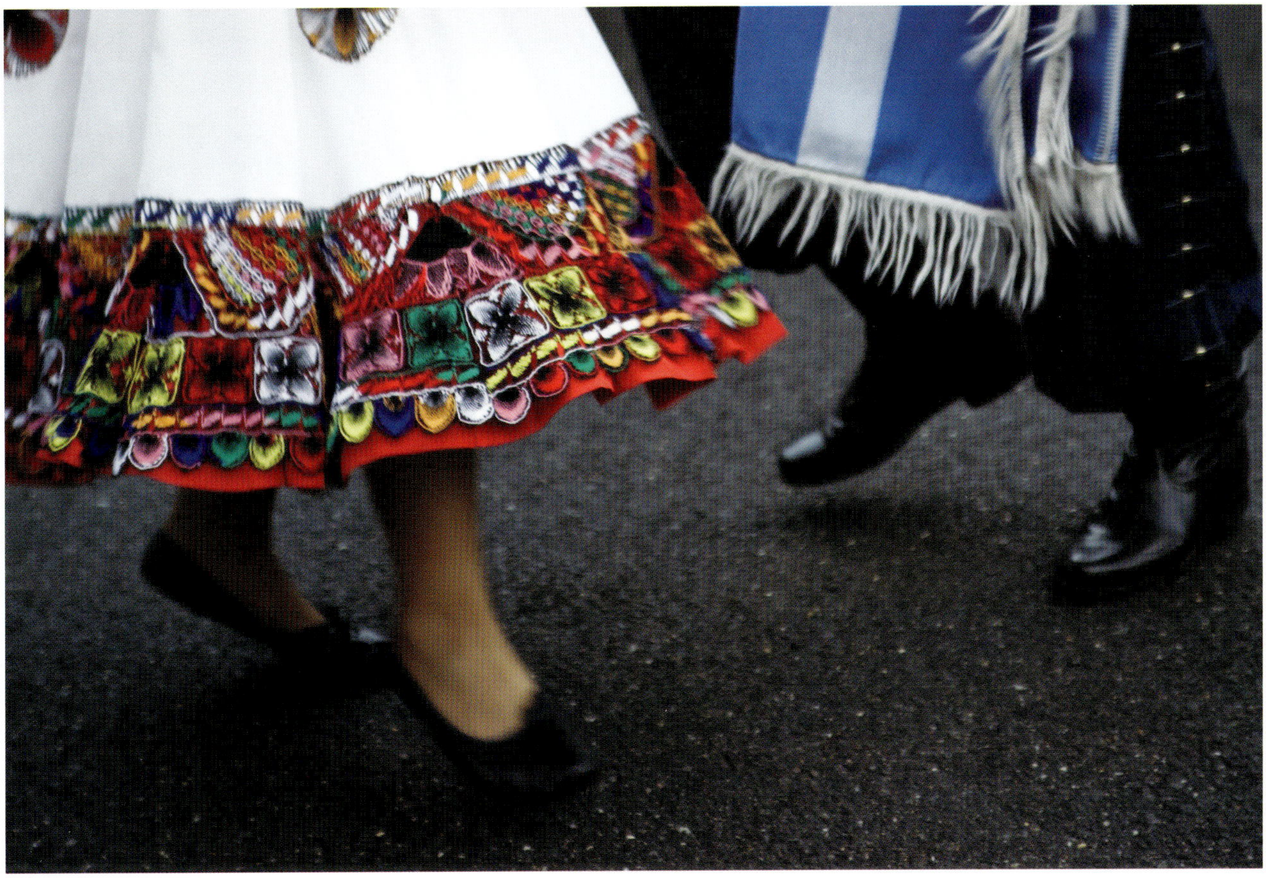

Dancers, Randolph School

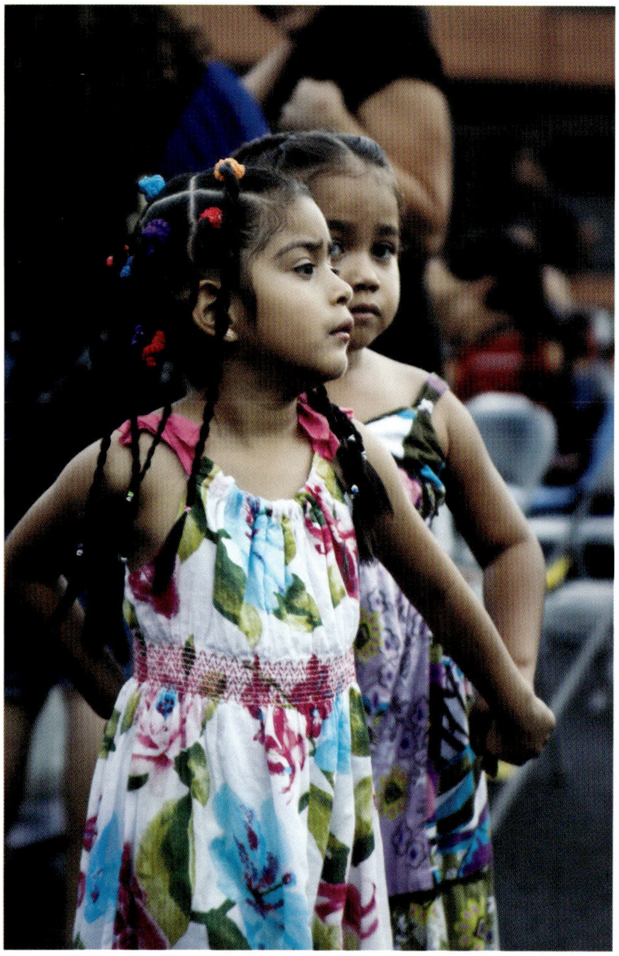
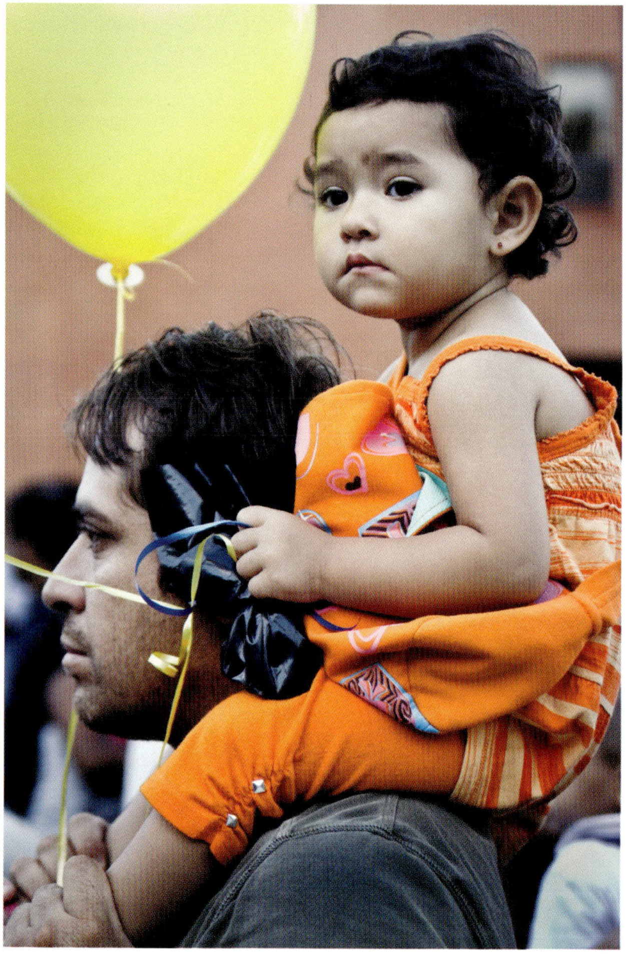

Community Gathering, Randolph School

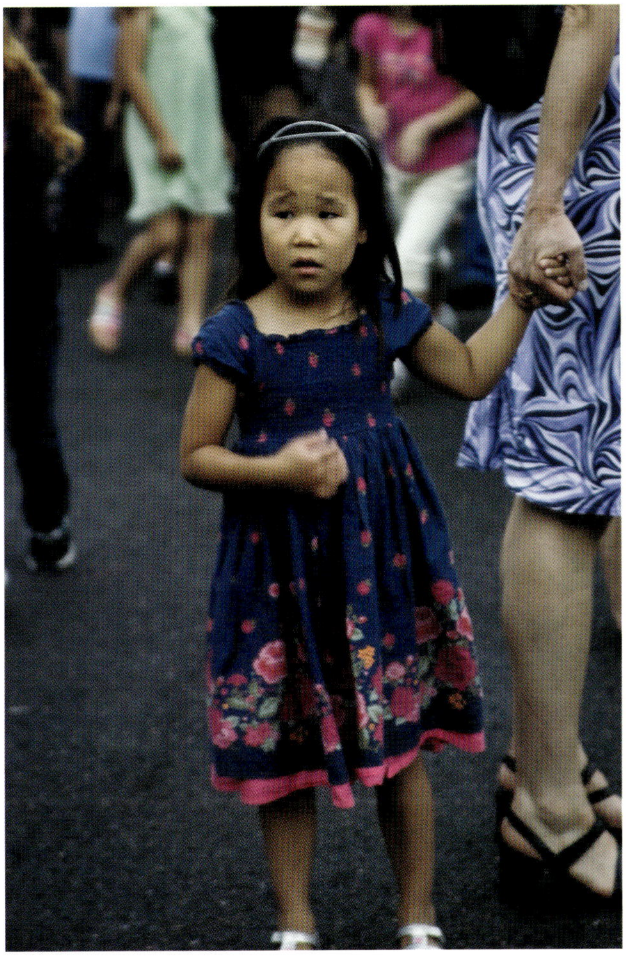

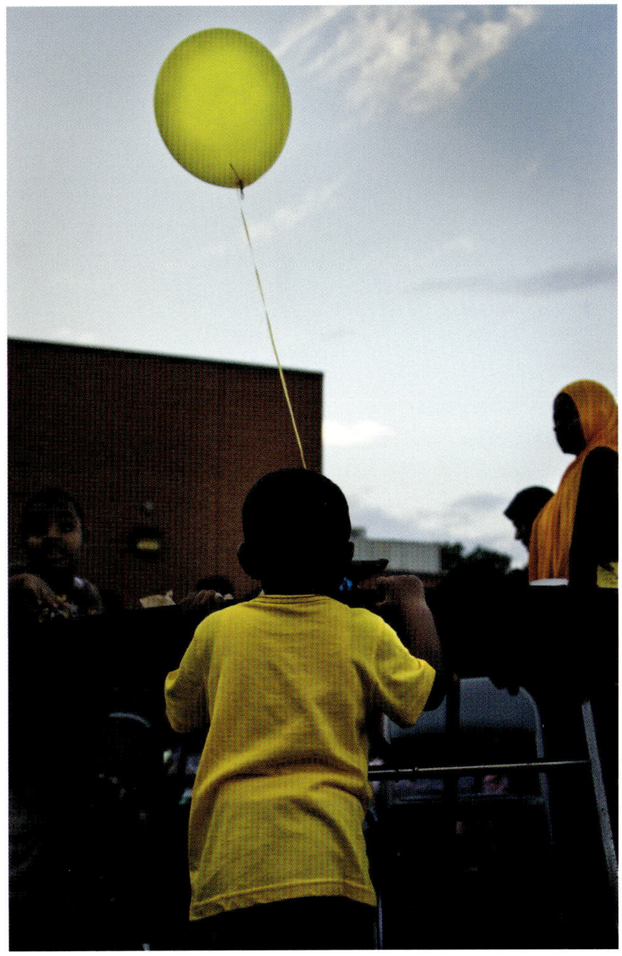

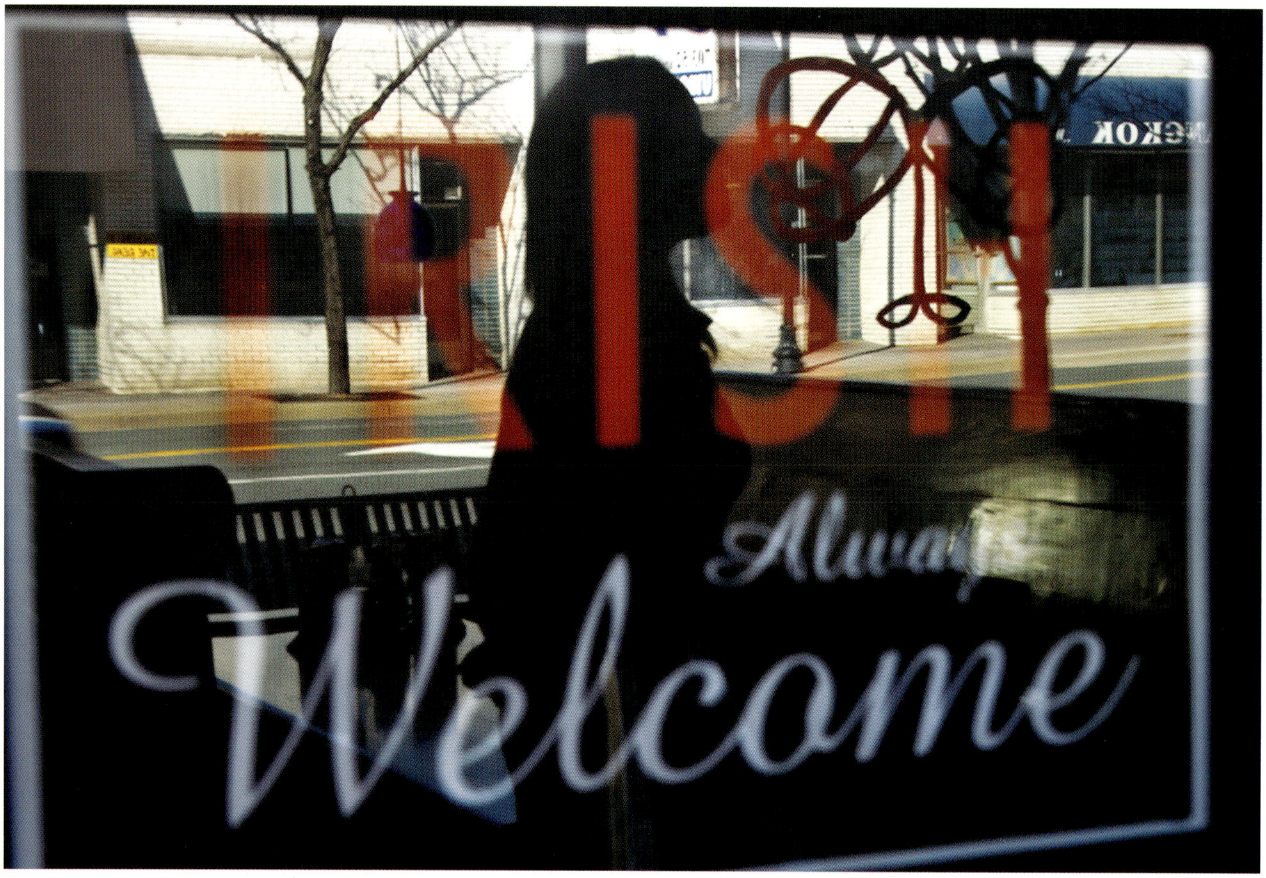

Shop Window, 2600 block Columbia Pike

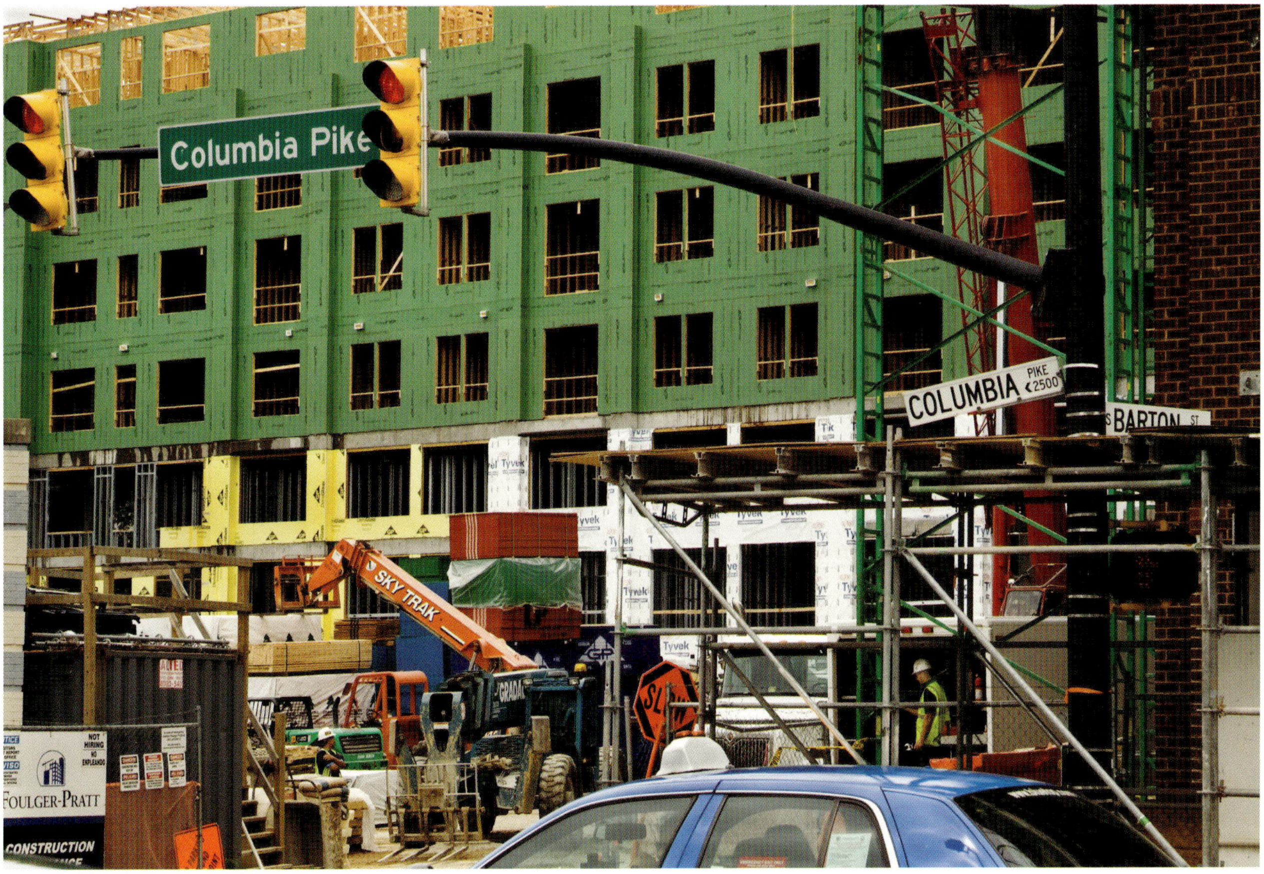

Construction, Penrose Square Shopping Center

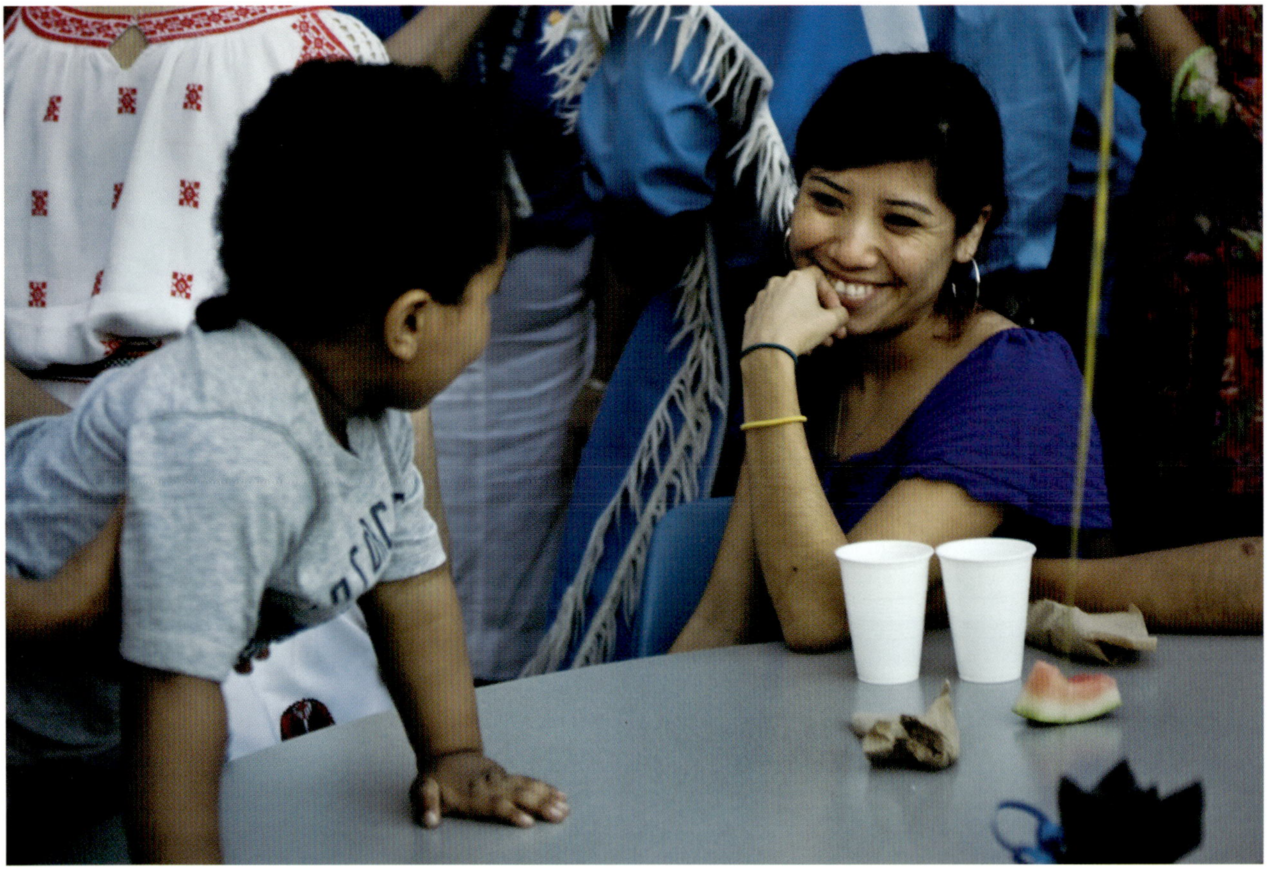

Community Gathering, Randolph School

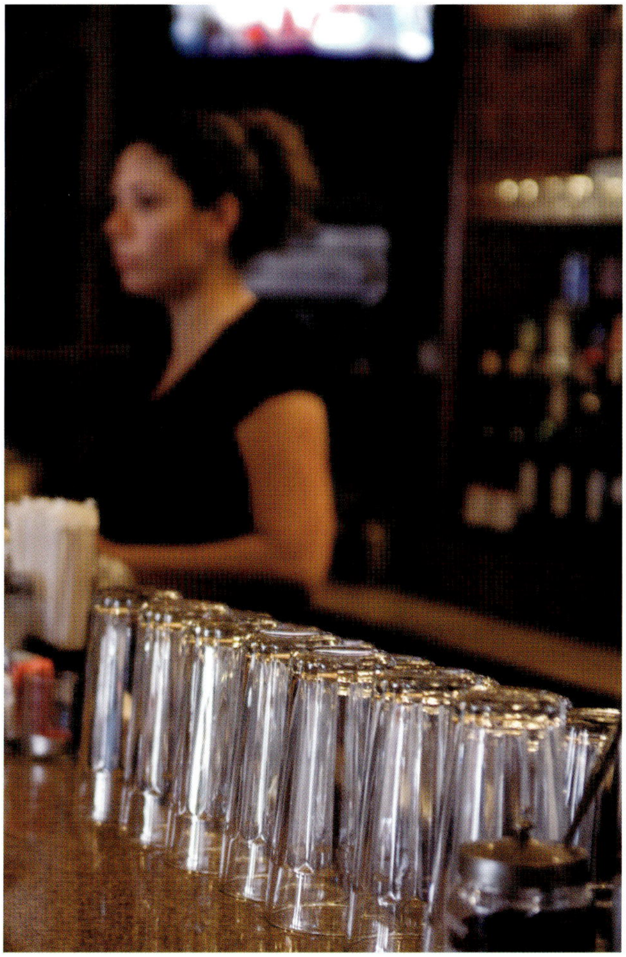

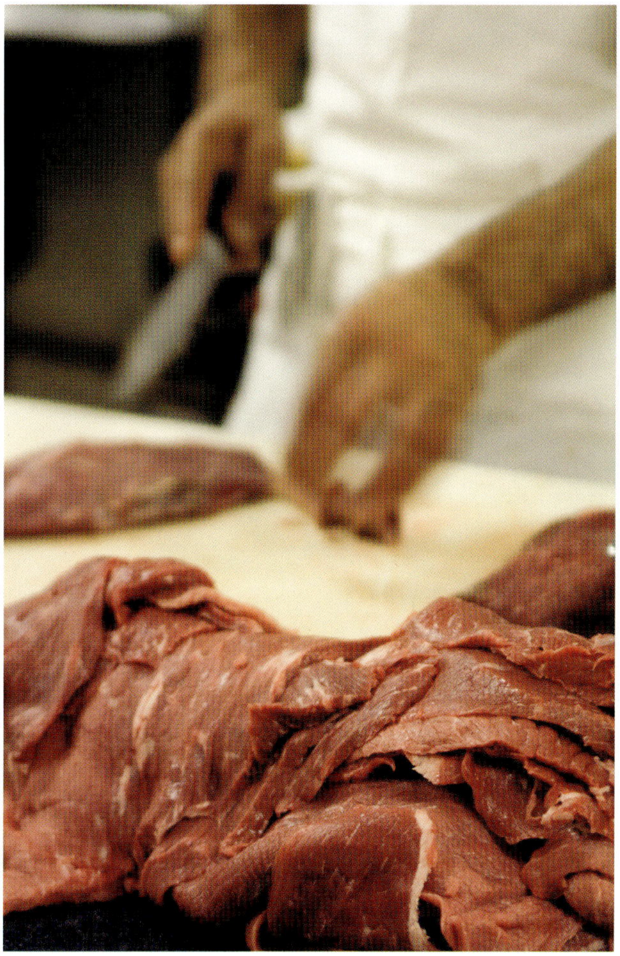

Atilla's Restaurant

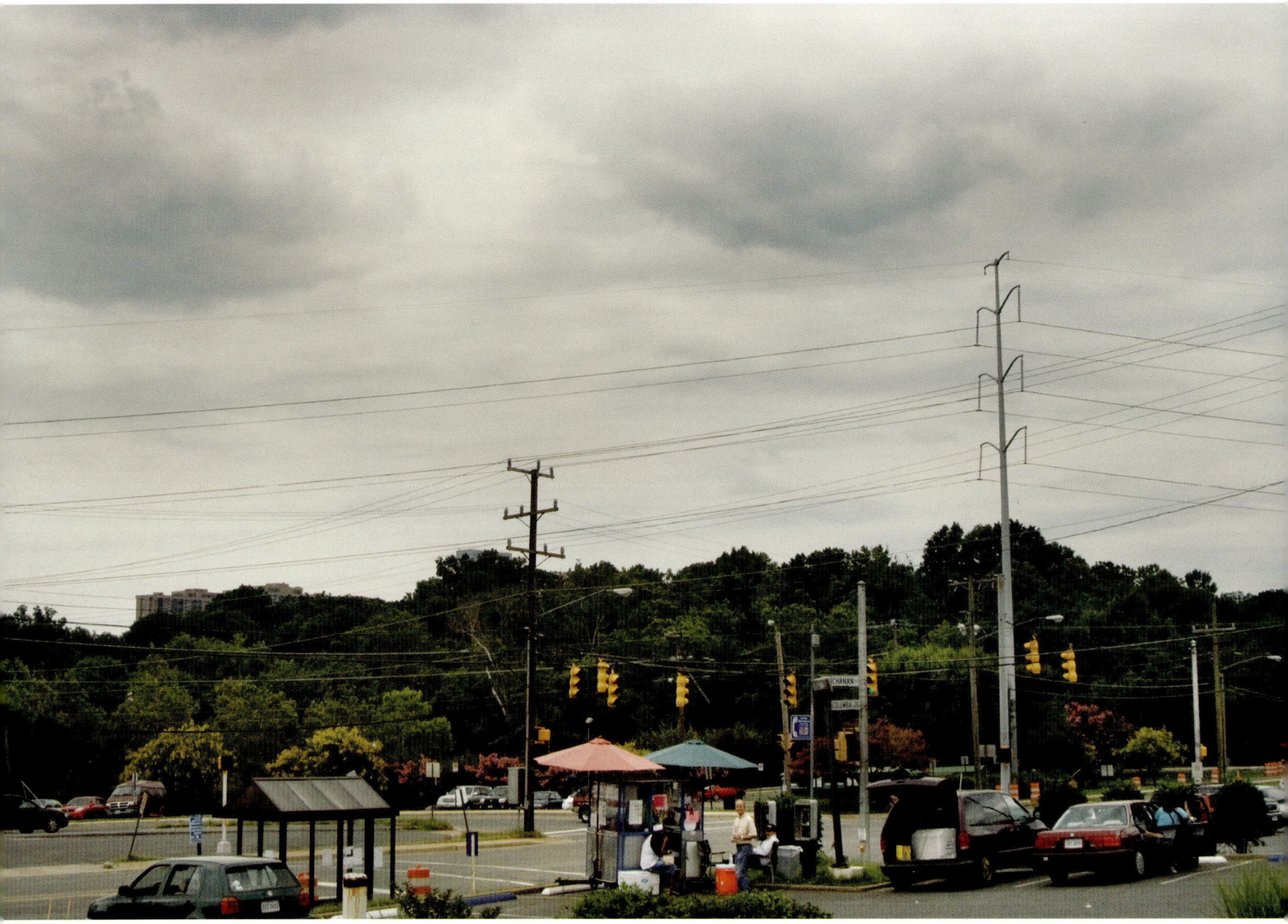

Columbia Pike at South Four Mile Run Drive

PAULA ENDO

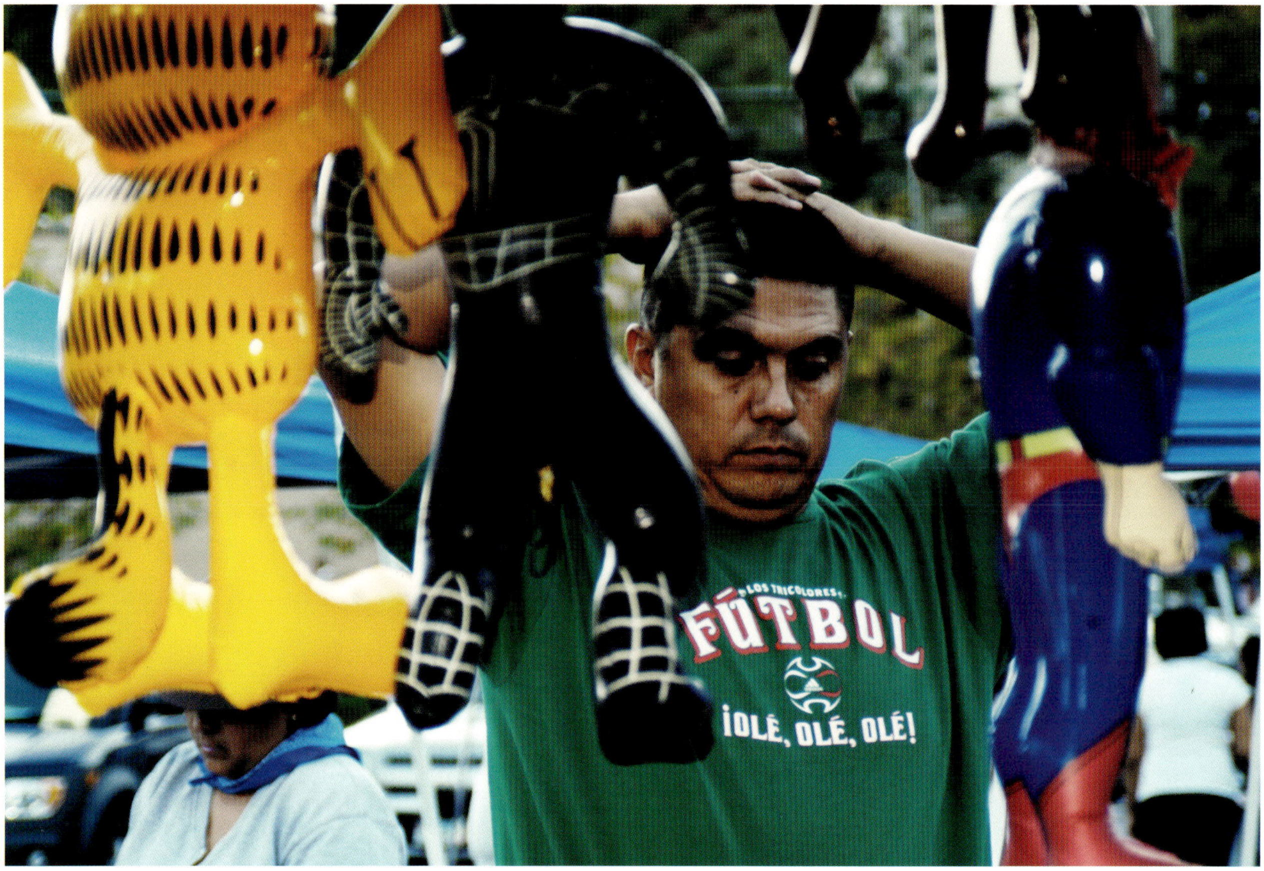

Taste of the Pike Festival

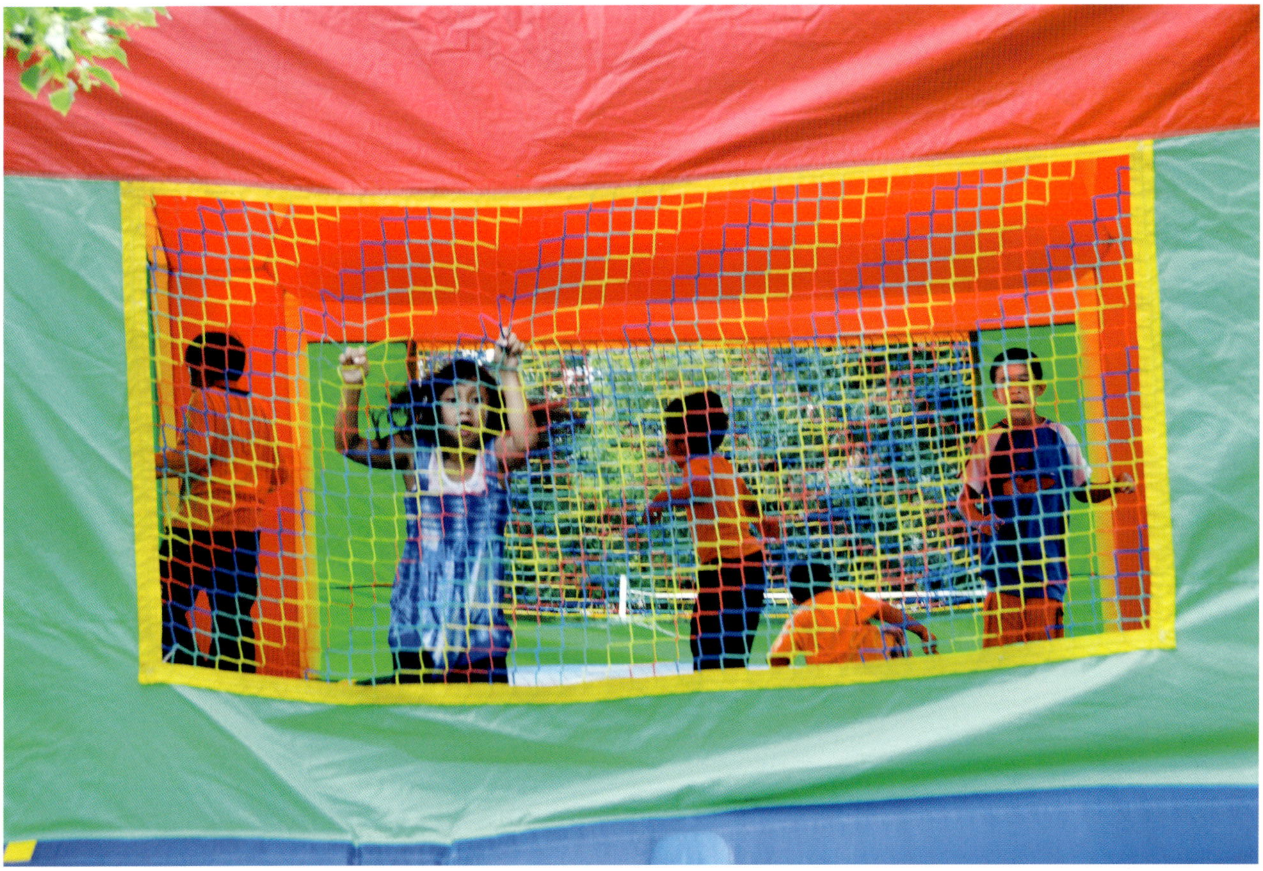

Taste of the Pike Festival

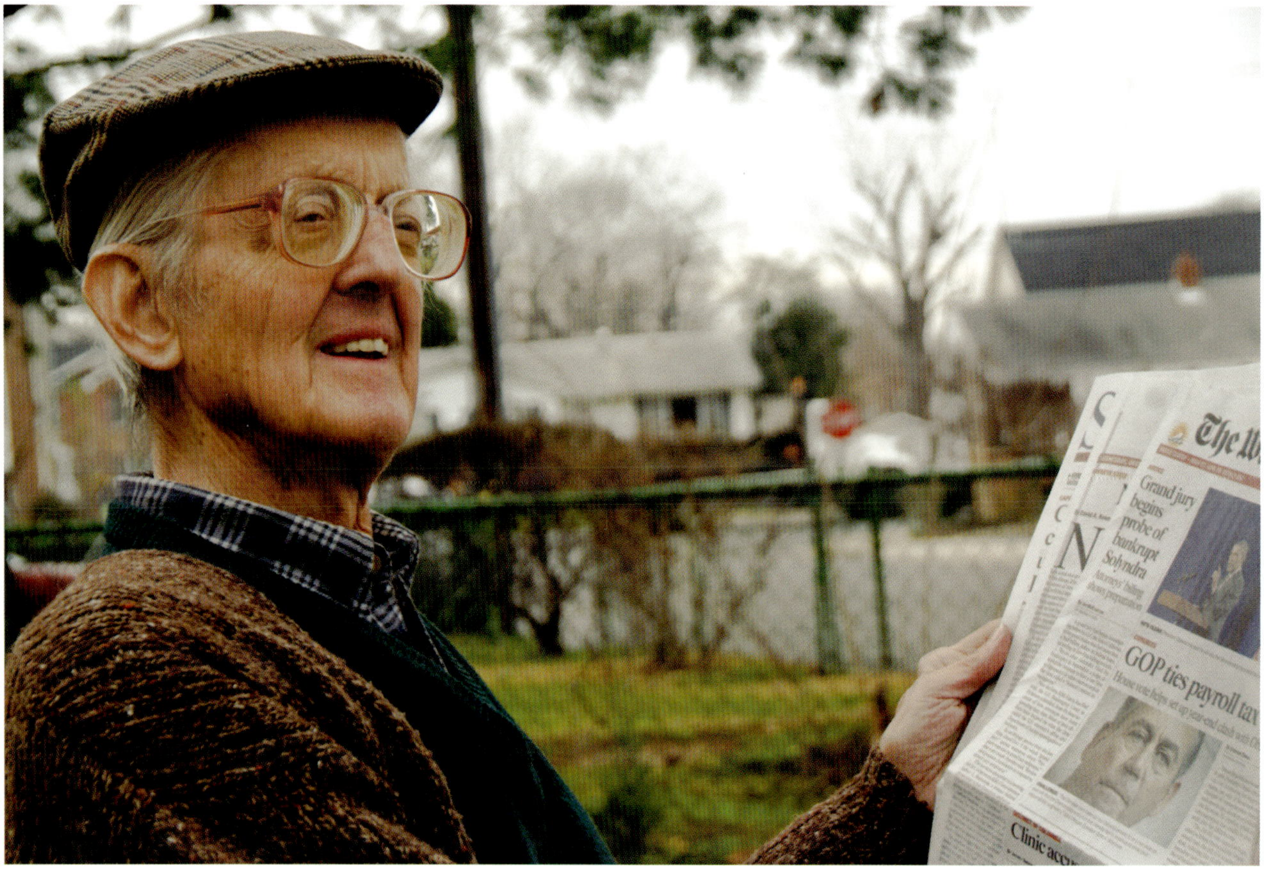
Grand jury
begins
probe of
bankrupt
Solyndra
GOP ties payroll

Sedge Moss

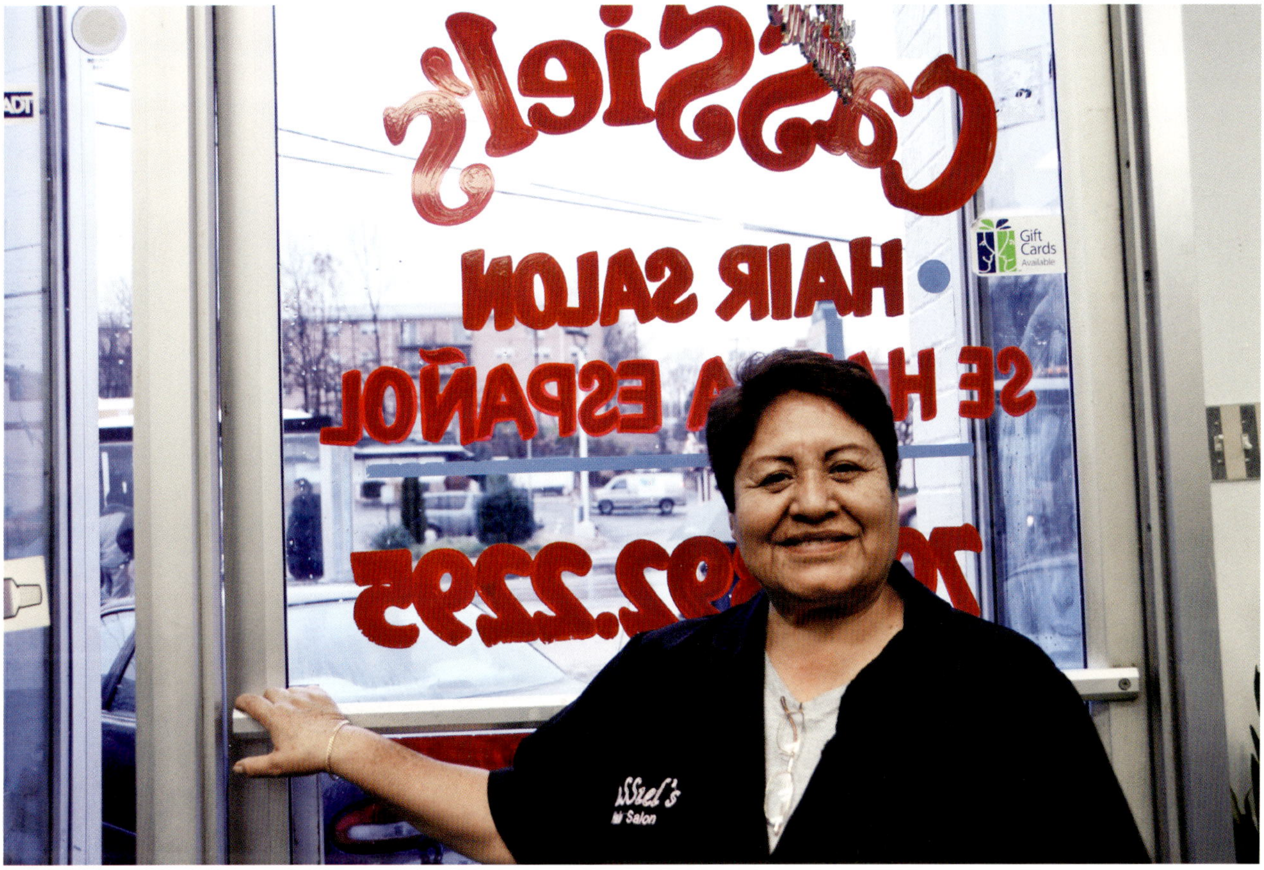

Eva Torres, Owner, Cassiel's Salon

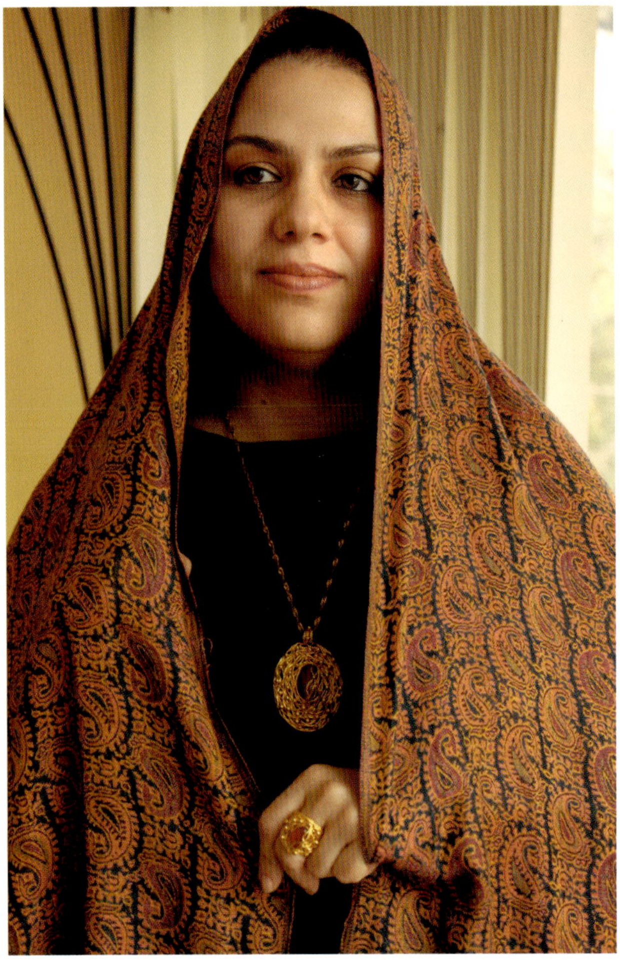

Huda Hussein

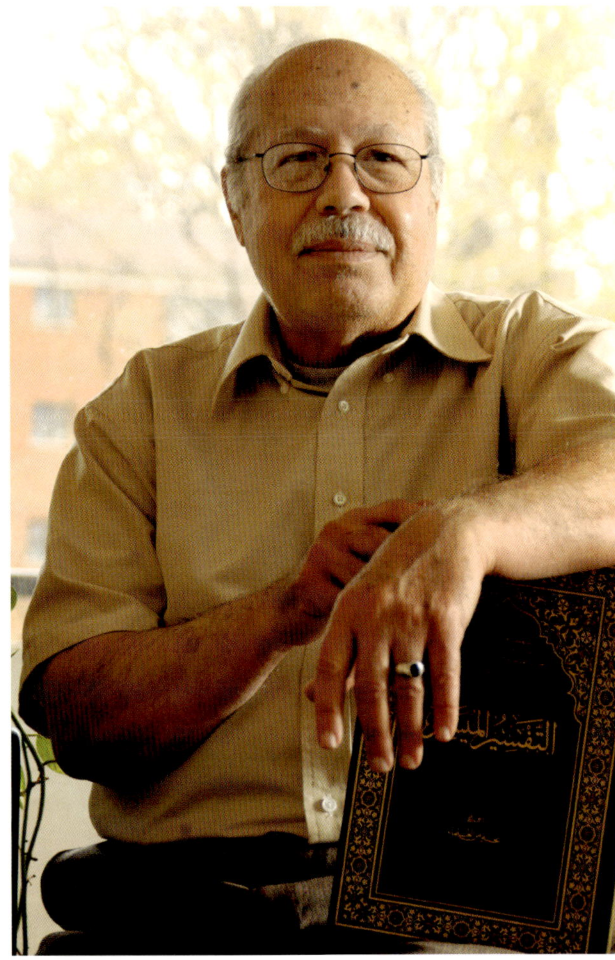

Omer Hussein

I was born in the Sudan in 1946. I came to the USA in 1960. My daughter Maha was born here in 1965. My husband, Riad Omer, was a student here.

When I came here I didn't know any English. I went to school to learn English. I volunteered with Miss Hawa Warsame in Arlington Mill Community Center and practiced my English, and I took care of my four grandchildren. I cook for them, watch as they come from the public school, take them to their buses.

I have many friends, Mary Kay, and my neighbor, Suzanne. We take tea together. Sometimes they take me to the hospital if I need, sometimes they take me to the store when my daughter is working. They are from America. We also have many many friends from my country. Sometimes they make a party for the holidays, like Ramadan and Eid.

Now I can talk and understand English, but when I came to this country I didn't know anything, just like table, chair, but now I can talk with my grandchildren, with teachers, with the people, much better, much better!

I have my grandkids' dreams. Abdul wants to be a doctor. Gigi wants to be a doctor. Other one she wants to be a doctor. I want to see them there in a hospital with a white jacket. Opportunities... many opportunities. I ask my children - we are in the big forest. You have to be strong and work hard and they found what they want after they work hard.

Raaga Hussein Abdul

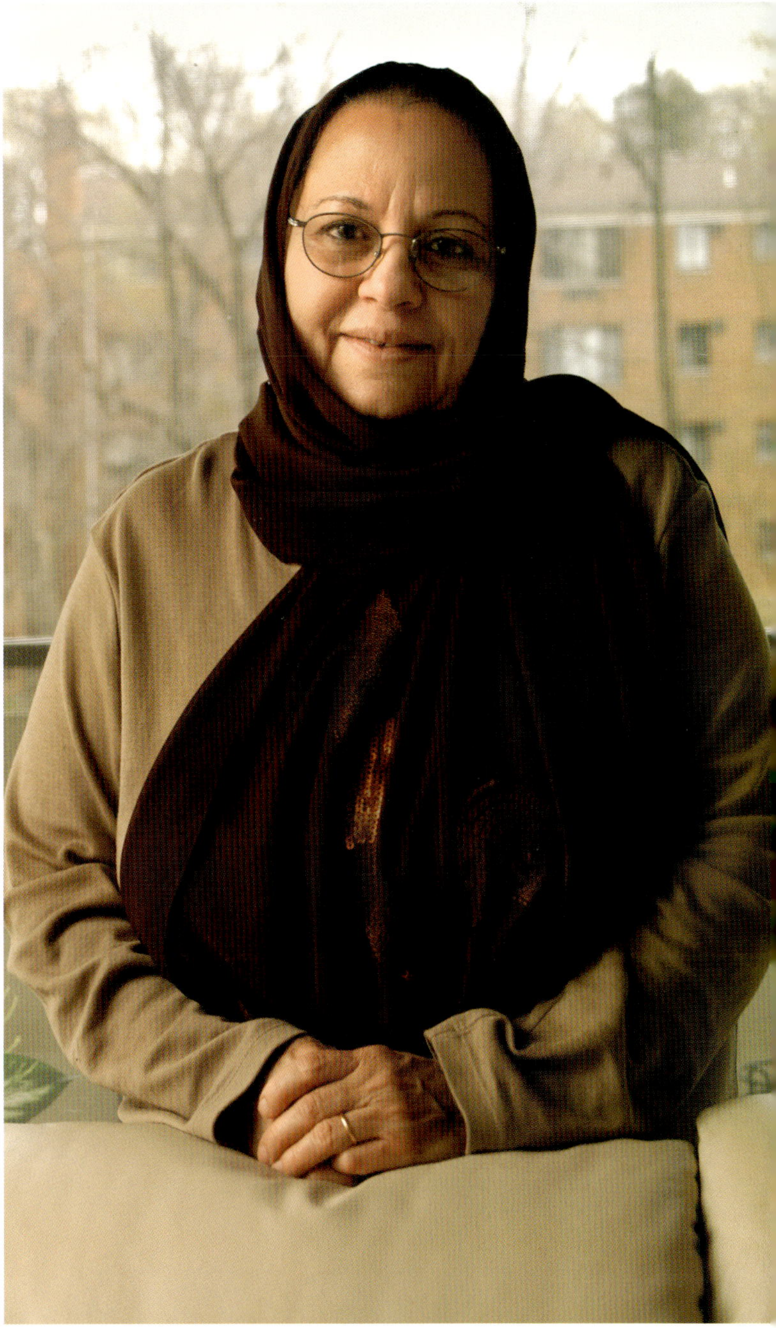

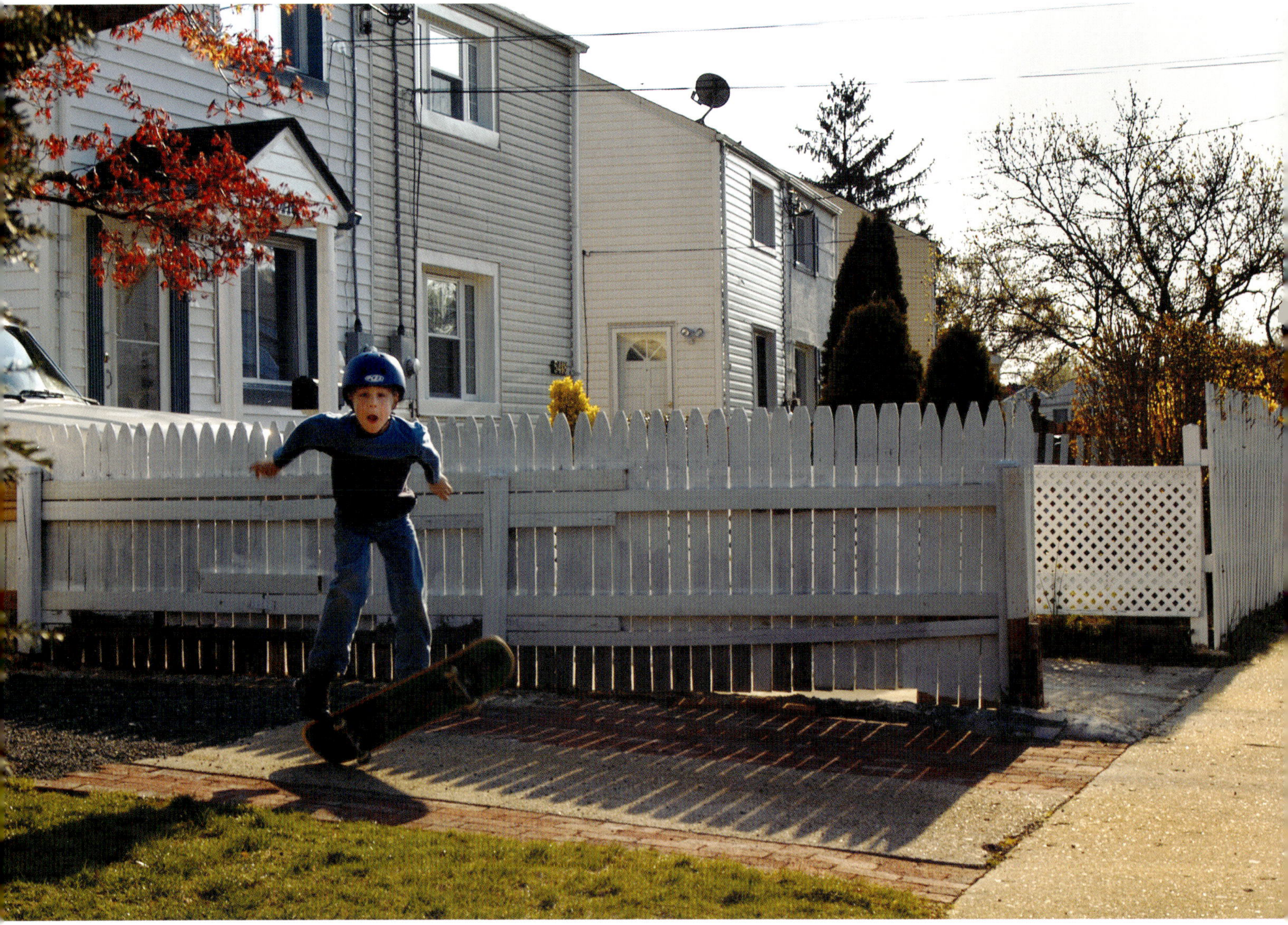

Luke Anderson

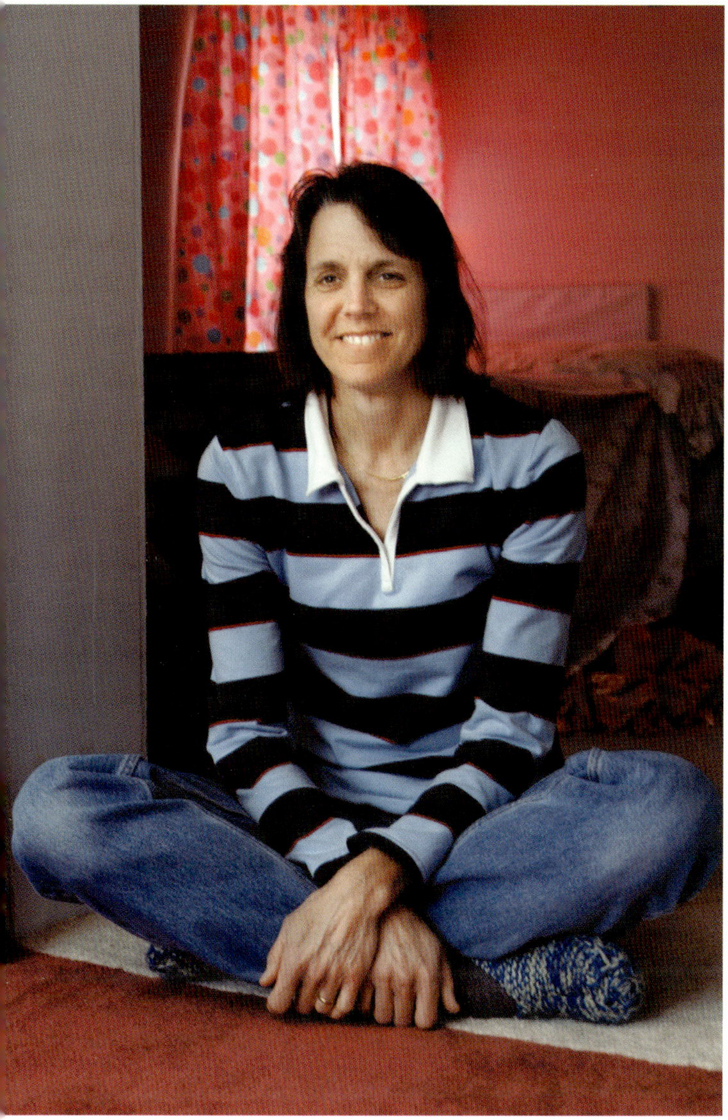

Linda Anderson

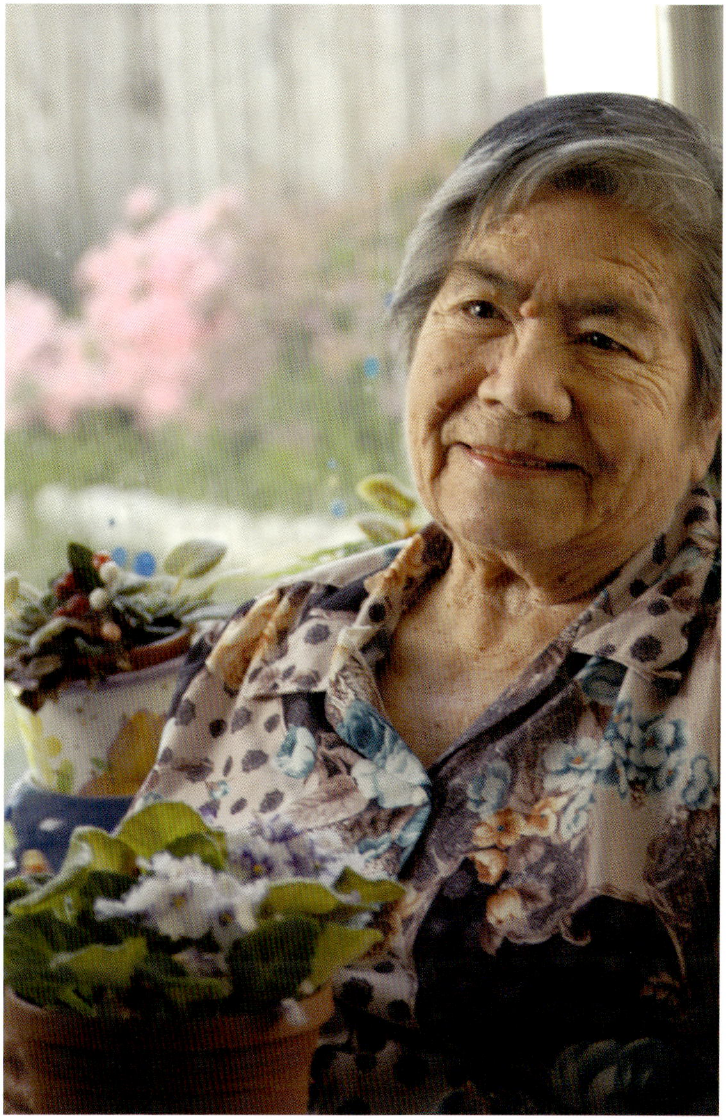

Eudora Barrios

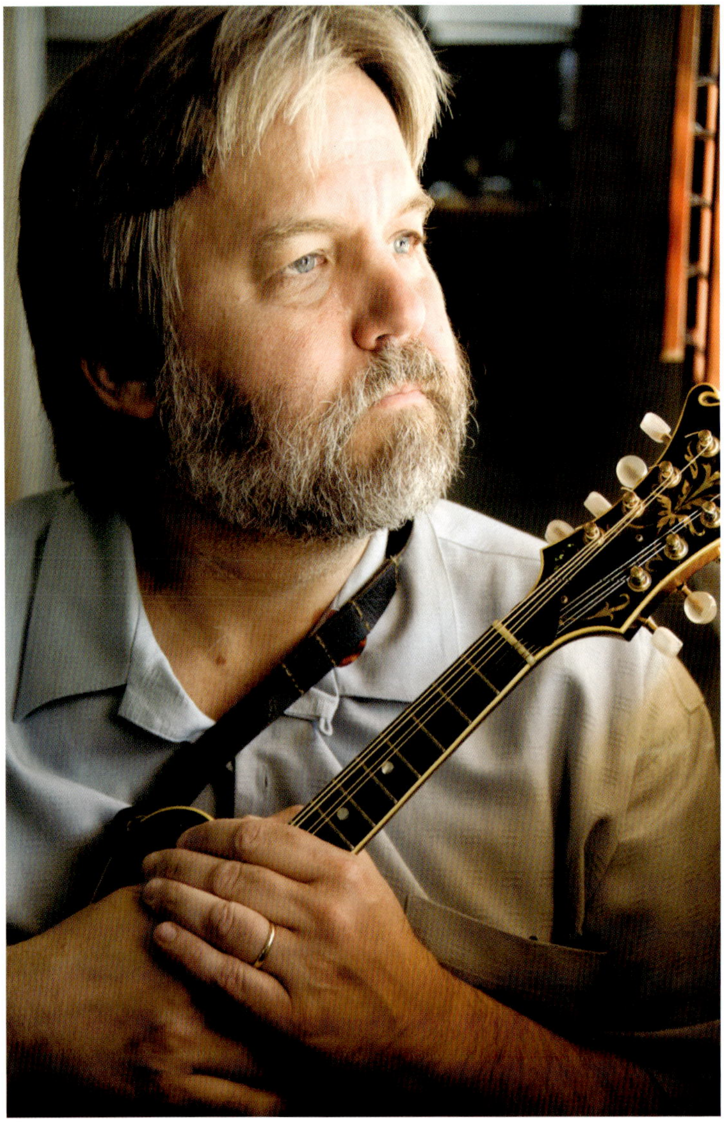

Jamie Daly

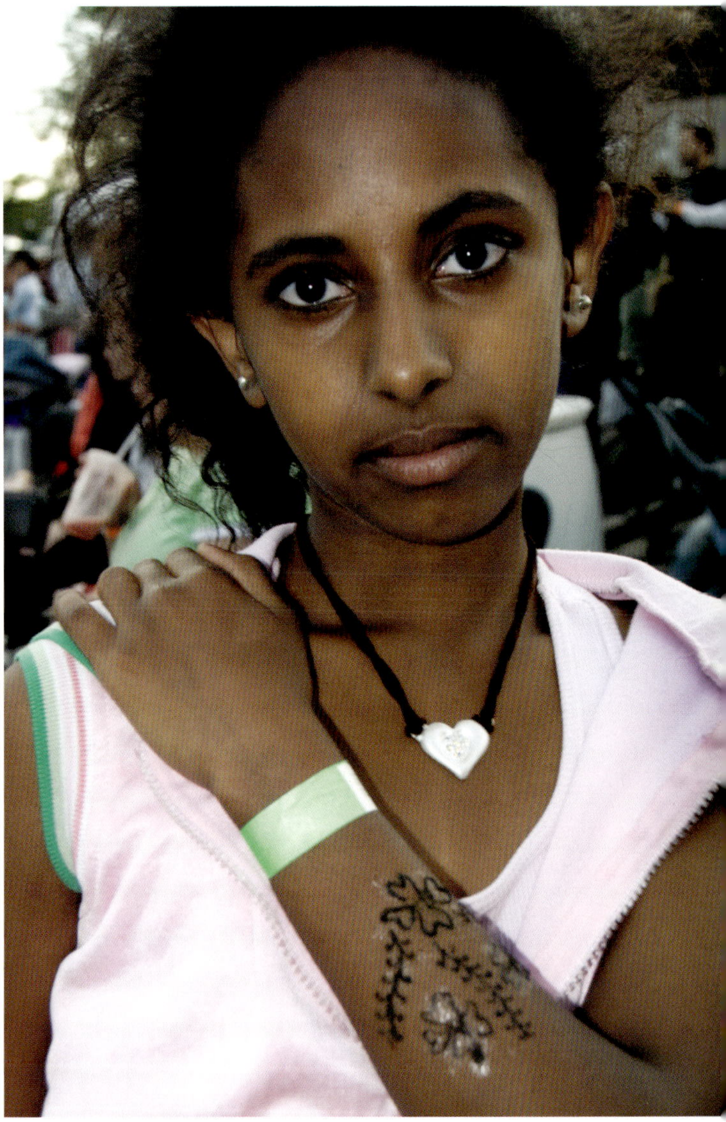

Eritrean Girl

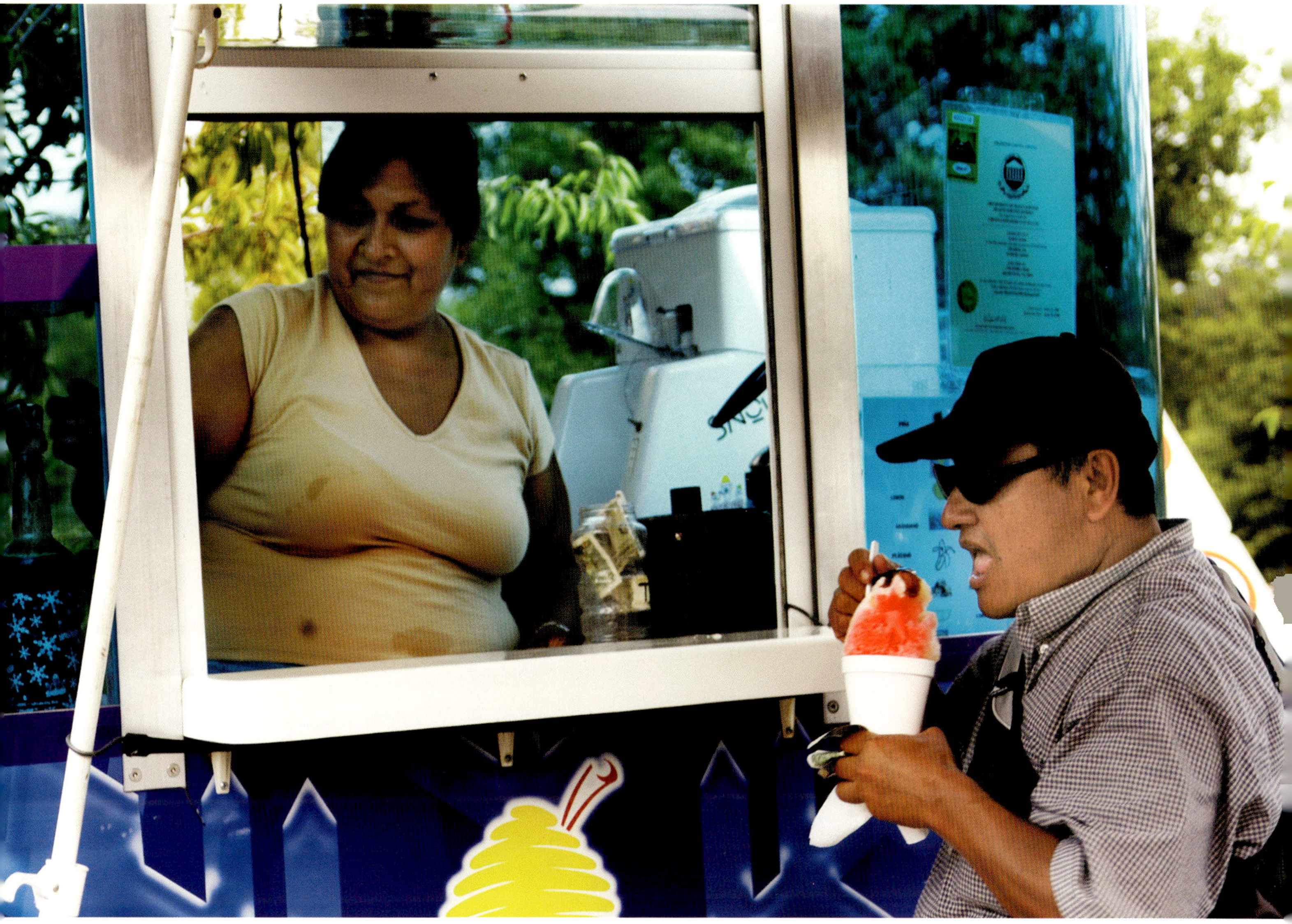

Latin Ice Stand

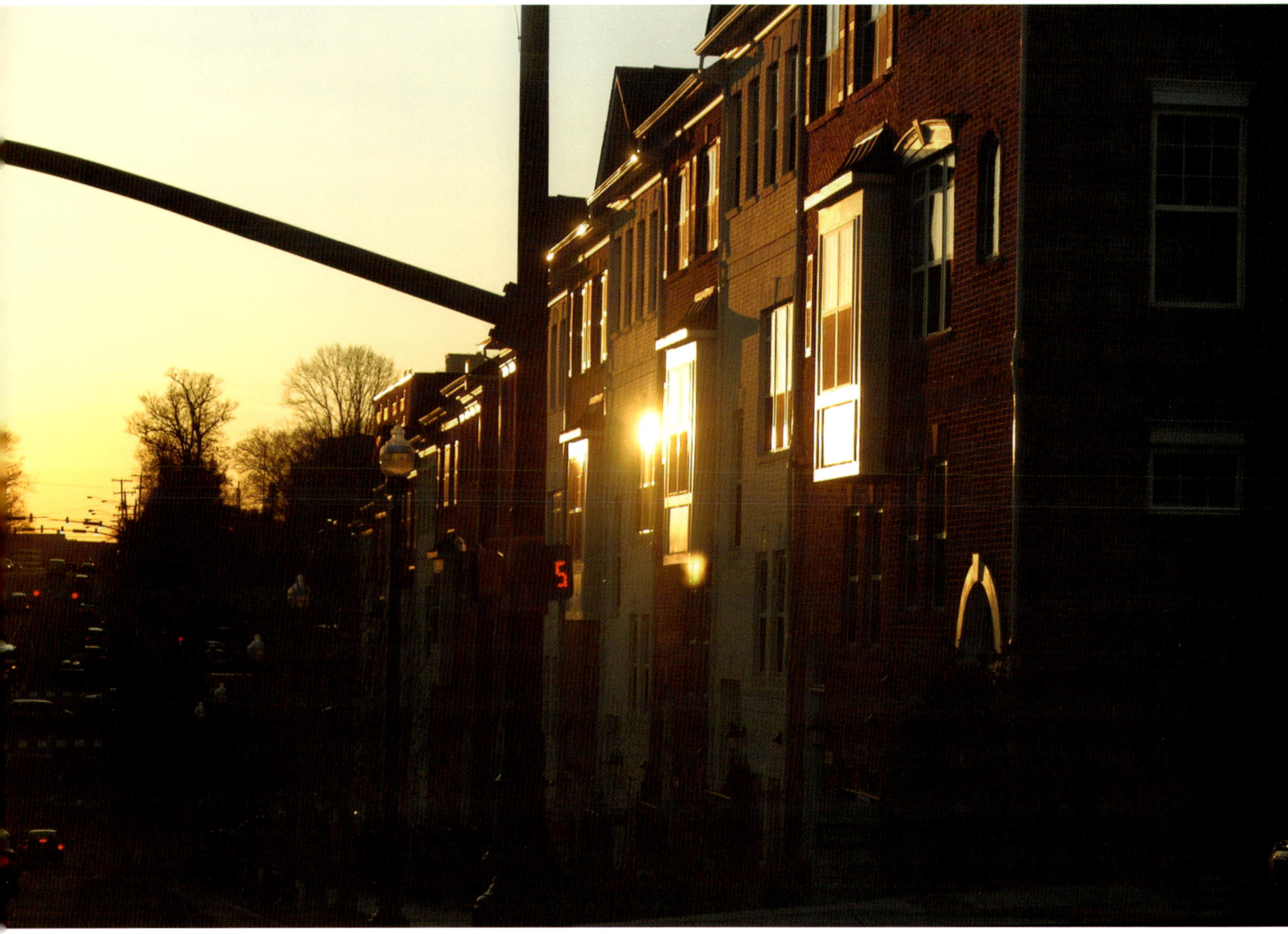

Sunset, 4000 Block of Columbia Pike

XANG MIMI HO

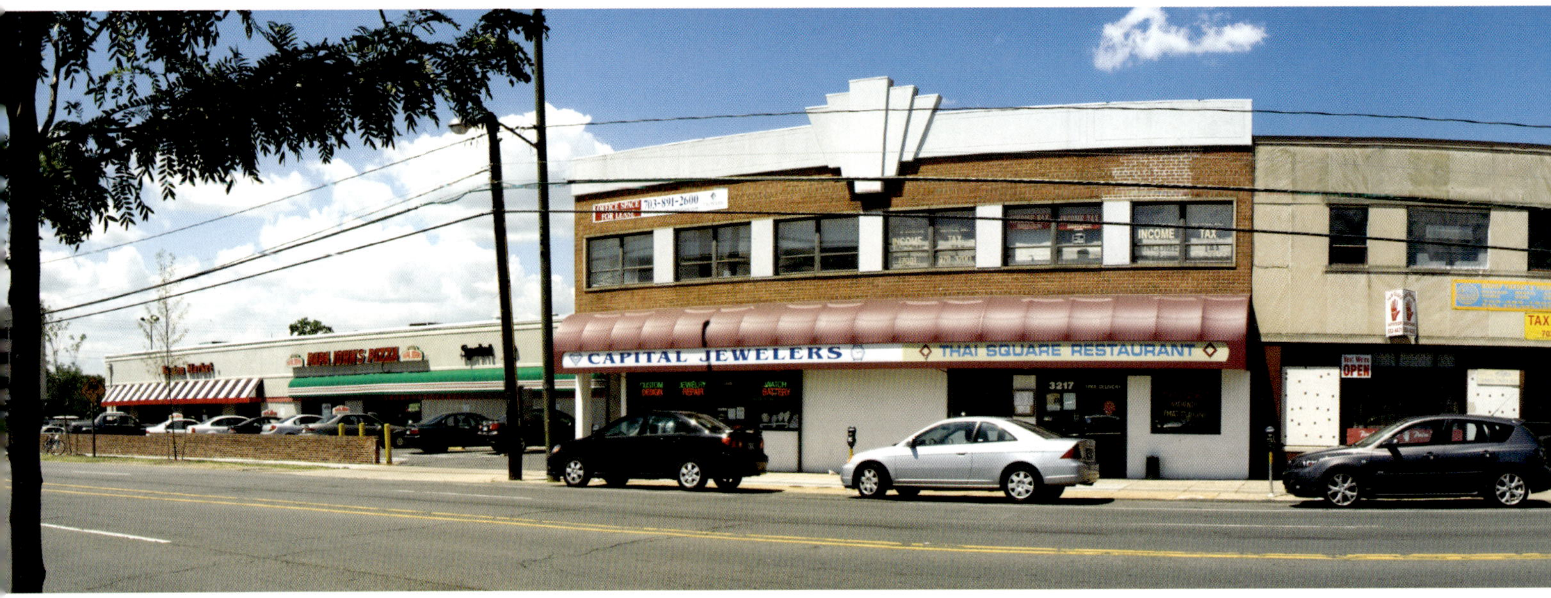

Panorama, 3200 block of Columbia Pike

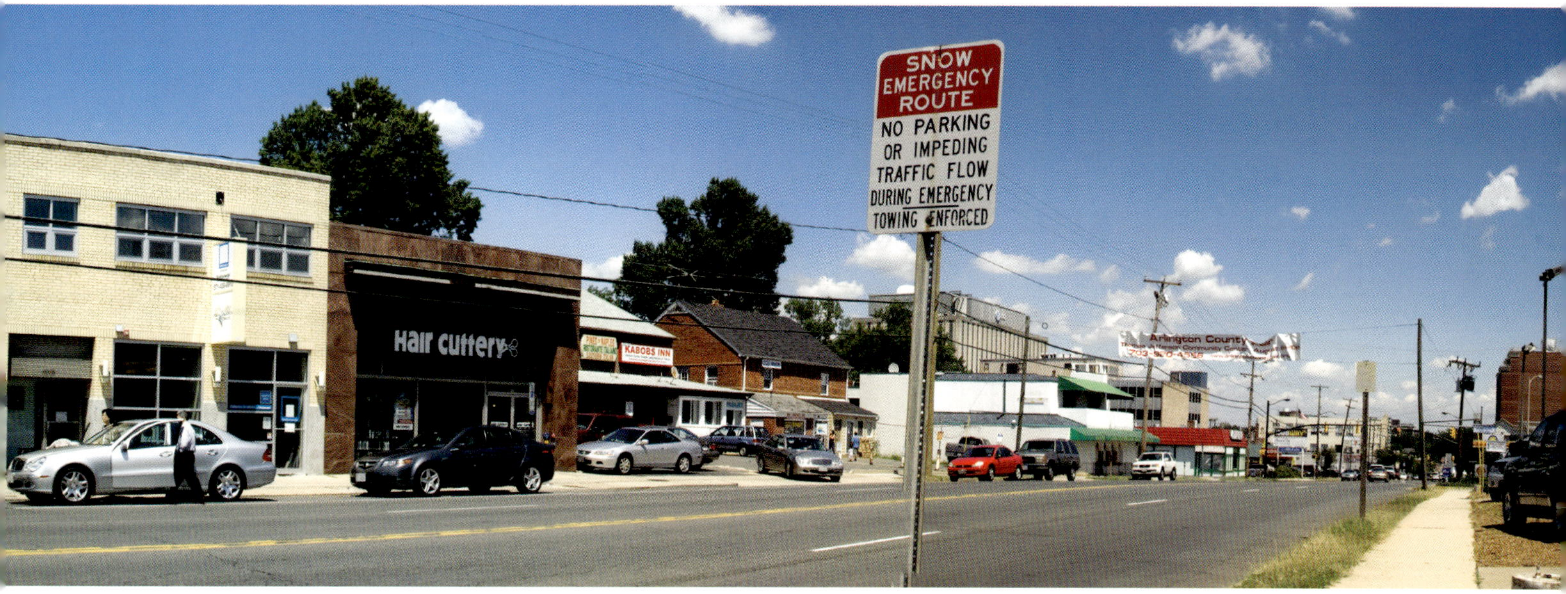
SNOW
EMERGENCY
ROUTE
NO PARKING
OR IMPEDING
TRAFFIC FLOW
DURING EMERGENCY
TOWING ENFORCED
Hair cuttery
KABOBS INN
Arlington County

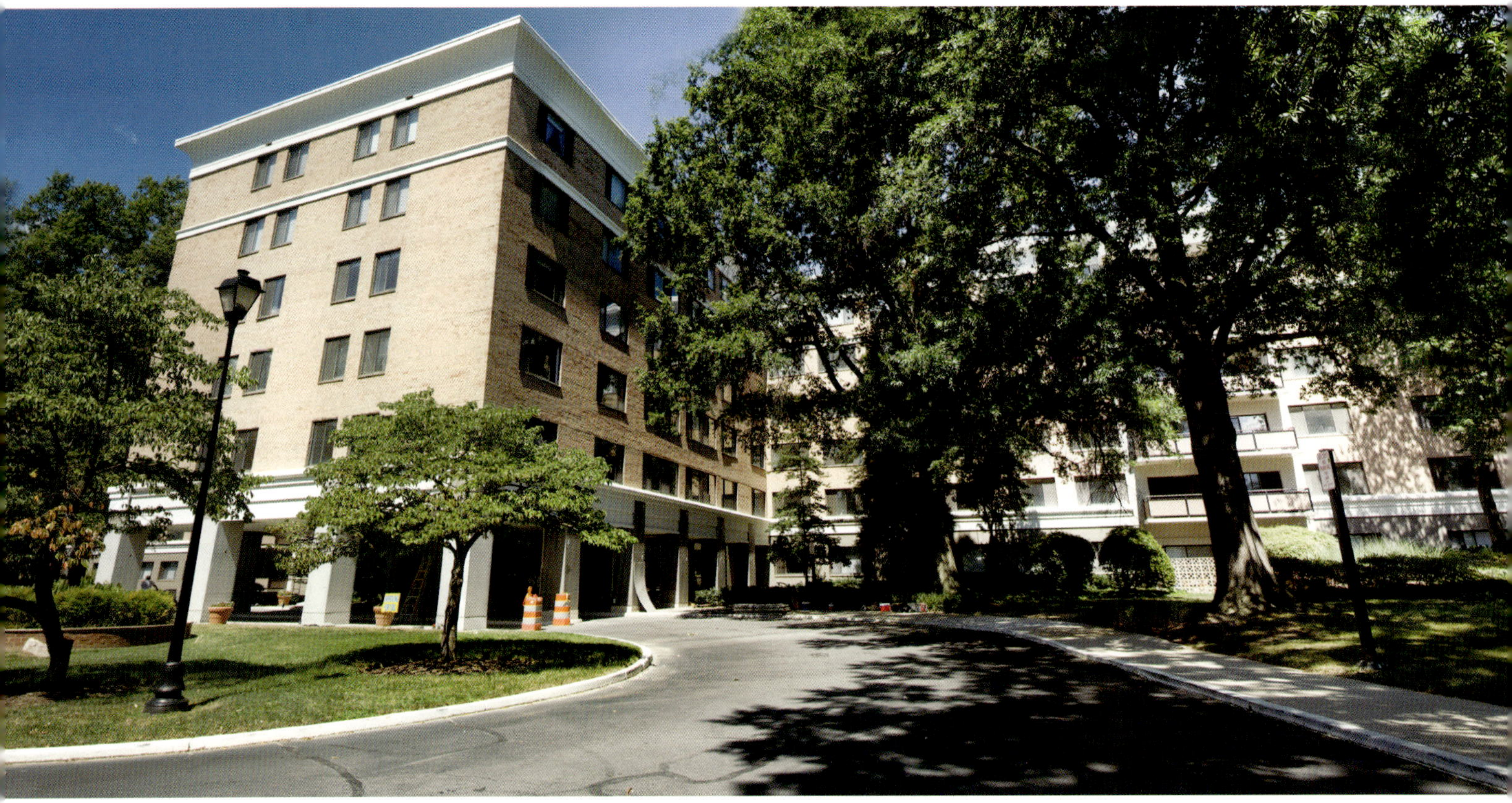

The Whitmore Apartments, 4301 Columbia Pike

The Broiler Restaurant, 3601 Columbia Pike ››

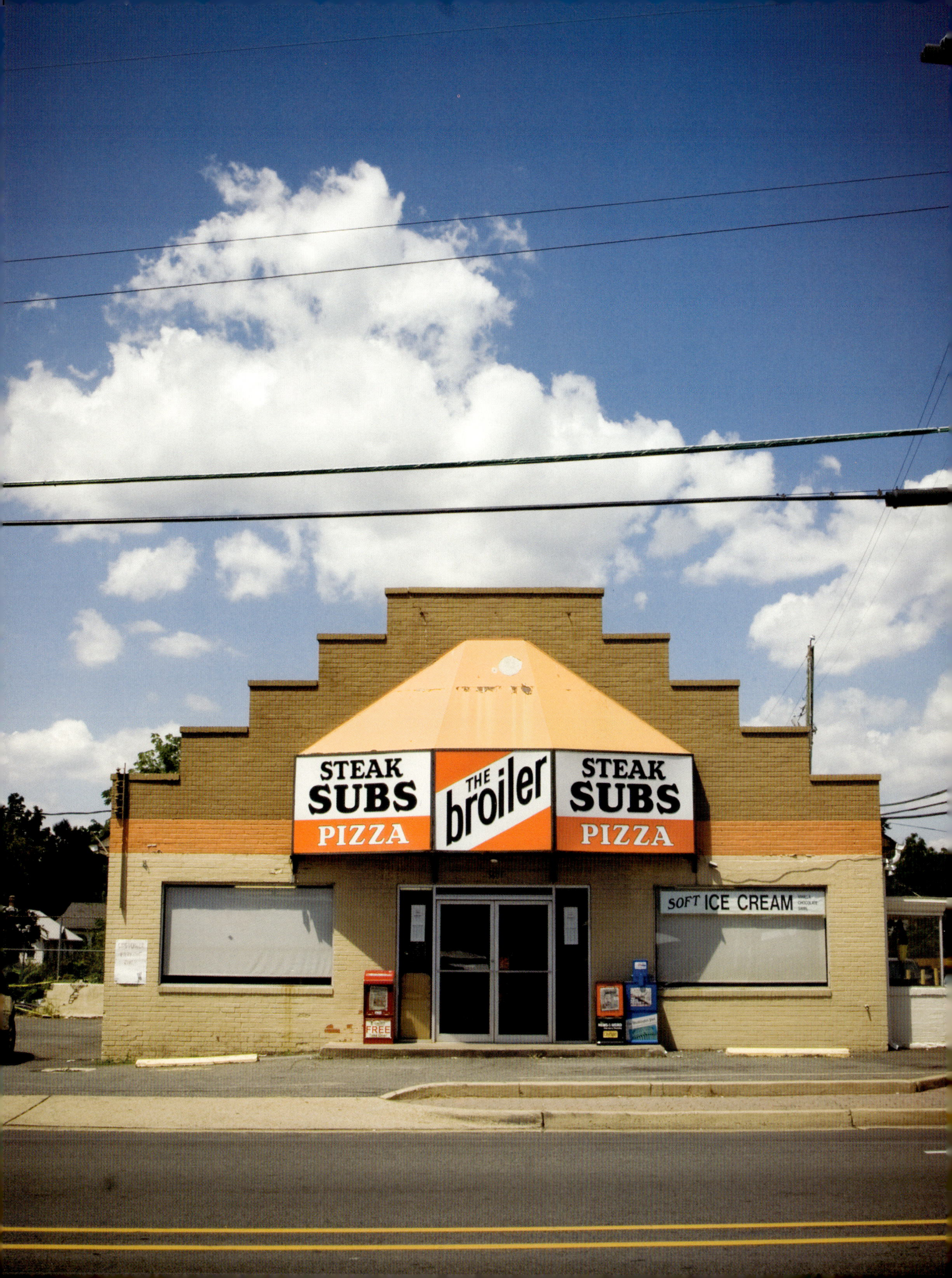
STEAK
SUBS
PIZZA
THE
broiler
STEAK
SUBS
PIZZA
SOFT ICE CREAM
FREE

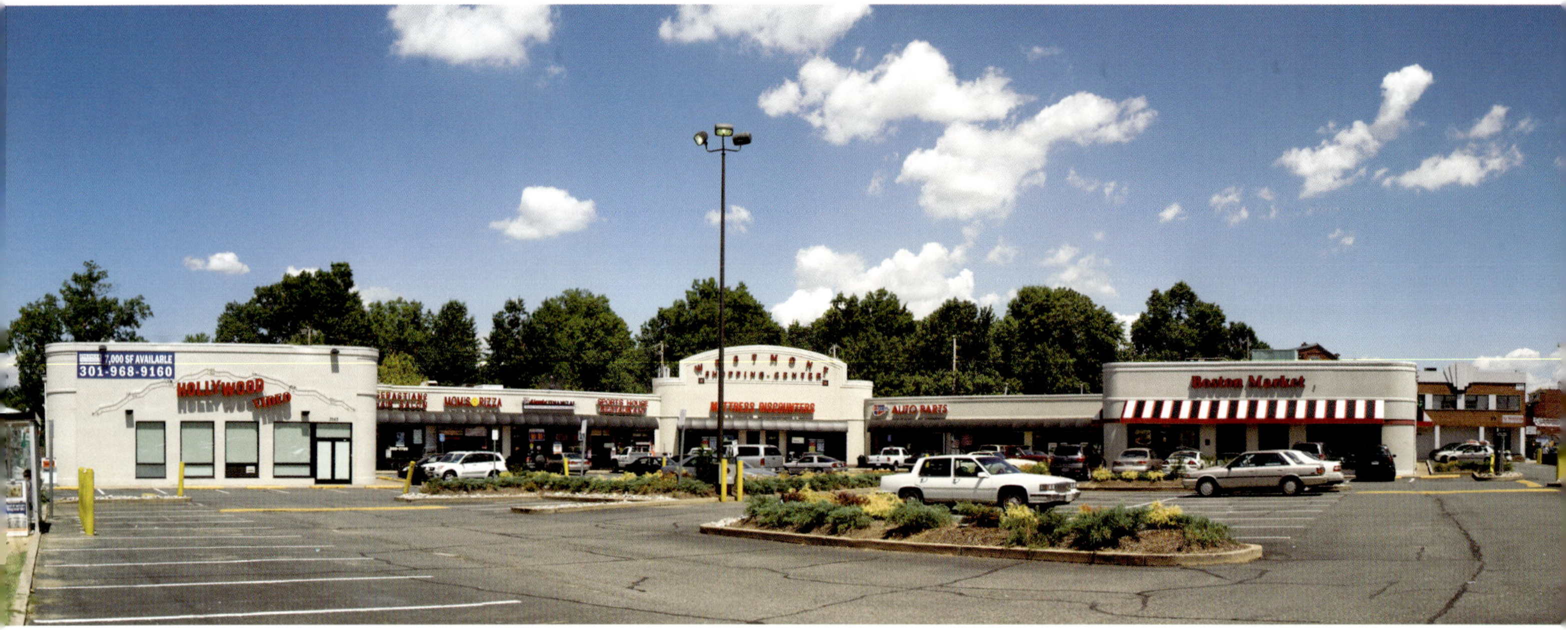

Westmont Shopping Center, 3200 block of Columbia Pike

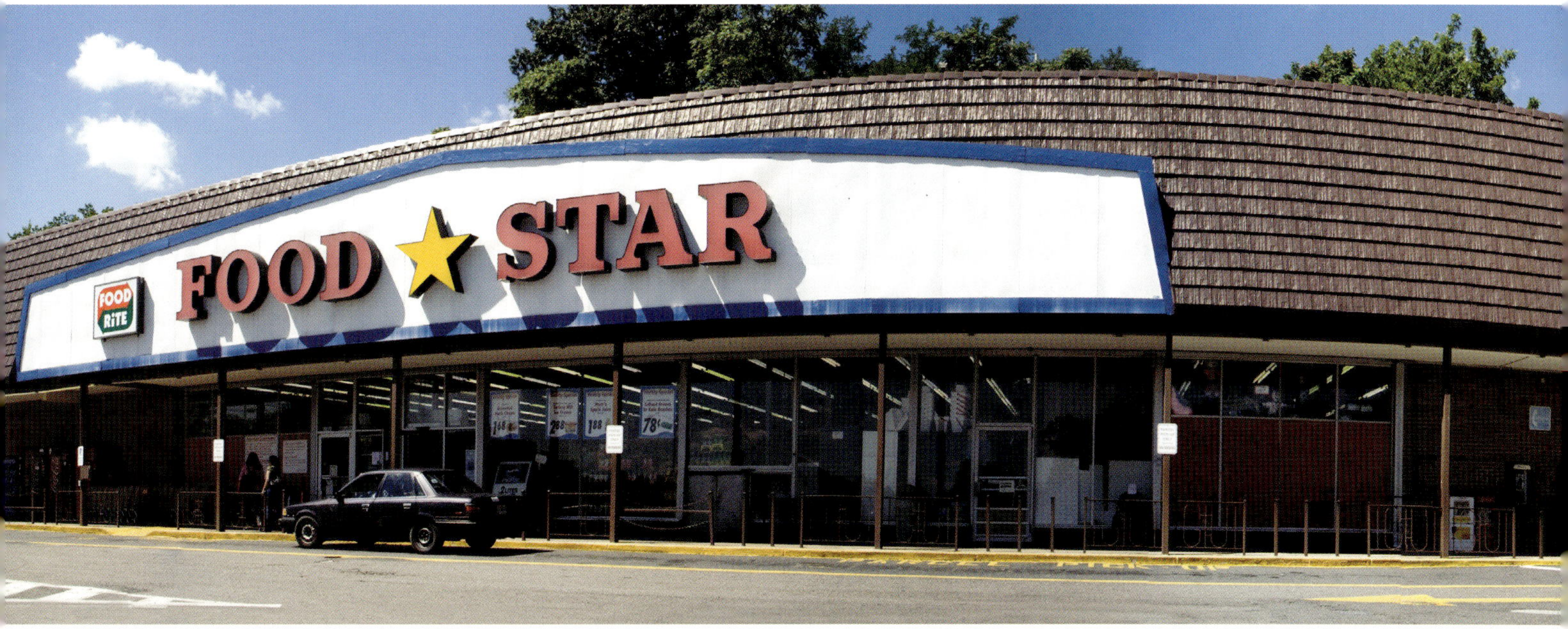

Food Star Grocery

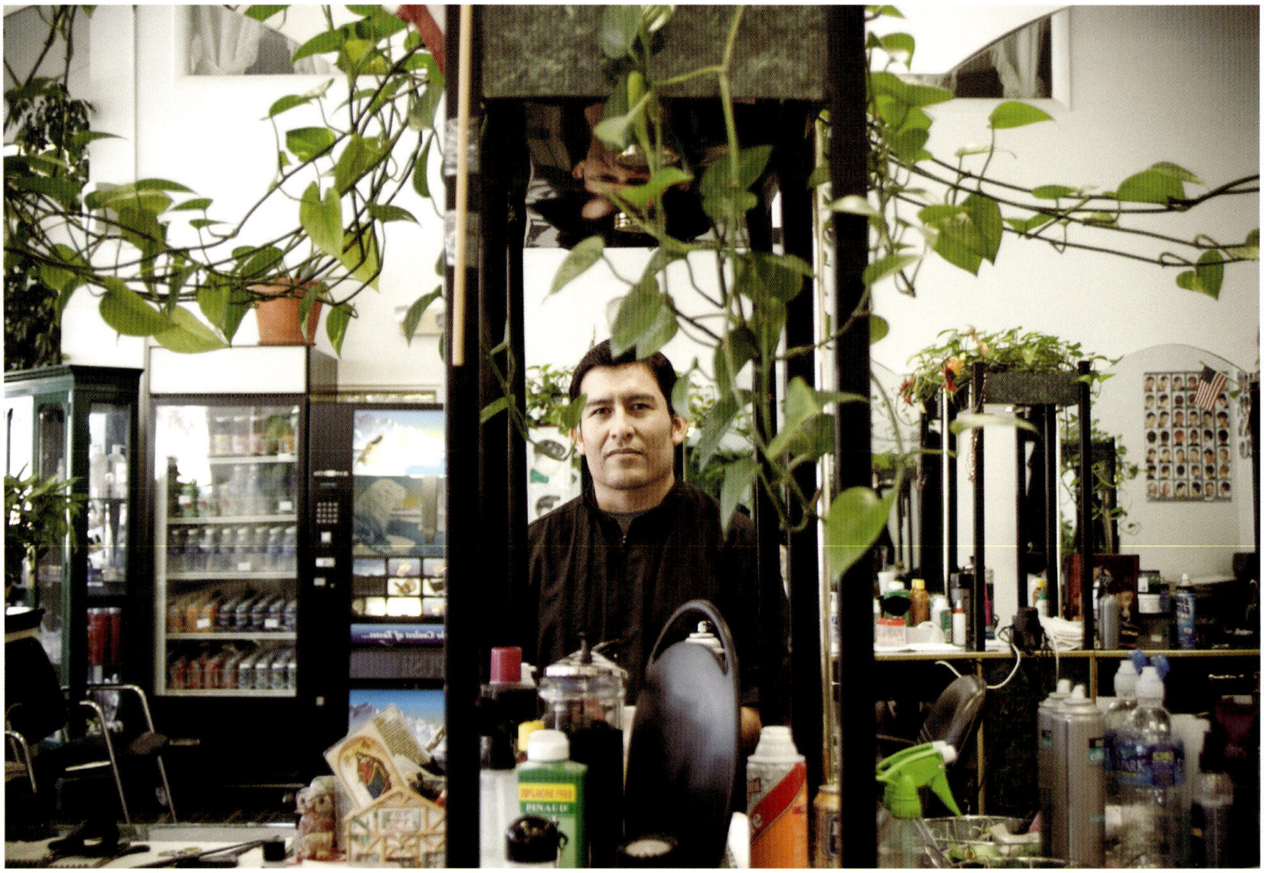

hairdresser, Cassiel's Salon

Seated, Claudia Salazar. Standing, left to right:
Ottoniel Portillo, Nuvia Lopez, Immer Garcia, Gladis Cardona, Ingry Hernandez, Delmis Argueta ››

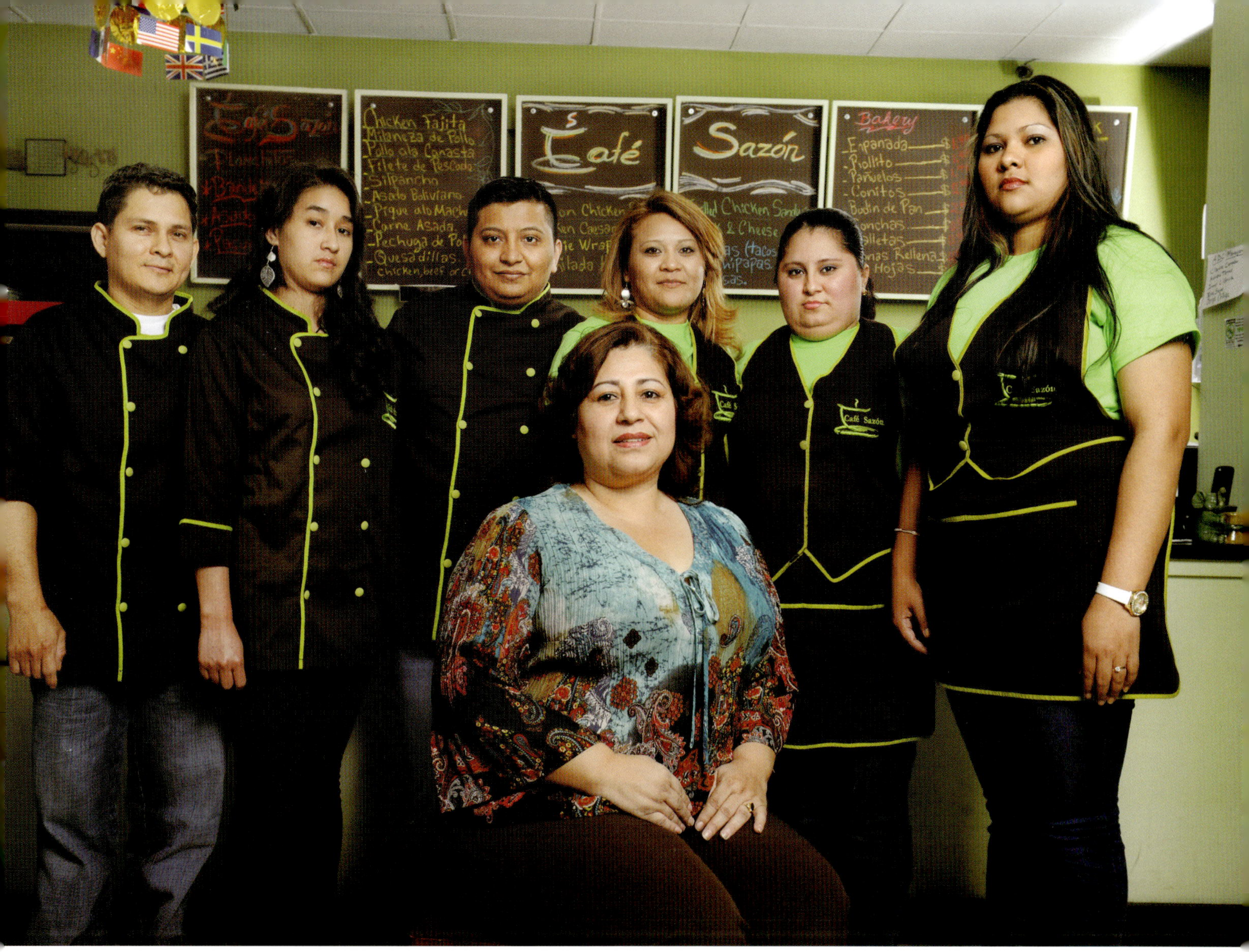

Claudia Salazar: I am originally from Cochabamba, Bolivia. I came with my mom and sister Adriana to find something different. We lived in Greenbrier, along the Pike. Through my cousins, I got a job as a babysitter. I was busy working and going to school to learn English.

After their child had grown, the family I worked for referred me to a job at SunTrust Bank. I started as a cashier, and at night went to American University. I worked at the bank for ten years, and became an assistant manager.

I started Café Sazon with my sister and mother. The menu has a mostly Bolivian influence, plus we have dishes from El Salvador and Mexico. The pastries especially are Bolivian.

My family does traditional Brazilian dancing. I started dancing when I came here. It's a way to remember home. I was in the group Raíces de Bolivia - "Roots of Bolivia." We did caporales dances, a particular style. In the beginning we made our own costumes, family and friends would come over to work on them. After the sewing, there were always lots of little beads that had fallen on the floor, and you could hear them go 'ping ping ping' when we vacuumed up afterwards.

When I came here I saw diversity of all kinds. I felt accepted here, and found the dancing group right away. We did not experience prejudice. Arlington is good for that.

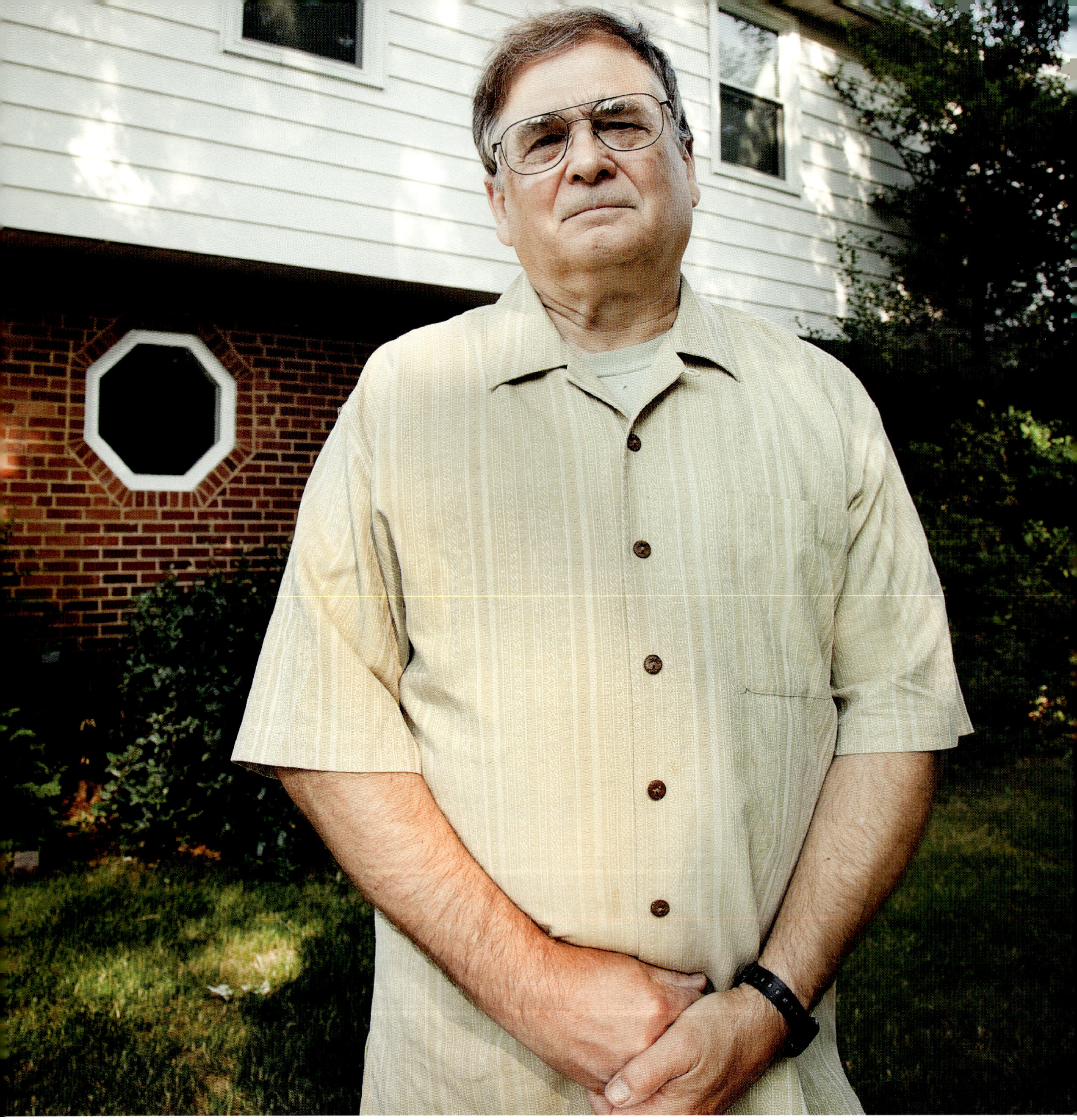

Randy Kelly

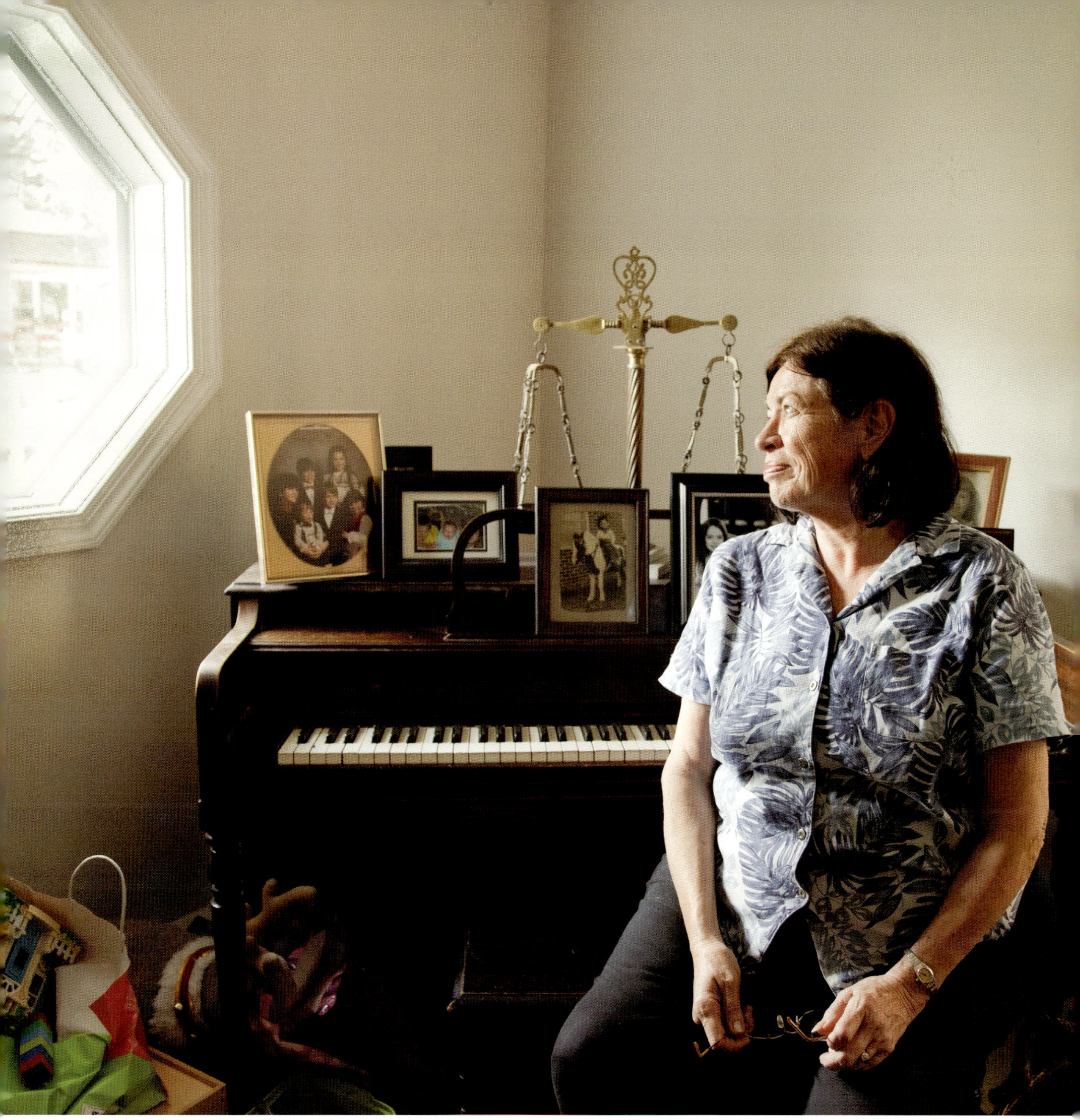

Anne Kelly

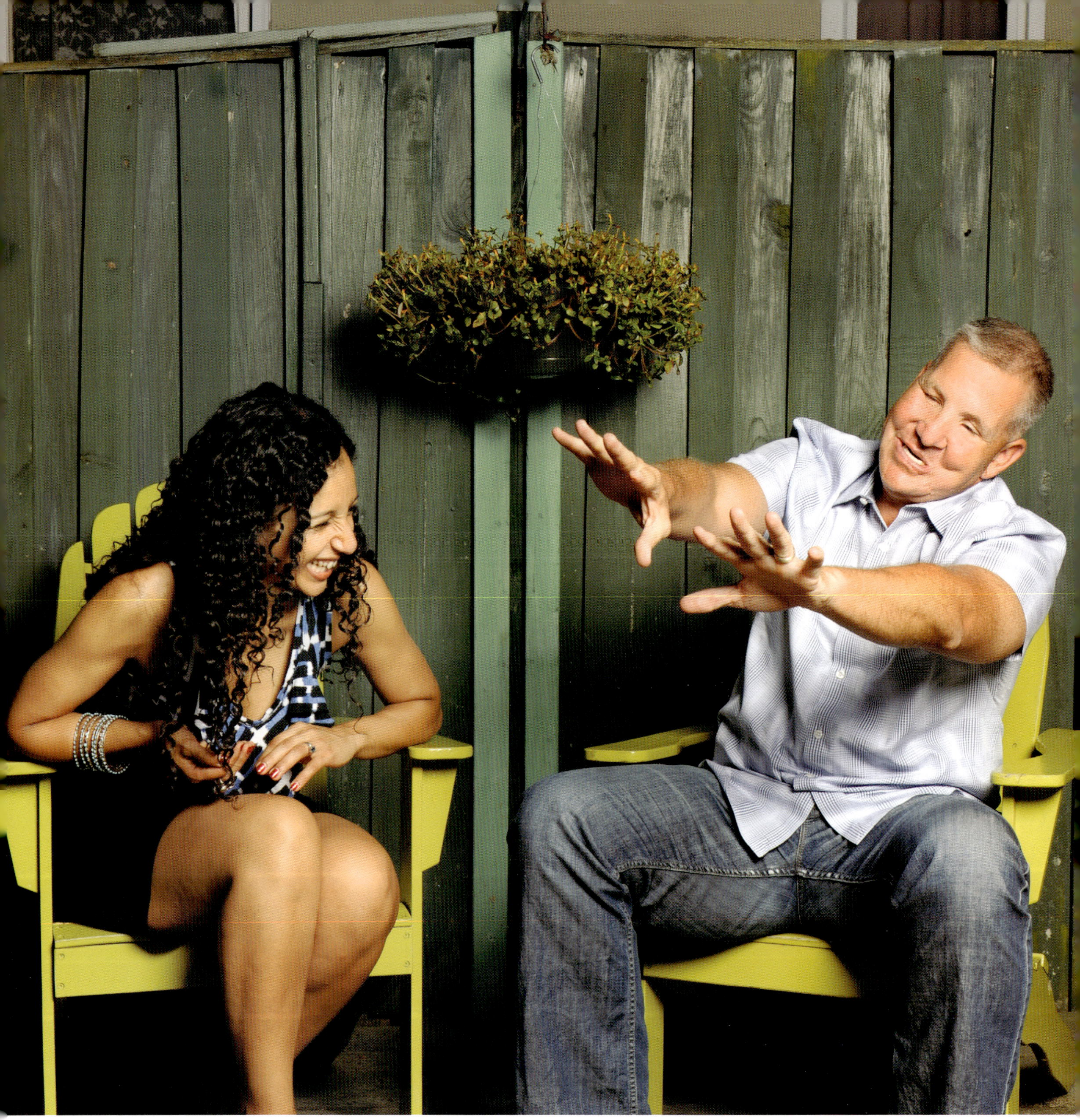

Dahlia and Justin Constantine

Dahlia and Justin Constantine

Justin Constantine, a decorated Marine combat veteran, is an attorney and consultant who grew up in northern Virginia. He is active with the Wounded Warrior Project. Dahlia Constantine, his wife, was born in Cairo Egypt, and grew up in California. She teaches third grade at Patrick Henry Elementary School.

Justin: I was deployed to Iraq in 2006, assigned to the Anbar province, attached to an infantry battalion. Our mission was to rebuild infrastructure that had been destroyed both by us and the insurgents. We found it hard to work with Iraqis, as many who cooperated with us in building things back up were given death threats, and were scared even when we offered security to them. The insurgents were so powerful.

Dahlia: Justin was wounded about six weeks after he got there. He was shot in the head by a sniper... We had spoken the night before, and had texted. I got an email from his mother, "Justin is OK." That was how I learned that he'd been wounded.

Justin: I proposed to Dahlia in July 2007. I got down on one knee at the Iwo Jima memorial, just a day before another surgery. I had the ring with me. Dahlia got out of class at 10 o'clock, it was late, and was wondering why we were hanging around so long. I was waiting for a quiet moment, and then I proposed to her.

Dahlia: Justin figured out somehow to get the ring organized, and to get me to the memorial, on his own. We got married in 2008. We bought the house here on South Ivy Street from a Croatian family who was moving back to Croatia. They made us lots of Croatian food. I met the principal of Patrick Henry School and she asked me to apply for a position at her school. It's worked out, and I can walk to work, too. I love teaching here.

This neighborhood is diversity nutso. I got to know the neighborhood when I started teaching. Almost every house here has kids, which is new. It used to be more older couples. It's a changing demographic. Different blocks have different ethnic mixes. There are more white families than when we first moved in. I am concerned about the new condos going up near Glebe Road and the Pike. They are so big, close to the road

Justin: Most families are still immigrants, at least in the duplexes where we live. The single family detached homes are mostly white.

Dahlia: Diversity in California is very different than here. There it was black, white, and Hispanic, and most of the Latino people were Mexican. Here there are many layers of diversity.

Our students' parents like the diversity; they fight for low-income housing, and are concerned about the changes; both the dilution of diversity, and the increased traffic.

Our school is a Title 1 school, which means that 50% or more of our students receive free or reduced-cost lunch. I, and many of our teachers and parents are committed to Title 1 schools. We may not be Title 1 in a few years, due to gentrification. The older grades in our elementary school are more diverse than the lower grades, which are becoming wealthier and whiter, as young well-to-do couples from north Arlington move in and buy houses, and send their kids to our school, which has a good educational reputation.

Justin: My grandfather came from Romania. My last name sounds Greek, but it is a Romanian name. This area has been good for me. I am finishing my advanced degree in law, worked on Capitol Hill for the Senate Veterans Affairs Committee, and as counsel for the FBI. I have my own business working with veterans' employment issues. I was presented with an unusual opportunity as a result of my injury. I have something to talk about, to share.

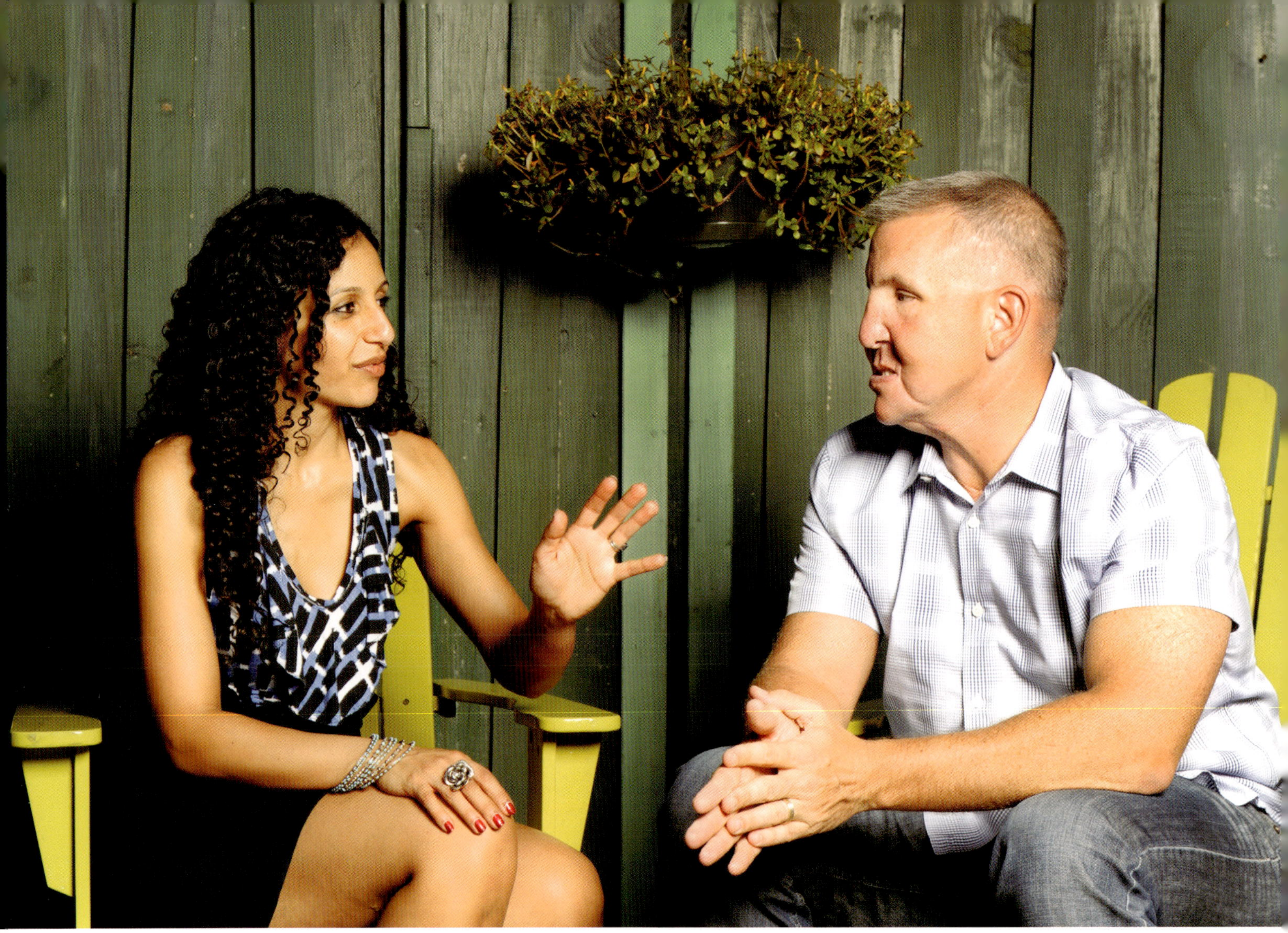

Dahlia: My parents both came from Cairo. We moved here for good when I was in third grade. This was during the time of Sadat. My parents are not political or economic immigrants. They had a comfortable life in Egypt. They were professional people, both working as veterinarians. They were big John F. Kennedy, Martin Luther King, and Malcolm X fans. To them, the US symbolized freedom, a more ideal kind of society. The idea of America attracted them, not need. They came under a Professional Act that allowed special skilled workers into the country.

I attended pre-K and kindergarten in the US, then we moved back to Cairo, then we moved back to America when I was in third grade. My parents sent me to public school, not to a functionally-segregated private school. They wanted me to have a wide mixture of experiences. I got these values from my parents. My Dad is working in in Iraq right now. He's good with languages and dialects.

There are nine languages spoken in my class of twenty-one kids, ten really. Between the students and me, we have Bengali, Spanish, Arabic, English, Tagalog, Farsi, Amharic, Portuguese, and Quechua, which is the language of the native peoples in Bolivia, plus one student knows and uses ASL, American Sign Language.

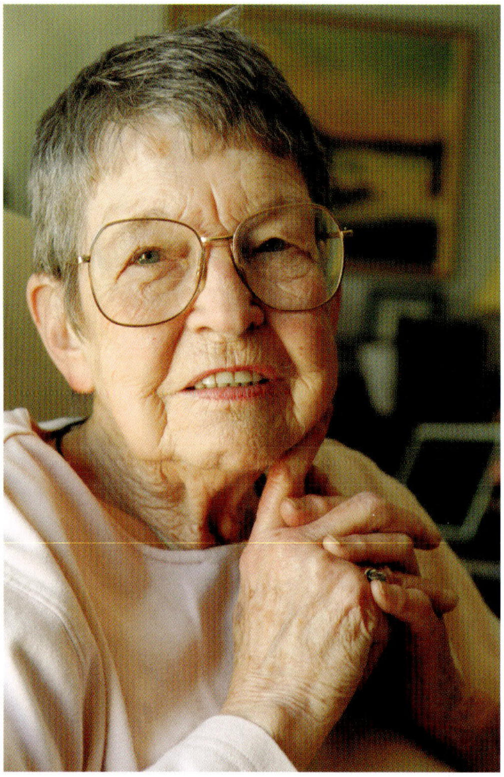

This book is dedicated to the memory and spirit of Sara Collins (1929 -2014).

A long-time resident of Columbia Pike, Sara was a leader in exploring, preserving, and sharing our local history. Her pioneering work as the Arlington County Public Library's historian in creating the Arlington Community Archives within the Center for Local History, including extensive in-depth oral histories of our diverse neighborhoods, will have meaning for the ages.

Her cheerful generous spirit inspires us all. May her memory, and her work, be for a blessing.

Columbia Pike: Facts & Figures

Columbia Pike built and incorporated:	1810
Length of Columbia Pike inside Arlington County from Carlin Springs Road to the S. Joyce Street intersection:	3.5 miles
Daily traffic count:	34,000
Public transit weekday ridership:	16,000

2013 Census Data for the 22204 zip code:

Population	51,262
Total Households	19,775
Average House Value	$426, 600
Average Annual Household income	$75,135.00

Population Data:

White	26,449
Black	8,568
Hispanic	14,433
Asian	6,131
American Indian	823
Hawaiian	155
Two or more races (2010 data)	2,335
Other	7,603

Median Age	33.9 years
2010 Social Security beneficiaries	3,565

Real Estate

Residential mailboxes	21,539
Business mailboxes	599

Total housing units	21,078
Owner occupied units	8,205 (41.5%)
Renter-occupied units	1, 570 (58.5%)
Vacant housing units	1,303
Population density	11,489.13 sq/m
2013 Average home selling price,	$409,875
Average monthly rent	$1,246

Employment

22204 Zip Code (16 years And over)	39,852
In labor force	80%
Civilian labor force	79.7%
Employed	75.3%
Armed Forces	1.2%
Not in labor force	19.1%
Unemployment rate	5.5%

Education (25 years or older):

Less than High School	5, 621
High School Graduate	5,702
Some College/Associates Degree	6,244
Bachelor Degree	10,595
Master, Doctorate, or Professional Degree	7, 5111

Place of origin/citizenship

Native to USA	30,690
Foreign-born with US citizenship	7,092
Foreign-born without US citizenship	11,566
Born in Europe	1,139
Born in Asia	4,827
Born in Africa	2,734
Born in Oceania	57
Born in Latin America	9,698
Born in Northern America	158

Language spoken at home:

English	11,077
Spanish	4,647
Other Indo-European languages	1,585
Asian & Pacific Islander languages	1,257
Other	1,218

Languages spoken in Arlington Public Schools ESL classes, in the 2204 zip code, 2013:

Spanish, Arabic, Amharic, Mongolian, Bengali, Urdu, Tigrinya, Chinese (Mandarin), Russian, Vietnamese, Tagalog, Hindi, Thai, French, Indonesian, Dari, Portuguese, Turkish, Pashto (Northern), Somali, Farsi, Uzbek, Georgian, Bulgarian, Kurdish, Tamil, Czech, Panjabi, Tajiki, Ukrainian, Dutch, Khana, German, Lao, Oromo, Pashto (Southern), Samoan, Singhalese, Chinese (Min Nan), Malayam, Telegu, Kannada

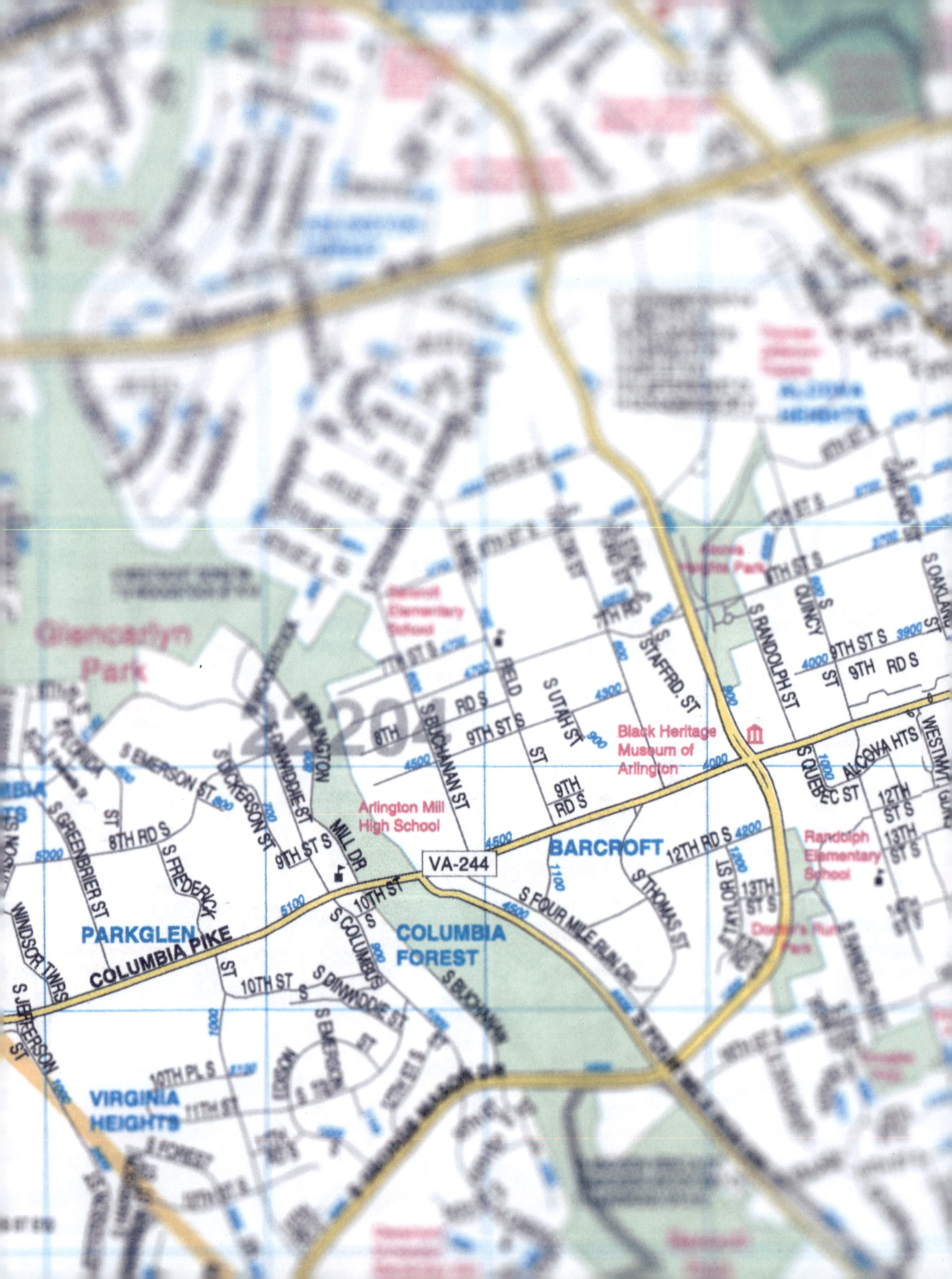

Glencarlyn Park
22204
S EMERSON ST
S DICKERSON ST
S DINWIDDIE ST
MILL DR
Arlington Mill High School
VA-244
BARCROFT
Black Heritage Museum of Arlington
S BUCHANAN ST
9TH ST S
S UTAH ST
9TH RD S
S STAFFORD ST
S RANDOLPH ST
S QUINCY ST
S OAKLAND ST
ALCOVA HTS
12TH RD S
S THOMAS ST
S TAYLOR ST
13TH ST S
S FOUR MILE RUN DR
Randolph Elementary School
PARKGLEN
COLUMBIA PIKE
COLUMBIA FOREST
S COLUMBUS ST
10TH ST
S GREENBRIER ST
8TH RD S
S FREDERICK ST
WINDSOR TWRS
S JEFFERSON ST
10TH PL S
11TH ST
VIRGINIA HEIGHTS